DAY by DAY

CHRIST AND HIS APOSTLES

Day by Day

Christ
and His Apostles

Edited by
KEN TOTTON

PRECIOUS SEED PUBLICATIONS

© Copyright Precious Seed Publications 2012
The Glebe House, Stanton Drew, Bristol, UK, BS39 4EH

First published September 2012

ISBN 978 1 871642 46 9

This is the fifteenth book in the Day by Day series.

The others are:

Day by Day through the New Testament
Day by Day through the Old Testament
Day by Day in the Psalms
Day by Day Moments with the Master
Day by Day in Prayer
Day by Day with Bible Characters
Day by Day Christ Foreshadowed
Day by Day Bible Promises
Day by Day Divine Titles
Day by Day Bible Commands
Day by Day Paradise to the Promised Land
Day by Day Bible Pictures and Parables
Day by Day Bible Questions
Day by Day Living in the Promised Land

Printed in China

Contents

	Page
Acknowledgements	7
The Contributors and their Contributions	9
Biographies of the Contributors	11
The Readings	15

Acknowledgements

The Day by Day series seeks to promote daily meditation in the word of God. The original volume *Day by Day through the New Testament* was published in 1979, and in this fifteenth volume we revisit this most important portion of scripture. In an era of religious pluralism we bow to the fact that Jesus Christ the Son of God is God's unique and final communication to man. He came not to destroy the law, or the prophets . . . but to fulfil. Supremely, that 'fulfilment' is seen in His death and exaltation. Moreover, the inspired writings of His apostles are no less authoritative than Christ's own words, for according to Paul 'the things that I write unto you are the commandments of the Lord'. This is the faith that was once for all delivered to the saints.[1]

We are indebted to an international team of writers who share the conviction that the New Testament (and, indeed, all of scripture) speaks authoritatively to the needs of God's people today, and is essential for our individual and collective edification. As we use this book alongside scripture may we know the gracious Spirit's help in guiding us into all truth.

This production was once again a true team effort. John Scarsbrook compiled the daily passages and their titles, as well as assisting with the proof reading. John Bennett provided valuable advice and encouragement at every stage, but especially with proof reading, assisted by Brian Clatworthy and Michael Sparkes.

Typesetting was carried out by Derek Hill, while the cover design is the work of Barney Trevivian. Roy Hill, in addition to helping with proof reading, managed the printing process. All are deserving of our thanks for their valued expertise, commitment, and contribution.

On behalf of the Precious Seed Committee,

Ken Totton   July 2012

---

[1] Heb. 1. 1-2; Matt. 5. 17; Acts 13. 29; 1 Cor. 14. 37; Jude 3 ESV

The Contributors and their Contributions

Richard Catchpole*	England	Jan 1 – 15
William Burnett	Canada	Jan 16 – 31
John Scarsbrook	England	Feb 1 – 15
Jack Hay*	Scotland	Feb 16 – 29
Jeremy Gibson	England	Mar 1 – 15
David McAllister*	Ireland	Mar 16 – 31
Ian Rees	Wales	Apr 1 – 16
Douglas Mowat	Scotland	Apr 17 – May 1
David Newell*	Scotland	May 2 – 17
Scott Dunn	Australia	May 18 – Jun 3
Mark Kolchin*	USA	Jun 4 – 18
Richard Collings	Wales	Jun 19 – Jul 4
Simon Sherwin	Scotland	Jul 5 – 20
Ian Jackson*	England	Jul 21 – Aug 3
John Bennett*	England	Aug 4 – 19
Keith Keyser*	USA	Aug 20 – Sep 3
Alan Gamble*	Scotland	Sep 4 – 18
Ken Totton*	England	Sep 19 – Oct 2
Wesley Ferguson*	N. Ireland	Oct 3 – 15
Roy Hill*	England	Oct 16 – 28
Bernard Osborne*	Wales	Oct 29 – Nov 14
Colin Lacey*	England	Nov 15 – 28
Thomas Wilson*	Scotland	Nov 29 – Dec 13
Malcolm Davis	England	Dec 14 – 31

* Contributor supplied Introduction

Biographies of the Contributors

Richard Catchpole lives in South Norwood, London, with his wife Judith. He is in fellowship at Clifton Hall, South Norwood. He was commended in 1989 to the grace of God for the work of the Lord and travels extensively in the UK in a Bible teaching ministry.

William Burnett was raised in Scotland, and spent his professional life in the oil refining business. His employer seconded him to Canada in 1972. He ministers throughout North America, and abroad. He sits on the board of *Counsel* magazine, and contributes regularly to various assembly publications. He and his wife Beth reside in Oakville, Ontario, where they are in happy fellowship in Hopedale assembly. They have three married sons, and eight grandchildren.

John Scarsbrook is an elder in the Killamarsh assembly, Derbyshire, England. He is active in ministry throughout the UK. He is a self-employed finance broker, married to Ruth, with four married sons and ten grandchildren; he is Secretary to the Precious Seed Trust.

Jack Hay is in fellowship in the assembly at Perth, Scotland. He is a commended full-time worker preaching the gospel and teaching the word throughout the UK, North America, and the Far East. He is also the author of numerous magazine articles.

Jeremy Gibson was converted while studying at University. He is currently in assembly fellowship in Derby, UK.

David McAllister and his wife Priscilla were commended to the work of the Lord by the Parkgate assembly, Belfast. They worked in Zambia for 18 years, and are now in Donegal, Ireland. They have four children.

Ian Rees, with his wife Rebecca, served the Lord in Botswana for a number of years, and saw an assembly planted in Francistown. Upon his return to Bath, he served as an elder in the Manvers Hall assembly for several years. He and his family now live in Narberth, West Wales, and hope to see an assembly planted in Pembrokeshire.

Douglas Mowat is an elder in the Culloden assembly in Inverness, Scotland. He is employed as a Chartered Surveyor in the Highlands and is actively involved in preaching and teaching throughout the UK.

David Newell is in fellowship in the assembly at Eastpark Gospel Hall, Glasgow, Scotland.

Scott Dunn was in fellowship in the Wallingford assembly in Oxfordshire, England, but has relocated to Perth, Australia. He is married to Elaine and has two children.

Mark Kolchin, along with his wife Cynthia, was commended to the Lord's work in 1993 by the assembly in Toms River, New Jersey, USA. He is currently engaged in an itinerant Bible teaching and conference ministry, and maintains an evangelistic and Bible teaching web site, www.knowtheword.com. He has written on a variety of topics in the Christian life.

Richard Collings is in fellowship in the assembly at Caerphilly, Wales and is a committee member of Precious Seed Trust.

Simon Sherwin is in fellowship at the Innerleven Gospel Hall, Lower Methil, Fife, Scotland. He is married to Jennifer and has four children.

Ian Jackson is in fellowship with the assembly meeting at Marine Hall, Eastbourne, England. He is married with three married children, and five grandchildren. He is a commended full-time worker travelling widely as an evangelist and Bible teacher.

John Bennett is an elder at the Gospel Hall, Kirkby-in-Ashfield, Nottinghamshire, England. He is active in ministry in England and has written numerous articles for assembly magazines. He became a trustee of Precious Seed in 2002, publications editor in 2004, and ministry articles editor in 2010. He is married to Rachel and has three children, one of whom is married.

Keith Keyser is a commended full-time worker and is in fellowship in the assembly meeting at Gilbertsville, Pennsylvania. He ministers throughout North America and spent some time in Spain. He also regularly writes material for assembly magazines.

Alan Gamble is in fellowship in the assembly at Bethesda, Linthouse, Glasgow, Scotland. He is active in Bible teaching in the UK and North America. He serves as a trustee of Interlink, a missionary service group. He is married to Elizabeth, and they have three adult children and two grandchildren. His professional background is in law.

Ken Totton is an elder in the Roseford assembly, Cambridge, England. Following a career in telecommunications, he now engages in Bible teaching in the UK. He is also Publications Editor for Precious Seed Publications. He is married to Kate and has two sons.

Wesley Ferguson is an elder in the assembly in Antrim in Northern Ireland. He is the author of numerous magazine articles. He authored Genesis in the Ritchie series *What the Bible Teaches*. He was previously a teacher and a schools' inspector.

Roy Hill is in fellowship in the assembly at Pensford Gospel Hall, near Bristol, and is well known as an international Bible teacher. He is married with five children and ten grandchildren. Having spent his life in the printing trade he is currently chairman of Precious Seed Trust, general editor of *Precious Seed International* and a board member of Gospel Folio Press in Canada. He also writes extensively for assembly magazines.

Bernard Osborne is retired from a career in education and is in fellowship in Ebenezer assembly, Cardiff, Wales. He travels extensively in ministry throughout the UK and North America. He also writes for *Precious Seed International* and other assembly magazines.

Colin Lacey was headteacher of a large secondary school. He is married to Alison, and has two sons and six grandchildren. Now retired, he lives in Bath and meets with the believers in Manvers Hall. He travels throughout the UK teaching the word of God. He is the author of the commentaries on Judges and Nehemiah in the John Ritchie *What the Bible Teaches* series.

Tom Wilson is an elder in the Springburn assembly in Glasgow and ministers the word throughout Scotland. He was for many years editor of *Believer's Magazine,* and is a recently retired principal of a specialist college in Glasgow.

Malcolm Davis, together with his wife Ruth, is in fellowship at Harehills Gospel Hall, Leeds. A retired academic librarian, he has written two concise commentaries: one on the book of Revelation, *The Climax of World History* (2009); the other, on the book of Daniel, *Anticipating the End Times* (2010). He also writes for several assembly magazines.

The author is mentioned by the name of 'Matthew' some five times in the New Testament, twice in the Gospel that bears his name, 9. 9; 10. 3. Most commentators also identify him with a man named 'Levi' referred to by Mark and Luke, Mark 2. 14; Luke 5. 27-29. Comparing the accounts of his conversion we find he was in the employment of the Roman Government, gathering taxes, when he heard the Saviour's call, 'Follow me', Matt. 9. 9. His response was immediate, leaving all to 'follow him', Luke 5. 28-29. His testimony began with a feast to the Lord and continues still today in his Gospel about the Lord.

Matthew was initially writing for a Jewish readership, his purpose being to provide irrefutable proof that the Lord Jesus is Israel's long promised Messiah, the 'king of the Jews', Matt. 2. 2; 21. 5. A king must have a kingdom and so some thirty-two times Matthew speaks of 'the kingdom of heaven'. Not surprisingly there is a strong 'Jewish' character to the Gospel. Eight times Matthew refers to the Lord as the 'Son of David'. Twice reference is made, and only in this Gospel, to 'the lost sheep of the house of Israel', 10. 6; 15. 24. Of all the New Testament books, only Matthew describes the country of the Lord as 'the land of Israel', 2. 20-21. Matthew alone records the Lord's extensive condemnation of the Pharisees, ch. 23. Certain expressions, characteristic of this Gospel, continually direct the reader's attention back to the Old Testament, the 'oracles of God' of which the nation had been made the custodians, Rom. 3. 2, expressions such as 'that it might be fulfilled', 'it is written', 'have ye never read', and 'it was said of them of old time'.

A very simple division of the Gospel can be linked to its opening verse, where the Lord is described as 'the son of David, the son of Abraham'. Solomon, the wise sovereign was the son of David, Isaac the willing sacrifice the son of Abraham. The first twenty-five chapters of Matthew focus attention on five major teaching discourses that all conclude on a similar note 'when Jesus had finished'; here we are listening to the *wise Sovereign*, the powerful words of a king, Eccl. 8. 4. The final three chapters of the Gospel record Christ's arrest, trial, death and resurrection; here we view Him as the *willing Sacrifice*, whose blood was shed 'for the remission of sins'.

His Apostles

January 1st

Matthew 1

The books. At the beginning of the Old Testament reference is made to 'the book of the generations of Adam', the first man, the head of the original creation, Gen. 5. 1. As the New Testament opens we have 'the book of the generation of Jesus Christ', the last Adam, the Head of the new creation. We might well say the message of the whole Bible revolves around the history of these two men, Adam and Christ, and all men fall under one of these two heads. Any Jew confronted with the claim that Jesus of Nazareth is the promised Messiah would immediately enquire, 'Does He have the right genealogy?' Whilst Luke traces the Lord's genealogy through Mary, Matthew in this opening chapter traces it through Mary's husband, viewing the birth of the Lord primarily from Joseph's standpoint, his perplexity and intention, v. 19, the revelation given to him, v. 20, and finally his obedience, vv. 24-25. Matthew divides the genealogy into three sections: first, from Abraham to David, the period of the Jewish nation's growth and development; second, from David to the captivity in Babylon, a period of decline and departure from God; third, from the captivity to Joseph, a period witnessing to the preservation of a remnant and a return to the land, vv. 2-17. The name of 'David' is prominent in the genealogy. Twice he is referred to as 'David the king'; Joseph is identified as a 'son of David'. God gave David promises concerning his house, kingdom, and throne and, born of David's line, the Lord Jesus is the One through whom those promises will be fulfilled, 2 Sam. 7. 16.

The birth. The word 'begat' is used thirty-nine times in the first sixteen verses but a distinction is made when the chapter records the coming of Christ: not now 'begat', but the words 'born' and 'birth' are used, Matthew thus guarding the truth of the virgin birth, vv. 16, 18. The unique character of the conception was announced by an angel; the unique character of the birth was foretold by a prophet, vv. 20, 22-23. In light of what He would *do* He was to be called 'Jesus', but in light of who He is His name would be called 'Emmanuel . . . God with us'. Surely we must bow our heads in worship and adoration! 1 Tim. 3. 16.

The book of the generation of Jesus Christ

Christ and

Matthew 2 — January 2nd

Only Matthew records the visit of these wise men from the east. The word for 'wise men', Gk. *magos*, is of Persian origin, indicating that these men were Gentiles, and the fact they were given an audience with Herod suggests they were men of high standing and wealth. Although the record of scripture is brief what we do know about them is instructive and challenging.

Their desire. They came to Jerusalem asking, 'Where is he that is born King of the Jews?' There has been much speculation concerning the star they saw. This we at least can say, that whatever the means employed, a divine revelation had been given to them and they acted upon it. The journey they undertook must have been considerable, possibly involving several months of travelling, their one objective was to see the King. What a rebuke to the Jewish nation that it was Gentiles who brought to Jerusalem news of its Messiah's birth. What a rebuke to the religious leaders who, informed of the fact, made no effort to find the King themselves. Would the wise men's diligence in seeking after Christ, put us to shame in our day? In response to the demand of Herod as to where 'Christ should be born' the Jewish leaders quote Micah chapter 5 verse 2, identifying the place as 'Bethlehem' in 'Judaea'. One commentator has perceptively said 'It is strange how much these scribes knew, and what little use they made of it', R. Glover. Could such a charge be levelled against us?

Their devotion. Two parties spoke of worshipping the new-born King: the wise men and Herod. With the former it was a genuine desire; with the latter, a mere pretence, Matt. 2. 2, 8. When the wise men saw the Child they did two things: 'they fell down and worshipped him'; and 'they presented unto him gifts'. Are these things true of us? As Christ is brought before us are our hearts always moved in adoration towards Him? Think of what things we can present to Him: our person, our praise, our possessions, Rom. 12. 1; Heb. 13. 15; Phil. 4. 18.

Their direction. 'Warned of God they departed . . . another way'. They were in a world hostile to Christ so that other 'way' involved a path in separation from it, cp. Rom. 12. 2.

Wise men from the east

His Apostles

January 3rd Matthew 3

Prepare ye the way of the Lord

In chapter 1 Matthew demonstrated that the genealogy of Jesus Christ could be traced back to Abraham and David. In chapter 2 the circumstances of His birth fulfilled prophetic announcements, see vv. 5, 15, 17, 23. Now in chapter 3 Matthew shows He had the prescribed forerunner.

The man. 'In those days', when Jesus was living in obscurity in Nazareth, 'John the Baptist' came 'preaching in the wilderness' in fulfilment of the words of the prophet Isaiah, and everything about the life of this man added weight to his testimony. Though of the priestly line, his sphere of ministry was in the wilderness, outside of the established camp of Judaism, v. 1. He was content to occupy the place appointed to him in scripture, as a 'voice' crying in the wilderness, his own identity being of secondary importance to the message he brought, v. 3. His clothing and character of life all conformed to the solemn words he spoke, v. 4. Is the clarity and consistency seen in John's witness equally evident in our own life and testimony?

The ministry. As the forerunner, the focus in John's ministry was to prepare the way for the coming of the Lord by making a straight path – one in which every obstacle that might hinder His coming to, or blessing of, the nation has been removed. In the quotation from Isaiah the word for 'Lord' in Hebrew is 'Jehovah', and used as it is here in connection with the ministry of John the Baptist it is a testimony to the essential deity of the Lord Jesus, the One for whose manifestation John prepared.

The message. Since the sins of the nation had issued in the glory of the Lord departing from Israel, repentance and confession of sins was foremost in John's message, vv. 2, 6. He was fearless in exposing sin, forthright in speaking of 'repentance', 'wrath to come', and 'unquenchable fire', and was faithful in his testimony to Christ, asserting that a man's relationship to the Lord determines his future destiny, vv. 7-12. This was not the message the Pharisees and Sadducees wanted to hear. Later, the Lord said to them, 'John came . . . and ye believed him not', Matt. 21. 32. It might have been unpalatable, but John did not shrink from preaching it, and neither should we, 2 Tim. 4. 2.

Christ and

Matthew 4 — January 4th

Both the Lord and the devil, in drawing attention to the scriptures said, 'It is written', but while the evil one misquoted and distorted the written word, the Lord Jesus bound Himself to it.

In his quotation from Psalm 91 the devil omitted the words 'in all thy ways', the promise of the psalm being thus linked to the regular pathways of one living in dependence upon God and not, as the tempter was suggesting, to some spectacular display, entirely for self-promotion, v. 6; Ps. 91. 2, 9-12. Today, Satan has many emissaries, men and women who profess to be Christians, who go forth with a Bible in their hand, but only to misquote and misinterpret it to the ruin of souls. Warning the Corinthian believers lest Satan should gain an advantage over them Paul said, 'We are not ignorant of his devices'. Let's make sure that we are not ignorant either, 2 Cor. 2. 11.

When the Lord Jesus said 'It is written', He affirmed the **authority of the scriptures**, with men responsible to take heed to their teaching and truth. Equally, His appeal to the sacred writings asserted the **finality of the scriptures**, their precepts and principles providing the final ground of appeal in determining and vindicating actions. Further, in addressing the devil thus, the Lord demonstrated the **sufficiency of the scriptures** to answer and silence every attack of the tempter. In view of His deity the Lord could have simply used His divine power and glory to dismiss the devil but instead, as the dependant Man, He used 'the sword of the Spirit . . . the word of God' – an example we are exhorted to follow, Eph. 6. 17. So, acquaintance with the scriptures is absolutely vital if we would be well equipped to withstand the assaults of the devil.

The passages quoted by the Lord all came from the book of Deuteronomy, and quite apart from silencing the tempter each quotation gives an insight into the personal priorities and perfections of our Saviour. He was the obedient Man, living by 'every word of God'. One with implicit faith and confidence in God who shunned all thought of testing or challenging God, and a Man of undivided devotion in service to God, Matt. 4. 4, 7, 10. Are all these things priorities with us?

His Apostles

January 5th   Matthew 5. 1-20

This is the beginning of the Lord's first teaching discourse in this Gospel, and one in which the King sets forth the principles of His kingdom. The nine beatitudes begin with poverty and end with persecution, and can be viewed as following a logical sequence in spiritual experience. The lowliness of spirit, with which they commence, results in mourning over failure. That produces a meekness of heart so that we accept and submit to God's ways with us, culminating in an intense hunger and thirst for righteousness, vv. 3-6. The next three beatitudes describe the practical outcome of the first four – the reflection of the very character of God in those thus exercised, in being merciful, pure in heart, and peacemakers, vv. 7-9. The remaining two beatitudes both concern persecution, the reaction of a hostile world toward those who are 'called the children (Gk. *huios* 'sons') of God', vv. 9-12.

The persecution is twofold. In verse 10 it is for a principle, 'righteousness' sake', and in verse 11 for a Person, 'my sake'. The Lord would later warn His disciples to expect such opposition, John 15. 19-20. Comparing the two verses in Matthew chapter 5 the description of the sufferings for Christ's sake is far more extensive than those for righteousness' sake, 'revile you . . . persecute you . . . say all manner of evil against you falsely'. If men are hostile towards what is righteous in God's sight, that hostility is only increased when a person's conduct is linked to the name of Christ. But even though such persecution might come, and intense persecution at that, it is not to be viewed as a disaster, but instead, as a basis for rejoicing, and three reasons are given. Firstly, in relation to the past, we are following in the steps of prophets 'persecuted' before us, men who spoke for God, and following their example we are maintaining in our own day a testimony for God. Secondly, in reference to the present, since it is suffering for His 'sake' we become 'partakers of Christ's sufferings' and though others might speak ill of Him, on our part 'he is glorified', 1 Pet. 4. 12-14. Thirdly, in connection with the future, there is the promise of 'reward in heaven'. The apostles rejoiced to suffer 'for his name', Acts 5. 41. Do we?

Christ and

Matthew 5. 21-48

January 6th

I say unto you

At the end of chapter 7 Matthew writes of the Lord, 'The people were astonished at his doctrine: for he taught them as one having authority, and not as the scribes'. In today's passage six times the Lord says, 'But I say unto you', the Lord drawing a sharp contrast between what had formerly been said respecting the Mosaic law and His own teaching concerning it. Here we are listening to the voice of the Lawgiver Himself. The Lord asserted that the law was inviolable, the least of its commandments was important, and that its righteousness exceeded the standards espoused by the scribes and Pharisees, vv. 18-20. The righteousness of the scribes and Pharisees was based upon an external adherence to the law, but the teaching of the Lord was concerned not just with the 'letter' of the law and external conduct, but the 'spirit' of the law embracing the desires and motives of the heart.

In verses 21 to 26 the teaching concerns brotherly relationships, a warning against holding wrong attitudes towards brethren, and the importance of being at peace and at one with our brethren. In verses 27 to 30 the subject is purity of mind and the importance of excluding everything that acts detrimental to the wellbeing of the soul. In verses 31 to 32 the focus is upon faithfulness in marriage, maintaining the sanctity of the marriage bond. In verses 33 to 37 the theme is the taking of oaths, while the scribes warned against swearing falsely the Lord said, 'Swear not at all', the principle being that our words should be so dependable as to make such affirmations unnecessary. Verses 38 to 42 concern a readiness to give way when unfair demands are made upon us, a spirit of generosity and forbearance. Finally, in verses 43 to 47 love for all is commanded, even to enemies.

Here is the righteousness that exceeded the standards of the scribes and Pharisees, a righteousness reflecting the very character of the Father Himself, v. 48. Today, a believer is not under law but under grace, but Paul does speak of the 'righteousness of the law', that which the law required, being 'fulfilled' in those who walk 'not after the flesh but after the Spirit', Rom. 8. 4. Is our conduct reflecting the Father's character?

His Apostles

January 7th   Matthew 6. 1-18

When thou prayest

While the Lord's teaching in these verses covers the three themes of almsgiving, prayer, and fasting there is one lesson common to each: namely that our life is to be lived as unto God and not as unto men. Yet how easy it is to be more concerned with how we appear unto men rather than with pleasing God, and gaining the praise of men rather than the approval of God.

Three times in today's passage the Lord says *'when* [thou] prayest', not *'if* thou prayest', it being assumed that every true believer will be thus exercised to call upon God. Is it something that is characteristic of us? The teaching on prayer is divided into two sections: firstly, how not to pray; secondly, how to pray. We are not to pray as the *hypocrites,* men guilty of insincerity. The Lord is not condemning praying in public, for the Bible has many examples of godly men who prayed thus, men such as Solomon and Ezra. What the Lord condemns is the hypocrites' motive, praying 'that they may be seen of men'. Instead of seeking the most public place the disciple is to seek the most private place – 'thy closet'. Again, they were not to pray as the *heathen* men, condemned for their ignorance. They think God is unaware of their needs, reluctant to hear their requests, and this can be overcome only by prayer being reduced to a kind of repetitive incantation. Instead of praying with a view to informing God as the heathen do, the believer prays with a spirit dependent upon God, conscious that He knows what things we have need of even before we ask. In verses 9 to 15 the Lord shows **how** to pray. This 'pattern' prayer is a model of brevity, yet embraced within it there is praise of God, desire for the fulfilment of divine purpose, and petition for daily needs. At the heart of the prayer is a personal relationship, the privilege of knowing God as 'Father'. Next, is **reverence**, the focus in the opening statements being on God's interests and glory, His Name, kingdom, and will. Then four **requests** for personal needs are made, these petitions reflecting the Father's interest in the material and spiritual needs of His children, and a concern for their preservation and protection. May we heed the Lord's instruction and exhortation, and 'after this manner' pray.

Christ and

Matthew 6. 19-34   January 8th

While the first part of this chapter focused attention upon the practices of the disciple, almsgiving, prayer, and fasting, the remaining verses consider what the priorities in the life of the disciple should be: to lay up treasure in heaven, and to seek first the kingdom of God.

'Treasures in heaven' are contrasted with 'treasures upon earth', the Lord sounding a note of warning lest the acquisition and possession of material things should become the goal and ground of confidence in the believer's life. That the Lord gives the warning indicates there is a real possibility of such a thing happening, and perhaps especially so today when success is often measured by a man's wealth and riches. What we esteem to be treasure is an index to where our desires and affections lie, where our 'heart is', and that in turn determines the path we will pursue in life, vv. 21, 22-23. Moses esteemed 'the reproach of Christ greater riches than the treasures in Egypt: for he had respect unto the recompense of the reward', Heb. 11. 26. Could such words be written of us?

If the desire to acquire riches can become a distraction to a believer, having too little can equally become detrimental to him, a hindrance to 'seeking first the kingdom of God'. The concern for food, clothing, and the maintenance of life can dominate his mind, filling him with anxious thoughts and so deflect him from giving attention to the interests and will of God. Since God has given us life can we not trust Him to give us food to maintain it? Since God has given us a body can we not trust Him to provide clothing to cover it? Matt. 6. 25. Birds do not work, have no harvest to gather, and no storehouse to draw upon, yet they are fed by the provision of the Father in heaven. Solomon was the most affluent of all Israel's kings, but his glory is not to be compared to the glory with which God clothes the wild lilies. If our Father does that for birds and lilies what will He not do for us? He knows our needs and if we put God's kingdom first, we can count upon Him ministering to them. He adds His benefits to our day, whereas all anxious care will give only an additional burden to our day, vv. 33-34.

Seek ye first the kingdom of God

His Apostles

January 9th　　　　　　　　　　　　　Matthew 7. 1-14

Ask, and it shall be given you

The first six verses of this chapter centre around two exhortations: the first, 'judge not'; the second, 'give not'. The first concerns the treatment of brethren, a warning against applying to our brother a standard we have failed to apply to ourselves, something that is so easy to do, 1 Sam. 12. 1-12. The second exhortation concerns conduct towards the unregenerate and profane, the folly of setting sacred truth before those who have neither the desire, nor capacity, to receive it – men like Herod to whom the Lord answered nothing, Luke 23. 9.

The next section of Matthew chapter 7 concerns the Father's treatment of us, vv. 7-11, and our treatment of others, v. 12. The words 'ask', 'seek', and 'knock' are, in the Greek text, all in the present tense, denoting what is to be ongoing and constant, and thus importunity in praying. Again, the content of the request is not specified, so the emphasis is upon the attitude to be adopted in prayer, rather than on any one specific request and the assurance is given that all who pray thus shall receive. We are not however to assume that we can ask for anything we like, and are guaranteed to be given it. Paul prayed three times for the removal of the 'thorn' in his flesh, but instead of its removal the Lord said, 'My grace is sufficient for thee', 2 Cor. 12. 7-9. Other scriptures connect answered prayer to the petitioner keeping His commandments, asking according to His will, and asking in faith, 1 John 3. 22; 5. 14; Jas. 1. 6. The thrust of the Lord's assurance in Matthew chapter 7 is simply that a dependent and persistent spirit of waiting upon God will not be disappointed. Now, if such praying will result in a receiving, what kind of answer can we expect? If men who are inherently 'evil', members of Adam's fallen race, know how to give good gifts to their children, how much more can we expect God, who is intrinsically holy, to give good things to His children, especially when we remember He knows what we have need of, Matt. 6. 32? The concluding two verses of today's reading draw a contrast between two ways: one leading to life; the other leading to destruction – a reminder to us that to wait upon God and to live in prayerful fellowship with God is the pathway of life.

Christ and

Matthew 7. 15-29   January 10th

It has ever been the object of Satan to imitate what is of God, and the New Testament gives many warnings of the coming of those who are false: false prophets, false Christs, false apostles, false brethren, and false teachers, Matt. 24. 24; 2 Cor. 11. 13, 26; 2 Pet. 2. 1. To these we can add the warning of Paul who, writing of the last days said, 'Evil men and seducers shall wax worse and worse', 2 Tim. 3. 13. How timely then the call with which today's reading begins, 'Beware'!

Speaking of 'false prophets', the Lord indicated how easy it is to be deceived. Such men act subtly, coming in 'sheep's clothing' when in nature and character they are 'ravening wolves'. Later, when commissioning the twelve the Lord said, 'I send you forth as sheep in the midst of wolves', Matt. 10. 16. The false prophets present themselves as 'sheep', men called and sent by the Lord, but it is only a mask. In reality they are like greedy wolves, seeking unsuspecting victims to catch and devour. But how can we identify them if their true character is veiled? There is something that cannot be hid – the character of the fruit they produce, Matt. 7. 16, 20. In the world of horticulture the nature of the fruit corresponds to the nature of the plant or tree that produced it, a principle that goes back to creation when the earth brought forth 'herb yielding seed after his kind, and the tree yielding fruit whose seed was in itself, after his kind', Gen. 1. 12. Applying the Lord's teaching, expecting to receive what is edible and wholesome from false prophets is akin to looking for grapes on thorns, or figs on thistles. The false prophet is represented by things that are a result of the fall, thorns and thistles, and by a corrupt tree in which the foliage might be abundant, but the fruit bad. Thus it is with these unregenerate prophets. Just as corrupt trees are dispensed with, so the false prophet is to be rejected, Matt. 7. 19. Any man can confess 'Lord, Lord', but the evidence of reality will be seen in such departing from iniquity, vv. 21-23; 2 Tim. 2. 19.

Because there are spiritual imposters we must act wisely towards all who approach us claiming to be servants of the Lord, for sometimes appearances can be deceiving.

Ye shall know them by their fruits

His Apostles

January 11th — Matthew 8. 1-27

What manner of man is this!

Matthew chapter 5 began with the Lord going up into the mountain; chapter 8 begins with His descent from the mountain. In between those two points, in the Sermon on the Mount, the King has revealed the principles by which He will govern. In chapters 8 and 9 the focus now is not upon His teaching but upon His miracles, and His power to implement the manifesto of His kingdom. Five times in today's passage, and for the first time in Matthew's Gospel, He is directly addressed as 'Lord', vv. 2, 6, 8, 21, 25. For the first time the Lord refers to Himself by the title 'Son of man', v. 20.

One effective way of answering the query, 'What manner of man is this?' is to consider what the miracles recorded in these verses reveal about the Saviour. Firstly, in a miracle **in the countryside**, a leper was cleansed by His touch and word, vv. 1-4. In the second, a miracle accomplished **in the town**, a centurion's servant was healed by His word from a distance, the servant not seeing the One who healed him, vv. 5-13. Thirdly, in a miracle **in the home**, with no word, only a touch, Peter's mother-in-law was enabled immediately to rise from bed and minister unto them, vv. 14-15. In the stilling of the storm we see Christ's power **in the realm of nature**, vv. 23-26. Here was a 'man' who was master of every situation, able to meet the need of all who came to Him, v. 16. But is He only a man? The king of Israel confronted with Naaman the leper cried, 'Am I God . . . to recover a man of his leprosy', 2 Kgs. 5. 7? Equally, what man could rebuke the 'winds and sea' and from 'a great tempest' produce 'a great calm'? Of the Lord God of hosts Ethan wrote, 'Thou rulest the raging of the sea: when the waves thereof arise, thou stillest them', Ps. 89. 9. Here are things which are the prerogative of God alone, these miracles bearing testimony to the essential deity of the Lord Jesus.

Having thought of the greatness of the power of the Lord Jesus, and the glory of His Person, the quotation of the words of Isaiah, 'himself took our infirmities', reminds us of His grace, Matt. 8. 17. With reverent and grateful hearts we must surely exclaim with the disciples, 'What manner of man is this?'

Christ and

Matthew 8. 28 – 9. 17   January 12th

For the first time in the New Testament the Lord Jesus is directly confessed to be the Son of God and that from a most unexpected source. In chapter 4 the language of the tempter was, 'If thou be the Son of God'; now in chapter 8 two demon possessed men address him as 'Jesus, thou Son of God'. Speaking as one with these men the demons acknowledged who the Lord was, that they were powerless to resist His command, and that there was an appointed time for their judgement, vv. 29, 31. The plight of the two men was indeed desperate but 'the Son of God was manifested, that he might destroy the works of the devil', 1 John 3. 8. Just one word, 'Go', from the lips of the Saviour was sufficient to cast them out. How sad that while demons acknowledged and feared Him, men besought Him to depart, their darkened minds valuing a herd of swine above the help of the Saviour! cp. Eph. 4. 18; 2 Cor. 4. 4.

In contrast to those who desired His departure from them, others came to Him, Matt. 9. 2. Their faith that the Lord could meet their need and their determination to bring their friend to Him should surely challenge us, as to how far we are prepared to go in seeking to bring others to the Lord. While those men were occupied with the physical need of the one they brought, the Lord Jesus was concerned with his far greater *spiritual* need, the two things having in common that only Christ could minister to each need. John would later write, 'He was manifested to take away our sins', 1 John 3. 5, and as evidence of His power to forgive sins the man was healed. What a blessing to know that although we are 'altogether born in sins', through Christ and faith in Him our sins are forgiven also! Eph. 1. 7; Col. 1. 14. What a meditation to think of the One who 'died for our sins', who 'gave himself for our sins', and who 'by himself purged our sins'! 1 Cor. 15. 3; Gal. 1. 4, Heb. 1. 3. What a privilege to preach 'the forgiveness of sins' that by Him 'all that believe are justified from all things'! Acts 13. 38-39.

In Matthew's narrative, after the theme of forgiveness we see a man 'following', Matt. 9. 9. Has the forgiveness of sins resulted in such commitment to Christ on our part?

His Apostles

January 13th — Matthew 9. 18-38

Healing every sickness and every disease

Commenting on the ministry of the Lord Jesus as recorded in the latter part of this chapter J. C. RYLE wrote, 'He was an eye-witness of all the ills that flesh is heir to; He saw ailments of every kind, sort, and description; He was brought into contact with every form of bodily suffering. None were too loathsome for Him to attend to; none were too frightful for Him to cure'. Several Old Testament prophets spoke of the blessings that would attend the coming of Israel's Messiah, amongst which are the words of Isaiah, 'The eyes of the blind shall be opened, and the ears of the deaf shall be unstopped . . . the tongue of the dumb [shall] sing', Isa. 35. 5-6. This prophecy is looking on to the second advent of the Lord and to millennial days, but the very fact the Lord accomplished such miracles at His first advent bore testimony to His identity as the Messiah.

As the Lord began His public ministry Matthew spoke, in chapter 4 verse 23, of the Lord 'healing all manner of sickness and all manner of disease among the people'. Now in chapter 9, in almost identical words, the same observation is made. But why? Despite the references to the spreading of His fame and the testimony of the people, 'It was never so seen in Israel', it is nevertheless evident that on the part of the religious authorities there was a growing animosity towards the Saviour, vv. 26, 31, 33-34. The reminder of the power of the Lord to heal *all* demonstrates that even after adequate testimony was given to them, still they rejected Him. Truly He could say, 'They hated me without a cause', John 15. 25.

Reviewing the verses before us today, not only is there an emphasis upon the power of the Lord, but also equally upon His compassion. Consider His condescension in agreeing to follow the ruler of the synagogue, His words of comfort and assurance to the woman, His attention to those who cried, 'Have mercy on us', His willingness to receive those brought to Him for help. Even the cruel insinuations and false accusations of His enemies produced no change within Him. Still He 'was moved with compassion' seeing the multitudes as sheep without a shepherd.

Do the multitudes without Christ similarly move us?

Christ and

Matthew 10. 1-22 — January 14th

At the conclusion of chapter 9 the Lord said, 'The harvest truly is plenteous, but the labourers are few', exhorting the disciples to pray to 'the Lord of the harvest' to 'send forth labourers into his harvest'. Thus it is our responsibility to pray; His prerogative, to send. As we come into chapter 10, as 'Lord of the harvest' He calls and sends forth the Twelve. Those sent were men who had followed Him, had learnt from Him, and to whom the need to pray for labourers had been made known. Are we spending time with Him, learning of Him, praying in the light of His revealed will, as individuals He could choose and send forth today?

The commission given to the Twelve was distinctly Jewish in character, and while it embraces principles that are equally applicable today, the literal details can only be rightly understood when viewed in connection with the ministry of the apostles, and the witness of a future Jewish remnant living in tribulation days prior to the manifestation of Christ in glory. Specific mention is made of the 'house' and 'cities' of Israel, vv. 6, 23. The content of the message, 'the kingdom of heaven is at hand', concerned the kingdom promised by God through the ministry of the Old Testament prophets, v. 7. To demonstrate the authority and validity of the message the preaching would be accompanied by the working of miracles, 'the powers of the world to come', v. 8; Heb. 6. 5. As encouragement to the preachers the promise is given, 'He that endureth to the end shall be saved': the 'end' being a reference to the coming of 'the Son of man' in power, Matt. 10. 22-23, cp. 24. 13.

While we must not ignore the literal interpretation of these verses, neither should we overlook some of the very practical lessons for ourselves today. The Lord not only calls men, He empowers and equips those called, and determines the sphere of their ministry and the message to be preached, 10. 1, 6-7. Those called will need to act with wisdom and prudence, and although opposition is to be expected, the Holy Spirit will give help, vv. 16-22. An anticipation of the Lord's coming and kingdom imparts a sense of urgency to the work, 2 Tim. 4. 1-2.

The kingdom of heaven is at hand

His Apostles

January 15th   Matthew 10. 23-42

He that loseth his life for my sake

   The Lord never sought to hide from His disciples the demands that would be made upon all who resolved to follow Him in a world where He has been rejected. Such must expect to be exposed to verbal abuse and false accusations, and potentially even martyrdom, vv. 25, 28. Open confession of Christ might lead to division, even making enemies of family members, those from whom, on a natural level, they might have expected to receive some measure of interest and care, vv. 34-36. Unless a man is prepared to take up his cross, saying, No, to self and giving to Christ the pre-eminent place in his life and affections, that man is not fit to follow the Lord. The disciple's sole objective is to follow Christ and to exalt His name, vv. 37-39. Do we know anything of such a pathway, 'losing our life' in the interests of Christ? Is the Lord Jesus so precious to us and knowing Him so esteemed by us that we can say with Paul, 'I count all things but loss for the excellency of the knowledge of Christ Jesus my Lord', Phil. 3. 8? The Lord Jesus gave up His life for us, but what have we given up for Him?

   There was always a perfect balance to the teaching of the Lord and against this background of warnings regarding the difficulties to be expected, the Lord gave words of counsel and encouragement. His disciples are not wilfully and deliberately to seek to be divisive and contentious, hence the call to 'flee', but neither are they to be found fearful of men, Matt. 10. 23, 26, 28, 31. They are to remember that these sufferings will bring conformity to Christ, the disciple treading the same path as He trod. Could there be a greater privilege than that, vv. 24-25? Though hated of men they are the object of their Father's care. A care extended to the sparrow, and if to them how much more to His own? Such is the Father's interest in every detail of their life, even the hairs of their head are numbered by Him, vv. 28-31. No confession of Christ will be unrewarded; it might be despised on earth but it will be owned in heaven. Every sacrifice made for Christ will be honoured, vv. 32, 39.

   These verses present us with just two alternatives: to live for self or to live for Christ. Which one have you chosen?

Christ and

Matthew 11

January 16th

The chapter before us introduces us to an unexpected development in the life of John the Baptist. John had been the forerunner of the Lord Jesus – 'that Elias, which was for to come', v. 14. The same had introduced the Lord Jesus as the 'Lamb of God, which taketh away the sin of the world.' John 1. 29. But by this time John is in prison, and like his counterpart Elijah, following his greatest moments of service and at the end of his public ministry, he is plunged into doubt and depression, wondering if indeed the Lord Jesus is the Messiah. The Lord asks John's disciples to go and tell him all they had heard and seen – namely the mighty works being performed by the Lord Jesus as the prophets had anticipated regarding the coming Messiah.

We might have expected that the Lord would have been guarded in His endorsement of John in light of this seeming lapse, but rather, the Lord Jesus takes occasion to give John the highest of accolades. He describes him as 'more than a prophet', v. 9; 'the greatest born of women', v. 11; 'Elias, which was for to come', v. 14. The Lord then goes on to say that Israel had not responded to the strict asceticism of John, nor the sociability of His own ministry, but had condemned the one as having 'a devil', v. 18, and the other as 'a friend of publicans and sinners', v. 19. The Lord showed that rejection of God's overtures will lead to the most catastrophic of judgements, even as Sodom, with eternal consequences.

Some of God's greatest servants have had seasons of doubt and depression as their ministry comes to its close, and as adverse circumstances overtake them in the form of old age, ill-health, isolation, and loneliness. However, this does not depreciate the value of their ministry to His people over the years. Just as the Lord gave honour to John, He also has taken note of all that has been done by His servants, and the day of accolades is coming, when their service will be seen in its true light, and heaven's awards will be given. Meanwhile, the closing verses of the chapter could be applied to wearied servants like John, 'Come unto me, all ye that labour and are heavy laden, and I will give you rest', Matt. 11. 28.

Art thou he that should come?

His Apostles

January 17th

Matthew 12. 1-21

Lord even of the sabbath day

In this meditation, we find the Pharisees in conflict with the Lord regarding what was permissible on the sabbath day. Under the Law, the sabbath was prescribed to be a day of rest in which no work could be done. The Pharisees had taken this commandment and had added their own traditions, and in doing so, introduced human strictures that violated the spirit of the law.

In the first instance, the Lord's disciples were hungry, and had plucked ears of corn to eat them. The Pharisees designated this act as 'work' in the context of the commandment, and were quick to condemn. The Lord showed the error of their thinking by taking an illustration from the life of David when he was fleeing from Saul and was hungry. David had gone to Ahimelech the priest, and was given the hallowed bread that had been taken from the table of showbread, NKJV. By using this illustration, the Lord showed the Pharisees that the meeting of legitimate need was within the spirit of the law, v. 7.

In the second instance the Lord comes into the synagogue, and sees a man with a withered hand. The Pharisees then asked Him, 'Is it lawful to heal on the sabbath days?' v. 10. The Lord revealed their hypocrisy by showing that they would deliver one of their sheep if it fell into a pit on the sabbath day, then He reasoned, 'How much then is a man better than a sheep? Wherefore it is lawful to do well on the sabbath days', v. 12. He then healed the man.

The Pharisees could not resist the wisdom of the Lord's responses, but rather than admit their wrong, they begin to plot how they might kill Him. Note that, as opposed to the hostility of the Pharisees against the Lord, Matthew chooses to tell about the infinite pleasure and delight that Jehovah had in Christ. Matthew quotes from the prophet Isaiah where Jehovah expresses His pleasure in His perfect Servant saying, 'Behold my servant, whom I have chosen; my beloved, in whom my soul is well pleased', v. 18. In the final analysis, man's condemnation of the Lord was of no account, when He had the commendation of God. May we take comfort from this as we face an increasingly hostile world.

Christ and

Matthew 12. 22-50 — January 18th

Matthew introduces his Gospel with the words, 'The book of the generation of Jesus Christ, the son of David, the son of Abraham', Matt. 1. 1. The Lord Jesus was the Messiah anticipated by prophets of old, who foretold the things that He would do to demonstrate His credentials as Son of David, with right to the throne of Israel. Matthew shows that the Lord Jesus had all of the Messianic features identified by the prophets, indeed one of the recurring phrases in Matthew's Gospel is 'that it might be fulfilled which was spoken of the Lord by the prophet'. It is evident that, unlike the blind Pharisees, the common people accepted that the Lord was fulfilling what the prophets had said concerning the Messiah, hence we hear them say, 'Is not this the son of David?', v. 23.

The Pharisees could not refute that the Lord was doing these mighty works, and the accolades of the people towards the Lord raised their anger. To counter this, they tried to undermine the Lord's works, by claiming that His power was coming from Beelzebub, the prince of demons, v. 24. The Lord showed that if this was true, then Satan would be casting out Satan, which was completely illogical, v. 26, and that ascribing the work of the Holy Spirit done through Him to Satan, was blasphemy of an unforgiveable kind, vv. 31-32. Of course, the exception among the Pharisees was Nicodemus, who came to the Lord and said, 'No man can do these miracles that thou doest, except God be with him', John 3. 2. Nicodemus was honest enough to acknowledge the Lord's mighty works, as coming from God.

There are some practical lessons we can learn from these events. Firstly, that the realm of fulfilled prophecy is one of the strongest bulwarks against assaults being made upon the divine inspiration of the scriptures. Secondly, many religious leaders in Christendom today are no different from the Pharisees, and deny the power of God as witnessed in the works of the Lord Jesus. Finally, we find encouragement to continue with the spread of the gospel, knowing that as in our Lord's day, there are still many who are ready to accept Him for who He is – the Saviour of the world – even among the Pharisees.

His Apostles

Is not this the son of David?

January 19th

Matthew 13. 1-17

Matthew chapter 13 marks a significant watershed in the ministry of the Lord Jesus. We see Him leave the house, v. 1, and go to the seaside, v. 2. This was a highly symbolic move, and foreshadowed the time, when shortly afterwards, the unique privileges of the house of Israel would be set aside, and the gospel would be preached to the nations, as signified by the sea. The Lord's ministry now takes on a universal character, where He shows in the Parable of the Tares that 'the field is the world', v. 38.

Thereafter, the chapter describes the progress of the kingdom, the character of which, at present, is spiritual rather than visible. It is worthy of note that the Lord adopted the parabolic method in His teaching concerning the kingdom. This prompted the disciples to ask the question, 'Why speakest thou unto them in parables?' The Lord showed them that speaking in parables was a judgement upon the nation of Israel, 'because they seeing see not; and hearing they hear not, neither do they understand', v. 13. We must not take this to mean that the Lord had imposed this blindness and deafness on them, but rather as the Lord said, 'For this people's heart is waxed gross, and their ears are dull of hearing, and their eyes they have closed', v. 15. They were the ones who were deaf and unseeing by their own choice, and the Lord simply takes them up on the position they had already adopted. But to the ready-minded and open-hearted the Lord made His teaching known, vv. 11-12.

In the same manner, when speaking about the impotence of worldly wisdom in the spiritual realm, the apostle Paul wrote, 'Eye hath not seen, nor ear heard, neither have entered into the heart of man, the things which God hath prepared for them that love him. But God hath revealed them unto us by his Spirit', 1 Cor. 2. 9-10. Fallen man has shut God out of his mind and heart, and consequently he is completely insensitive to spiritual things. But those who have come to Christ and have the indwelling Holy Spirit are able to comprehend spiritual things that are beyond the capacity of the world's greatest intellects. This is one of the great blessings that the Lord has bestowed upon us, and we must take advantage of it in our spiritual lives.

He spake many things . . . in parables

Christ and

Matthew 13. 24-43

January 20th

Matthew chapter 13 verse 35 reads, 'I will open my mouth in parables; I will utter things which have been kept secret from the foundation of the world', cp. Ps. 78. 2. The Old Testament prophets foretold a literal kingdom – the millennial reign of Christ – but they did not anticipate developments leading to a spiritual kingdom being established, following the rejection of the King, nor did they anticipate the hiatus in the prophetic programme that would be filled by the church.

In the parables of Matthew chapter 13 the Lord Jesus describes the progress of the spiritual kingdom on earth during His absence. In them the Lord refers to 'the mysteries of the kingdom of heaven', v. 11. In the New Testament, a 'mystery' is a truth which human reason could never discover, but is revealed by God; once revealed it is an 'open secret' and thus for the edification of all of God's people. To avoid confusion it must be said that the mysteries of this chapter are not related to the 'mystery' that the apostle Paul refers to when he wrote, 'What is the fellowship of the mystery, which from the beginning of the world hath been hid in God', Eph. 3. 9. The former relate to the kingdom, the latter relates to the church. Whilst there are some commonalities between them, as to their constitution and destiny, they are quite different. In the kingdom parables of Matthew chapter 13 we find wheat and tares, good and bad, false and true, profession and reality, whereas in the church which is His body, there are only true believers. Also in the kingdom, dealing with evil is to be postponed until the Lord returns to earth. By contrast, the local church is expected to take action against such now, 1 Cor. 5. Again, prophecy anticipates a visible kingdom in the world when the Lord returns to earth in power and glory. However, this is not the hope of the saints. They look forward to the Lord's return to the air, to take them to be with Him for eternity. The kingdom has Christ as its King, but for the church He is her Lord, her beloved, her bridegroom. These then are two of the many 'mysteries' found in scripture: the mystery of the kingdom, and the mystery of the church – both once hidden, but now made manifest.

His Apostles

January 21st

Matthew 13. 18-23; 44-58

The kingdom of heaven is like unto . . .

Of the seven parables in Matthew chapter 13, the first four are spoken by the seaside, but the last three are spoken privately to the disciples, in the house. The first four relate exclusively to the kingdom, but the last three anticipate the church which would come into being after the Lord had ascended, and the Holy Spirit had come. Let's consider a select few of these parables from each of these groups.

The Sower and the Seed, vv. 3-23, is a lesson in evangelism. In this parable, the Lord is showing how the gospel should be propagated in the world, and it is given from the perspective of the evangelist. We learn that the seed – the word – is sown without regard to the kind of reception it will receive. The gospel is for everyone. We also learn that satanic agents will be busy when the seed is sown to snatch it away. Also, to keep us from being discouraged, the Lord shows that we can expect the responses to vary considerably, and it is not for the evangelist to be concerned about results; he must leave that to the Lord. But to encourage, He also tells about good results in fertile soil. All these lessons are invaluable to those involved in spreading the gospel.

We next consider the parables of the Treasure in the Field and the Goodly Pearl. These parables were spoken privately and anticipate the church. Note that in both these parables, the cost to the seeker was that he had to sell all that he had to purchase the treasure and the pearl. And indeed, for the church to be claimed, it cost the Lord everything – even unto death. We read, 'For ye know the grace of our Lord Jesus Christ, that, though he was rich, yet for your sakes he became poor, that ye through his poverty might be rich', 2 Cor. 8. 9. Note also that in the case of the treasure the whole field was bought to secure it. Such is the scope of the gospel – it embraces all humanity. There is no idea of 'limited atonement' here, but the work of the Lord Jesus on Calvary has the potential for the whole world to be saved through faith in that atoning work. It is only refusal to accept the gospel message by faith that will doom souls to a lost eternity.

Christ and

Matthew 14. 1-21　　　　　　　　　　January 22nd

Give me here John Baptist's head

This narrative describes a horrendous act of spiteful vengeance perpetrated by Herodias, King Herod's wife. Herodias had been the wife of Herod's brother Philip, and Herod had taken her for himself. John, in his fearless forthright way, condemned Herod for doing so. Herod, under pressure from Herodias, had him arrested, intending to execute him, but he feared an uproar from the people who thought John was a prophet; therefore he imprisoned him instead. However, Herodias' desire for vengeance overrode any concerns she might have had about the reaction of the people, and she waited her time to get her way. The opportune time soon arrived. Herod was having a birthday party, and Herodias' daughter danced for him, and Herod foolishly promised to give her whatever she desired. Prompted by her wicked mother, she asked for the head of John the Baptist on a platter. Herod was shocked and saddened by this request, but rather than lose face with the party attendees, he gave instructions that the deed should be done, and John was executed.

What a sad and ignominious end for such a great servant of God – put to death, not for any great cause, but to satisfy the calculated vengeance of a wicked, immoral woman. But even in such dire circumstances, we must acknowledge that in all of this, the sovereign purposes of God were being fulfilled. John's time had come to depart the scene, and Herodias was but the instrument used to accomplish God's intended purpose. It is true as the psalmist wrote, 'Surely the wrath of man shall praise thee', Ps. 76. 10.

We also see this principle at work in the death of the Lord Jesus. On the day of Pentecost, Peter addressed the elders of Israel saying 'Him (Christ), being delivered by the determinate counsel and foreknowledge of God, ye have taken, and by wicked hands have crucified and slain', Acts 2. 23. The sovereign purposes of God were fulfilled in that dreadful act, but the elders of Israel were not absolved from guilt.

May we take comfort from the fact that God's sovereign purposes for our lives can never be thwarted. We will find great peace by leaving things in His hand.

His Apostles

January 23rd

Matthew 14. 22-36

Lord, save me

In this incident the disciples, acting in obedience to the Lord's command, launched out into the sea, whilst He retired to the mountain to pray. Soon, the disciples encountered a great storm and found themselves in dire straits. Strangely, it was only when the disciples had reached the limits of their endurance that the Lord appeared walking on the waves. This further added to their terror, thinking they had seen a spirit. The Lord calmed their fears saying, 'Be of good cheer; it is I; be not afraid', v. 27.

Circumstances like these are also common in our lives, and there are some helpful and comforting lessons that we can learn from them. Firstly, we learn that walking in obedience to the Lord does not grant exemption from the severest of trials. Secondly, in the trial the Lord may not respond to our cries as quickly as we would like, and we may be taken to the very limits of our faith. Thirdly, the Lord will never abandon us, and will intervene to terminate the trial before we are overwhelmed. The apostle Paul reminds us, 'There hath no temptation taken you but such as is common to man: but God is faithful, who will not suffer you to be tempted above that ye are able; but will with the temptation also make a way to escape, that ye may be able to bear it', 1 Cor. 10. 13.

Subsequent to the Lord's appearing, Peter asked the Lord to bid him come to Him, and at His bidding he stepped out of the ship and was walking on the sea. But when he took his eye off the Lord, and became occupied with the wind and waves, his confidence was shaken, and he began to sink. In his distress he cried, 'Lord, save me.' The Lord immediately responded, chiding Peter for his 'little faith'.

From this final scene we learn that if we invite the Lord to test our faith, as Peter did, we must be prepared to face the consequences, and to trust Him in the test that comes along. It is so easy to have strong faith when we are in the ship. But even if, like Peter, we embark on a certain course with over-confident bravado, and discover that our faith is not as robust as we thought, in His love He is always ready to answer that urgent prayer, 'Lord, save me'.

Christ and

Matthew 15. 1-28 — January 24th

Blind leaders of the blind

In this passage, the Lord finds Himself being criticized by the scribes and Pharisees, because His disciples were eating bread without first washing their hands. This had not to do with personal hygiene, but the man-made traditions of the Pharisees demanded a ceremonial washing before one ate. The Lord rebuked them, showing that whilst they criticized the disciples for the violation of their traditions, they seemed to have no problem with violating the commandments of God in relation to things much more serious – honouring father and mother. The Lord used very strong language, calling them 'hypocrites', v. 7, and 'blind leaders of the blind', v. 14.

The Lord then identified the real source of defilement. He showed that it is not what enters a man that defiles, but what proceeds from him, and He describes the terrible things that emanate from the unregenerate heart as being the real source of defilement, v. 19.

The Lord is teaching that to be content with external compliance, yet to neglect the more serious issues of the inner condition, is nothing short of hypocrisy. On this same note, the Lord later described the Pharisees as 'whitened sepulchres . . . full of dead men's bones', Matt. 23. 27. They looked so pure and holy externally, but were full of rottenness and corruption within. This is a sobering thing for the Christian to contemplate; be warned against ever becoming like the Pharisees.

The chapter closes with the story of a Gentile woman who came to the Lord asking Him to heal her son. At first the Lord seems to rebuff her, reminding her that He had not been sent 'but unto the lost sheep of the house of Israel', and that as a Gentile 'dog' she had no right or claim to His ministrations. At this point the woman showed remarkable humility, accepting the place of the 'dog', but reminding Him that even dogs eat the crumbs that fall from their master's table. The Lord commended her for her great faith and healed her son. In this the Lord shows that humility of spirit combined with faith in Him, apart from merit, worth, or claim, will bring blessing. What a message for sinners!

His Apostles

January 25th   Matthew 15. 29 – 16. 12

Beware of the leaven of the Pharisees

In this passage, the Lord continued to demonstrate by His mighty works that He was indeed the long-promised Messiah, and that He had come from God. He performed miracles of healing across a wide spectrum of acute medical problems. He also fed the four thousand using the meagre resources available, and the surplus was greater than the original supply. Faced with all this evidence, the voice of unbelief is still heard to say, 'Show us a sign from heaven', cp. Matt. 16. 1. The Lord rebukes these religious leaders by saying that they could discern from the heavens whether the weather will be fair or foul, and yet they were unable to discern the fact that His mighty works were indeed the ultimate 'sign from heaven' they were seeking. The Lord shows that unbelief will never be satisfied, no matter how conclusive the evidence presented.

After this confrontation with unbelief, the Lord says to His disciples, 'Beware of the leaven of the Pharisees and of the Sadducees', v. 6. But the disciples misunderstood, thinking that the Lord was referring to the fact that they had not brought bread with them. The Lord reminds them that He had just demonstrated the adequacy of heaven's resources in the absence of adequate supply, and that He could not be referring to the lack of bread, but that He was referring to the doctrine of the Pharisees and Sadducees.

Leaven is consistently portrayed in scripture as the propagation of evil. It permeates silently and insidiously until the whole mass is irreversibly affected. The apostle Paul likened the tolerance of immorality in Corinth to leaven saying, 'And ye are puffed up', 1 Cor. 5. 2. And again, 'Know ye not that a little leaven leaveneth the whole lump? Purge out therefore the old leaven', vv. 6-7. Likewise he likens the false gospel, being propagated among the Galatians, to leaven, saying again, 'A little leaven leaveneth the whole lump', Gal. 5. 9.

The Lord would have us be diligent in our watchfulness against the inroads of 'leaven' in any assembly, whether doctrinal or moral, and to have the courage to deal with it promptly, before all is affected.

Christ and

Matthew 16. 13 – 17. 13   January 26th

Matthew chapter 16 marks another significant watershed in the life and ministry of the Lord Jesus. Up until this time, He has been presented as 'Son of David,' with a demonstrated right to the throne, but from this point on, He is presented as 'son of Abraham', Matt. 1. 1. We read, 'From that time forth', 16. 21, and the Lord proceeds to show that like Isaac of old, He is bound for the altar. He tells His disciples 'that he must go up unto Jerusalem, and suffer many things of the elders and chief priests and scribes, and be killed, and be raised again the third day', v. 21. Not only so, but far from encouraging the expectation of an immediate arrival of His earthly kingdom, He shows His disciples that each must take up his cross, and follow Him, v. 24. A pathway of suffering and rejection was to be their lot. In view of this, and lest they should be discouraged, the Lord took Peter, James, and John up to 'an high mountain apart, and was transfigured before them', 17. 1-2, thus giving them a preview of the glory of the future kingdom. In the meantime they had to realize that the promise of an earthly kingdom was not being abandoned, but simply postponed, during which time He would build His church, 16. 18.

But the highlight of these verses is surely the divinely inspired confession of Peter when he declared, 'Thou art the Christ, the Son of the living God', v. 16. Others were prepared to see the Lord Jesus as being on a par with some of the great prophets of the past such as Elijah, Jeremiah, or the more recent John the Baptist, but Peter sees beyond all of these and identifies Him as possessed of full deity – 'Son of the living God'. It is this that separates the Lord Jesus from all other men, and leaders of world religions. He alone is the eternal Son of the eternal God.

> Thou art the everlasting Word,
> The Father's only Son;
> God manifestly seen and heard,
> And heaven's beloved one.
>
> JOSIAH CONDER

His Apostles

January 27th
Matthew 17. 14 – 18. 11

One of the constant preoccupations of the Lord's disciples was 'Who is the greatest in the kingdom of heaven?' 18. 1. The mother of James and John approached the Lord on one occasion and requested, 'Grant that these my two sons may sit, the one on thy right hand, and the other on the left, in thy kingdom', 20. 21. All this took place, even as the shadow of the cross lay heavily across the path of the Lord Jesus.

It is noteworthy how the Lord responded to this spirit of pride. He placed a little child in their midst and said, 'Verily I say unto you, Except ye be converted, and become as little children, ye shall not enter into the kingdom of heaven', 18. 3. This must have been a stinging rebuke to these grasping disciples. They had to learn that prominence in the kingdom does not come to those seek it, but rather to the humble in spirit, who have no ambitions for self-glory, and who are prepared to take the lowest place in the society of men. This is why the Lord used a little child as His object lesson on this subject. Children do not vie for position or glory. They are humble in heart and accepting of the lowly place they occupy.

The Lord Himself is the greatest exponent of this humility of heart and mind. The apostle Paul writing to the Philippians reminded them that the Lord Jesus was 'equal with God', and yet did not think this something to be grasped after, but 'made himself of no reputation', Phil. 2. 2-7. He proceeded step by step to go lower and lower, until we read 'obedient unto death, even the death of the cross.' v. 8. The grand sequel is this, 'Wherefore God also hath highly exalted him', v. 9. The pride that motivated these disciples is still at work today. Many of the problems that plague local churches have nothing to do with the defence of fundamental truth, but rather, the clamour for prominence and self-glory. May the Lord give us the spirit of humility and self-abasement that characterizes the 'little child', and Himself. In the world of men the way to glorification is self-exaltation, but in the spiritual world the way to glorification is self-abnegation.

Matthew 18. 12-35

January 28th

The passage under consideration has to do with the matter of problems between brethren, and how to remedy them. In the first section, vv. 15-17, we learn how to proceed when offence is given by one brother to another, and three steps are described.

Firstly, an attempt should be made by the two parties involved to put things right privately. We read, 'Between thee and him alone', v. 15. If this approach is not successful, then the offended brother has to take two or three more with him, for a second attempt at reconciliation, v. 16. If this is not successful then the church has to be involved, and if the offender will not hear the church, he is to be considered 'as an heathen man and a publican', v. 17. We learn therefore that every attempt should be made to reconcile within as small a circle as possible.

The second section, vv. 21-22, has to do with how often should one go through the process described in the first section before one should refuse to forgive the offender. Peter asks the question, 'Lord, how oft shall my brother sin against me, and I forgive him? till seven times?' The Lord surprised Peter by saying, 'Until seventy times seven', v. 22. Now the Lord was not teaching that we must keep an account of every time a brother sins against us, and when it reaches 'seventy times seven' that we can refuse to forgive any further. No! The Lord is teaching that in the matter of forgiveness of an offender, where there is true repentance, there must be no limit to that forgiveness. Concerning forgiveness, J. N. DARBY (*Synopsis*) wrote, 'We must pardon to the end, or rather, there must be no end; even as God has forgiven us all things'.

The third section of this passage, vv. 23-35, shows why our forgiveness must be without limit. The Lord tells of a man who owed 10,000 talents, and when he could not pay his lord forgave him. This man then took a fellow-servant by the throat, who owed him a mere 100 pence, and demanded payment. His lord was 'wroth', and he took severe action against him.

May we heed the words of the apostle, 'Forgiving one another, even as God for Christ's sake hath forgiven you', Eph. 4. 32.

His Apostles

January 29th   Matthew 19

Is it lawful for a man to put away his wife?

This chapter deals with matters concerning the sanctity of marriage, and the protection of children who result from that union. We are living in days when marriage is taken lightly by so many in the world, to the extent that more and more are ignoring the necessity for it, and choosing to cohabit, thus leaving the door open for a quick exit without the complications of divorce proceedings. Also, many who have taken marriage vows do not treat them seriously. At the first indication of marital disharmony, they readily turn to the idea of divorce, rather than to work through the problems with each other. This reflects the way in which society has rejected God's intention regarding marriage. Marriage was never intended to be a convenience, but a commitment to each other for a lifetime.

It is evident from the passage under consideration, that the marriage problems which plague today's society were also present, even if on a lesser scale, in New Testament times. The Pharisees tried to put the Lord on the spot regarding the problem of divorce and whether it should be allowed. In those days a man could divorce his wife for some trivial reason – 'for any cause'. The Lord made it clear that it was God's intention that marriage should be a commitment for life, as it is God who joins together. He also made it clear that Moses did not introduce the bill of divorcement to accommodate an easy way out of marriage, but 'because of the hardness of their hearts', and He follows this by adding, 'but from the beginning it was not so', v. 8. In other words, Moses introduced the bill of divorcement as an exception, and as a protection against those who thought they could break the marriage bond for some trivial reason – 'for any cause'. The obtaining of a bill of divorcement would demand that 'just cause', e.g., fornication, v. 9, be presented, versus 'any cause', before it would be granted, thus giving protection to the wife and the children of the union.

In conclusion, marriage is intended by God to reflect that indissoluble eternal union between Christ and His church and this must always be borne in mind within every Christian marriage.

Christ and

Matthew 20. 1-16   January 30th

In this section we find a parable where a householder went out early in the morning and hired labourers to work in his vineyard. At the eleventh hour he went out again to the market place, and hired others who were still unemployed. At the end of the day, he gave one penny to those who had worked all day, and also to them who had worked only part of the day. The early workers complained that since they had worked longer, and under much more arduous conditions, they should receive more. In response, the householder reminded them that they had agreed to work for a penny, and that he had honoured his word. Also, because no one had hired the second group earlier, through no fault of their own, they did not have the same opportunity to work as long as the others. In these circumstances, he had opened his heart to them and paid them for the whole day.

This, being a kingdom parable, primarily relates to the Lord's second advent, when He will come to the earth, and judge Israel and the nations, but the principles involved can be applied to the coming day of reckoning, when saints will stand before the judgement seat of Christ. We learn here that the Lord in His sovereignty chooses to use us in His service. Many dear saints have borne the heat of the day, and laboured for a lifetime, but others have served well, but for a shorter time due to ill-health, premature death, martyrdom, or the Lord's predetermined tenure for their service. Consider, for example, John the Baptist. Also, the rapture of the church will mean that the work of younger servants will be cut short. In such circumstances, the criteria for reward will not be the length of service given, but the willingness to serve when opportunity was available to serve, and the faithfulness with which that service was exercised.

In light of these facts, how important it is that we do not compare our service with the service of others, or assume entitlement to greater glory! We must humbly accept that the Lord, who could have done His work without us poor earthen vessels, has chosen to use us, and to give us reward according to His sovereign grace. To Him be all the glory!

A penny a day

His Apostles

January 31st   Matthew 20. 17-34

It is against the background of the disciples' vying for position and power in the kingdom that the Lord makes the statement, 'The Son of man came not to be ministered unto, but to minister, and to give his life a ransom for many', v. 28. He had not come into the world to seek earthly glory at this time, but to lay down His life as a ransom, and the implication is that the disciples should also be prepared to suffer in the present, and have patience with regard to coming glory.

It should be noted that the Lord describes Himself in this context as 'the Son of man'. This title is one that embraces all that was involved in the great stoop when He took upon Himself flesh and blood. He had been Son of God from all eternity, but the work of redemption required that He become 'Son of man' – not that He ceased to be what He ever had been. The incarnation was not a *subtraction* from His person, but rather an *addition* to it. He became something that He had not been before – 'Son of man'. We read, 'But we see Jesus, who was made a little lower than the angels for the suffering of death, crowned with glory and honour; that he by the grace of God should taste death for every man', Heb. 2. 9.

Note the grand purpose of becoming Son of man: 'to give His life a ransom for many'. There are three important things we must note in this statement. Firstly, the voluntary nature of His death. It is not that men will take His life from Him, but that He gives His life. The Lord could say, 'No man taketh it from me, but I lay it down of myself. I have power to lay it down, and I have power to take it again. This commandment have I received of my Father', John 10. 18. The second thing we should note is that in His death the 'ransom' price was paid in full to redeem us from the slavery of sin. We could not pay it ourselves, but He took responsibility for it at Calvary. Thirdly, it was for *'many'*. The apostle Paul also wrote, 'Who gave himself a ransom for *all'*, 1 Tim. 2. 6. This reminds us that the gospel is *'unto all* and *upon all* them that believe [the many]', Rom. 3. 22. We should ever praise God for His grace and mercy in giving His Son.

Christ and

Matthew 21. 1-32 — February 1st

The journey to Jerusalem was almost completed. It was from the top of the transfiguration mount that the Lord turned His steps toward Jerusalem for the final time. With the assurance of heaven's interest in His decease clearly impressed on His heart, the Saviour set His face toward the city that He knew would reject Him; the appointed hour was drawing near.

Yet the nation must be given one more opportunity to acknowledge that the prophet from Nazareth of Galilee was indeed the promised One, the King of Zechariah's prophecy, 'just, and having salvation; lowly, and riding upon an ass', Zech. 9. 9. The cry of the 'very great multitude' echoed from the city walls, 'Hosanna to the Son of David: Blessed is he that cometh in the name of the Lord': words taken from Psalm 118, that great Hallel psalm of praise. The Lord would later quote from this psalm to emphasize that His rejection was the subject of prophetic scripture, Matt. 21. 42, and some have suggested that the hymn sung by the Lord and His disciples before leaving the upper room was this same psalm. If that is so, then the words, 'bind the sacrifice with cords, even unto the horns of the altar', Ps. 118. 27, would strike a very poignant chord in the heart of the Saviour.

The initial acclaim of the multitude soon faded however, and with the temple cleansed, the innocent tribute of the children heard in the courts soon incurred the displeasure of the authorities. Significantly, we read, 'he left them', and journeyed to Bethany, where He knew a welcome would await Him.

As He returned to Jerusalem the fruitlessness of the nation, epitomized by the barren fig tree, occasioned the only judgemental miracle by the Lord Jesus; nevertheless, He used it to teach His disciples a lesson in faith and prayer.

On entering the temple, the chief priests and elders seized the opportunity to question His authority, no doubt as a result of His action in removing the market traders the previous day. But, with the wisdom of omniscience, the Lord Jesus countered their question with one of His own, rendering them confused and speechless! So putting to silence the ignorance of foolish men.

His Apostles

February 2nd
Matthew 21. 33 - 22. 14

The two parables in the reading today underline the inevitable sentence passed upon the nation in view of persistent refusals to accept their Messiah. The illustration of the householder and the vineyard draws substantially on chapter 5 of Isaiah's prophecy. There the nation is seen as a choice vine, nurtured, protected, and given every opportunity to produce the best of fruit. The heartbreak and disappointment of the householder is tangible when the privileged vine produced only wild grapes and the cry is heard, 'What could have been done more to my vineyard that I have not done?' The retribution which followed left the once cherished vine broken, trodden down, and laid waste. In the Lord's application of this prophecy He focuses on the husbandmen, rather than the vineyard, revealing their despicable treatment of the householder's servants and, above all, of the son and heir.

In the second parable He likens the provision offered to the nation as an invitation to a wedding feast, with no expense spared. Their base ingratitude was revealed by the Lord's words that many 'made light of it, and went their ways', while others even ill-treated and slew those who brought the invitation! Again, just reprisals followed and ultimately the wedding was seen to be 'furnished with guests', not least with those who once seemed to have no chance of a place at the table. The parable, of course, has dispensational and kingdom implications, with the guest not having a wedding garment an example of profession without possession, like the tares among the wheat.

The clear teaching of the Lord was not lost on the chief priests and Pharisees, 'they perceived that he spake of them', and they 'sought to lay hands on him'. The Lord would later say to Pilate, speaking particularly of Caiaphas the representative of the nation, 'he that delivered me unto thee hath the greater sin'. Abundant evidence of His credentials had been placed before them and they still resolutely rejected Him. To sin against light and opportunity will inevitably result in severe judgement, whether it be on the nation of Israel or upon those who refuse the gospel of grace in our day!

Matthew 22. 15-46 February 3rd

What think ye of Christ?

Pressure was mounting. Pharisees, Herodians, Sadducees, and scribes all pressed upon the Saviour seeking occasion against Him. Yet, as each attempt to trap Him failed, men were left marvelling, astonished, and ultimately silenced!

The first attack was political. The question seemed innocuous, but in truth it was barbed and baited. It was really a matter of allegiance and subjection: would the Lord risk alienating the nation by condoning the tribute paid to the hated Roman occupiers, or would He provide ammunition to be used against Himself by suggesting that payment be withheld? His response was masterly. He called for the tribute coin, not primarily because of His poverty, though the thought is appropriate, but rather, had He produced the coin bearing Caesar's image, they would have immediately accused Him of idolatry, since the Jews used their own temple coinage. 'Render', He said, 'to Caesar . . . and to God', the thought is to *give back*, to each their rightful due, and it was abundantly clear that the nation's leaders had persistently failed to honour the God of their fathers with their obedience! They hastily withdrew, defeated.

The next attempt was theological. The Sadducees came with a question about resurrection, a truth they refused to accept. Their hypothetical reasoning was based on ignorance and unbelief, the same ground from which many in our day attack the word of God. Again, the Lord dismisses their fatuous argument with challenging words, 'Ye do err' and, 'have ye not read?' vv. 29, 31.

The final approach was legal. An attempt was made to coerce the Saviour into taking sides in a rabbinical dispute which divided the scholars of the day. His reply, straight from the scriptures, condemned their behaviour both toward God and their neighbour!

The Saviour's question in response to their scheming was in the spiritual realm, 'What think ye of Christ? whose son is he?' They must have thought, Ha! that's an easy one, 'The Son of David'. Quoting directly from Psalm 110, the Lord silenced them by pointing out that the promised One was both David's Lord and David's son, 'the root and the offspring of David'. He stood before them; very soon they would cast Him out!

His Apostles

February 4th   Matthew 23

Woe unto you!

The verses before us today are a catalogue of woes! Eight times the Lord pronounced woe upon the scribes and Pharisees, the blind guides of the nation. But before He denounced them for specific hypocrisies, He reminded both them and His audience of the solemn responsibilities these scribes and Pharisees had placed themselves under by sitting 'in Moses' seat'. They claimed to teach the law, yet, by additions and adaptions of their own they had made the law burdensome to others, while they proudly flaunted their status and standing in society.

In Ephesians chapter 4 verse 26, the apostle allows that there are circumstances where anger is a justifiable reaction for the believer; he cautions, however, of the danger that this might lead to sin. With the Lord there was, of course, no possibility that His withering condemnation would amount to vindictive and malicious anger. It flowed out from the righteous indignation He felt within His own soul on seeing the disadvantaged, the poor, the widows and the common people toiling under burdens 'grievous to be borne', while those who should have been shepherds fed themselves from the flock.

In rapid succession the scribes and Pharisees were denounced as hypocrites, fools, blind, serpents, vipers, and, finally, murderers! The Lord ended this perceptive exposure with a prophetic statement in verses 34 to 36. Of those prophets sent to them, some they would kill and crucify, clear evidence that He knew what lay before Him, since crucifixion had no place in the Jewish legal system. But just retribution would undoubtedly fall on these ungodly men in order to vindicate the blood of righteous martyrs from Abel right through the course of their national history.

The closing verses mark a significant point in the pathway of the Saviour. Of Zion, the city of David, He had declared through the prophet, 'I have graven thee upon the palms of my hands; thy walls are continually before me', Isa. 49. 16. He viewed the city, considered its past and future; the house of God was soon to be left as their house and rendered desolate. As He turned away the tears streamed down His face.

Christ and

Matthew 24. 1-28 — February 5th

As the Lord Jesus left the temple for the final time, the disciples sought to draw His attention to the beauty and magnificence of the building which had been constructed over the past forty-six years under the jurisdiction of the Herods. The disciples' interest provided opportunity for the Lord to reveal one of the most important prophetic outlines found in scripture.

He began by announcing the utter destruction of the temple, 'not one stone left upon another'. The disciples were amazed and questions came flooding out, 'Tell us . . . when? . . . what?' Before addressing the questions directly, however, He spoke of conditions which would prevail in anticipation of the end times.

Many attempts have been made and much has been suggested to try and equate the Lord's words to historical and present events. However, we need to bear in mind that the 'coming' referred to throughout is not the rapture of 1 Thessalonians chapter 4. It has often been taught, and rightly so, that the present church age is not the subject of prophecy. The Lord is here speaking of events leading up to His return 'with power and great glory', Matt. 24. 30; Rev. 19. 11-16. There is no doubt that history is scarred by false Christs, wars, famines, and earthquakes; these, however, are not the 'signs' referred to in our chapter, but rather, a marked intensity of these things will follow the rapture of the church as the seals are broken in Revelation chapter 6.

The Lord then outlined a timetable of events which will accompany those days of tribulation, yet future, of which the scripture clearly speaks. It is important to understand that before that time commences the church will be gone, 1 Thess. 5. 9; Rev. 3. 10. Jeremiah the prophet calls those days 'the time of Jacob's trouble', Jer. 30. 7, hence, the context of Matthew chapter 24 is clearly Jewish and relates to conditions on earth, and particularly in the Middle East, centred upon Jerusalem. The latter part of the seven years of tribulation, which concludes the remarkable prophecy of Daniel chapter 9, will be marked by events or signs which will clearly indicate to the suffering nation of Israel the imminent return of their Deliverer, their once-rejected Messiah, the Son of Man.

His Apostles — *What shall be the sign of thy coming?*

February 6th

Matthew 24. 29-51

Continuing His discourse from the Mount of Olives, the Lord Jesus described the immediate events surrounding His return to earth. It will be swift, eye-catching, and accompanied by disruption in the stellar heavens; angels will summon the elect of Israel with 'a great sound of a trumpet'.

A parenthesis follows in the Lord's teaching before the narrative is again taken up in chapter 25 verse 31. The intervening verses emphasize the practical responsibilities of watchfulness, readiness, and patience.

The Lord's words which follow from verse 32 of chapter 24 have been the subject of various interpretations, some of which seek to determine a date for the Lord's return; such speculation is, however, futile, and was never the intended purpose of these verses. It is clear, nonetheless, to those who embrace the entirety of prophetic truth taught in scripture, that the imagery applied in these verses and in the chapter which follows refers to events concerning the nation of Israel just prior to, and at the time of, the Lord's return to the earth. His reference to the fig tree points, as in other scriptures, to the nation, set aside in view of their fruitlessness, 21. 19, yet to be restored in a coming day. In confirmation of this, the Lord's reference to 'this generation', 24. 34, may indicate His preserving hand upon the seed of Abraham through the course of history and on into times yet future. Should any doubt, as many do, the certainty of Israel's restoration, the Lord verifies it by emphasizing the immutability of His words, which 'shall not pass away', v. 35.

The days of Noah were days of unbelief, resulting in rejection of the revealed word of God in respect of impending judgement. The return of the Lord in glory will take many by surprise, even though it is clearly indicated, and with some detail, in the scriptures. The ones in the field and at the mill who are left are examples of those who have endured faithfully through tribulation days, they will enjoy millennial blessing. The careless and unbelieving are summarily judged at the Lord's return. The chapter closes with a parable to emphasize these truths.

Christ and

Matthew 25. 1-30 — February 7th

Watch therefore

The word 'then' which opens this chapter links the teaching in the following verses to the events outlined by the Lord in chapter 24. Many a gospel message has been preached from the parable of the ten virgins, and doubtless it has led souls to salvation. However, whereas the principles found in portions of scripture such as this can be used as illustration and application, we need to take into account the context and details to arrive at an interpretation. The Lord is speaking of events associated with the coming of the Son of Man, a title linked with His earthly pathway and purpose. He illustrates His coming as that of a bridegroom and the parable portrays the ceremony and culture of a Middle Eastern wedding. The virgins cannot represent the bride, she has already been claimed by the bridegroom; they do, however, indicate the watchfulness or otherwise of the remnant of Israel in anticipation of millennial blessing when the Lord Jesus inaugurates His kingdom on earth.

The parable which follows places emphasis, not so much on preparation and watchfulness, but on faithfulness in service. The prophetic timeframe still anticipates the Lord's return to the earth, but the principles and the pattern can be applied to every age: the absent lord, the servants entrusted with the means to engage in profitable employment, the period of opportunity given until their lord's return, and his assessment of service, followed by appropriate reward or loss.

This parable is often compared with the parable of the pounds, Luke 19. 12-27. There are similarities but also differences, not least being the occasion on which each was spoken. Here also, the amount entrusted to the servants was 'according to his several ability', whereas in Luke the amount given was the same to each, with emphasis being placed on the rewards gained by prudent management of the master's assets. Both parables look forward to the kingdom reign of the Lord Jesus, but we in our day have been likewise entrusted with both ability and opportunity to serve a returning Master. There will be for us a time of assessment and reward, 2 Cor. 5. 10; we do well to heed the Lord's words, 'Occupy till I come', Luke 19. 13.

His Apostles

February 8th

Matthew 25. 31-46

Before Matthew concludes his record of the great prophetic discourse given by the Lord Jesus, he reminds us that His sovereignty is not restricted to the nation of Israel. On a number of occasions in his Gospel, Matthew recalls that Gentiles acknowledged the authority of the Lord Jesus. In chapter 2, the wise men came from the East and worshipped Him. Then in chapter 8, the centurion, a man who had travelled from the West, owned His authority. In chapter 15, a woman of Canaan, one from the land, but a Gentile, a 'stranger to the covenants of promise', came and worshipped Him. Matthew does not record the ascension of the Lord Jesus; He is last seen with the Eleven in Galilee, 'Galilee of the Gentiles', Matt. 4. 15, where, from a mountain top, and in anticipation of a kingdom, the 'King of all the earth', Ps. 47. 7, proclaimed, 'All power (authority) is given unto me in heaven and in earth'.

Our reading today underlines the need to appreciate that scripture explains God's purposes for three companies of people. The nation of Israel, the Gentile nations (often referred to as 'the heathen'), and the church. The last of these, comprised of all believers of this present age, is not in view in Matthew chapters 24 and 25; the rapture of the church will have taken place before these events begin to unfold. The greater part of prophetic scripture in both Old and New Testaments has to do with God's purposes for Israel. To a lesser degree there are prophecies which relate to Gentile nations, but these are usually determined by their association with, and influence upon Israel.

The judgement described in our verses relates to Gentile nations, following the Lord's return to earth. The nation of Israel will have already passed 'under the rod' of judgement, Ezek. 20. 33-44; now a similar assessment is made of Gentiles to determine entrance into the millennial kingdom for some (the sheep), or rejection for others (the goats). The decisive factor will be their attitude and behaviour towards the faithful remnant of Israel during tribulation days, 'Inasmuch as ye have done it unto . . . these my brethren, ye have done it unto me', Matt. 25. 40.

Matthew 26. 1-30

February 9th

Our reading today is one of dark conspiracies alleviated by bright shafts of light as the storm clouds gather around the Saviour. It begins with fear of an uproar and ends with the singing of a hymn. We read of Mary's worship of her Lord expressed in the pouring out of that which was 'very precious', in contrast to Judas' paltry estimate of the Lord Jesus, just thirty pieces of silver. The Passover is kept, looking back to redemption from Egypt, but pointing forward to Calvary. Then bread and wine from the Saviour's hands is given to His own for a remembrance which looks back to Calvary and onward to His coming; between these two memorials the betrayer leaves to carry out his nefarious plan.

The malevolent scheming of the Jewish authorities to try and find an appropriate time to apprehend the Lord Jesus was futile. He knew exactly both the time and the manner of His death, v. 2, their devious plans only contributed to their guilt; as the Lord would later say to Pilate in reference to Caiaphas and his allies, 'He that delivered me unto thee hath the greater sin', John 19. 11.

Of the three Gospel writers who record the costly expression of devotion to the Lord seen in these verses, only John identifies the worshipper as Mary of Bethany, John 12. 3. We know that this incident took place after the raising of Lazarus. Mary, unlike others, understood that the Lord must die, 'she did it for my burial'. But had Mary also grasped the truth which evaded the disciples, that 'in him was life' and resurrection? Did she appreciate that to anoint His body after death would be unnecessary? She worshipped, as we do today, a living Saviour!

All the Gospel writers record, as though barely credible, that Judas was 'one of the twelve' – so close, so privileged, so unforgivable. Yet all recall his heinous act of 'lifting up his heel' against One who had shown him only kindness.

Now to the Eleven, the Lord reveals something entirely distinct from the Passover rituals, the enduring memorial of His pathway to the cross symbolized in bread and wine, our constant reminder also that it is only 'till he come'.

My time is at hand

His Apostles

February 10th — Matthew 26. 31-56

Could ye not watch with me one hour?

It is John who recalls with inspired guidance, clarity, and detail the words spoken by the Lord Jesus as the little group made their way from the upper room to the slopes of Olivet. Matthew passes over those precious truths, though spoken in his hearing. His mind is focussed, as so often in his Gospel, on Old Testament prophecy applied on this occasion by the Lord to the events about to take place that night, Matt. 26. 31; Zech. 13. 7.

We have no eye-witness account of the Lord's Gethsemane experience. John was the evangelist closest, but the Lord had gone that stone's cast further. John and his two companions slept, and in his Gospel he does not mention the agony of the olive press. The Spirit of God has, however, left us a record through the pens of the other Gospel writers and we find ourselves transfixed, overwhelmed, almost with a sense of intrusion as we hear the Son addressing the Father 'with strong crying and tears', 'If it be possible . . . nevertheless . . . thy will be done', Matt. 26. 39, 42. Gethsemane is truth for the heart, not the head. Its depths are imponderable, its mystery inexplicable, and its detail unforgettable, as in the words of hymn writer JAMES MONTGOMERY:

> Gethsemane can I forget?
> Or there Thy conflict see,
> Thine agony and blood-like sweat,
> And not remember Thee?

The Lord had taken Himself to where He knew Judas would find Him, for, 'Jesus ofttimes resorted thither with his disciples', John 18. 2. Events now begin to move quite swiftly. We watch the 'great multitude with swords and staves' emerge from the darkness and we witness with contempt the traitor's kiss. We admire brave Peter's efforts to defend his Lord, being unaware that more than twelve legions of angels, ready and prepared, waited for the briefest word of command.

Again, we notice Matthew's interest in the fulfilment of Old Testament scripture. In verse 54 and again in verse 56 he recalls the theme of the prophets that the Promised One would be despised and rejected. He found none to take pity or give comfort, Ps. 69. 20; they all 'forsook him, and fled'.

Christ and

Matthew 26. 57-75 — February 11th

It had been a long sleepless night for the Saviour. He had fulfilled His desire to keep the Passover with His disciples, and we know that night had fallen when Judas left the upper room. In the darkness of Gethsemane the Lord had gazed into the cup that He must drink and, though the night was cold, the ground where He lay in agony was saturated with sweat. Luke tells us that 'there appeared an angel unto him from heaven, strengthening him', Luke 22. 43, He would need every ounce of that strength to face the hours that lay before Him, as into that darkness came the traitor with those carrying lanterns and torches to arrest the Light of the world!

The hurried assembly in the palace of the high priest bore no resemblance to a trial; it was at best an arraignment. The only qualification considered necessary of the witnesses was that they were false! Caiaphas had already determined the sentence and would consider his thirty pieces of silver well spent, as the Saviour, seemingly helpless, stood before him. The Lord's prophetic words regarding 'the temple of his body' were spoken right at the commencement of His public ministry, John 2. 19.

For over three years vindictive minds had retained His words to use against Him when occasion arose. The refusal of the Lord to offer any word of defence incensed the high priest, causing him to demand a response, under oath, 'whether thou be the Christ, the Son of God'. The reply was in the affirmative, 'Thou hast said', Matt. 26. 63-64. The rending of the high priest's garments, contrary to the Mosaic law, had particular significance in marking the imminent end of the Aaronic priesthood. What Caiaphas did not know was that the bound and beaten man standing in his courtyard that day would shortly take His place 'sitting on the right hand of power', the great High Priest of a higher and more noble order.

The Gospel writers all record Peter's denial of the Lord. We do well to consider, without a critical spirit, the steps which led Peter to lie, to curse and finally to weep bitterly, mindful of the warning, 'Let him that thinketh he standeth take heed lest he fall', 1 Cor. 10. 12.

His Apostles

February 12th — Matthew 27. 1-26

Barabbas

In Psalm 1 we are introduced to a man who is both blessed and righteous. In contrast to this man there are those whose activities are marked out as ungodly. Our reading today adequately illustrates this difference as the Lord Jesus stands in silent dignity while unrighteous men plot and scheme against Him.

As the sun rose upon the most significant day in human history, the 'counsel of the ungodly' was heard planning how best to put the Lord Jesus to death. Verses 3 to 10 of this chapter are a parenthesis in which 'the way of sinners' is clearly seen in the actions of Judas, and then of the chief priests as they gathered up the 'reward of iniquity', Acts 1. 18, from the temple floor and purchased the potter's field as a salve to their conscience. 'The seat of the scornful' is occupied by Pontius Pilate, no doubt in ill humour, having been called upon to give judgement at such an early hour. With a curl of the lip he asked, without any serious interest in the reply, 'Art thou the King of the Jews?'

Pilate no doubt thought that by invoking the tradition of releasing a Passover prisoner, he could soon be rid of this case. Surely the chief priests would not take sides with Barabbas, one condemned for capital crimes even by their own law? To show support for an insurrectionist was to oppose the Roman authorities openly. However much they hated the occupying power in private, the rulers and chief priests were not troubled too much under Rome, and sympathy for Barabbas could easily jeopardize their position.

The message brought to Pilate from his wife served only to increase his irritation. The superstitious Romans placed great emphasis on dreams, and this was not helping! Pilate no doubt felt that he was being out-manoeuvred, and for the second time he offered the choice, Barabbas or Jesus. The chief priests had, however, persuaded the multitude to unite in their preference, causing Pilate to exclaim in frustration the words which have echoed down the centuries, 'What shall I do then with Jesus which is called Christ?' Many today are still saying, 'Let him be crucified', and no amount of water would cleanse the blood from Pilate's hands or dilute his responsibility, Acts 4. 27.

Christ and

Matthew 27. 27-44   February 13th

A place called Golgotha

Under Roman law, the scourging of a man condemned to death was not considered necessary. There was, however, a law which took precedence over the legislation of Caesar. Some 700 years before, the Spirit of God, through Isaiah the prophet, had decreed that such brutality and the shameful treatment endured in the soldier's common hall, would be the portion of the One who, 'was not rebellious, neither turned away back', Isa. 50. 5.

No doubt taking the accusation provided by Pilate as their motivation, the soldiers derided the very thought that the prisoner before them was a king. These were callous, cruel men, insensitive to the suffering of others. Without a thought for His dignity, they stripped Him and cast a robe of mockery around His lacerated shoulders. Then with a crown of vicious thorns beaten into His brow, anointed with their loathsome spittle, and with their derision ringing in His ears, He was led by them to Golgotha. Never did a man seem more at the mercy of others; never was the reverse more true!

As the day unfolded, scripture after scripture was being fulfilled. Psalms came to life; seemingly enigmatic prophecies revealed their purpose and ancient writings took on a new vitality as ignorant men unwittingly moved at the impulse of a living word!

Whether Golgotha, the 'place of a skull', is descriptive of the natural features of the location, or a name given to identify it as a place of execution, matters little; the events of that remarkable day supersede their setting. If the place were known for certain, man would only make of it an excuse for idolatry. Suffice it to say that as in birth, so in death, and still in many hearts, the Lord Jesus was given the outside place.

Strong bulls of Bashan gathered at Golgotha that day, elders of the nation, rulers and priests. Gentile 'dogs', the assembly of the wicked, pierced His hands and feet before sitting down to watch Him there and gamble for His clothes. Satanic forces energized and orchestrated the venomous hatred directed against Him. While above, legions of angels awaited the command that was never issued; He 'endured the cross', Heb. 12. 2.

His Apostles

February 14th　　　　　　　　　　　Matthew 27. 45-66

Three men died that day at Golgotha. For one man with shattered legs and tortured frame, death was a welcome release as his soul entered the promised Paradise. For his erstwhile companion in crime, though death ended the agonies of crucifixion, it also secured against him the door of hope as he entered the darkness of hell!

The death of the Man on the centre cross was accompanied by strange and remarkable events. For three hours an unnatural darkness enveloped the land. No human eye would penetrate that mid-day night as His soul was made 'an offering for sin'. From that darkness a cry was heard which has reverberated through time, as the scapegoat, laden and bowed beneath a load of iniquity, entered a land not inhabited. Maybe with a touch of human sympathy, one by the cross placed a sponge filled with vinegar to His lips, little realizing that his actions had been well documented a thousand years before, Ps. 69. 21. The living word continued to exert its force on the actions of men.

The darkness receded, a loud voice proclaimed that the suffering was ended, but still the life must be given. Not taken by the soldiers of Rome, or by the scheming of the Jews, but at the appointed moment, fully knowing there was 'a time to die', He exercised the divine prerogative and dismissed His spirit.

Some hours before, the high priest had rent his garments. Now the veil of the temple was rent from above. The earth shook and the rocks rent, fracturing the tombs of sleeping saints – significant events which announced the fulfilment and end of Levitical ritual and priesthood. The law also, engraved in rock, would no longer proclaim 'This do and thou shalt live'; it was now not 'do', but 'believe'. Three days later, reliable witnesses testified that some who were known to have died were seen walking in Jerusalem; the effects of Golgotha were astounding! The rich man came at the appointed time as foretold by Isaiah, Isa. 53. 9, and laid the precious body 'in his own new tomb'. Not content with His death and burial, the chief priests then determined to prevent any suggestion of resurrection – how futile!

'Vain the stone, the watch, the seal',

C. WESLEY

The veil of the temple was rent in twain

Christ and

Matthew 28 — February 15th

The Saviour had already risen, early, on the first day of the week, when the angel came, rolled back the stone and sat on it! Just one angel in Matthew's Gospel; only one from those legions who stand in the presence of God, yet his coming caused an earthquake and rendered the guards unconscious; we wonder what effect 'more than twelve legions of angels' would have had!

The invitation to the women to witness the empty tomb was sufficient to assure them that the Lord was risen. The instruction is similar to that which we are given, 'Come and see': be assured of the absolute certainty of the truth we believe. 'Go and tell': make it known to others that they also may believe.

On rising from the dead, the Lord did not make a spectacular appearance on the steps of the temple to challenge the unbelief of those who had pursued Him to Golgotha; their day will come! Instead, He departed into Galilee to be with His own. The rulers of the nation despised His Galilean connections; the Lord was never embarrassed about His humble circumstances, 'He made himself of no reputation'.

It was, of course, only to His disciples and followers that He showed Himself in resurrection. Faith alone is that which grasps the truth upon which all else depends. We recall the apostle's words to the Corinthians, 'If Christ be not raised' all else is vain. Then he will say, 'But now is Christ risen', 1 Cor. 15. 17-20, so everything for the believer's future is secure!

Matthew takes time to record the dilemma of the Jewish elders: inventing a story, buying the silence of the guards with 'large money', no doubt rather more than the thirty pieces of silver, in fact pursuing any avenue rather than accept the truth!

There is no mention of the ascension in Matthew's Gospel. The earthly people of God, the Jews, are much in his mind, and it is to establish a kingdom on earth that the Lord will return. Before that time, however, the Lord is building His church, a heavenly people, and the guarantee we have as a motivation for service is in Christ's closing words, 'All power is given unto me in heaven and in earth. Go . . . make disciples . . . baptize . . . teach: and, lo, I am with you always' – blessed assurance!

His Apostles

Introduction to Mark's Gospel

The Gospel by Mark is the shortest biblical record of the life of the Lord Jesus and, as such, could be recommended reading for any new believer wondering about where best to start their exploration of scripture. The narrative is fast-moving and holds our interest.

There is no internal statement of authorship but there is general agreement that the Spirit used John Mark to pen its pages. He features occasionally in the book of Acts and is generally remembered as the man who abandoned Paul and Barnabas on their first missionary journey, Acts 13. 13. Despite this breakdown in his service, ultimately he was fully restored, 2 Tim. 4. 11. It has often been remarked that God used a failing servant to write about His perfect Servant.

A time-honoured way of describing the book is, 'The Gospel of the Perfect Servant', and there is virtue in that description. The pages are filled with *activity*; less of the Lord's teaching is recorded than in the other Gospels. A frequently used word is 'immediately', sometimes translated by other words such as 'straightway' or 'forthwith'; He moves quickly from one incident to the next. So He is portrayed as a busy Servant, who experienced weariness, or who, on an occasion had 'no leisure so much as to eat', 4. 35-38; 6. 31; He had come 'to minister', 10. 45. Right to the last verse He is seen as being active, 'the Lord working with them', 16. 20.

Mark records no genealogy; who is concerned with a servant's pedigree? He commences with a clear statement of the true identity of the subject of his narrative, 'Jesus Christ, the Son of God', 1. 1. He teaches us that the Servant is the Son, 'his own son that serveth him', Mal. 3. 17. We could write over Mark's account, 'Behold my servant', Isa. 42. 1.

Mark's Gospel divides into two large sections. The first ten chapters deal with the Lord's public ministry, mainly in Galilee. The remainder of the book focuses on His arrival at Jerusalem for the last time, and the subsequent week, culminating in His death and resurrection. As with the other Gospels, considerable space is devoted to these crucial events.

Christ and

Mark 1. 1-20 — February 16th

Thou art my beloved Son

Without noting the genealogy or birth of the Servant, Mark launches into details of His activity. He records preparatory events including the ministry of John the Baptist, His baptism, and the temptation in the wilderness.

Interestingly, the supremacy of the Servant is stressed at the outset. He is the Son of God, v. 1. He is the Lord, Jehovah, v. 3, a quotation from Isaiah chapter 40 verse 3. He is 'mightier than' John, Mark 1. 7, who was the greatest born of women, Matt. 11. 11. The day would come when He would 'baptize . . . with the Holy Ghost', Mark 1. 8. How amazing that someone so majestic should then be portrayed as One who had come, 'not to be ministered unto, but to minister', 10. 45! What marvellous grace!

The triunity of God is disclosed in the first verse of the Bible with the usage of the plural name Elohim. It is inferred in the cries of the seraphim, 'Holy, holy, holy', Isa. 6. 3. Here, Father, Son, and Holy Spirit feature at the baptism of the incarnate Son. 'Jesus . . . was baptized', Mark 1. 9. From a rent heaven, the Spirit descended, v. 10. The Father's voice declared, 'my beloved Son', v. 11. Once more, it is touching to think that the one on whom the Spirit abode so contentedly, the one who had attracted such warm appreciation from the Father, was soon to be closely involved in service to broken humanity. What condescension!

How suddenly circumstances change! From the Jordan to the wilderness; from fellowship with the Father and the Spirit to confrontation with the devil; from association with John the Baptist to the company of wild beasts. The devil encouraged Him to simulate an emergency to test the promise of angelic assistance, Matt. 4. 6. With the devil in retreat, the reality of the promise was proved: 'the angels ministered unto him', Mark 1. 13.

Without eclipsing John who was already sidelined, the Lord Jesus embarked on His ministry. He then solicited the help of those who would be 'fishers of men', Andrew the personal evangelist, and Peter the public preacher. 'Menders' were needed as well, and so James and John were summoned. He still calls to various aspects of service. Be available!

His Apostles

February 17th — Mark 1. 21-45

He healed many

Scripture speaks of 'the *days* of his flesh', Heb. 5. 7, and Mark details one of those days, a busy Sabbath day. Firstly, there was preaching in the synagogue; even the untutored Galileans distinguished between His authoritative message and the lifeless lectures of the scribes. Authority was the keynote that day, for even the demons were subject to His power, Mark 1. 27. Both His words and His works created astonishment, vv. 22, 27.

The next port of call was Peter's home where there was an emergency; his mother-in-law was in the grip of a fever. 'Anon (immediately) they tell him', v. 30. In the difficulties of life speaking to Him should be the first resort and not the last. In the first of numerous occasions in his Gospel, Mark mentions the hand of the Servant. When He took her hand, the fever was dismissed. With immediate effect she served them, a delightful illustration of the familiar maxim 'saved to serve'.

In this first chapter of the Gospel there is a sunset scene, v. 32. In the last chapter there is a sunrise scene, an appropriate accompaniment to the triumph of resurrection, 16. 2. Here, at the close of day 'he healed many'. Matthew says He 'healed all', Matt. 8. 16. Doctor Luke stresses that they each received individual attention, 'he laid his hands on every one of them', Luke 4. 40. No case was too hard for the Great Physician!

He rose early after the busy day, Mark 1. 35, and the lesson for our own lives is that public activity and private devotion must be kept in balance. Synagogue preaching and solitary place praying should never be divorced. He started the new day with God, communing with the Father, and, indeed, taking instructions for the day, Isa. 50. 4. Further, the adulation of the men of Capernaum did not deflect Him from His purpose to cover new ground with the gospel, Mark 1. 38.

A leper was next to experience His touch, v. 41. A word would have cleansed him, but compassion moved the Saviour to touch the untouchable! When a high-ranking leper arrived at Elisha's door, he sent him instructions via a messenger, 2 Kgs. 5. 10; the Lord made physical contact with this outcast. His authority, ability, humility, and pity are all in evidence here.

Christ and

Mark 2. 1-22 — February 18th

Once more a visit to His adopted hometown created a stir, vv. 1-2, and the Lord took opportunity to '[preach] the word unto them'. Amidst amazing stories of healing power, Mark gives these constant reminders of the main focus of His ministry: to preach the word of God. It should still be at the heart of Christian service, the major activity among all our labours.

It took four men co-operating to bring the palsied man to the Saviour, just as today it requires believers to be 'striving together for the faith of the gospel' if souls are to be won for Him, Phil. 1. 27. For the first time in this Gospel, we get a hint of resentment and opposition; His authority to forgive sins was questioned but the healing of the paralysed man confirmed that authority. Forgiveness is a prerogative of deity, Ps. 103. 2-3.

The seaside was another venue for preaching, Mark 2. 13, and it was in that vicinity that Levi (Matthew) was called. Mark discloses what Matthew in his modesty does not divulge, that it was he who hosted the meal for the Lord, to which he invited publicans and sinners. It appears that Matthew was as concerned for the salvation of his colleagues as Andrew was for 'his own brother Simon', John 1. 41. Sadly, we are not so burdened today! 'He that winneth souls is wise', Prov. 11. 30.

The cowardly scribes and Pharisees attacked Him through His disciples, but as ever, the Shepherd sprang to the defence of the sheep. Eating with the outcasts was no indication that He condoned their sin. On the contrary, His mission was to call 'sinners to repentance', Mark 2. 17. By contrast, these self-righteous religionists would never hear His call.

At verse 18, the narrative switches from feasting to fasting. People were questioning what they probably deemed to be lack of devotion and earnestness on the part of the Lord's disciples as compared with John's. He showed that there was no need to display signs of sobriety and self-denial when the bridegroom was still with them! The time for that would come, but even after the bridegroom would be 'taken away from them' the joyful wine of Christianity could never be contained in the old wineskins of legalistic Judaism; they are incompatible, v. 22.

His Apostles

February 19th Mark 2. 23 – 3. 12

The Pharisees … took counsel … against him

Opposition to the Lord Jesus was hardening, and the disciples plucking and eating the corn on the Sabbath day was a further cause for criticism, v. 23. The Shepherd once more defended His sheep. This time, He appealed to the occasion when a hungry David ate shewbread, a precedent that demonstrates that humanitarian considerations take priority over ceremonial laws; that principle still holds good today.

On occasions in the Gospels we read that 'they watched him', the first here in Mark chapter 3 verse 2. He was under constant scrutiny as we are too. The belief seemed to be that He would heal the man with the withered hand; His history of compassion aroused that expectation. What about our track record? What do people expect of us? The Lord faced His critics head-on, and in commanding the man to 'stand forth' performed the miracle in a very public fashion. On other occasions He took people out of town or healed at a distance but there would be no secrecy when withstanding a hardness that angered Him. As demonstrated here, anger can be legitimate, but for us, extreme caution is necessary: 'Be ye angry, *and sin not*', Eph. 4. 26. The incident enflamed His opponents, and an unlikely alliance was formed with the object of destroying him, Mark 3. 6.

In the face of such virulent opposition, He 'withdrew himself', v. 7. His hour had not come and there was no need to precipitate a crisis. The withdrawal involved the disciples. They were still fledgling followers, and, at that early stage, He again shielded them from the excesses of murderous intent. Similarly, when Israel fled Egypt, 'God led them not through the way of the land of the Philistines', Exod. 13. 17; it was too early for a confrontation with such a warlike people. 'He knoweth our frame; he remembereth that we are dust', Ps. 103. 14.

There was magnetism about the Lord that drew crowds from many districts. He who had dwelt 'in the light which no man can approach unto', 1 Tim. 6. 16, was now in a position where He was thronged, 'pressed upon', and touched, Mark 3. 9-10. He banished disease and demons, vv. 10-12. Coming from heaven to Galilee did not diminish divine power.

Christ and

Mark 3. 13-35 — February 20th

How can Satan cast out Satan?

Today's reading contains various groups of people: disciples, vv. 13-19, 'the multitude', v. 20, 'friends', v. 21, 'scribes', vv. 22-30, and 'his brethren and his mother', vv. 31-35.

From His many disciples, twelve were chosen to 'be with him'. He appreciated human society, but for them, being with Him was a necessary prerequisite for effective service. That is how it has to be for us too. These men were diverse in background and temperament, for God's servants are not clones; we all have potential for His service.

The demands of the multitude deprived Him of a meal break. He always ensured that others were fed, whether it was a solitary little girl, 5. 43, or vast crowds, 6. 37; 8. 2, but here the interests of others took priority over His own needs.

Such was His dedication and selflessness, that His friends questioned His sanity. Be prepared for misunderstanding if your spirituality and devotion are well above average. He experienced it from the age of twelve, when Mary misconstrued His commitment to His 'Father's business', Luke 2. 49.

The scribes took their cue from the criticism of His friends and suggested a more sinister reason for what was regarded as extreme behaviour; they said He was energized by Satan. Firstly, the Lord showed how illogical their attitude was – Satan would never expel his own kind; a divided kingdom is doomed – a lesson we all need to learn. Secondly, someone as strong as the devil has to be bound by a superior power. Frequently, the omnipotent Christ robbed him of his captives: people like the man of Gadara, or Mary Magdalene. Thirdly, by making their absurd suggestion, these scribes crossed a line that placed them beyond pardon; they had blasphemed against the Holy Spirit by implying that the Spirit's power by which He performed His miracles was the devil's. That unforgivable sin was committed exclusively by people who saw Him when He was here.

The arrival of His mother and brethren gave Him opportunity to explain that it is possible to have a closer relationship with Him than with those whose connection was purely natural. Doing God's will places us close to His heart!

His Apostles

February 21st Mark 4. 1-20

Behold, there went out a sower to sow

In an earlier study, it was stated that Mark's Gospel focuses on *activity* rather than on sermons, but chapter 4 does contain some of the Lord's teaching. In particular, the early verses highlight the Parable of the Sower and the Seed, with an explanation to the disciples. Sometimes we are given the impression that the Lord told parables to elucidate spiritual truth; in fact, it was to obscure it from eyes that were already blinded, vv. 11-12.

'There went out a sower to sow'. This sower was diligent; he got on with his business, the sowing of seed. 'In the morning sow thy seed, and in the evening withhold not thine hand', Eccles. 11. 6. Be busy, and enjoy the blessing of involvement, for 'Blessed are ye that sow beside all waters', Isa. 32. 20.

'The sower soweth the word'. Sowing, whether in preaching or in witnessing, involves quoting the texts of scripture and explaining its truths. There is no substitute for that, for it is the means by which God promotes faith, and effects regeneration, Rom. 10. 17; 1 Pet. 1. 23. 'Preach the word', 2 Tim. 4. 2.

Some seed falls on the hard-packed path, and is immediately devoured by birds, a picture of hard, careless hearers from whose minds Satan 'immediately' snatches the truth preached. He is present with malicious intent at every gospel meeting.

There are listeners who are more thoughtful, and seeing the benefits of salvation 'immediately receive [the word] with gladness'. There is no mention of sorrow for sin, or repentance, but merely an emotional response to the preaching. The test of persecution proves the profession of these stony ground hearers to be shallow and empty.

Thorny ground hearers are distracted by anxieties, preoccupied with materialism or obsessed with worldly things, all of which blunt the cutting edge of the preached word. Like the previous two, this soil is unproductive.

Happily, there is good ground, with fruit as evidence of reality. The yield rate varies, but, in this Servant Gospel, increase is anticipated in ascending order, for a servant will always expect the maximum possible. Being practical, if we have responded to the word, are our lives productive for God?

Christ and

Mark 4. 21-41 — February 22nd

Having spoken about the responsibility to sow, the Lord now teaches that disciples ought to disseminate received truth. There is only one suitable place for a lamp and that is on a lampstand! Do nothing to obscure the truth that has been committed to you. Listen to God, v. 23. Communicate what you hear, and there will be further enlightenment, v. 24. Fail to impart your knowledge, and that knowledge will be lost to you, v. 25.

The next little parable has various cogent applications, but the interpretation has to do with the growth of God's kingdom in this world. From small beginnings it moves to eventual maturity without any human instrumentality. The Creator has put agricultural laws in place that are beyond human understanding. Similarly, the development of His kingdom defies the human intellect. He Himself superintends it through its various stages of growth; it is all a divine work.

The parable of the mustard seed is a wake-up call. Presently, God's kingdom is a sphere of profession in which Satan is active. 'The fowls of the air' have featured earlier, and were interpreted as illustrating the work of the devil, vv. 4, 15. The great monstrosity that we call 'Christendom' harbours a great variety of satanically-inspired error that corrupts the pure gospel of Christ, and compromises devoted Christian living.

Verses 33 to 34 contain a practical lesson for preachers. He spoke 'as they were able to hear it'. Paul also tailored his ministry to suit the spiritual condition of his hearers; spiritual babies cannot digest the strong meat of the word, 1 Cor. 3. 1-2. We have to be sensitive to the needs of audiences. In this passage, the disciples were enlightened privately, and today, as possessors of the Spirit, we have the capacity to understand what is obscure to the unregenerate mind, 1 Cor. 2. 14.

At verse 35, the narrative switches back to activity and miracles, the first being the stilling of the storm. The weariness of Christ demonstrates His true manhood, and yet His power over the elements is evidence of His essential deity. At a practical level, let us be encouraged that He cares for us in the storms of life, and that if He so wills, He can calm these storms.

His Apostles

Without a parable spake he not unto them

February 23rd — Mark 5. 1-20

Clothed, and in his right mind

The Lord Jesus had instigated the voyage to 'the other side', Mark 4. 35, and yet the whole venture bristled with difficulties. There was the storm, and then there was a satanic assault; ultimately He was expelled from the district, v. 17. The lesson is that to move at His bidding does not guarantee an easy road, or ensure success.

Attention has been drawn to the recurrence of the word 'immediately' in describing the ceaseless activity of the Perfect Servant. To keep us on our guard, at times Mark shows us that the devil is alert and busy also. No sooner had the Lord Jesus set foot on land, than 'immediately' the demoniac confronted Him, cp. 4. 15. Observe too how swiftly the daughter of Herodias and the executioner did Satan's work in chapter 6.

We are confronted here by a man whom evil spirits had made reclusive, morbid, violent, self-destructive, and untameable; he possessed superhuman strength. This was an extreme case that only the power of Christ could put right, and wonderfully, as the narrative proceeds, that restless, naked, demented being was 'sitting, and clothed, and in his right mind'. It should have been a source of great rejoicing for the community, but they seemed to be more concerned about the loss of the pigs; it gives us an insight into the warped values of the human heart. Happily, when the Lord Jesus was next in Decapolis, their attitude had altered significantly, Mark 7. 31-37. The testimony of a transformed life had made an impact! Similarly, many 'believed on Jesus' because of Lazarus, John 12. 10-11.

The liberated soul wanted to be an instant missionary, but his first sphere of responsibility had to be his own home territory, 'Go home to thy friends, and tell them'. The Lord always employs people in their own district before widening their field of activity. The apostles were used extensively in the spread of the gospel, but it started in Jerusalem before ever it radiated to 'the uttermost part of the earth', Acts 1. 8. Labour where you live, and it may be that the Lord will relocate you to some other area of service. Years ago men used to tell us that we must 'cross the street before we cross the sea'.

Christ and

Mark 5. 21-43 — February 24th

Be not afraid, only believe

The three miracles in Mark chapter 5 involve a man, a woman, and a child. The Lord Jesus meets the need, irrespective of age or gender. He is omnipotent, and shows His power over demons, disease, and death. Each case was beyond human help; the man was untameable, the woman had exhausted her capital and her condition was still worsening, and the girl had died. In the three incidents the Lord was rejected by the Gadarenes, v. 17, rebuked by the disciples, v. 31, and ridiculed by the mourners, v. 40. What amazing patience on His part!

'The wisdom that is from above is . . . easy to be entreated', Jas. 3. 17, and Jairus' appeal met with an immediate response. This must have heartened him, but the delay *en route* would have sent his hopes plummeting; his daughter was 'at the point of death'! A roller coaster of emotions is a common feature of life, and the news of his daughter's death would have removed any vestige of hope. But he was in the company of One who knew 'how to speak a word in season to him that is weary', Isa. 50. 4. 'Be not afraid, only believe'. As in the storm, the Lord was teaching that faith and fear are mutually exclusive, Mark 4. 40. We all know this, but it is difficult to implement in our lives for so many circumstances alarm us. May we all learn the truth of this biblical promise, 'Thou wilt keep him in perfect peace, whose mind is stayed on thee: because he trusteth in thee', Isa. 26. 3. Today's passage illustrates it. The faith of the woman resulted in her going 'in peace', Mark 5. 34.

The healing of the woman and the raising of the girl hold lessons regarding the sequel to conversion. It appears that the woman attempted to slip away undetected, but the Lord wanted an open confession of what had transpired. He does not desire secret disciples, people who are ashamed of Him in this sinful generation, 8. 38. Be open in acknowledging Him.

The girl gave evidence of life by walking, 5. 42, and she required nourishment to sustain the new life. Similarly, genuine believers will 'walk, even as he walked', 1 John 2. 6. For their spiritual nourishment, they will 'desire the sincere milk of the word', 1 Pet. 2. 2. What about our conduct and our appetite?

His Apostles

February 25th — Mark 6. 1-29

He marvelled because of their unbelief

Nazareth was 'his own country' just as Capernaum became 'his own city', Matt. 9. 1. In incarnation the omnipresent Son of God became linked with specific geographical locations. The people of Nazareth could not fathom that one of their own could possibly be the Messiah even although 'wisdom' and 'works' were noted, Mark 6. 2, *'mighty works'* that were 'wrought by his hands'. Those hands now touched the needy, but the Nazarenes had watched them handle saws and chisels and planes, and could see only 'the carpenter', v. 3. Further, He belonged to a local family without status. Their unbelief stifled blessing, vv. 5-6. Learn two lessons: first, we should never be prejudiced on account of a man's location, trade, or family; second, unbelief will inevitably staunch the flow of divine blessing. 'They could not enter in because of unbelief', Heb. 3. 19.

In verses 7 to 13, the Lord Jesus commissioned His twelve apostles, and while their function was unique, there are general principles here relating to service. The fact that they went two by two emphasizes the value of fellowship in service, Eccles. 4. 9-12. The instructions to travel light indicate the need for dependence on God to supply the resources for the work, and there is encouragement to be content with what is provided, Mark 6. 10. The Lord indicated that we should never expect universal acceptance of the message, and hence the need at times to 'shake off the dust', v. 11. The final lesson is that of implicit obedience: having been sent, the disciples simply 'went out, and preached', v. 12.

News of the proliferation of miracles was a jolt to Herod's conscience. Could it be that John had been raised from the dead? At the instigation of the ruthless Herodias, Herod had been responsible for his martyrdom. 'He had married her', but from God's standpoint, she was still 'his brother Philip's wife', v. 17, and John had been firm in his condemnation of that adulterous relationship. Herod's respect for John's integrity, v. 20, could not save him in the face of such uncontrollable hatred. Be like John: earn the respect of the ungodly without compromising your convictions, and regardless of the cost.

Christ and

Mark 6. 30-56 — February 26th

The feeding of the 5000 is the only miracle that is recorded by all four evangelists so it must have great significance. Elisha used twenty loaves to feed a hundred men and that was regarded as miraculous, 2 Kgs. 4. 42-44; how much more the satisfying of such a massive crowd! It is another evidence of the superiority of the Son over the prophets, Heb. 1. 1-2.

Rest from labour in the company of Christ is necessary and legitimate, Mark 6. 30-32, but we must be prepared for the intrusions of needy humanity. The Saviour's compassion, v. 34, can never accommodate the 'send them away' attitude, v. 36; the weary disciples were pressed into organizing the people, and then feeding them. Are we happy to be available at times when we may feel under par, or are deprived of anticipated leisure?

The mention of sheep in verse 34 inevitably transports us to Psalm 23, and the 'green pastures' of the psalm has a counterpart in the 'green grass' of our passage. How considerate the Lord is, always taking physical comfort into account! Scripture is wonderfully accurate in that at the feeding of the 4000 there is no mention of grass, but simply 'the ground', Mark 8. 6; by then, the summer sun had scorched the green grass.

Even though it was a public place, the Lord Jesus gave thanks for the food, 6. 41, a lesson for us all. He was bountiful yet economical: 'they did all eat, and were filled', and yet the fragments were gathered, vv. 42-43. Never be mean, but never be wasteful.

His shepherd care was once more in evidence as the disciples were excused the task of dismissing the crowd; He undertook that personally, and then resorted to prayer, vv. 45-46. They would need His prayers, for the men who had been so busy were to face another storm. Commitment to Christ does not exempt us from the storms of life. He not only prayed for them but He saw them, and came to them, 'walking upon the sea' v. 49. It is still the same; the great High Priest who intercedes on high, Heb. 7. 25, knows our 'tribulation', Rev. 2. 9, and does not leave us comfortless, but comes to us, John. 14. 18. Let us be encouraged.

His Apostles

February 27th Mark 7. 1-23

The commandments of men

The last book of the Bible has a warning for those who would add to the book or subtract from it, Rev. 22. 18-19. Mankind has always had the inclination to tinker with divine instructions, right from the day when Eve misquoted God's original command, Gen. 3. 3. This was never more apparent than when the Lord Jesus was here, and the nation was dominated by the hypocritical religious thinking of the Pharisees. A glut of man-made rules was superimposed upon God's law.

Frequently, the Lord and His disciples fell foul of these strictures, and, on this occasion, criticism was levelled at the disciples because they ignored elaborate ceremonial ablutions before eating. In responding, the Lord Jesus systematically exposed their hypocrisy. Firstly, He showed that their mind-set amply illustrated the prediction of Isaiah chapter 29 verse 13. Let us learn the lesson that paying lip-service to God from a cold and wayward heart is totally unacceptable, and portraying human regulations as divine laws renders our worship vain.

Next, He exposed their inconsistency; they were giving human traditions precedence over God-given commands. This was particularly objectionable in respect of their attitude to their parents. A human tradition was giving them licence to neglect them, and thus ignore one of the basic commandments of the ten. That was just one example of their actions: 'many such like things do ye', v. 13. Never allow man-made rules to supersede divine directives, or even to rank alongside them.

Thirdly, He made the clear point that from God's standpoint it is not what we put into our mouths that defiles us. It proceeds through the alimentary canal, and the impurities are dealt with. What defiles us are the things that proceed from the heart, and the Lord lists an appalling range of evil in thought, word and deed. 'The heart is deceitful above all things, and desperately wicked', Jer. 17. 9. Our corrupt human nature is a deep well from which every foul evil is discharged. As believers, we are grateful for the cleansing provided by precious blood, 1 John 1. 7; Rev. 1. 5; we 'purified [our] souls in obeying the truth', 1 Pet. 1. 22. But, practically, 'keep thyself pure', 1 Tim. 5. 22.

Christ and

Mark 7. 24-37 — February 28th

Readers who are unfamiliar with the geographical locations in the verses have little concept of the distances that the Lord Jesus travelled to alleviate human need. It involved many, many miles on foot to travel from Galilee to the Tyre region, and then away over to Decapolis. He 'went about', said Peter, Acts 10. 38, but the phrase masks the weariness, the searing heat, the thirst, and the dust of every journey that He took.

In the vicinity of Tyre and Sidon, 'he could not be hid', v. 24. He was like the 'city that is set on an hill' of which He preached, Matt. 5. 14. His fame had spread to that remote Gentile district, and His branches would 'run over the wall', Gen. 49. 22, to bring blessing to a needy family. Matthew takes note of the woman's faith, Matt. 15. 28, but while it is not mentioned here, it is evidenced in her response to the Lord. She was willing to take the place of an outcast Gentile dog, and be content with an undeserved crumb of blessing! Her obedience to Christ was unquestioning; accepting His promise, she simply returned home and found things as He had said. May God help us all to have such implicit faith, and the same submissive obedience.

The incident of the deaf man is unique to Mark. A deaf man could never hear of Christ, and 'faith cometh by hearing', Rom. 10. 17. However, the compassion of the Saviour was such that by sign language, Mark 7. 33, He indicated His intentions, and faith was engendered. The single Aramaic word 'Ephphatha' could be easily lip-read, another aid to faith. How considerate He was!

From the very first miracle, when water became *'good* wine', John 2. 10, everything that the Lord did was done perfectly. Thus it was here: of a man with 'an impediment in his speech' it was said, 'he spake *plain'*. No wonder the reaction was, 'He hath done all things well'!

> We muse on more than heart can hold,
> On more than tongue can tell,
> And simply say like those of old,
> 'He hath done all things well'.

I. Y. EWAN

February 29th — Mark 8. 1-21

Bread

If the huge crowd were to be dismissed as it was, the people would faint with hunger, v. 3, hence, 'I have compassion on the multitude', v. 2. His compassion was the spring from which all His actions flowed. How is it with us? The noblest acts, if not motivated by love, are profitless, 1 Cor. 13. 1-3. Have 'compassion one of another', 1 Pet. 3. 8.

At the feeding of the 5000, the disciples had made a blunder; they had expressed doubt as to how such an enormous crowd could be fed, and the doubt resurfaced here, v. 4. Abraham duplicated his error when he portrayed Sarah as his sister, Gen. 12. 13, 19. We should learn from our mistakes, but we rarely do!

To their credit, the disciples knew that their Lord would want to 'satisfy' the multitude, v. 4, and so He did, v. 8. They had constantly observed His generosity; He 'giveth to all men *liberally*', Jas. 1. 5. He 'giveth us *richly* all things to enjoy', 1 Tim. 6. 17. Divine gifts are always lavish, and the disciples' expectations of their Lord were never disappointed.

Despite the background of such a mighty miracle there was still the clamour for 'a sign from heaven', Mark 8. 11. The Lord Jesus was not insensitive, and so 'he sighed deeply', v. 12. Ominously, verse 13 records, 'he left them'. There are times when people cross the line and place themselves beyond mercy.

An oversight regarding provisions occasioned a warning against the corrupting attitudes of both the Pharisees and Herod, describing them as 'leaven', v. 15. In scripture, leaven invariably symbolizes evil in its various guises, but the disciples were slow to detect that He was teaching them spiritual truth. They rather thought that His remarks related to their carelessness in forgetting to bring loaves, and the anxiety that this had caused. But why should they be anxious? He had provided for both the 5000 and the 4000 with considerable surplus; where was the problem? They were so slow to remember His power and His faithfulness. 'Beware of the leaven . . .'. The cold, legalistic, demanding teaching of the Pharisees withers the soul. The liberal, worldly, ostentatious mind-set of Herod destroys moral fibre. Beware!

Christ and

Mark 8. 22-38

March 1st

Christ's power to heal blindness proved that He was Israel's Messiah. Isaiah predicted that when the glory of the Lord would appear on earth 'then the eyes of the blind shall be opened', Isa. 35. 5. When the faith of John the Baptist wavered and he sent two of his disciples to ask the Lord, 'Art thou he that should come, or do we look for another? Jesus answered and said unto them, Go and shew John again those things which ye do hear and see: The blind receive their sight', Matt. 11. 3-5. This blind man at Bethsaida might have suffered from two separate eye pathologies. Christ healed the first instantly; a second touch cured the man's severe short-sightedness which caused him to see 'men as trees, walking', Mark 8. 24.

The Saviour was unafraid of scrutiny and, when appropriate, acted powerfully before large crowds. However, when public display was unwarranted He acted in private. Christ had taken the blind man tenderly 'by the hand, and led him out of the town', v. 23, and having cured the blind man, said, 'Neither go into the town, nor tell it to any in the town', v. 26. Such modesty on the part of the Son of God is worth emulating. Whenever possible, avoid shining the spotlight on your service.

The crowds recognized that the Lord Jesus preached repentance (like John the Baptist), worked miracles (as Elijah), and spoke with divine authority (much like an Old Testament prophet), but they fell short of recognizing Him as the Christ. Nevertheless, despite their shortcomings, the disciples knew in their hearts that He was the Christ, God's anointed Prophet, Priest, and King, v. 29.

Even though the Lord Jesus foretold His suffering and subsequent resurrection, v. 31, the disciples failed to grasp this important teaching. Peter went so far as to rebuke Him, v. 32. Christ in turn 'rebuked Peter, saying, Get thee behind me, Satan: for thou savourest not the things that be of God, but the things that be of men', v. 33. The very suggestion of avoiding the cross was satanic in nature.

Following Christ is difficult. It demands rigorous self-denial and living as though dead to this present world, vv. 34-38.

Whom do men say that I am?

His Apostles

March 2nd — Mark 9. 1-29

He was transfigured before them

Christ told His disciples 'that there be some of them that stand here, which shall not taste of death, till they have seen the kingdom of God come with power', v. 1. Within one week 'he was transfigured before them', v. 2. 'His clothes became radiant (like 'a gleam from polished surfaces', M. R. VINCENT), intensely white, as no one on earth could bleach them', v. 3 ESV. Thus the transfiguration gave these privileged disciples a temporary, miniature preview of the glory and splendour of Messiah's coming kingdom.

Moses had reflected the divine glory, Exod. 34. 29-35. Christ's radiance was the outshining of His intrinsic excellencies. This glory of the Lord will be displayed throughout the millennial kingdom and beyond into the eternal state when 'the city [will have] no need of the sun, neither of the moon, to shine in it: for the glory of God [will] lighten it, and the Lamb is the light thereof', Rev. 21. 23.

The disciples were 'aghast by dread', Mark 9. 6 WYCLIFFE, at the glorious sight. Uncertain of what to say, Peter inadvertently placed the Lord Jesus on an equal footing with Moses and Elijah, 'Master, it is good for us to be here: and let us make three tabernacles; one for thee, and one for Moses, and one for Elias', v. 5. Peter was, however, quite correct in connecting the feast of tabernacles with the future kingdom, Zech. 14. 16.

The 'cloud that overshadowed them' signified the presence of God. Out of this cloud God the Father spoke, 'This is my beloved Son: hear Him', Mark 9. 7. Suddenly the vision was over and the disciples 'saw no man any more, save Jesus only', v. 8, emphasizing His pre-eminence.

The disciples responded to this vision of the future kingdom by asking, 'Why say the scribes that Elias must first come', v. 11. The Saviour clarified that Elijah will spiritually restore Israel prior to Messiah's coming, v. 12; see Mal. 4. 5, 6. If the nation had accepted the Lord Jesus as Messiah the kingdom would have been established then. However, since Israel mistreated John and Christ, there now needs to be another forerunner – Elijah himself – before the return of the King to rule.

Christ and

Mark 9. 30-50 — March 3rd

The Saviour now sought privacy to instruct the disciples about His coming suffering, vv. 30, 31. This teaching was so important that He exhorted them, 'Let these sayings sink down into your ears', Luke 9. 44. And yet the disciples were saddened and 'understood not that saying, and were afraid to ask him', Mark 9. 32; Matt. 17. 23. Christians also feel sorrow in place of joy when they fail to appreciate vital Christian truths.

The disciples 'had disputed among themselves, who should be the greatest', Mark 9. 34, no doubt in the coming kingdom, Matt. 18. 1. But true greatness in the things of God is the very opposite of what this world perceives as great. The little child represented the simple faith and humility required not just to enter the kingdom of God but also to be great in it, because 'if any man desire to be first, the same shall be last of all, and servant of all', Mark 9. 35, 36.

Moreover, since each child of God is intimately linked to Christ and the Father who sent Him, our response to humble believers reflects our view of Christ, v. 37. While the smallest kind act shown to God's people will not go unrewarded, v. 41, 'whosoever shall offend one of these little ones that believe in [Christ]' will not escape punishment. A horrible death – 'a millstone were hanged about his neck, and he were cast into the sea', v. 42 – is a better fate than 'the fire that never shall be quenched', v. 43, which awaits those who offend God's children. The word translated 'offend' is *skandalizô*, which means 'to entrap' (J. STRONG), and probably includes tempting believers to sin as well as overtly opposing them.

Since the punishment is so severe for ensnaring a child of God – eternal fire and exclusion from the coming kingdom, v. 47 – the Lord Jesus exhorted His disciples to exercise ruthless self discipline to avoid ensnaring others, and thus themselves, vv. 43-48. The language is so severe because the stakes are so high. The apostle Paul applied this same principle to the Christian life, writing, 'If meat make my brother to offend, I will eat no flesh while the world standeth', 1 Cor. 8. 13. May we do our utmost to 'have peace one with another', Mark 9. 50.

His Apostles

March 4th   Mark 10. 1-31

He taught them again

While Christ taught the multitudes, the Pharisees asked their question, vv. 1, 2. It held great danger because of where it was asked: in 'the coasts of Judaea by the farther side of Jordan (Peraea)', v. 1. This region was under the jurisdiction of Herod Antipas, who had recently divorced his own wife to marry his brother Philip's wife, and then imprisoned and executed John the Baptist for criticizing him, 6. 14-29. If the Lord Jesus openly condemned divorce He risked provoking Herod's wrath and suffering the same fate as John. The Pharisees' question also leaned on conflicting Jewish interpretation of what exactly a woman's 'uncleanness' was which permitted divorce under Mosaic law, Deut. 24. 1, and assumed that divorce frees a man to remarry. Stricter Jews permitted divorce only for moral transgressions, whereas the liberals allowed divorce for tiny offences. Even if the Saviour permitted divorce, whichever view He took concerning its grounds would alienate some of His followers. These factors made the Pharisees' question very difficult to answer.

Christ avoided the Pharisees' trap by directing their attention to God's original ideal, which did not even contemplate divorce. Marriage is a creatorial institution which originated in the heart of God and is as old as time itself. Through marriage God graciously gives to one man one female companion to help and complement him, Gen. 2. 18, bringing them into a relationship that is closer than that of children to parents, 'For this cause shall a man leave his father and mother, and cleave to his wife; and they twain shall be one flesh', Mark 10. 7, 8; Gen. 2. 24. Adam verbalized this oneness with the expression, 'This is now bone of my bones, and flesh of my flesh', Gen. 2. 23.

Marital infidelity fails to break this one flesh union. Hosea's marriage still held good despite his wife's unfaithfulness, Hos. 1. 2. The Lord Jesus affirmed the complete indissolubility of marriage by saying, 'What therefore God hath joined together, let not man put asunder', Mark 10. 9. In fact, 'Whosoever shall put away his wife, and marry another, committeth adultery against her', v. 11.

Christ and

Mark 10. 32-52

March 5th

As the Lord Jesus approached Jerusalem His disciples sensed looming catastrophe, for 'they were amazed; and as they followed, they were afraid', v. 32. He answered their concerns with another prediction of His passion, vv. 32-34. He foretold Judas' betrayal, the sentence of the Sanhedrin, and His deliverance unto Gentiles who would mock, scourge, and spit upon Him. With a note of triumph He concluded that 'the third day He shall rise again', v. 34.

Sensing the nearness of the kingdom, James and John requested 'that we may sit, one on thy right hand, and the other on thy left hand, in thy glory', v. 37. However, their ambition was misguided. It betrayed an ignorance of God's electing purposes, v. 40, as well as a misconception of the character of Christ's kingdom, and how greatness is measured in it, vv. 43, 44. The Lord Jesus replied, 'Ye know not what ye ask: can ye drink of the cup that I drink of? and be baptized with the baptism that I am baptized with?' v. 38. These two figures represented Christ's expiatory sufferings at Calvary: the drinking of a cup indicated their voluntary nature, while baptism – picturing His immersion in God's judgement – suggested their intensity. Even though James and John confidently affirmed, 'We can', v. 39, they could never participate in Christ's atoning work. What they could do was, in measure, taste Christ's sufferings in a similar vein to that of the apostle Paul who saw his own suffering as filling 'up that which is behind of the afflictions of Christ in my flesh for His body's sake, which is the church', Col. 1. 24. James was eventually martyred, Acts 12. 2, and John exiled, Rev. 1. 9.

The remaining disciples revealed their own selfish ambitions when 'they began to be much displeased with James and John', Mark 10. 41. The Saviour reacted quickly to this self-seeking spirit amongst His disciples by explaining the huge difference between present worldly greatness and future greatness in the kingdom. Great saints stoop low in self-sacrificing service for others, vv. 43, 44. By taking this humble approach to the Lord's service many divisions sparked by pride can be averted.

His Apostles

March 6th — Mark 11. 1-26

Have faith in God

Christ's triumphant entry into Jerusalem suitably climaxed His earthly ministry, which largely consisted of preaching, 'the kingdom of God is at hand: repent ye, and believe the gospel', Mark 1. 15. By riding a colt into Jerusalem the Lord Jesus declared Himself to be Israel's Messiah and invited national recognition.

The practical and verbal adulation of the crowds was full of messianic implications. 'Many spread their garments in the way: and others cut down branches off the trees, and strawed them in the way', as though welcoming a worthy monarch. They cried out, 'Hosanna (save now); Blessed is He that cometh in the name of the Lord: Blessed be the kingdom of our father David, that cometh in the name of the Lord: Hosanna in the highest', vv. 9, 10. The worship of the multitudes clearly identified the Lord Jesus as Israel's Messiah.

But instead of rejoicing in their Messiah, Zech. 9. 9, the religious leaders were envious of His popularity, Mark 15. 10, and filled with fear, they sought to destroy Him, 11. 18. Within a few days the crowds demanded His crucifixion.

Returning to Jerusalem the morning after His triumphant entry and feeling hungry the Saviour saw a fig tree. Although from a distance it had leaves, suggesting fruitfulness, on closer inspection it bore no figs. Christ cursed it so that by the following morning it was 'dried up from the roots', v. 20. Like the fig tree the majority in Israel bore little spiritual fruit. But individuals could move mountains and achieve the impossible, through believing prayer: 'have faith in God', vv. 22-26.

'Jesus went into the temple, and began to cast out them that sold and bought in the temple, and overthrew the tables of the moneychangers, and the seats of them that sold doves', v. 15. This anticipated His future return when He will come suddenly to His temple with irresistible power 'to purify the sons of Levi', Mal. 3. 3. As in those 'last days . . . out of Zion shall go forth the law, and the word of the Lord from Jerusalem', Isa. 2. 2, 3, the people were 'astonished at [Christ's] doctrine'.

Christ and

Mark 11. 27 – 12. 17

March 7th

Having repelled the religious leaders' challenge to His authority, vv. 27-33, Christ exposed their malevolent intent through the vineyard parable. In Isaiah's song 'the vineyard of the Lord of hosts is the house of Israel', Isa. 5. 7; in the Gospel parable the vineyard symbolizes the kingdom of God as entrusted to Israel, Mark 12. 9. God gave Israel every possible advantage to induce fruitfulness, Isa. 5. 1, 2, 4. The 'fruitful hill' where God planted this choicest vine stands for the land of Canaan, while the surrounding hedge, Mark 12. 1, corresponds to God's protective care for the nation. The removal of stones, Isa. 5. 2, speaks of the extermination of the Canaanites. The 'winepress' may refer to the temple where God was worshipped, and the tower may represent Jerusalem the capital city itself.

Sadly, when God 'looked that [His vineyard] should bring forth grapes, it brought forth wild grapes', Isa. 5. 2. In the Gospel parable the problem was not the vineyard's fruitlessness, but the refusal of the farmers (Israel's leaders, past and present) to give over the fruit. With escalating violence they rejected God's servants the prophets, Mark 12. 2-5, their rebellion culminating in the slaying of His Son, vv. 6-8. In Isaiah's song God punished Israel's persistent sinning by allowing Gentile nations to plunder and destroy the Holy Land, Isa. 5. 5. Here Christ warned that those guilty of His death would also be judged most severely, and the vineyard given to others: a repentant generation of Israelites, Mark 12. 9.

The symbolism now alters so that the murdered Son becomes the rejected Stone, soon to be exalted, to the delight of genuine believers, vv. 10, 11. This primarily refers to Christ's exaltation in relation to His kingdom, for He is the stone 'cut out without hands' who will smite all earthly kingdoms. His kingdom, like a great mountain, will fill the whole earth, Dan. 2. 34, 35, 44, 45. He is also exalted in the church to be 'the chief corner stone', Eph. 2. 20.

Israel's leaders dared not apprehend Him; instead, they sent others to 'catch him in His words', Mark 12. 12, 13. But those who were sent 'marvelled at him', v. 17.

This is the heir; come, let us kill him

His Apostles

March 8th

Mark 12. 18-44

The Lord's enemies had come out in full force, attempting to ensnare Him. However, every fresh effort they made to discredit the omniscient Christ served only to highlight His infinite wisdom more clearly. The Sadducees, who denied resurrection, v. 18, based their question on the levirate marriage, which required a man to marry a widowed sister-in-law and raise seed to his dead brother, Deut. 25. 5, 6. If one woman had seven brothers this way 'in the resurrection therefore, when they shall rise, whose wife shall she be then?', Mark 12. 23. The Lord Jesus had previously taught the indissolubility of marriage in this life, Mark 10. 8, 9. He now affirmed that marriage is only for this life; death terminates it. 'For when they shall rise from the dead, they neither marry, nor are given in marriage', v. 25. Furthermore, when God at the burning bush said, 'I am the God of Abraham, and the God of Isaac, and the God of Jacob', v. 26, He was claiming to be the God of people who were very much alive, not dead. These patriarchs still live in God's presence, awaiting the resurrection of their bodies and the fulfilment of God's promises to them, Heb. 11. 13.

The question asked by the scribe had been long disputed by students of the law of Moses, 'Which is the first commandment of all', Mark 12. 28. Christ's elevation of two commands above all others, which in essence summarized the entire law, required a perfect knowledge of the whole law. The first commandment called for a man to be completely devoted to God, from the affections of his heart to the thoughts of his mind and the physical energy of his body, v. 30. The second command demanded selfless love for others, v. 31. When the scribe concurred – such a life 'is more than all whole burnt offerings and sacrifice', v. 33 – he showed true insight into the spirit of the law of God. Of course, the only man who ever fully magnified the law and made it honourable, Isa. 42. 21, was the Lord Jesus Christ, our flawless example, 1 Cor. 11. 1.

Critics were silenced, Mark 12. 34, but 'the common people heard him gladly', v. 37. The widow's two mites show us that what men despise can be highly valued by Christ, vv. 41-44.

Mark 13

March 9th

After the disciples had pointed out the magnificent temple structure, Christ predicted its total destruction, vv. 1, 2. The disciples asked, 'When shall these things be? and what shall be the sign of thy coming, and of the end of the world?', Matt. 24. 3. They referred to His 'coming in the clouds with great power and glory', Mark 13. 26, to receive an indestructible kingdom, Dan. 7. 13, 14. Although the precise time of His coming cannot be accurately predicted – 'of that day and that hour knoweth no man, no, not the angels which are in heaven, neither the Son, but the Father', v. 32 – the Lord Jesus unfolded to His disciples events which will immediately precede it, vv. 28, 29.

The Olivet discourse is so named because Christ gave it while sitting 'upon the mount of Olives', v. 3, the mount upon which 'his feet shall stand' when He comes to reign, Zech. 14. 4. It details the period just prior to His return and takes a similar viewpoint to that of the Old Testament prophets who looked beyond Christ's suffering to kingdom glory, bypassing the entire church age, 1 Pet. 1. 11. The chronology of the discourse parallels the prophetic timetable revealed to Daniel, Dan. 9. 24-27. Christ addressed His disciples as representatives of godly Jews who will live during these turbulent times.

The events which are outlined in this chapter will begin following the rapture of the church, 1 Thess. 4. 16, 17. They are so certain of fulfilment that the Lord Jesus stated, 'Heaven and earth shall pass away: but my words shall not pass away', Mark 13. 31. And once they begin they will take place rapidly, within one generation, v. 30. During the tribulation there will be widespread deception in the form of false Christs, vv. 5, 6, international warfare, vv. 7, 8, and widespread natural disasters including earthquakes and famines, v. 8. Despite the intense persecution of believers, vv. 9, 11-13, there will be global evangelism, v. 10, and throughout the period genuine believers will live in the expectancy of a soon coming Messiah. Even though Christian believers do not look for Christ to return as King, we do live in the daily hope of His coming to the air for His church. Such a hope should lead to pure living, 1 John 3. 3.

Tell us, when shall these things be?

His Apostles

March 10th — Mark 14. 1-26

She hath done what she could

True worship is costly. Mary demonstrated this when she came 'having an alabaster box of ointment of spikenard very precious; and she brake the box, and poured it on his head', v. 3. She had kept this expensive ointment especially for the Lord, not even using it to anoint the body of her own brother Lazarus who had recently died, John 11. 14. Sadly, such Christ-centred devotion provoked the criticism of the disciples. Knowing the monetary value of the ointment they viewed her worship as waste, Mark 14. 4, 5. But we cannot measure worship in pounds and pence. Only the Lord assesses rightly the quality of our worship. He appreciated what Mary had done and He defended her, 'Let her alone; why trouble ye her? she hath wrought a good work on me', v. 6.

Mary did not have much time. The Lord Jesus was to be crucified shortly and this may have been her last opportunity to anoint Him, vv. 1, 7. Her expression of love for Christ was deeply personal. While the disciples misunderstood it, the Saviour commended her, 'She hath done what she could', v. 8. In the Jewish sacrificial system offerings ranged in size from small birds to large bullocks, Lev. 1. 5, 14. The important thing about our worship is not the size of our offering in comparison to others, but that we do what we can. Sitting over against the temple treasury the Lord Jesus drew the attention of His disciples to a poor widow woman who gave merely two mites. As far as Christ was concerned she had 'cast in more than they all', Luke 21. 3. Mary's worship was also highly intelligent. She had a greater understanding of what was to take place over the next few days than all the disciples put together. Knowing that the Lord Jesus was going to die and on the third day rise again 'she [came] aforehand to anoint [His] body to the burying', Mark 14. 8. She did not accompany the other women who went to the tomb to anoint Him, knowing He would not be there. She had developed such spiritual perception by sitting at His feet and hearing His words, Luke 10. 39. It is as we study the word of God that we too will be equipped to worship. God remembers His people's worship, and Mary's is not forgotten, Mark 14. 9.

Christ and

Mark 14. 27-52

March 11th

Gethsemane means 'place of olive presses'. Here, as Calvary loomed, the Lord Jesus felt extreme pressure, His soul being 'exceeding sorrowful unto death', v. 34. This pressure was so intense that 'there appeared an angel unto him from heaven, strengthening him. And being in an agony he prayed more earnestly: and his sweat was as it were great drops of blood falling down to the ground', Luke 22. 43, 44. Knowing every detail of His imminent sufferings only enhanced the heaviness of the Saviour's heart. But even at this difficult time His submission to the Father's will was unblemished, 'Abba, Father, all things are possible unto thee; take away this cup from me: nevertheless not what I will, but what thou wilt', Mark 14. 36.

He endured without human companionship. While He took Peter, James, and John further than the other disciples, alone 'he went forward a little' to pray. Three times over He returned to find the disciples sleeping, vv. 37, 40, 41, and despite their earlier protestations. He knew they would all forsake Him and flee. In fact, when the critical moment arrived it was He who allowed their escape, John 18. 8.

No detail of what took place at Gethsemane was incidental. His abandonment by the disciples fulfilled the prophecy, 'I will smite the shepherd, and the sheep shall be scattered', Mark 14. 27; Zech. 13. 7. The Lord Jesus was withdrawn from the disciples 'about a stone's cast', Luke 22. 41, the distance of a man condemned under the law of Moses. The betrayal by Judas had also been predicted, Mark 14. 21; Ps. 41. 9, and it took place at exactly the right time according to God's foreordained timetable. It was just as Judas entered the Garden that Christ said, 'The hour is come; behold, the Son of man is betrayed into the hands of sinners', Mark 14. 41. By securing the safety of His disciples the Lord Jesus fulfilled His own saying 'of them which thou gavest me have I lost none', John 18. 9.

Christ displayed inimitable majesty. The great multitude that came to arrest Him, armed 'with swords and staves', Mark 14. 43, were utterly feeble before His powerful word, see John 18. 6.

His Apostles

My soul is exceeding sorrowful

March 12th

Mark 14. 53-72

Peter denied the Lord Jesus in 'the palace of the high priest', v. 54. Several factors contributed to his denial. He was physically and emotionally exhausted. The fatigue felt by the disciples was seen in Gethsemane when they repeatedly fell asleep. Peter had also been overly confident in his devotion to the Lord, vehemently declaring, 'If I should die with thee, I will not deny thee in any wise', v. 31. Such boasting is extremely dangerous, because 'pride goeth before destruction, and an haughty spirit before a fall', Prov. 16. 18. Although Peter had swung out with his sword 'and smote a servant of the high priest, and cut off his ear', Mark 14. 47, he did not stay, but fled, and then followed 'afar off', v. 54. If Christians, who are expected to 'follow [Christ's] steps', 1 Pet. 2. 21, follow Him at a great distance they also will be left vulnerable to attack. Staying close to Christ ensures that Christians are safe. Peter's distance also caused him to company with the ungodly, for 'he sat with the servants, and warmed himself at the fire', Mark 14. 54. When Christians settle down with unbelievers they too are in grave danger. Better it is to live a separate life; truly, 'Blessed is the man that walketh not in the counsel of the ungodly, nor standeth in the way of sinners, nor sitteth in the seat of the scornful', Ps. 1. 1. Satan also played a part in Peter's denial, Luke 22. 31.

At Peter's third denial 'the Lord turned, and looked upon Peter', Luke 22. 61. That look reminded Peter of Christ's words and caused him to weep bitterly, Mark 14. 72. The look also showed that Peter's denial augmented Christ's suffering in the palace of the high priest. It was here that the Lord Jesus was thoroughly outnumbered by Israel's leaders, v. 53. Alone, far from the heat of the fire, He would have felt the night cold. Many lied about Him, v. 56. Frustrated by the Lord's dignified silence the high priest compelled Him to answer the question 'Art thou the Christ, the Son of the Blessed', v. 61; see Matt. 26. 63. The law of Moses required that He answer, Lev. 5. 1, and this He did. Using the words of Daniel's prophecy He confirmed that in the future He will return in the clouds of heaven with unlimited power, Mark 14. 62.

I know not this man of whom ye speak

Christ and

Mark 15. 1-23 — March 13th

Art thou the King of the Jews?

Four times over in this section the Lord Jesus is called the 'King of the Jews'. As David's descendant, He was 'born King of the Jews', rightful heir to Israel's throne, Matt. 1. 1; 2. 2. The angel Gabriel had promised Mary before she conceived that the son whom she would bear would be great and 'called the Son of the Highest: and the Lord God shall give unto him the throne of his father David', Luke 1. 32. This promise is yet to be realized when He returns from an opened heaven with 'his eyes as a flame of fire, and on his head many crowns . . . And out of his mouth goeth a sharp sword . . . And he hath on his vesture and on his thigh a name written, KING OF KINGS, AND LORD OF LORDS', Rev. 19. 11-16.

Whether He stood before the Jewish Sanhedrin who envied Him, Mark 15. 10, Pilate who feared Him, John 19. 8, or the Roman soldiers who mocked Him, Mark 15. 20, the Lord Jesus acted with the majesty and authority of a King. He clearly affirmed His royalty with the words, 'Thou sayest it', v. 2. His dignified silence before aggressive accusation caused Pilate to marvel; it also fulfilled the scripture, 'He was oppressed, and he was afflicted, yet he opened not his mouth: he is brought as a lamb to the slaughter, and as a sheep before her shearers is dumb, so he openeth not his mouth', Isa. 53. 7. With disdain these Gentile soldiers 'bowing their knees worshipped him'. In the future 'the Lord shall be king over all the earth . . . And it shall come to pass, that every one that is left of all the nations which came against Jerusalem shall even go up from year to year to worship the King', Zech. 14. 9, 16.

How people responded to the King of the Jews said a lot about them. Israel's leaders had witnessed His powerful miracles and listened to His authoritative teaching, Mark 1. 27, but instead of acknowledging His claims, they were determined to kill Him, 12. 7. Pilate found no fault with Him but for political expediency delivered Him to be crucified. Even though many Israelites had benefited from His powerful miracles, the crowd 'cried out the more exceedingly, Crucify him', v. 14.

His Apostles

March 14th

Mark 15. 24-47

Truly this man was the Son of God

The centurion had participated in the crucifixion of the Lord Jesus. He had seen first-hand Christ's faultless demeanour, 'Who, when he was reviled, reviled not again; when he suffered, he threatened not', 1 Pet. 2. 23. The centurion had felt the three hours of darkness during which the Saviour was hid from human eye, and after which He 'cried with a loud voice . . . My God, my God, why hast thou forsaken me', Mark 15. 33, 34. Instead of hanging on the cross for many hours, gradually weakening, suddenly 'Jesus cried with a loud voice, and gave up the ghost', v. 37. The earth shuddered in response, Matt. 27. 51, and 'when the centurion, which stood over against him, saw that he so cried out, and gave up the ghost, he said, Truly this man was the Son of God', Mark 15. 39.

The centurion was not the only one whose attention was fixed on Christ. Speaking of His physical body the Lord Jesus had said, 'Destroy this temple, and in three days I will raise it up', John 2. 19. Passers by mocked Him with these very words, Mark 15. 29. His earthly ministry had touched the lives of many. On one evening 'all the city was gathered together at the door. And He healed many that were sick of divers diseases, and cast out many devils', 1. 33, 34. Israel's leaders acknowledged this and jeered at Him because of it, 'He saved others; himself he cannot save', 15. 31. Even 'they that were crucified with him reviled him', v. 32. Others came to the cross out of wholehearted commitment to Christ. There were women who had followed and served Him in Galilee. When men had done their worst, Joseph of Arimathaea came and tenderly 'took him down, and wrapped him in the linen, and laid him in a sepulchre', v. 46. This action fulfilled the scripture, 'He made his grave with the wicked, and with the rich in his death', Isa. 53. 9.

Many other Old Testament prophecies were fulfilled in minute detail at Calvary, including His death by crucifixion, Mark 15. 24; Ps. 22. 16, the gambling of the soldiers for His garments, Mark 15. 24; Ps. 22. 18, and even His being crucified between two robbers, Mark 15. 27, 28; Isa. 53. 12.

Christ and

Mark 16 — March 15th

He is risen; he is not here

The resurrection of the Lord Jesus Christ is fundamental to Christianity, for 'if Christ be not raised, [our] faith is vain; [we] are yet in [our] sins . . . But now is Christ risen from the dead, and become the firstfruits of them that slept', 1 Cor. 15. 17, 20. For three days His body lay in 'the place where they laid him', Mark 16. 6. During that time His body, which was entirely free from sin, did not decompose, Ps. 16. 10. And as soon as three days had passed, Matt. 12. 40, He rose from the dead; death could not hold Him, Acts 2. 24. By the time the women came to the sepulchre 'very early in the morning the first day of the week', Mark 16. 2, He had risen.

Christ's resurrection took His followers by surprise. The women did not expect it. Full of devotion to the Lord Jesus they determined to 'anoint him', v. 1. It was only as they approached the tomb that they queried 'Who shall roll us away the stone?' The women 'trembled and were amazed' at the words of the angel, 'He is risen; he is not here', v. 6. Neither did the disciples expect Christ to rise from the dead. Despite the clear reports from Mary Magdalene and the two that 'went into the country' they refused to believe that 'he was alive', vv. 9-13. When the Saviour finally 'appeared unto the eleven as they sat at meat, [he] upbraided them with their unbelief and hardness of heart', v. 14. During His earthly ministry the Lord Jesus had repeatedly told His disciples that He would suffer and die and 'after three days rise again', 8. 31; 9. 31; 10. 34; 16. 7. But they had failed to understand His words.

An angel had heralded the birth of the Lord Jesus Christ, Luke 2. 10-12. Appearing as 'a young man', an angel now declared His resurrection, Mark 16. 5, 6. The angel had not rolled the stone away to allow Christ out, but to let others in to see that the tomb had been vacated. It was not totally empty because the linen clothes 'and the napkin, that was about his head' remained, John 20. 6, 7.

The absence of a body, the post-resurrection appearances, and the courageous preaching of the disciples – backed up by miracles – all confirmed that the Lord Jesus had truly risen.

His Apostles

Introduction to Luke's Gospel

The third Gospel and the book of Acts were written by the same person (Luke) to the same person (Theophilus, 1. 3; Acts 1. 1). The way Theophilus is addressed indicates that he was a man of dignity. Luke was a doctor, Col. 4. 14, who travelled much with Paul, and who was with him in his imprisonments, right to the end, 2 Tim. 4. 11. Comparing Colossians chapter 4 verses 10-11 with verse 14, it has generally been taken that Luke was a Gentile; likely the only Gentile to have written any of the Bible. Evidence points to a date for the Gospel of about AD 61.

Luke's purpose in writing his Gospel is clearly stated, 'That thou mightest know the certainty of those things wherein thou hast been instructed', 1. 4. This aim he certainly achieves.

Luke presents the Lord Jesus Christ as the perfect Man. His is the only Gospel to trace His genealogy right back to the first man, 3. 23-38. In the opening chapter, Luke recounts the announcement of Jesus' birth to Mary, and he closes the final chapter with His ascension. Thus he covers a greater span of the Lord's time here on earth than any other writer.

There are many incidents unique to Luke's Gospel, which highlight His perfect humanity. These include: Him in the temple as a young child, 2. 22-38, and as a boy of twelve, vv. 42-52; His message at Nazareth, 4. 14-30; Him raising the widow's son, 7. 11-17; the salvation of Zacchaeus, 19. 1-10; and the walk to Emmaus, 24. 13-35. Parables unique to Luke include the Good Samaritan, 10. 25-37, and the Prodigal Son, 15. 11-32, which show His lovely character. In Luke, many miracles, parables, encounters, and sayings are recorded. In it all, we see His devotion to His Father, His holiness, His righteous walk, His tender heart, and His desire for the blessing of people.

Luke portrays Him as being on a journey, whose goal is given in chapter 9 verse 51, 'He stedfastly set his face to go to Jerusalem', that He might do the work to 'save that which was lost', 19. 10. Having done that, Luke tells us that He took another journey – to Bethany, from whence He was 'carried up into heaven', 24. 50, 51. The perfect Man, having done His Father's will perfectly on earth, is now at His Father's right hand in heaven! We are privileged, like Theophilus, to have this precious treatise in our hands, and to be able to 'Behold the man'!

Luke 1. 1-25 — March 16th

What an honour was bestowed upon Zacharias! To have the angel who stands in the very presence of God Himself in heaven, v. 19 standing before him here on earth, v. 11 bringing a message of blessing from God to him. What were the characteristics of this man who received such a distinguished visitor?

Zacharias was a **sanctified** man, v. 5, a priest, one who was dedicated to the service of God.

He was a **separated** man, v. 5. He had married a woman who was also of the priestly tribe. His dedication to God was borne out practically in his being joined to a daughter of Aaron.

He was also a **spiritual** man, v. 6. Both he and Elisabeth were righteous, and it is stated that it was 'before God'. What mattered to them was being right in His sight.

Zacharias was a **submissive** man, v. 6. He and his wife were obedient to 'all the commandments and ordinances of the Lord'. They did not 'pick and choose' what to obey, but happily followed all that was written in God's word.

In addition, he was a **stable** man, v. 7. Doubtless, being childless was a big burden, but it did not prevent this couple from continuing in faithfulness to the Lord, and to each other, into their old age.

He was a **serving** man, vv. 8, 9. We see him busy carrying out the work that God had given him to do in the house of God.

Finally, he was a **supplicating** man, v. 13. His life was characterized by prayer. It is evident that he had not given up, despite the unlikelihood from the human standpoint, of ever receiving the answer for which he longed.

None of us will receive such a communication in such a dramatic manner today, but God does speak to us through His word. If we would hear His voice, and receive His blessing, we would do well to seek to be like Zacharias: live lives dedicated to God, know practical separation from the world, live righteously before God, be obedient to His word, be consistent in our lives as believers, be busy in service for Him, and continue faithfully in prayer.

I am Gabriel, that stand in the presence of God

His Apostles

March 17th   Luke 1. 26-56

As in yesterday's passage, a godly person receives a visit from Gabriel to be told of the birth of a son. There it was an old long-married man; here it is a young betrothed woman – not of the priestly family, but of the kingly family; not in the august temple in Jerusalem, but in the despised town of Nazareth.

In both cases, the birth of the child would need a miracle. For Elisabeth, it would involve the removal of barrenness, something which had happened before, as Zacharias well knew. In Mary's case, it would involve an event unparalleled in human history, described so beautifully in verse 35. Both sons would be 'great', vv. 15, 32, but Mary's son would be unique: He would be truly human, vv. 31, 35, yet divine: 'the Son of the Highest', v. 32; 'the Son of God', v. 35.

Godly man though he was, Zacharias did not believe, v. 20, but Mary does, v. 45. His question was an expression of doubt, v. 18, but hers, v. 34, asked in faith, is a request for an explanation. The implications for her are enormous, but she gladly and humbly submits to God's word and to His will, v. 38.

Her subsequent actions are interesting: having received a visit from the angel, she pays a visit to Elisabeth. Doubtless, the word of encouragement that Gabriel has given Mary regarding Elisabeth, v. 36, has given her a great desire to see her who would be able to appreciate, more than any other, the significance of what Mary has been told. And what a joyful three months it turns out to be! How encouraging to Mary are Elisabeth's words, vv. 42-45, and the fact that Elisabeth's unborn child leaps for joy in his mother's womb, v. 44! It produces great joy in Mary, causing her to burst out in a beautiful song of praise to her God and Saviour, vv. 46-55. It is an exemplary song – full of allusions to the scriptures. Evidently, Mary knew her Bible.

Doubtless, Zacharias would have been aware of these events taking place in his home. What a rebuke it must have been to him: his lack of faith had left him unable to speak; Mary's faith led her to utter these majestic words of praise to God. How blessed is the song born of faith, in contrast to the silence produced by unbelief!

Luke 1. 57-80 — March 18th

In the first part of today's reading, the main issue is the matter of what the new-born son of Elisabeth would be called. The community, the mother, and the father all have an input, and we can learn a lesson from each.

The general opinion of the relatives and neighbours is that he should be called Zacharias, after his father, vv. 59, 61. Here we see the danger of **consensus**. These people have not received a message from God, so they advocate the following of tradition rather than what God has said. We need to remember to base all our decisions on what we have received from God's word, and not on the opinions of well-meaning people who do not know God or His word.

Elisabeth says, 'He shall be called John', v. 60. Clearly Zacharias must have communicated to Elisabeth what he had been told by the angel. Thus they are united in their beliefs. Here we learn the importance of **communication**, whether in a couple, or among believers in general. They that fear the Lord should still speak often one with another, and be of one mind.

Zacharias writes, 'His name is John', v. 63. What an example of **conviction**! He is utterly persuaded of that which he had once doubted, and there is no room for negotiation or compromise! So his tongue is unloosed. What a joy it must have been to him to be able to utter this delightful prophecy, vv. 67-79, and it is wonderful to see his emphasis in it. Delighted as he is about the birth of his son, he knows that God is about to send One even greater of the house of David, v. 69, and He is the main subject of the prophecy. Zacharias starts and finishes with the fact that God has 'visited' his people, vv. 68, 78. The result will be redemption, v. 68, salvation, vv. 69, 71, 77, deliverance, v. 74, remission of sins, v. 77, and peace, v. 79, all of which allow people to serve God, vv. 74, 75.

Finally, some early details of John's life are given: the **presence** of the Lord with him, v. 66; the **predictions** of how he would serve God, vv. 76, 77; the **progress** he made, v. 80; the **power** given to him, v. 80; and the **place** he was in, v. 80. In obscurity, he was being prepared for the work which lay ahead.

His Apostles

March 19th

Luke 2. 1-21

She brought forth her firstborn son

What a momentous event is recorded in these verses for our consideration today! Mary's 'firstborn son', is also 'Jesus', the 'Saviour, which is Christ the Lord'. Yet He comes in humility, 'wrapped . . . in swaddling clothes', and there is an early hint of the rejection that will characterize His life, 'There was no room for them in the inn'.

The Lord Jesus is the focus of this passage. Yet the inspired writer also draws attention to other personalities involved. They contrast greatly: an immensely powerful individual in the imperial capital; a poor couple from Nazareth; a group of shepherds from Bethlehem; and a multitude of angels from heaven itself! We can learn something about God from each of them.

Caesar gives us an insight into the **government** of God. In making his edict that 'all the world should be taxed', v. 1, never did he imagine that he was setting in train the events that would fulfil the prophecy that the Christ would be born in Bethlehem, Mic. 5. 2. How comforting it is to know that God is over all, and that even ungodly men can unwittingly be used to carry out His purposes in human history!

In Joseph and Mary we see something of the **guidance** of God. Having trusted Him, and made themselves available to be used by Him, they could look to Him regarding the details as to how His great plan would be worked out. What a blessing it is to know that, if we are depending on Him, and obedient to His word, He will guide us, and ensure that we are in the right place, at the right time, to fulfil His will for us.

The shepherds illustrate the **grace** of God. He first made known the coming of the Saviour, not to the great and mighty of this world, but to these humble men. How lovely is their response to His gracious message: they hastened to find the baby, they told others about Him, and they gave glory to God! Our response to His grace should be thus, too.

In the angels we see the **glory** of God. The account of their visit begins with His glory being seen visually, and ends with glory being ascribed to Him verbally. Truly, as we consider these things, we like them can say, 'Glory to God!'

Christ and

Luke 2. 22-52 — March 20th

We can compare the two main incidents in today's passage. In both, Joseph and Mary go up to Jerusalem with Jesus, vv. 22, 42, in order to carry out rituals commanded in the Old Testament, vv. 23, 42. In both cases, the action is in the temple, vv. 27, 46, and the Lord Jesus is the focus of attention, vv. 28, 46.

The first event occurs when the Lord is just beginning His childhood; the second is as He is nearing the end of it. On the first occasion, Joseph and Mary enter the temple with the child; on the second, they enter without Him but both arrivals are due to parental care. In both cases, mature people come into contact with the child, and react very positively to Him. However, there is a big difference. Simeon, vv. 25-35 and Anna, vv. 36-38 are godly, devoted believers, who are in touch with God, are in the temple under divine direction, appreciate the enormous significance of what is taking place, speak wonderful words concerning Him, and tell others of Him. By contrast, the teachers in the second incident do not have this spiritual insight, and thus are 'astonished at his understanding and answers', v. 47.

In both instances, significant statements are made concerning the Lord: in the first, by Simeon; in the second, by the Lord Himself. Simeon emphasizes His **salvation**, 'mine eyes have seen thy salvation', v. 30, which will be for both Israel and the Gentiles, vv. 31, 32, and His **sufferings**, vv. 34, 35; the Lord Jesus emphasizes His **sonship** and His **service**, 'I must be about my Father's business', v. 49 – a gentle reminder to His mother that, while she spoke of 'thy father', v. 48, Joseph was in fact only His 'supposed' father, 3. 23, and that, while He was exemplary in His subjection to them, v. 51, yet His responsibility to do His Father's work was paramount.

There are also parallels in the closing of the two events: in both, Joseph and Mary return to Nazareth with the child, vv. 39, 51, and we are told of His godly development, vv. 40, 52. Also, in both cases we are told of His mother's response to the great words that had been said, vv. 33, 51. These words were certainly worthy of her contemplation – and they are worthy of ours, too.

Mine eyes have seen thy salvation

His Apostles

March 21st

Luke 3

The Lord is about to step out from obscurity into public service. His fitness for this great work is indicated for us in three ways.

Firstly, in the **description** of His **forerunner**, vv. 1-20. John the Baptist was a great man. Names are given: the emperor, the governor, the tetrarchs, and the high priests, but 'the word of God came' not to them in their palaces, but 'to John the son of Zacharias in the wilderness', vv. 1, 2. We see him **faithful** in declaring the need for repentance (and the acknowledging of it in baptism, and the evidence of it in a righteous manner of life), vv. 3, 8-14; **forthright** in warning of the coming judgement, vv. 7, 9, 17; and **fearless** in exposing hypocrisy and immorality, right to the highest echelons of society, vv. 7, 8, 19, 20. Yet he freely acknowledges that he is not the Messiah, v. 15. There is One mightier than he, whose work will be even greater, v. 16, and for whom he, John, was preparing the way, v. 4. By such a description of Him we are left without doubt as to the greatness of the One of whom we are about to read more.

Secondly, in the **declaration** of His **Father**, vv. 21, 22. Luke's brief description of the baptism of the Lord Jesus lays emphasis on the lovely words from heaven, 'Thou art my beloved Son; in thee I am well pleased', and on the descent of the Holy Spirit upon Him. We know little of the first thirty or so years of His time on earth, v. 23, but this united testimony, involving the Father, the Spirit, and the Son, shows us the perfection of His life during the 'hidden years' in Nazareth, and how His service will be with all the approval of heaven itself.

Thirdly, in the **details** of His **family**, vv. 23-38. Luke has already told us that the Lord Jesus is of the family of David, through both Mary, 1. 27, and Joseph, 2. 4. Now he gives us the details of the line through Mary, complementing Matthew's record of the kingly line, through Joseph, Matt. 1. But Luke does more: he traces the line right back to the first man Adam. Jesus Christ is not only the Son of David, He is also descended from Adam, but, coming by means of the virgin's womb, He is the perfect Man – the only One who could possibly undertake the work which lies ahead.

The word of God came unto John

Christ and

Luke 4. 1-14 — March 22nd

Forty days tempted of the devil

The Lord's temptations follow directly from His baptism, 3. 21, 22. He is 'full of' the same Holy Spirit who descended upon Him, v. 1. On the other side, doubtless the devil observed the Father's acknowledgement of Him as His 'beloved Son', and was eager to counter with 'If thou be the Son of God . . .', vv. 3, 9. Thus, from the devil's perspective, the temptations were an attempt to make Him sin; from the divine perspective, they were to prove that He could not sin. And the Lord did indeed triumph, so that having been 'led by the Spirit into the wilderness', v. 1, He 'returned in the power of the Spirit into Galilee', v. 14.

Three specific temptations are recorded for us. In the first, vv. 3-4, the devil is attempting to make the Lord use His powers to provide for His own bodily needs, outside the will of God. Unquestionably, He was capable of producing food miraculously, as all four Gospels show, but for the benefit of others, not to satisfy His own needs, and in accordance with the will of God: certainly not at the behest of Satan.

In the second, vv. 5-8, Satan offers the Lord the kingdoms of the world, if He will worship him. The kingdoms *will* be His, but the timing will be God's, not Satan's; they will be given by God, not the devil; they will be His on a righteous basis, not by giving allegiance to the 'god of this world'.

In the third, vv. 9-12, the enemy subtly uses scripture to try to make the Lord throw Himself from a height to the ground. How often still does he misapply scriptures in order to achieve his evil purposes! But the Lord will have none of it: the promises of preservation are there for the encouragement of the righteous, not as a basis for putting God to the test.

When Satan tempts us, he does not tell us to produce food, or take us up mountains, or to Jerusalem, but still he would have us go outside the will of God to satisfy our own desires. He would put us in positions where we are tempted to value the gains of this world above our service of God, and he would do his utmost to make us act contrary to the teaching of scripture. We should respond as the Lord did, 'It is written . . .', vv. 4, 8.

His Apostles

March 23rd — Luke 4. 15-44

No prophet is accepted in his own country

The details of this section are sandwiched between two statements regarding the Lord teaching and preaching in the synagogues of Galilee, vv. 15, 44. Within that general framework, Luke mentions four specific places to which He went. We will consider the differing responses to His presence in each place.

Firstly, v. 16, 'he came to Nazareth', where He read in the synagogue from Isaiah chapter 61 verses 1 and 2, telling of the great works that the Messiah would do, and of the words He would declare. He read what Isaiah wrote of Him preaching 'the acceptable year of the Lord', v. 19 – a time of blessing – but not the following phrase, 'the day of vengeance of our God' – a time of judgement. His comment, 'this day is this scripture fulfilled in your ears', v. 21, shows that His first coming was to bless; His second will be to judge. Nevertheless, the people violently refused both His words and His blessings.

Those who met Him in the other three places happily contrast with those who were **angry with Him** in Nazareth. In the synagogue at Capernaum, v. 33, the response to His releasing of the demon-possessed man is one of **acknowledgment of Him**, vv. 36, 37 – so different from 'Is not this Joseph's son?', v. 22, by which the inhabitants of Nazareth belittled Him.

Then He went to Simon Peter's home, v. 38, and He healed Peter's mother-in-law, and many others. Her **appreciation of Him** is seen in the willingness with which 'she arose and ministered unto them', v. 39. How unlike the people of Nazareth, who felt He was not doing enough to minister unto them! v. 23.

Finally, we see Him going into the desert, v. 42, where the people went after Him and **appealed to Him** to return to them – in marked contrast to the citizens of Nazareth, who 'thrust him out of the city', and would have killed Him, vv. 28-30.

Thus, while the residents of Nazareth fulfilled the Lord's words to them, 'No prophet is accepted in his own country', v. 24, happily, there were those elsewhere who welcomed Him gladly. As the Lord indicated in the references to the times of Elijah and Elisha, vv. 25-27, the great blessings of His ministry have extended even to us, who have received Him.

Christ and

Luke 5. 1-16 — March 24th

In today's section, we have two miracles of the Lord, both introduced with the words 'and it came to pass', vv. 1, 12. The first is a nature miracle, the second, a healing miracle. Twice we read of people coming to hear Him; this is what led to the first miracle, v. 1, and it is what resulted from the second, v. 15.

The first miracle culminated in the Lord telling Simon Peter, 'From henceforth thou shalt catch men', v. 10, showing that the Lord saw the fishing which had just taken place as picturing the work of soul-winning. Thus it affords us some lessons.

Despite a night of failure, they were washing their nets, v. 2, with the purpose of going out again. Likewise we should not give up if we have not seen any visible results from our efforts.

Just as Simon made his boat freely available to the Lord, v. 3, we, and all we have, should be available to Him for His use.

The Lord could produce a catch when the circumstances were not favourable, v. 4, and He can save souls today in what appear to be the most unfavourable of conditions.

Simon was happy to 'let down the net', v. 5, because he had the Lord's word for it. We too should depend only on His word, and be obedient to it, as we seek to win others for Him.

The co-operation between the fishermen, v. 7, pictures the need to work together in the winning of souls.

The great catch that the Lord used Simon to bring in did not cause pride; rather, it made him see his own unworthiness, vv. 8, 9. So it should be with us – if He uses us for blessing we should be humbled that He would deign to work through us.

In the light of this, 'they forsook all, and followed him', v. 11. Those who get a proper view of His greatness can see all else in true perspective, and they follow Him unreservedly.

Whereas the first miracle involved something which was empty being 'filled', v. 7, the second involved one who was 'full of leprosy', v. 12, being emptied of it, v. 13. The One who could fully provide the fish (picturing souls) could fully purge the filth (picturing sin). It is no wonder that His fame spread abroad, v. 15!

May we, like them, ever follow Him and spread His fame!

His Apostles

March 25th   Luke 5. 17-39

In today's reading, Luke brings before us the difference between what the Lord Jesus came to do, and what the empty religion of the scribes and Pharisees stood for, vv. 21, 30.

Firstly, it is seen in His **power**, vv. 17-26, in the healing of the paralysed man. The religious leaders are indignant that a man could tell another man that his sins are forgiven, vv. 20, 21. However, the fact that the Lord could make a paralysed man walk, vv. 24, 25, shows that He has power not only to 'heal', v. 17, but also to 'forgive sins', v. 24.

Secondly, we see it in His **purpose** in coming into the world, vv. 27-32. He states that He 'came, not to call the righteous, but sinners to repentance', v. 32. This is amply shown by the call of Levi, a despised tax collector, vv. 27, 28, and by the meal in Levi's home, where the Lord and His disciples eat with those whom the scribes and Pharisees despise, vv. 29, 30.

Thirdly, it is evidenced by His **presence** with His disciples, and the effect it has on them, vv. 33-35. The Jewish leaders cannot understand why Jesus' disciples do not fast, v. 33. The Lord points out that it would be unreasonable to expect His disciples to fast when they have the joy of His presence, just as one would not expect people to fast at a wedding, vv. 34, 35.

Finally, it is shown in His **parable**, vv. 36-39. The righteous character (pictured in a new garment, v. 36) and the joy (pictured in new wine, vv. 37, 38) which He gives are new and distinct from miserable, worn-out Judaism. But the Jewish leaders, in opposing what the Lord is offering, show that they prefer to hold on to their old religion, considering it 'better', v. 39.

These verses show us how blessed we are in having trusted the Lord Jesus Christ. We belong not to an empty religious system, but to One who has the full authority and ability to forgive sins. Our Saviour came to us sinners in all our need, that He might call us and cure us, making us righteous in God's sight, and filling us with joy. His presence with us means that our service is a delight, not a duty, so that life is like a feast, and not a fast! How thankful to Him we should be!

Why do ye eat and drink with publicans and sinners?

Christ and

Luke 6. 1-19 — March 26th

In this chapter, Luke focuses on the relationship between the Lord and 'his disciples', who are mentioned four times, vv. 1, 13, 17, 20. Today and tomorrow, we will consider: His response to the **criticism** of the disciples, vv. 1-11; His **calling** of the disciples, vv. 12-16; Him in the **company** of the disciples, vv. 17-19; and His **counsel** for the disciples, vv. 20-49.

The first eleven verses deal with two incidents in which there is conflict over the Sabbath. In the first, vv. 1-5, the disciples pick and eat corn: an act which the Pharisees regard as work. The Lord's reference to David and his men eating consecrated bread shows that the Sabbath law was not given in order to deprive people of basic human needs. In the second, vv. 6-11, the Lord emphasizes His stand by healing a man with a withered hand on the Sabbath, showing that it is not unlawful to do good on the Sabbath. Thus He has shown Himself Lord of the Sabbath, v. 5, and what is lawful on the Sabbath, v. 9. The attitude of His detractors is highly ironic: they consider themselves guardians of the Sabbath, but, by conspiring to kill Him, v. 11, they are doing on the Sabbath that which is unlawful, v. 9.

In verses 12 to 16, we see the Lord calling His disciples to Him, after He has had a night of prayer, and choosing the twelve apostles. These men had recently observed the Lord's support for them against the criticisms they had received, and His fearlessness in healing a man despite the opposition of the same adversaries. Without doubt, these incidents would have been an encouragement to them knowing that they would face more hostility in the days ahead.

Following this, the Lord comes down to the plain in the company of the disciples, vv. 17-19. Multitudes come to hear Him and to be healed by Him, and they do not go away disappointed. Hearing the Lord's words to the people and seeing His works of power would further strengthen the disciples.

But the Lord has further means of fortifying the disciples in words given directly to them. Those words will be the subject of tomorrow's consideration.

He chose twelve, whom also he named apostles

His Apostles

March 27th   Luke 6. 20-49

Love ye your enemies, and do good

In this message, the Lord Jesus shows how different from the standards of the world are the attitudes and actions of those who would seek to follow Him.

In verses 20 to 26, we see the **blessedness** of a godly life. Four times those associated with Him are called 'blessed', vv. 20-23, in contrast to those on whom 'woe' is pronounced four times, vv. 24-26. As most people view things, being poor and hungry, weeping, and being hated and reviled are not considered desirable. But when it is for His sake, v. 22, and will be greatly rewarded, v. 23, it is cause for rejoicing.

Verses 27 to 38 show much of the **behaviour** of a godly life. It includes loving one's enemies, vv. 27, 35, doing good in return for hatred, v. 27, responding to cursing with blessing, v. 28, praying for those who mistreat, v. 28, giving more instead of retaliating, v. 29, lending without expecting to be repaid, vv. 30, 34, 35, showing mercy, v. 36, avoiding a judgemental spirit, v. 37, and showing forgiveness, v. 37. This is the opposite of how the man of the world would act, but the Lord points out that there is no virtue in acting in the way sinners do, vv. 32-34. Rather, His followers are to behave like their Father. Those who conduct themselves according to these principles will also be rewarded in the same way, vv. 35, 37, 38.

Finally, in verses 39 to 49, the Lord gives the **basis** of a godly life. As He shows in the parable of the two houses, vv. 46-49, the key is obedience to what He says. His word is the rock on which godly character is built. Thus the disciple will show character like that of the Master, v. 40, and will act in a manner consistent with what he professes to believe, vv. 41, 42. Just as the fruit produced by a tree shows what sort of a tree it is, even so, what is seen and heard from a person shows the true state of his heart, vv. 43-45.

So there is a stark choice: either to follow the pervasive philosophy of this present world system, or to obey the Lord Jesus from the heart. To settle for the former is to be without foundation. To choose the latter is to have a sure foundation, to receive His blessing, and to look forward to a reward in heaven.

Christ and

Luke 7. 1-29   March 28th

The statement made in verse 16, 'God hath visited his people', is certainly borne out by the events in today's passage. In the healing of the centurion's servant, vv. 1-10, we see how the Lord can heal a **diseased** man, without even having to be in the same place. Then He proceeds to raise a **dead** man (the son of the widow in Nain), vv. 11-17. After that, He can help a **discouraged** man (John the Baptist), vv. 18-23.

We can profit by pondering the words of the Lord Jesus in this section. Both the centurion and John the Baptist receive words of **commendation**: 'I have not found so great faith, no, not in Israel', v. 9, and 'Among those that are born of women there is not a greater prophet than John the Baptist', v. 28. In verse 13 are words of **compassion**, 'Weep not'. The Lord sees the widow in all her need and distress, and gives her the words she needs. Words of **command** quickly follow in verse 14: 'Young man, I say unto thee, Arise'. It is a command which is immediately obeyed by the dead man, with much resultant joy. Then His message to John, vv. 22, 23, has words of **confirmation**. John has sent two of his disciples to the Lord. In His response, the Lord gives John's disciples evidence that He is the fulfiller of the messianic promises, so John can have every confidence that Jesus is indeed 'he that should come', v. 19.

At the end we see words of **comparison**, v. 28: 'he that is least in the kingdom of God is greater than [John the Baptist]'. How? Not greater in character or work, but greater in privileges and blessings. These are amazing words, and we are included in them. We should appreciate and appropriate our blessings. When we face sorrows, we should (like the widow) give heed to His words of comfort. When discouraged (like John) we should ever be reminded of who He is and what He has done. We should seek to have faith (like the centurion) and show faithfulness (like John), which will receive His commendation. Also, our privileges are not confined to this life: if (like the young man) we die, we will hear His voice of command, 'Arise', when He returns. Then we will immediately rise, and experience a reunion of even greater joy than that at Nain! 1 Thess. 4. 13-18.

His Apostles

March 29th — Luke 7. 30-50

Who is this that forgiveth sins also?

Yesterday's passage described those who heard the Lord's words and believed, v. 29. In today's, the focus is on those who rejected Him, v. 30. We can note some of their characteristics.

We observe a refusal of God's call in whatever form it came, vv. 31-35. John's message of judgement ought to have produced sorrow because of sins. The Lord's message of blessing should have produced the joy of salvation. However, they did not respond positively to either.

We can also see no sense of need as sinners. For example, Simon called another person 'a sinner', v. 39, implying that he did not see himself as such.

Further, we can detect in the company no love for the Lord. Simon invited the Lord for a meal, v. 36, but his failure to show the usual courtesies to a guest, vv. 44-46, showed that he had no love or gratitude towards Him.

Finally, there is rejection of His claims. Simon denied that Jesus was 'a prophet', v. 39, and the general company doubted His authority to forgive sins, v. 49.

How up-to-date the scriptures are! Are not these the features of the Christ-rejecter, even today? There is a stubborn refusal to accept the divine call, whether it comes as a warning of judgement or as a promise of blessing. There is a denial of one's need as a sinner. There is no love for the Lord Jesus, no appreciation of what He has done, and no acknowledgment of who He is.

The woman brought to our attention presents a happy contrast. She had responded to God's call, realizing, and turning from, her sins, which were many, v. 47. Like the debtor who owed much, vv. 41, 42, she was forgiven much, v. 48. So she loved the Lord greatly, v. 47, showing it by her actions, vv. 37, 38, 44-46. Unlike the others present in the Pharisee's house, she did not doubt the Lord's Person, nor His authority to forgive sins. With great gladness she would hear His words, 'Thy faith hath saved thee; go in peace', v. 50. Unlike the 'children sitting in the marketplace', v. 32, she had responded to the message of her sins as was fitting – with sadness. Now she could respond fittingly to the tidings of her salvation – with joy!

Christ and

Luke 8. 1-21 — March 30th

Luke begins this section with the news that the Lord was travelling extensively, 'preaching and shewing the glad tidings', v. 1. But what about the response to His words? The three paragraphs of today's reading each give teaching from Him about those who 'hear' His words.

The first paragraph contains the well-known Parable of the Sower, vv. 4-15, and from it we learn about **reception** of the Lord and His word. He gives four different types of people who 'hear' the word. Three are shown in: those who do not even give it attention ('by the way side', vv. 5, 12), those who show only a superficial and short-lived interest ('on the rock', vv. 6, 13), and those whose interest lasts only until the things of this life come in and take away their interest ('among thorns' vv. 7, 14). None of these is a true believer. But there are those who truly receive the word, believe it, and give evidence of it in the 'fruit' which they produce (on the 'good ground', vv. 8, 15). The lesson is clear: each one should make sure that he or she has truly received the word.

In the second paragraph, vv. 16-18, we see **responsibility** to the Lord and His word. He says, 'Take heed therefore how ye hear', v. 18. A professed believer is responsible for what he does with the word he has heard. A person who lights a lamp will put it where its light can be seen. Likewise, a true believer will make the word known. One's true state cannot remain hidden forever: if a person is truly saved, this will be plainly seen.

In the third paragraph, vv. 19-21, we are taught about **relationship** to the Lord and His word. He is not disowning His own mother and brothers who have come to see Him, but He is showing that there is a deeper relationship with Him. It belongs to those who 'hear the word of God, and do it', v. 21.

That brings us back to the beginning of this passage, where we see those who went with the Lord when He was preaching: 'the Twelve', v. 1, and 'certain women', vv. 2, 3. Perhaps the former answer to 'my brethren', and the latter, to 'my mother', v. 21. At any rate, they were producing 'fruit', v. 15, and shedding 'light', v. 16. Their faithful service was evidence that they had heard and truly received His word.

His Apostles

Preaching and showing the glad tidings

March 31st — Luke 8. 22-39

Legion

Today we ponder two dramatic miracles: the Lord Jesus calming the storm on the lake, and casting out the demons from Legion. In both, He overcomes ferocious forces: physical powers in the first, and spiritual powers in the second. In the first incident, people are rescued from drowning in the lake, v. 23; in the second, pigs drown in the same lake, v. 33. The death of the pigs should not worry us, for it is part of the rescue of a man from a fate far worse than drowning, and one soul is of immeasurably greater value than many pigs. These events show the relative worth of men and animals in their true perspective.

In both, there is an appeal made to Him: by fearful disciples in the first, v. 24; by fearful demons in the second, vv. 28, 31, 32. In both, He gives a word of command, which is obeyed, vv. 24, 25, 29, 32, resulting in instant peace, vv. 24, 35. Both miracles cause the observers to be afraid, but in the first it leads to Him being worshipped, v. 25, whereas in the second it results in Him being rejected, vv. 35, 37. The first event begins with Him taking a boat journey to Gadara on His own initiative, vv. 22, 26; sadly, the second one ends with Him sailing in the opposite direction, because of people imploring Him to leave, v. 37.

But perhaps the links between these miracles go even deeper. Satan does not want to lose his slaves. Could the cause of the storm have been the devil as an attempt to prevent the Lord from reaching Gadara and freeing Legion? If so, then both miracles show Christ's power to overcome satanic forces.

What a change is brought about in Legion! At the beginning, v. 28, due to being possessed by demons, he states that he wants nothing to do with the Lord. By the end of the account, the opposite is true: he wants to join Him in the boat and be with Him, v. 38. Such is the transforming power of Christ. But the Lord has a greater thing for him to do: to preach Christ to the very people who had so publicly rejected Him, a work which he proceeds to do zealously, v. 39. The words of the disciples, v. 25, would also have been apt for his use, 'What manner of man is this!' The Lord who can calm a violent sea can do something even greater: He can cure a violent sinner!

Christ and

Luke 8. 40-56 — April 1st

Who touched me?

In a series of four great miracles, starting with the stilling of the storm, the Spirit of God brings to our attention the Great Physician on the road, and in each vignette we see the compassion of our Lord. In the midst of a howling tempest, with winds and waves crashing over the side of the boat, it is the cry for help from His own which stirs Him. In the turmoil of voices from the multitude of demons possessing the man from Gadara, the man's unspoken need draws His power. In the crush of the crowd on the way to a desperate man's house, it is the breaking heart of a bereaved father that draws from His lips, 'Fear not'. Then in the crush of the throng pushing its way through the narrow streets, it is the touch of faith that brings Him to a halt.

The anonymous woman was in desperate need of help, having spent all her life's savings on medical treatment that had failed to cure her. This haemorrhaging would have made her ceremonially unclean in the eyes of the law, so that she would have had limited opportunity to socialize with others and to worship publicly at the temple. She faced an uncertain future, with limited funds left and no prospect of a cure. Yet she had heard of Jesus of Nazareth, and with an understandable desire to keep her condition private and to hide her unwanted presence in the crowd of people, she decided that if she could only touch the great Healer, without even asking Him to touch her, that in itself would be sufficient to cure her. In the throng, she bent down and touched the hem of His cloak.

Instantly, our Lord stopped and with Him the whole crowd ground to a halt. His question, 'Who touched me?' seemed to elicit a very grumpy response from Peter. Pushed, shoved, and poked in the bustle of the crowd, Peter is not amused. 'Master, the multitude press thee and crush thee and sayest thou, Who touched me?' RV. But the difference is this: her's was a touch of faith. In the throng, touched by a multitude of hands, feet and shoulders, the Lord nevertheless felt the touch of faith. He still does. Whatever your needs may be today, by faith reach out and touch Him. He always responds to the touch of faith.

His Apostles

April 2nd   Luke 9. 1-17

He sent them to preach . . . and to heal

Until now, our Lord has been the One who has taught and healed. Mark tells us He had chosen twelve 'that they should be with him and that he might send them forth', Mark 3. 14. Now our Lord makes a significant change by sending out His representatives – here those twelve disciples – to teach and to heal in His place. They have learned *of* and *from* Him. Now they are to go out and speak *for* Him. The message is the same – they are to preach the kingdom of God, calling their hearers to repentance and faith in view of the coming judgement of God.

Many another leader has sent out his 'disciples' to carry on disseminating his message. It is one thing, however, to endue one's disciples with authority; it is quite another to endue them with accompanying *power*. Even Elijah was able to pass on a ministry to his successor, but he could not pass on to him his spirit and his power. But here our Lord, being God Himself, is able to give His disciples the authority and the power to heal. This ability to heal was to confirm that they were His messengers. It is salutary to notice that even the unbeliever, Judas Iscariot, went out with them, having the same power from our Lord.

Our Lord also endues them with a sense of urgency that was characteristic of Him. The disciples once commented that zeal for His Father's work consumed Him. Here, He tells them they are to allow nothing to delay them in their task. No time was to be wasted on preparation of food and extra clothing for the task, and no time was to be wasted choosing the best accommodation once they were on the way. Even the work of healing was only to be a handmaid to that of preaching. They were to give utmost priority to the task of proclaiming the kingdom. Should they meet with opposition or unbelief, they were not to waste time with reasoning, but to make an immediate show of an eventual judgement by shaking off the dust from their feet as they left.

This zeal for God's work is something we could do with learning. Our Lord was not teaching that they, or we, should go into His service irresponsibly, unprepared. But we should not put off the going and the doing, by spending so much time on meeting our own needs that His work is neglected.

Christ and

Luke 9. 18-36 — April 3rd

The Son of man must suffer many things

In the Gospel of Luke there has been a gradual growth up to this point in the self-revelation of our Lord as the Messiah of God. Now He is going to add another part to His self-revelation, a part astoundingly unexpected; the Son of man is to suffer.

But firstly, He draws out of the disciples a confession of faith. He asks them the simple question, 'Who do men say that I am?', not because He did not know what men were saying, but so that He could make the question even more personal to the disciples. There had, no doubt, been endless debate in the nation as to who this preacher and healer really was. Even Nicodemus, a ruler of the Jews, had come to talk about this with our Lord, and Herod, a man with a conscience over the execution of John the Baptist, hazarded the opinion that Jesus of Nazareth was John come back from the dead. But then our Lord brought it home to His disciples: 'Who do *you* say that I am?' Faith in God has to be a personal thing in the end. 'What must I do to be saved?' is far more personal than 'What must man do to be saved?'

Peter, the great spokesman for the disciples, says, 'The Christ of God'. This clear profession of faith that Jesus of Nazareth was the Messiah, the Son of God, showed how much deeper was the conviction in the heart of those Twelve who had been with him, Judas apart, than in the hearts of many others. The high point of confession has been reached, and not through the auspices of flesh and blood either. Messiah, the disciples believed, had arrived in His glory and power.

Yes, He has, said our Lord. But the pathway to that glory and that kingdom lies through suffering. For the first time He specifically warns of the horror that lies ahead of Him. From now on, He will revert to this subject time and time again, but the shock news must be broken now, whether the disciples can accept it or not. We note that He said the Son of man *must* suffer. There was a divine necessity about it all. In fulfilment of the prophecies of old, the great Servant of God must be a suffering Servant. The One who said, when He was twelve, 'I *must* be about my Father's business', knows that scripture *must* be fulfilled. And He will not fail to do just that.

His Apostles

April 4th   Luke 9. 37-62

He stedfastly set his face to go to Jerusalem

The high point of our Lord's self-revelation has been reached on the top of the mount where He was transfigured before them, and the three disciples caught a startling glimpse of the intrinsic glory that was His but had been veiled from human view. A week earlier Peter had declared their belief in His deity, and this had been confirmed to him and his two companions. Yet another contrast is to be drawn here and now. Even in His transfigured and glorious state, the conversation had been about His decease. So our Lord veils His glory once more, comes down from the mount, and once again prepares to humble Himself to walk the long, lonely, dusty road to Jerusalem.

His face is set towards Jerusalem. Visibly, this meant that the Samaritans, through whose countryside He would find the most direct route to Jerusalem, would see just another Jew on the way to the great feast, and they would make life difficult for all such. Animosity between the Samaritans and the Jews, who had once been of the same stock, had broken out when the Jews under Ezra and Nehemiah had returned from exile to re-build Jerusalem and the temple. On their return, they found a nation of people who had inter-married with the pagans round about them and had developed a way of worship that was foreign to Moses and the law. The Jews, therefore, rejected any help from the Samaritans in rebuilding Jerusalem, and the breach was final.

Metaphorically, however, the phrase 'he stedfastly set his face to go to Jerusalem' speaks to us of His total acceptance of the path of suffering that lay before Him. 'He must suffer' had now become 'I *will* suffer'. The heights of the mount have been replaced with the lowlands of Samaria. The adulation and acceptance of the mount have been replaced with the shame and rejection of Samaria. Yet with what grace He accepts their rejection and rebukes James and John for their severe attitudes. These men had been selfish (wanting to sit on His right and left hand in the glory), sectarian (rebuking one who was not of their company) and severe in calling down judgement from heaven. But the Saviour is none of these things; nor should we be.

Christ and

Luke 10. 1-24 — April 5th

Our Lord has already sent out the twelve disciples to preach the kingdom of God and to heal. They were sent to Jewish villages and towns. Now he sends out Seventy others, but this time they are sent out to the villages and towns that may very well have had many Gentiles resident. The message, however, is the same: the kingdom of God. These Seventy were to show the same commitment as did the Twelve; they were to waste no time in unnecessary preparation, prolonged polite greetings on the road (as was the custom), or seeking the best hospitality they could find. The kingdom of God was to be a priority. The sign of rejection was to be the same, too: the shaking off of the dust from the sandals. But these residents are warned that the opportunity of hearing the message will lead to a greater responsibility in its rejection. Just as there are degrees of reward in heaven, so there will be degrees of punishment in hell. It will be 'more tolerable' for those who did not hear, and therefore could not believe, than for those who heard and *would* not believe. The responsibility to preach the gospel to the heathen of our day is as great as ever. 'How . . . shall they call on him in whom they have not believed? and how shall they believe on him of whom they have not heard?' Rom. 10. 14.

Great success followed. The Seventy returned to report power over demon possession, something which seemed to be heightened during our Lord's life on earth, as though Satan himself were out to oppose Him as much as he could. Yet our Lord indicated to them that the battle was already won. Satan was already a defeated foe. Was it right for those who exercised such spiritual power as to cast out demons and to heal sicknesses to rejoice in their power? Yes, it was. Whenever the forces of darkness are overcome all spiritual people should rejoice. But our greatest ground for rejoicing should be our own spiritual experience. Keep on rejoicing that your names are written in heaven. He brings it all back to the simple gratitude and rejoicing that all who are His should know and enjoy. It is not selfish to marvel that we are His; it should be a wonder.

His Apostles

April 6th   Luke 10. 25-42

Who is my neighbour?

Luke now presents a series of parables and incidents in the life of our Lord which none of the other Gospel writers mention. One much-loved parable is this one – about the Good Samaritan.

Our Lord faces, yet again, a hostile, or at any rate a leading, question; one which was designed to put Him on the spot rather than to find out the real answer. How often He had to endure the 'contradiction of sinners against himself'! A lawyer, no doubt full of his own good deeds and fixated with a religion of works rather than of faith, as so many still are today, asked our Lord what one has to do to inherit eternal life. Our Lord's reply, though correct as an interpretation of the law, dissatisfied the lawyer. Feeling that he may have fallen down on loving his neighbour, he comes back to the Lord with the technical question, 'Who is my neighbour?' v. 29. Jewish teaching of the day was that a Jew had to be neighbourly only to a fellow Jew. Samaritans and Gentiles were beyond the pale.

In reply, our Lord tells of a man who was in desperate need, having fallen among thieves who had stripped him, robbed him, and injured him, leaving him to die. Two Jews, both of them highly religious, good-living, God-fearing men, who should have shown him kindness, failed to do so. Instead, it was a Samaritan, an avowed antagonist to the Jews (for 'the Jews have no dealings with the Samaritans'), who came to his rescue, met his physical needs as much as he could, and then provided for the care he could not manage. We fail to appreciate the shock with which this parable was received by those who heard it. Years ago a version of this parable was put out in a more modern setting in Africa, where a member of the Tswana tribe was presented as the man fallen by the wayside, and a Bushman, a member of the despised San people, was portrayed as the Samaritan, to the consternation of all. That was most offensive!

Our Lord did not in answer show who our neighbours are, so much as to *whom* we should be neighbour. Kindness should know neither racial, nor tribal, nor social barriers. We are to be neighbours to all, even to our enemies. After all, where would we be if our Lord had not shown immense kindness to us?

Luke 11. 1-28 — April 7th

Ask, and it shall be given you

Showing hospitality was such a key part of society in the time of our Lord that His illustration about travellers arriving after midnight would have been most familiar to His hearers. People often travelled at night, in the cool of the darkness. Regardless of what time they arrived, there was a huge onus on the part of hosts to provide the best they could for their guests. Seeing as there were no 24-hour supermarkets in those days, the host who opened up his home to hungry travellers after midnight only to find an empty bread bin would have been most embarrassed. This is where friends came in handy, and no doubt many of our Lord's hearers that day had been called upon late at night to lend urgent food to neighbours. The custom was to provide it, without question. In Christ's illustration, however, the friend whose help was sought seemed reluctant to provide it, fearing that his children in bed in the same room as him would be disturbed. However, when faced with the likelihood of prolonged and persistent knocking and pleading from his neighbour, he decided to get up and provide the requested bread supplies. Friendship was being tested; so was neighbourliness.

Our Lord proceeded to use this illustration to describe the believer's attitude in prayer. He is not likening God to a reluctant neighbour; God is not like that. However, He is likening the believer to the persistent host, who will have an answer to his request no matter how long he has to ask. So, says our Lord, when you pray, don't give up easily. Those who come to God on the basis of an existing relationship (here, a friend asks a friend) can persist in their request knowing that God will give what is right, in due course. If your neighbour will give you what you ask on the basis of friendship, albeit reluctantly, how much more willing will your Father be, with a much closer degree of spiritual relationship! So, says our Lord, do not give in easily but, with increasing degrees of effort, ask, seek, and knock. God will, in due course and in His time, give what is right for us. If asked for something edible, He will not give something inedible; if asked for something wholesome He will not give something dangerous. He is, after all, a caring Father.

His Apostles

April 8th

Luke 11. 29-54

Woe unto you

Despite the occasional hospitality shown to the Lord by individual Pharisees, and that not always from the best of motives, our Lord faced determined and harsh opposition from the body of Pharisees as a whole. They resented His popularity with the common people, His ease and authority in teaching, and His refusal to give them the respect to which they thought they were entitled. Our Lord, of course, saw the nefarious influence they had as teachers of the law, and He also saw their immense hypocrisy, and was not afraid to expose them publicly. This only deepened their hatred of Him.

In a series of 'woes' which He pronounced upon them, He showed them how well He could see through them. Men saw their public professions of purity and holiness; our Lord saw the inward decay of sinful thoughts and jealousies. As men clean the outside of a dish, but leave the inside dirty, and as men whitewash the outside of the grave, but leave the inside full of decay, so did the Pharisees: their public face of godliness being in huge contrast to their private state. They tithed the minutest of things (herbs, for instance), for this tithing was visible to all. Yet they did not care for the inward relationship of love to God. Moreover, said our Lord, in order to ensure absolute observance of the law of Moses, they added to the burdens of the common people. A man could not work on the Sabbath day, said the law; but to drag a chair through the dust and so make a groove in the earth, they said was to break the Sabbath rest, for you had 'ploughed'. All these burdens were added to the people, but no attempt was ever made to make it easier for them to keep the law.

Hypocrisy was found everywhere with these Pharisees. According to our Lord, they made huge memorials to Jewish fathers of old, from Abel in the first book of the Jewish scriptures to Zacharias in the last, showing an outward regard for them and their ministry, yet they were just the same as previous generations, willing to kill today's men of God who rattled their cages. The thrust of our Lord's teaching is that what we are in private, before God, is what we *really* are. The public face is but a show. God 'looks at the heart', though men cannot.

Christ and

Luke 12. 1-21 — April 9th

It may seem a little strange that a successful businessman, a diligent farmer, one who embodies all the characteristics the Bible commends, such as hard work, thrift, and patience, should be called a fool. The whole tenor of scripture is that men and women ought to work hard, to please God in everything and to provide for one's own. The fool in the book of Proverbs is idle, slothful, unmotivated. 'As a door turns upon its hinges so does the sluggard upon his bed' Prov. 26. 14 ESV. This farmer was no sluggard.

He, however, is called a fool not because he worked hard, but because he failed to realize that hard work is not everything. Nowhere does the Bible condemn wealth or success. There is nothing wrong with building larger barns if larger barns are needed. The farmer's folly did not lie in accumulating wealth, or even in preserving it, but in *trusting* in it. It is for neglect of the spiritual that he is condemned. There was a huge imbalance in his life. It is when he said, 'Much goods for many years. Take your ease, eat, drink and be merry,' that he is reproved.

The main lesson our Lord wished to convey is given clearly at the beginning of the parable – a man's life does not consist in the abundance of possessions he may have. Treasure down here on this earth may be a good thing, but treasure with God is better. Being rich before men is one thing; being rich before God is another. Moreover, the financial wealth I may enjoy down here can only be left behind; the spiritual wealth I have before God in heaven is yet to be enjoyed. The former will pass away, the latter will not.

There is yet one more lesson the farmer (and we through him) must learn. We are neither guaranteed the 'many years' nor the few. Our lives are in God's hands, and who knows when we shall hear the word, 'tonight'? To go out into eternity unprepared and unready is the greatest folly of all, trusting in earthly riches and neglecting a trust in God. Even the most diligent, hard-working businessman or woman must learn the wisdom of giving God His place, both in trust and respect for Him and in the use of wealth for His cause. Let us be diligent in both our work and our worship.

His Apostles

April 10th   Luke 12. 22-40

Fear not, little flock

Having addressed the crowds in general with His parable of the rich fool, our Lord now turns his attention to His beloved disciples, giving them an indication of the care their Father would show them. They were not to spend time and effort on the things of this life – food, clothing, wealth – as the rich man had. Their Father would care for their interests, if they cared for His. Neither were they to waste energy on anxiety about the needs of this life, for their Father, who was able to care for the least of His creation could, and would, care for them. The treasure they, and we, should seek is treasure in heaven.

These disciples of His were much loved and very dear to Him. Tenderly, He addresses them as a 'little flock'. What a lovely picture this is of His disciples! They were inclined to be **fearful**, so He tells them not to be afraid of anything. In the grand scheme of things, they were **few**, just a little flock. Those that love the Lord and His word, who seek to be faithful to Him and to follow Him, may very well be always in the minority. They were **favoured**, too, by His great grace. To them was the kingdom of God 'given'. Spiritual blessings are never inherited, nor are they earned. They are always gifts from God, given to whom-so-ever He will, when-so-ever He will.

They were also a **flock** to Him, and He, their shepherd. God's people have often been called sheep. Individuals have called themselves God's sheep. David could say, 'The Lord is my shepherd'. Jacob could speak of the God 'that shepherded me all my life long'. As a nation, Israel of old was God's flock, 'the sheep of his pasture'. And the church, today, is referred to as a flock. Elders are reminded to 'feed the flock of God', 1 Pet. 5. 2, over which the Holy Spirit had made them overseers, and they were told not to 'lord it over the flock', but to be examples to them. The Good Shepherd gave His life for the sheep and will also care for them. 'He will tend His flock like a shepherd; he will gather the lambs in his arms; he will carry them in his bosom, and gently lead those that are with young', Isa. 40. 11 ESV.

With such a Shepherd, and such shepherd care, why should that little flock, and we too, fear, little though we be?

Christ and

Luke 12. 41-59 — April 11th

I am come to send fire on the earth

There has been much debate about the nature of the fire to which our Lord here alludes. Is it the fire of the judgement of God that will eventually fall on sinners in the end times? He has hardly already kindled that! Is it the fire of persecution that had already begun and will find its most vehement expression at the cross? Is it the fire of the preaching of the gospel, as some speculate? It would appear to be linked to the baptism He tells his disciples He must yet undergo: a spiritual baptism of suffering and anguish, a baptism where all God's waves and billows will go over His soul. Fire and water are often mentioned together in the scriptures. Here our Lord mentions the fire He has come to bring and He speaks of its beginning; in alluding to the water of baptism He longs for its ending. Both together, therefore, probably relate to His sufferings on the cross.

He knew that ahead of Him lay the prospect of His being made an offering for sin. 'Thou shalt make his soul an offering for sin'. Such an offering necessitated the burning of fire. Fire speaks of the judgement of God, which His beloved Son endured on our behalf. How He longed for that to be kindled so that it would be soon accomplished! The baptism of suffering was one He also knew He could not avoid. Someone has rightly said that the prospect of His sufferings was 'a perpetual Gethsemane'. He tells His disciples He would be overwhelmed with anguish until it was accomplished. He knew He would sink in deep mire where there was no standing. He is not here complaining about what lies ahead of Him; but bears the burden of it long before it comes to pass. He must be about his Father's business.

Also, would the disciples be of the same mind as others that, when the Messiah comes, there will be a time of great peace upon the earth? 'No', said He. 'I am come to bring division'. There were many occasions when there was a division of the people because of Him. It will ever be so. Even families will be torn asunder by the Prince of Peace. Fire, suffering, strife. The work of God for Him was a natural thing to do, but surely not an easy one. Should it be any less for us?

His Apostles

April 12th   Luke 13. 1-21

Behold, these three years I come seeking fruit

Great care has been taken by the owner of the vineyard to plant a fig tree that would bear fruit; not only has he planted it in a vineyard, a place where there is likely to be fertile soil and much care, but also he causes it to be tended by a gardener and he himself comes to it each year, looking for fruit. But after three years, the expected time given for strong growth and abundance of fruit, he finds none. His patience is now at an end. He may as well plant something else. The fig tree must be cut down and thrown out. The gardener seems quite overcome at the thought. He has no doubt done much to cultivate this fig tree. He pleads with the owner to allow him to give it one more year. During this year he will once more tend the tree, loosening the soil, applying a fertilizer and giving the fig tree every chance to produce figs. 'If', says he, 'There is nothing at the end of the year, then the time will have come to cut it down'.

The parable illustrates the patience of God with His earthly people, Israel. The fig tree usually speaks of Israel. God had shown great patience with them, providing everything they needed to bring forth fruit for His pleasure. Yet they had failed to do so. The parable would also remind His hearers, and us too, that although God is supremely patient, there is a limit to that patience. The axe may yet fall on the unfruitful tree. Though God may cut off instantly some sinners, as the people thought He had done when the tower fell on them, this was not because they were particularly sinful sinners. God showed patience to others who had not been so suddenly taken from this world to the next, but continued refusal to repent would bring the judgement of God on individuals and on a nation.

'This year also'. How often God has given us one more year to put things right, to bring forth the fruit He has longed to see in our hearts and lives! And will it be this year also that His patience is extended to us? 'But if not'. Ah! But if not! What if this is the last year He gives us, the last year when He cultivates our dry roots, tends them, fertilizes them with His goodness, His longsuffering. 'Nothing but leaves?' Please God, let it not be so!

Christ and

Luke 13. 22-35 — April 13th

Are there few that be saved?

Would the whole nation of Israel be saved, as the Rabbi's taught? Or would there be few, as it would seem Jesus of Nazareth taught? The question comes to Him and is answered in His usual way. To paraphrase His reply somewhat, 'It does not matter whether there be few or many that will be saved, just make sure you are one of them'.

And it is not the appeal of entering in that matters; it is the attitude shown. To enter into heaven may appeal to many – 'many . . . will seek to enter in' – but not many will make it a priority. Our Lord tells His hearers they needed to strive to enter in. The word 'strive' means to agonize, as do sportsmen. It is to struggle, to exert oneself, to put oneself out. The way to secure the spiritual blessing of God necessitates going through a narrow doorway. One cannot pass through that doorway laden with indifference, pride, arrogance, and the burdens of materialism and riches. Sin must be left at the gate, as must all self-reliance and sense of self-worth.

Our Lord does not teach here that we will be saved through our works, through our striving. God's salvation is always a result of grace and not graft. Yet, nonetheless, it is those who have striven to win God's ear who will be saved. And God will not always leave the door open. As in Noah's day, Gen. 7. 16, there will come a time when the Lord Himself will shut the door. Then, when it cannot again be opened, it will be too late to begin to exert oneself, to knock and knock, seeking admission. God's patience will not last forever.

Those that are left outside continue to seek admission on the basis of their works, for they have learnt nothing of grace. They may well have done all sorts of things in His name, but if He does not know them as His they will be left on the threshold. How challenging this ought to be to us all! Are we as keen as we should be to seek God's ear, to strive to be as humble and sin-free as we can? And are we so full of our own assessment of what we have done in His name that we have failed to see that being His is far more important than doing His work? There may not be many that learn this lesson.

His Apostles

April 14th — Luke 14. 1-24

Come; for all things are now ready

Although Matthew records for us a parable about a wedding supper, Matt. 22. 1-14, Luke gives us a similar parable, told on a separate occasion, highlighting the feebleness of some people's excuses. One is hardly likely to buy a piece of ground one has not seen, to buy ploughing oxen without first having proved them, or to decline an invitation to a supper because one has just married. Behind each feeble excuse lay a more deep-seated problem: a reluctance to accept an invitation. Each excuse seemed, on first hearing, to be acceptable but subsequently proved not to be.

The exclamation from the lips of the pious, 'Blessed is he that shall eat bread in the kingdom of God!' indicated his assumption that it was his right to be there, as it was for all God-fearing Jews like him. In response, our Lord indicated that presence at that feast depends upon two things: a generous invitation, and a willing acceptance. An invitation to a supper was followed up by a personal visit to special guests announcing that the time for the supper had come and all was prepared and ready. Yet, an unspoken prejudice seems to have arisen in the intervening time, for none of those invited, accepted. Were they now indifferent to their would-be host? Were they just too pre-occupied? Were they hoping for another invitation which would make them feel more important? Their reasons for refusal were too pathetic to be genuine. Instead, the host sent out his servant into the hedgerows and lanes of the city inviting, nay cajoling, others to come so that the feast was full. No further invitation to the initial guests was forth-coming. By this our Lord first of all challenged the assumption that presence at the heavenly feast is dependent upon worth or birth. It is not. It is dependent upon a willingness to be there, which is shown by an acceptance of an invitation. Those preoccupied by other things will be passed over. He then challenged received opinion that that banquet will be reserved for Jews only; those who eventually filled the banqueting hall were from the highways and hedges, a metaphor for Gentiles. In much the same way, the gospel goes out now to men and women of all races, but only those willing and humble enough to accept will be in heaven.

Christ and

Luke 14. 25 – 15. 10 — April 15th

This man receiveth sinners

Our Lord was unlike any other 'Rabbi' of His day. His *knowledge* of the Hebrew scriptures was different from theirs, even at the age of twelve when He astounded men with His understanding. 'How is it that this man has learning, never having studied [at one of our schools]?' they queried. His *authority* was unlike theirs too, teaching with a quiet, dignified, 'I say unto you' which they could not match. His *method* was different as well. He made things so easy to understand when they needed to be so, using everyday things He saw round about Him to illustrate divine truths, whereas they made everything so complicated and hard to understand. Yet, He was winsome with it all.

The result was that the common people, those unversed in scripture, heard Him gladly and flocked to listen to Him. There were always crowds to hear and to be healed. He seemed to be able to soften hearts hardened by sin, to bring understanding where there was confusion, to draw out faith where there was none, and to bring to repentance the most unrepentant. He was a Man of the people. Where other teachers withdrew into their self-righteous huddles, refusing to touch and be touched by the mass of people, our Lord loved to sit among such, touching the leper, being touched by the harlot, eating meals in the homes of outcasts, and picking up children in His arms. The self-righteous of His day thought they insulted Him by calling Him the friend of sinners. 'This man receives sinners and eats with them!' they exclaimed. 'If this man were a prophet, he would know what sort of woman this is', they said, with the curl of the lip.

The basic problem was that men still looked on the outward, and only our Lord looked on the heart. He saw the pride and arrogance of the self-righteous, dressed in their symbolic whites, but He also saw the hypocrisy of their hearts and turned away from it all. Yet, He also saw the repentant hearts, and grieving souls of those who outwardly were far from God, yet who heard His word, and whose hearts burned within them. He had not come 'to call the righteous, but sinners to repentance'. How glad we are that it is so! 'Jesus, the sinner's friend, we hide ourselves in Thee', CHARLES WESLEY.

His Apostles

April 16th — Luke 15. 11-32

When he was yet a great way off

It is remarkable that the parable of the two sons, which initially was told in response to the Pharisees' self-righteous attitude against our Lord, judging Him for being so approachable to the unworthy, has become known as 'the Parable of the Prodigal Son', rather than 'the Parable of the Petulant Son'. The parable is, of course, much loved because it illustrates a number of truths we find moving: that a rebellious child can change his attitude; that a proud, self-indulgent one can return to a parent in humility and self-deprecation; that a parent never gives up hope, and is usually not only willing to forgive and restore, but is longing to do so; that all this illustrates the fact that God Himself waits patiently for the returning, humbled, repentant sinner.

Yet, the thrust of our Lord's parable was that the son who remained behind was just as lost to the father as the one who had left home; that the one who was careful and disciplined in doing his father's will was just as wrong as the one who was indulgent and disobedient; that a parsimonious, unforgiving spirit is just as regrettable as a generous but sensual one. The Pharisees felt that God owed them something as did the older brother in the parable. By their careful living they thought they had done God a favour and could not understand how Jesus of Nazareth could seemingly take more pleasure in the company of the sinners of the day than in theirs.

The father of the prodigal seems to have spent many an hour looking for the return of his errant son, for he saw him come 'when he was yet a great way off'. Physically, of course, the prodigal was still afar off, but in spirit the son was close to his father from the moment he 'came to himself', humbled himself, and repented of his folly. The opposite was true of the petulant son. Physically he had always been close to his father, yet in spirit 'he was yet a great way off'. The kind, generous, forgiving spirit of his father was not displayed in the son. Self-righteousness and a jealous spirit always destroy. Should we ever be called upon to come along side another overtaken in a fault, may we always be willing to restore such in a spirit of humility, and with a desire for true restoration.

Christ and

Luke 16 — April 17th

How much owest thou?

This chapter begins with a parable and ends with an anecdote – both of which concern 'a certain rich man'. The parable of the unjust steward, vv. 1-8, is followed by application, vv. 9-13. The condemnation of the covetous Pharisees, vv. 14-18, is followed by illustration, vv. 19-31.

We must not think that the Lord Jesus in any way approved of the dishonest practices of the unjust steward! It is the 'lord', v. 8, i.e., the 'certain rich man', who is forced to reluctantly admire the strategy of his unfaithful steward. The Lord Jesus makes the point that ungodly men know how to use their money now for benefit in the future.

The Lord draws three important lessons from this parable. Firstly, a believer's wealth invested wisely in this life can reap dividends in the life to come, vv. 8b-9. Secondly, faithfulness in money management qualifies a disciple to handle spiritual wealth, vv. 10-12. Thirdly, money should be mastered in the service of God and never allowed to become the master, v. 13.

The Lord's teaching immediately draws the scorn of the Pharisees. The Christian's attitude to wealth will always seem crazy to the ungodly. The Lord reminds them of three important facts. Firstly, what was precious to them was abhorrent to God, v. 15. Secondly, the Lord's teaching harmonized with the Old Testament scriptures and, despite the fact that John's ministry had signalled a dispensational change, God's standard had never changed, v. 16. Thirdly (and this was a 'hot topic' in Pharisaic circles), illegitimate divorce was simply a grosser expression of what motivated them – covetousness, v. 18.

The final illustration of the chapter, vv. 19-31 shows that a covetous lifestyle indicates a total absence of divine life and the certainty of future judgement. The rich man is not condemned for being rich; rather his selfish abuse of his wealth was proof that he had no living link with God.

Today presents an opportunity to revisit my attitude to money. Am I carefully using it to invest in spiritual, eternal things? Is it my servant, or has it become my master? Is my use of my wealth consistent with my profession of faith?

His Apostles

April 18th Luke 17. 1-19

Increase our faith

The disciples were often rebuked for having 'little faith'. In today's reading the lack is acutely felt by the disciples themselves. What aroused this desire for greater spiritual power and capacity?

The Lord had raised the subject of *causing offence,* vv. 1-2, and *dispensing forgiveness,* vv. 3-4. Possibly no other subject has caused as much distress among believers. No wonder the disciples felt their need of increased faith!

The word 'offences' is literally 'occasions of stumbling'. The believer will inevitably encounter stumbling blocks, but the Lord severely condemns any who place them in the believer's path. Some Christians are very easily offended – imagined slights and perceived injuries cause them continual grief – but this is not really what the Lord had in mind. Rather He condemns the deliberate attempt to trip up or impede the progress of a child of God.

In verse 3 the Lord turns from the *offender* to the *offended*. The steps are clear: rebuke him and, if he repents, forgive him. The offended believer must, however, maintain a forgiving disposition, regardless of the attitude of the offender. The point here is that forgiveness cannot be enjoyed in reality by the offender until he repents. And the Lord states that forgiveness must be extended without limit, v. 4. 'Seven times' refers to complete forgiveness and does not condone refusing to forgive the eighth trespass!

In response to the disciples' plea the Lord uses the illustration of a mustard seed – incredibly small, but with tremendous potential. Small faith, placed in the Lord, can achieve disproportionately great things. The removal of the sycamine tree illustrates the power of faith: in the context, to forgive my offending brother.

The illustration of the servant and his master, vv. 7-10, teaches that such demands are not unreasonable. We are under obligation to forgive, and in a sense it is our *duty*. Reflecting on this principle we are reminded of Paul's words, 'even as God for Christ's sake hath forgiven you', Eph. 4. 32.

Christ and

Luke 17. 20 – 18. 14 — April 19th

The Lord addresses the Pharisees, vv. 20-21, and the disciples, vv. 22-37, on the subject of the coming kingdom of God.

In response to the Pharisees' demands concerning timing, the Lord directs them to the kingdom's present moral dimension. They were interested in the externalities of the kingdom. The Lord reminds them that the kingdom must first be internal and moral, before it can be external and visible, and it must begin by them recognizing and accepting the King Himself.

The Lord then turns to His disciples with further detail about the approach of the visible kingdom.

Firstly, the arrival of the King will be *unmistakable:* as spectacular as lightning flashing across the sky, v. 24. This is His manifestation in glory at the end of the tribulation period. His rejection will precede, but not preclude, His coming in glory, v. 25.

Secondly, the coming of the kingdom will be *unexpected*. Conditions on earth at that time are described, vv. 26-30, and parallels are drawn with conditions prior to two great displays of judgement in the past: the flood, v. 26, and the overthrow of Sodom, v. 28. The predominant feature of both periods was the continuance of normal living and the total surprise when judgement fell.

The next section, vv. 31-37, emphasizes the *immediacy* of the coming of the kingdom, underlined by the expressions 'in that day', v. 31, and 'in that night', v. 34. The Lord warns of *delay*, vv. 31-33, and *division*, vv. 34-36. The 'one taken' refers not to the rapture, but to summary removal in the judgements associated with the Second Advent.

The Lord then turns, in chapter 18, to the subject of prayer. However, this is directly linked with the subject of His return, see verses 6 to 8.

The two prayer parables teach us the need for continuance in prayer, vv. 1-8, and humility in prayer, vv. 9-14. The first parable assures us that God will avenge His own elect at the coming of the King; the second assures us that repentant sinners will comprise the subjects of the kingdom.

April 20th — Luke 18. 15-43

What shall I do to inherit eternal life?

The Lord's treatment of individuals in this passage stood convention on its head. He completely overturned the prejudices and ideas of the time and society in which He lived.

Firstly, children were received by the Lord, vv. 15-17. His disciples rebuked those who brought the children; they thought children were not important enough to secure the Lord's attention. The disciples had to learn that child-like features are prerequisite to entering Christ's kingdom, v. 18. Spare a thought for children today, and pray for the Sunday School or Children's Meeting.

Secondly, the rich ruler, seeking eternal life on the basis of his own efforts, was rejected, vv. 18-30. His riches did not disqualify him from blessing, but they proved a serious impediment. He valued possessions more than eternal life and leaves the Lord with his purse full but his soul empty. The disciples are utterly astonished. To the Jew, material blessings indicated the favour of God. If the wealthy could only 'with difficulty' (v. 24 Newberry margin) enter into the kingdom, what hope was there for others? Yet, seemingly impossible things are possible with God, v. 27.

Thirdly, a blind beggar was blessed, vv. 35-43. Like the children earlier in our reading, he is judged unworthy to claim the Lord's notice, v. 39. To the popular mind, his blind state and poverty were indications of divine disfavour, and possibly personal or parental sin, cp. John 9. 1-3. Nevertheless, the Lord will stand still for such a suppliant. The contrasts between the rich man and the beggar are striking and extend beyond their bank balance and social status. The rich man addresses the Lord, 'Good Master'; the beggar addresses Him, 'Jesus, Son of David'. The rich man talks of *merit*; the beggar appeals for *mercy*. The rich man leaves the Lord sorrowful; the beggar follows the Lord, glorifying God!

The lessons of the passage are clear. Blessing depends on a child-like attitude, is obtained through grace alone, and is freely dispensed to needy souls who 'call upon the name of the Lord', Rom. 10. 13.

Luke 19. 1-28 — April 21st

Occupy till I come

This is a tale of two cities: *Jericho* – the city of the curse, v. 1, and *Jerusalem* – the city of the King, v. 11.

The people expected the Lord to head to Jerusalem and immediately set up His kingdom, and this is the key to the parable which forms the main part of today's reading, vv. 11-27.

Notice firstly, the nobleman's absence, v. 13, and rejection, v. 14. There would be a period when Christ would be absent from the nation and rejected by the nation. The kingdom would not 'immediately appear' v. 11; in fact, the King would be rejected. The parable then focuses on the behaviour of the servants during the nobleman's absence.

Each servant is given the same amount, ten pounds, and told to 'occupy (or trade) till I come', v. 13. This surely indicates gifts that every believer shares in common – life, time, energy, to name but a few – which we are expected to use as stewards for our absent Lord.

When the nobleman returns there is a day of *review* and *retribution*. Although this refers to events at the manifestation and not the judgement seat of Christ, the principles of stewardship and reward are equally applicable to our dispensation.

The amounts gained by faithful use of the pounds vary. One servant saw an increase of 1000%, another an increase of 500%. Rewards are given in proportion to faithful service – ten cities and five cities, vv. 17-18. One servant has gained nothing, and simply returns the original pound unused. The napkin, or sweat cloth, is an appropriate symbol of the servant's idleness. His distorted estimate of his master's character is offered as an excuse for his inactivity, but is rejected by the nobleman. There is no excuse for neglecting to use our gifts. A proper appreciation of the character of our Lord will surely stimulate zeal in His service!

The parable closes with *retribution*. The enemies who rejected the nobleman are slain, v. 27, prefiguring the judgement of apostate Israel at the Lord's manifestation.

Only when these lessons have been learned does the Lord continue His journey to Jerusalem, v. 28.

His Apostles

April 22nd — Luke 19. 29-48

The Lord hath need of him

The entry of the Lord into Jerusalem on an unbroken colt was an accurate fulfilment of a prophecy, Zech. 9. 9, and a dramatic foreshadowing of a future reality.

The procession began, significantly, at the Mount of Olives. From this spot the Lord will one day enter Jerusalem as the King, Zech. 14. 4, and set up His millennial kingdom. He descended the slopes of the mountain, pausing as the panorama of Jerusalem unfolded below. The Lord wept loudly over the city, vv. 41-44, reminding us of all the sorrow Jerusalem will experience before she truly welcomes her King. The procession at last reached its destination: the temple. The King will one day eject every unsuitable element from God's house and establish true worship at the heart of His kingdom, Zech. 14. 16-21.

In order to fulfil scripture and foreshadow future realities, the Lord needed a colt, v. 34. The role played by the colt teaches us important lessons regarding service.

Firstly, it was tied and untamed, v. 30, reminding us that by nature we are both captive and rebel. The predominant characteristics of the colt are self-will and stubbornness. Paradoxically, this colt needs to be both set free, and broken to the will of another – liberty and submission.

Secondly, the colt is covered, v. 35. It was not meant to be the central object of attention in this drama. It is at least partially hidden by the clothing of the disciples. Every true servant wishes self to be hidden.

Thirdly, the Lord is set upon the colt, v. 35. Its function is to bear and elevate the Saviour: to make Him visible and to raise Him high! The colt, or ass, is the mount of a king in time of peace; the horse is the mount for war and battle. Peace is a predominant theme of this passage, vv. 38, 42, and perhaps the colt illustrates for us the Bearer of the gospel of peace.

The colt had fulfilled a role that angels would gladly have undertaken, yet probably nobody gave it a second glance as it was led back to its owner! It had fulfilled its function.

Christ and

Luke 20. 1-19 — April 23rd

In questioning the Lord's authority, the chief priests and scribes were not genuinely seeking instruction; rather they attempted to undermine the Lord's teaching, Luke 19. 47. In response the Lord questions them about the ministry of His forerunner, John, and tells a parable to illustrate His own authority and the consequences of rejecting Him.

The Lord does not avoid their question, but He answers indirectly. He goes back specifically to John's baptism. The Lord asks whether that baptism was valid. Was it from heaven or from men? The spiritual leaders had rejected John's call to repentance, yet the people regarded him as a prophet. To discredit John's baptism would be to incur the wrath of the multitude. On the other hand, to acknowledge his ministry would condemn themselves. If they had believed John they would never have questioned the Lord's authority. The Lord will not debate with those who are unrepentant and have deliberately rejected the light. They *'could not* tell', v. 7; He *would not* tell, v. 8.

However, the Lord addresses the people (His questioners listening, v. 19), and by parable clearly states the basis of His authority and the dire consequences of flouting it.

The parable graphically illustrates God's dealings with the nation of Israel. The vineyard speaks of the privileges the nation enjoyed: a 'favoured nation status enjoyed by no other race. God, like the owner of the vineyard, looked for a return from the husbandmen. Despite repeated and gracious visitations, each servant is rejected – a disturbing commentary on Old Testament prophetic ministry. Last of all, the owner sends his son – the legitimate heir. The husbandmen recognize that he is in fact the heir, v. 14, but refuse to submit to his authority.

The parallel with the Lord's experience scarcely needs commentary. He has all authority because He is the Son, and the consequences of refusing to submit to His claims are far-reaching. The Stone rejected by men has been exalted by God, and one day will fall in judgement on His rejecters, vv. 17-18.

Let us gladly own His authority over our lives!

By what authority doest thou these things?

His Apostles

April 24th — Luke 20. 20 – 21. 4

Why tempt ye me?

Today's reading focuses on the futile attempts of scribe and Sadducee to trip up the Lord Jesus in His teaching.

The scribes brought a seemingly unanswerable *political* question; should they give tribute to Caesar? To answer 'Yes' would alienate the masses who hated paying tribute; to answer 'No' would expose the Lord to the charge of political rebellion.

The Lord's answer, 'Render . . . unto Caesar the things which be Caesar's, and unto God the things which be God's' has rightly become proverbial. There are two different spheres of authority: civil and religious. The disciple is obligated to submit to both, providing the demands of the civil power do not infringe on what belongs to God, Acts 5. 29.

There then follows a *theological* question from the Sadducees regarding resurrection, Luke 20. 27-39. In His answer the Lord exposes their ignorance both of the future state of existence and the teaching of scripture in the past.

In the resurrection, marriage distinctions will no longer apply. Marriage is an earthly arrangement severed by death. Gender distinctions will no longer apply. In that sense, the blessed will be 'equal unto the angels', v. 36. It would appear that in glory there will be recognition, but no resumption of marriage relationships. The Lord then reminds the scribes that scripture implies resurrection in referring to God as the God of the patriarchs – at a time when all the patriarchs had died.

The Lord now has a question for *them*, v. 41. It relates to His own Person and identity – the paradox of being both David's son and David's Lord. The real issue was whether they would recognize that the Man standing before them was God manifest in flesh. As at the beginning of the chapter, it appears that the scribes are unwilling to answer the question, and this leads to the Lord's public denunciation, vv. 45-47.

The actions of the 'poor widow', 21. 1-4, contrast directly with the attitude of the scribes. Despite opponents' hostility and selfishness, there is still a faithful remnant which pleases the Lord. May we bring Him pleasure today, regardless of the cynical and selfish attitudes of a hostile world!

Christ and

Luke 21. 5-38 — April 25th

These be the days of vengeance

Often, our ideas of vengeance include elements of vindictiveness or spite. Nothing could be further from the truth when we consider divine vengeance. According to Vine's *Dictionary of New Testament Words*, the word 'vengeance' means 'that which proceeds out of justice'. It denotes measured judgement flowing from impartial justice.

It must have astonished the disciples to learn that their impressive temple, and its associated religious system, was earmarked for divine judgement! Having rejected the Messiah, the nation inevitably faces the vengeance of God.

There appear to be two outpourings of divine vengeance referred to in this passage; firstly, the destruction of Jerusalem by Titus in AD 70, vv. 12-24, and secondly, the judgements prior to the Lord's coming in power and glory, vv. 5-11, 25-28. Both are centred on Jerusalem and its temple.

The Lord accurately foretold events that would unfold shortly after His ascension. This would be a period of widespread witness by, and persecution of, the disciples, vv. 12-19. The Lord encourages them to *endure*, v. 19. This period would cover the witness and sufferings of saints recorded in Acts, and would culminate in the destruction of Jerusalem by the Roman general Titus, vv. 20-24. This event would usher in 'the times of the Gentiles', during which Jerusalem would be subdued and its people led captive into all nations, v. 24.

The destruction of Jerusalem by Titus appears to be a parenthesis in this discourse, vv. 12-24. It is preceded and followed by descriptions of the final judgement of God on the nation.

The Lord enumerates the signs marking the approach of the final judgement on apostate Israel. These will include the appearance of false messiahs, v. 8, international tension and warfare, vv. 9-10, natural and unnatural catastrophes, v. 11, and astronomic phenomena, vv. 25-26. Ultimately the Lord Himself will appear 'with power and great glory', v. 27. The generation that behold these signs will witness the fulfilment of the Lord's prophecy, v. 32.

In light of this, the Lord says, 'Watch . . . pray', v. 36.

His Apostles

April 26th   Luke 22. 1-30

Behold, the hand of him that betrayeth me

In revealing the treachery of Judas the Lord speaks of his *hand*, v. 21; elsewhere He speaks of his *heel*, John 13. 18. The hand reminds us of his treacherous deeds; the heel of his total disdain for the Saviour.

The actions of Judas give rise to three contrasts. Firstly, his planning and preparation contrast dramatically with the preparations made for the keeping of the Passover, vv. 3-13: his avarice stands opposed to the generosity of the 'goodman of the house'; his scheming with the enemies of the Lord contrasts with the simple guidance involved in following the man with the pitcher of water, the activity of Satan, v. 3, is set over against a lovely picture of the activity of the Holy Spirit, v. 10.

Secondly, his participation in the Passover contrasts with his exclusion from the Lord's Supper. It would seem that Judas was present for the Passover feast but left the room before the Lord's Supper was instituted, John 13. 27. Luke records these incidents in a moral order, not chronological. Judas is connected with the Passover, and represents the state of the nation: hypocritically enjoying the feasts of Jehovah, yet at the same time harbouring evil intentions towards the Lord. The Passover cup was shared by all the disciples, Luke 22. 17, and symbolizes the joy of a redeemed nation. Because of Israel's treachery and rejection, the sharing of that joy is put on hold until the visible kingdom is established, v. 18. According to John, Judas 'went out' when he had received the Passover 'sop' from the Lord. When Judas leaves the company the Lord institutes a new feast – based on, but distinct from, the Passover. The last Passover gives way to the first Lord's Supper.

Thirdly, the Lord's startling revelation gives rise to contrasting speculation among the disciples: which disciple would be the *worst*, and which would be the *greatest*? vv. 23-27. Perhaps each felt that *he* could never be guilty of betrayal, and of course such a superior attitude leads inevitably to pride and strife, v. 24. The Lord reminds them that true greatness lies in selfless service, and He Himself would demonstrate that perfectly during the next few hours.

Christ and

Luke 22. 31-53 — April 27th

Not my will, but thine, be done

We cannot read these words without reflecting on the deliberate self-will of the first man in another garden. When our blessed Lord breathed 'not my will', v. 42, we understand of course that His will was not opposed to the Father's. Rather His prayer reveals to us His holy dread at the thought of what lay ahead.

Luke's account of this sacred garden scene contains four unique features which reveal the extent of His sufferings.

Firstly, only Luke tells us that the Lord withdrew from them 'about a stone's cast', v. 41. This intimates that His sufferings would be penal. Stoning was the method of capital punishment among the Jews. What the Lord would bear at Calvary would be penal and judicial, and it could not be shared with any other. He must go that distance alone.

Secondly, only Luke reveals that an angel from heaven appeared, 'strengthening him', v. 43. What a demonstration of the true humanity of the Lord Jesus! What privileged angelic service! Here are sufferings which are beyond human bearing and would sap the strength of even the Perfect Man.

Thirdly, only Luke describes the sweat of the Lord in the intensity of His agony, v. 44. Again our minds go back to the sweat resulting from Adam's fall, Gen. 3. 19. The Lord Jesus is truly associating Himself with the effects of sin on humanity, although Himself remains absolutely sinless. Sweat like blood indicates that this is no normal sweat, but rather proceeds from a deep-seated agony, v. 44. We dare go no further, but simply bow in worship.

Fourthly, only Luke records the words of the Lord, 'This is your hour, and the power of darkness', v. 53. Satan personally was involved in the activities of this dark night. Having entered into Judas, v. 3, and demanded Peter, v. 31, he now vents his full fury on the Lord Himself. Satan once defeated the first man in a garden; will he now succeed with the Second Man?

Praise God, the outcome of this contest was never in doubt! John 12. 31. Let His enemies do their worst; let all the powers of hell assail Him: He will never waver from submission to the Father's will!

His Apostles

April 28th — Luke 22. 54 – 23. 12

I find no fault in this man

While emphasizing the true manhood of the Lord Jesus, Luke in his Gospel is at pains to assure us that the Lord's humanity is *holy* humanity. In this passage he calls three witnesses to testify to the faultless Man. Each witness has his own reason for testifying, and this is the subject of our meditation today.

Pilate testifies, 'I find no fault in this man', v. 4. Here is the voice of *human justice*. Rome prided itself in its legal code, aspects of which have influenced our own legal system. This corrupt Roman governor was forced to acknowledge on three separate occasions that the Lord was guiltless, vv. 4, 14, 22. Accustomed to judging all types and classes, Pilate had no doubt as to the Lord's innocence. Incidentally, the trial of the Lord is without parallel in this respect, that the condemned Man is thrice unequivocally declared faultless by the judge!

The **repentant thief** declares, 'This man hath done nothing amiss', v. 41. This is the voice, not of human justice, but of *criminal experience*. The thief has been watching the Lord's reaction to His suffering and listening to His words. What he sees and hears results in a dramatic turnaround in his thinking. From his brief acquaintance with the Lord (possibly only three hours) he is able to make such a startling statement.

The **centurion** glorifies God and exclaims, 'Certainly this was a righteous man', v. 47. His is the voice of *military assessment*. As a Roman soldier, the centurion would have been no stranger to violent death and execution. Rome ruled with an iron rod, and the martial discipline and severity of her troops was legendary. Perhaps he was experienced in this very duty – the execution of criminals. He had no doubt seen many in their last moments, but none had died like this Man! Scripture says he 'saw what was done', v. 47.

Pilate testifies to the absence of evil: the Lord is *without fault*. The repentant thief testifies to His perfect actions: the Lord *has done not one thing out of place*. The centurion testifies to the positive aspect of His character: He is a *righteous man*. An unjust trial, dreadful sufferings, and death by crucifixion served only to reveal the perfections of this Man!

Christ and

Luke 23. 13-46 — April 29th

Father, forgive them

Luke records the first and last of the sayings of the Lord from the cross. Both are prayers addressed to the Father, vv. 34, 46.

Verse 34 commences with the poignant word, 'then'. It was at the very moment when man's cruelty reached its zenith – the moment of crucifixion – that the Lord breathed this fragrant prayer. In the privacy of the upper room He prayed for His own, John 17; here He publicly prays for His enemies.

For whom was the Lord praying at this point? Was it for the Roman soldiers? Certainly they were in ignorance of what they were doing. To the execution soldiers the victim was probably nothing more than another Jewish criminal. Was He praying for the unjust religious and civil judges who had condemned Him to such a death? Paul certainly assures us that had the rulers of this world known the wisdom of God, 'they would not have crucified the Lord of glory', 1 Cor. 2. 8. Was it for the nation of Israel? Peter says to the Jews, 'I wot that through ignorance ye did it, as did also your rulers', Acts 3. 17. In a sense the nation was acting in complete ignorance. The possession of the oracles of God was no guarantee of spiritual wisdom or perception.

The answer is that this prayer probably embraces the whole of guilty humanity. Ignorance, darkness and blindness are characteristics of fallen mankind. John reminds us, 'He was in the world, and the world was made by him, and the world knew him not', John 1. 10. Mankind as a whole crucified the Lord Jesus, and we acknowledge with shame our part in this ignorant rejection.

Ignorance does not excuse responsibility. The sin offerings of the Old Testament teach us that sins committed in ignorance still require blood sacrifice, Lev. 4. 2. The One who *prayed* for forgiveness would also *pay* for forgiveness.

The Lord's final prayer is the confident, trusting repose of the Son as He voluntarily steps into death, Luke 23. 46. His foes were ignorant, His friends bewildered, angels and demons uncomprehending; His Father alone understood what He was doing.

His Apostles

April 30th Luke 23. 47 – 24. 12

A sepulchre . . . wherein never man before was laid

The focus now shifts from the cross to the sepulchre. Both are essential for our salvation, Rom. 4. 25, and Paul emphasizes the fact 'that he was buried', 1 Cor. 15. 4. The burial of Christ underlines the reality of His death, and is the platform for His glorious resurrection.

Luke earlier emphasized the virgin womb, Luke 1. 27; now he speaks of a virgin tomb. No one had occupied it before. This of course was literally true, but it also points to the deeper truth – the tomb had never known such a man before! There were no forerunners, no predecessors.

Linked in this passage with the sepulchre are: Joseph, the women, and Peter.

Joseph fulfils the Old Testament picture and prophecy. Just as Old Testament Joseph was trained to handle great responsibility, so Joseph of Arimathaea takes responsibility for the most precious thing on earth – the body of the Lord. How reverently he handled it! How carefully he laid it in the tomb! Perhaps he little understood the vital role he played in the purposes of God, but surely he is the 'rich man' of Isaiah chapter 53 verse 9.

Luke's Gospel emphasizes the value of women. It begins with unbelieving men and believing women, Luke 1. 20, 45, and it ends in precisely the same way. Women are the first to hear the news of His resurrection, 24. 1-9, but the men regard their report as 'idle tales' and refuse to believe them, v. 11. The intentions of the women were commendable, although perhaps misguided, v. 1. However, their actions sprang from a deep devotion to the Lord and they were rewarded with a wonderful revelation. God knows our motivation and reads our hearts, though often we may act ignorantly.

Peter sees the linen clothes lying by themselves and departs, 'wondering in himself', v. 12. We can imagine the turmoil in his heart: the thrill of dawning hope; the deep remorse at the memory of his denials. Was there a longing, as well as a kind of dread? Peter need not fear meeting the Lord, v. 34, and neither need we, despite our failures.

Christ and

Luke 24. 13-53 — May 1st

In this wonderful passage three things are opened: 'he *opened* . . . the scriptures', v. 32, 'their eyes were opened', v. 31, and 'then opened he their understanding', v. 45. These openings prefigure the ministry of the resurrected Christ through the Holy Spirit.

Luke begins and ends his Gospel with a journey from Jerusalem. In chapter 2, the travellers are unaware of the Lord's *absence*; in this chapter they are unaware of His *presence*, v. 16.

How tenderly 'Jesus himself' draws near to this sorrowful pair! We picture the scene reverently, and listen with wonder to their conversation. Our hearts, with theirs, burn as He unfolds the types and figures of the Old Testament: 'the things concerning himself', v. 27. Passages, which before had been perplexing and unclear, are now plain. A suffering Saviour is entirely consistent with 'all the scriptures', v. 27. What a rich treasure store of picture and prophecy we have in the Old Testament! We, too, need Him to draw near and open the scriptures to us.

As they invite the Lord into their home, the Guest assumes the role of the Host and breaks the bread at their table, v. 30. Surely, this is a sweet picture of fellowship with Him. 'Their eyes were opened, and they [fully] knew him', v. 31. We, too, can testify to experiences of when our eyes have been opened to recognize Him. May we know Him today as we meditate on the word of God!

Later, the Lord appears to the disciples in Jerusalem. After demonstrating the reality of His physical resurrection, the Lord 'opened their understanding', v. 45. Can we imagine the thrill that must have filled their hearts as the redemptive plan of God became clear? The Lord not only explained the past, v. 46, but also set out an evangelistic programme for the future, v. 47. This programme would be empowered by the Spirit, v. 49, and the intercession of a heavenly High Priest, vv. 50-51.

In the act of blessing them, the Lord is taken up into heaven. Today, those hands are still uplifted in blessing. Like the disciples, we worship and praise! vv. 52-53.

His Apostles

Introduction to John's Gospel

Written by the 'disciple whom Jesus loved', 21. 20, 24, John's Gospel is both a first reader in Christ and the most advanced textbook in Christology ever penned. Its vocabulary and style are deceptively easy yet inexhaustibly sublime. Said LUTHER, 'Never in my life have I read a book written in simpler words than this, and yet the words are inexpressible'.

John's narrative has several distinctive features. Firstly, he contrasts man's ignorance with the Saviour's infallible divine knowledge, 2. 23-24; 4. 29; 16. 30. To read this book is to grow in spiritual understanding and in the knowledge of God, 17. 3.

Secondly, while the Synoptic Gospels hint at the truth of the Trinity when reporting the Lord's baptism, John goes much further, unfolding the family secrets of heaven, unveiling the special activities of Father, Son, and Holy Spirit. Indeed, the most detailed teaching in the Gospels about the Person and work of the Spirit of God is contained in John chapters 14 to 16. To grasp this is to be guarded against charismatic error.

Thirdly, with references to Jewish feasts John, alone among the Evangelists, establishes a time sequence for the earthly ministry of the Lord Jesus, 5. 1; 6. 4; 7. 2; 10. 22; 11. 55. The pervasive allusions to 'his hour', 2. 4; 17. 1, are a reminder that with God there are no accidents, no hastes and no delays.

Fourthly, John's account is back-to-front, because it ends where Luke begins (with a statement of the writer's purpose, 20. 30, 31; Luke 1. 1-4) and begins where the Synoptics end (with Israel's rejection of its Messiah). The nation's failure is revealed early, for 'his own received him not', John 1. 11, so that John can introduce a different 'his own', the disciples, 13. 1.

Fifthly, John presents a careful selection of the Lord's miracles as proofs of His Person. Although aware that He did much more, 2. 23; 3. 2; 21. 25, John chooses those best suited to demonstrate His deity, 20. 30-31. Avoiding the normal word for 'miracle' (*dunamis*, power) he uses a term (*semeion*, sign) that emphasizes the credential value of each action. Every sign then is a living lesson, a testimony to the Lord's identity as promised Messiah and eternal Son, 2. 11; 5. 36; 12. 37. Let us not be like those who read about a miracle yet miss its underlying meaning, 6. 36, for everything is designed to spotlight Christ.

Christ and

John 1. 1-18   May 2nd

John's Gospel begins with neither salvation nor prophetic fulfilment but with the Word in all His divine excellence.

About this grand Person John teaches seven great lessons. Firstly, His **eternal reality**: 'In the beginning was the Word', v. 1. He was always 'from everlasting', Mic. 5. 2, 'before the world was', John 17. 5, 24. There never was a time when He was not. This is the mark of deity, Ps. 90. 2. Secondly, we learn of His **distinct personality**: 'the Word was with God'. The preposition 'with' intimates plurality within the Godhead, a truth to be enlarged upon in verses 32-34. Yet it could not be plainer, thirdly, that the Word possessed **full deity**: 'and the Word was God'. He 'was another and yet not other than God', LENSKI. We have only to compare Romans 9. 5 and Titus 2. 13.

Fourthly, the repetition in verse 2 underlines the **blessed society** of heaven, for from all eternity the Word enjoyed complete harmony, mutuality, and affection within the Godhead, Prov. 8. 30. Jehovah cannot be lonely, so any suggestion that God created man to satisfy a felt need of companionship is a denial of divine self-sufficiency. Fifthly, we learn of **unambiguous creativity**, John 1. 3. Despite all man's efforts to account for the universe 'without him', the New Testament insists that Genesis chapter 1 verse 1 be read in the light of its additional information about the Son's activity in creation, Col. 1. 16. The sixth, is **essential vitality**: 'in him was life', John 1. 4. Unlike creatures, whose existence is derived and dependent, the Son ever has 'life in himself', 5. 26, inherent, independent, and immutable, for He truly is 'the life', 11. 25; 14. 6. Finally, John's prologue introduces us to His **gracious ministry**: 'the life was the light of men', 1. 4-5. The Word, viewed in relation to God, vv. 1-2, and to creation, v. 3, is now seen in relation to men, acting on their behalf and for their good. The darkness in which man dwells because of sin could neither appreciate nor extinguish that light, v. 5.

And in order to accomplish this gracious work for men – marvel of marvels! – 'the Word was made flesh, and dwelt among us', v. 14. He who was eternally Son of God became Son of man. Can you think of a better reason for worship?

His Apostles

May 3rd   John 1. 19-51

John records the events of four consecutive days to help us grasp the supremacy of Christ.

On **Day One,** vv. 19-28, John the Baptist faced challenges as to his own person and ministry. His progressively crisper negatives indicate that he had no wish to speak about himself at all. Rather, his desire was to exalt Christ. He was but 'a voice', heard and not seen, directing attention to the Word. Here is a model for us; in his honesty, humility, clarity, authority, and pertinacity John the Baptist is a pattern servant.

Day Two, vv. 29-34, brought the great announcement of the Saviour's mission as 'Lamb of God', v. 29. John's language draws on a range of Old Testament passages that associate the lamb with spotlessness, submissiveness, sacrifice, and divine selection, Gen. 22. 7-8; Exod. 12. 5; 29. 38-42; Isa. 53. 7. The stupendous task in view was to bear away the sin of the world, for through the propitiatory sacrifice of Christ man's sinfulness would be for ever dealt with to God's glory. This grand purpose is the work of the triune Godhead, for the Father spoke to John (to identify His Son), the Holy Spirit descended to abide on Christ, and the Son Himself would baptize with the Spirit.

Day Three, vv. 35-42, records individuals being drawn to the Saviour, 6. 44. On this occasion, the Baptist's abbreviated announcement, 1. 35-36, focussed exclusively upon Christ's Person, because the Lord Jesus, God's perfect Lamb, is Himself greater than all His works. John, last of the prophets, appropriately illustrated the function of the Old Testament – to direct men to Christ. His hearers therefore changed their allegiance and 'followed Jesus', v. 37, language implying reverence, obedience, and persistence. We are not to emulate mere men but Christ Jesus, 1 Cor. 11. 1. Their desire for His company, John 1. 38, teaches the value of communion, for we cannot effectively go out for Him until we learn to spend time with Him, Mark 3. 14.

Day Four, vv. 43-51, fittingly climaxes with Nathanael's exclamation of wondering worship, v. 49. John's Gospel displays Christ's essential glory as 'Son of God'; at His return all creatures will behold His official glory as 'King of Israel'.

John 2 — May 4th

This beginning of miracles

The Saviour's first recorded sign miracle is memorable for several reasons. For a start, it was low key. It had none of the razzmatazz of the arena; the Son of God did not hire a stadium for a healing campaign or blitz the area with glossy self-promoting posters. Indeed, the setting was the insignificant and still unidentified Cana, rather than the prestigious capital of Israel, the city of the great king. The manner of the Lord's activity was wonderfully quiet, v. 9; there was no show or performance to appeal to the flesh. Instead, all was marked by sublime unostentatiousness, for only the servants, disciples, and presumably Mary knew that a miracle had taken place at all.

Second, like everything the Lord did, it was genuine. Performed in the context of normal daily life (at a wedding, by a pool, on a hillside, on a lake, in the street, at a cemetery) His signs were devoid of all the shady features of showmanship. Further, they were free from any suspicion of trickery, for at Cana the Lord Jesus never even handled the water pots.

Third, it was verifiable. It could be put to the test and investigated; in fact the Lord encouraged it, vv. 8-10, making sure that an unprejudiced, expert witness testified to the excellence of His work, Matt. 8. 4; John 20. 27. This contrasts with the blasphemous nonsense of transubstantiation and with the fraudulence of many so-called healing miracles. A real work of God will stand up to the most robust examination. Those who claim to be saved must demonstrate the reality by changed lives, 8. 30-32.

Fourth, it was economical. The Lord of glory condescended to use lowly human instruments, thus teaching the principle that in all Christian service we are to do what we can while He alone does the impossible. And how dutiful were those servants! They obeyed the Lord's words without question. After all, who was He to give orders in someone else's house? But Mary's advice must have struck home, 'Whatsoever he saith unto you, do it', 2. 5. They therefore obeyed without delay and without stinting, filling the pots 'to the brim', v. 7. Their total surrender to what must have seemed an absurd command stands as a model of godly obedience to the word. May we be as diligent.

His Apostles

May 5th   **John 3. 1-21**

How can a man be born when he is old?

Israel's great Bible expositor was stumped! He just could not make sense of what this new 'teacher come from God', v. 2, was saying about the entrance requirements for the coming kingdom. Of course Nicodemus knew all about the great kingdom promised Israel under the terms of the Davidic covenant, 2 Sam. 7. 12-16, and he had doubtless many times read Daniel's amazing end-times prediction that 'the God of heaven [would] set up a kingdom, which shall never be destroyed', Dan. 2. 44. This language underlay the Saviour's proclamation that 'the kingdom of heaven' and 'the kingdom of God' (synonymous terms) were at hand, Matt. 4. 17.

But what about being born again? 'Except a man be born of water and of the Spirit, he cannot enter into the kingdom of God', John 3. 5. It seems that Nicodemus, like many believers today, had overlooked Ezekiel in his scripture reading programme. The Lord gently rebuked him: 'Art thou the teacher of Israel, and understandest not these things?', v. 10 ASV. Nicodemus should have recognized that the Lord was echoing a description of Israel's future national regeneration which used the key words 'water' and 'spirit', 'Then will I sprinkle clean water upon you, and ye shall be clean: from all your filthiness, and from all your idols, will I cleanse you. A new heart also will I give you, and a new spirit will I put within you . . . And I will put my spirit within you, and cause you to walk in my statutes, and ye shall keep my judgments', Ezek. 36. 25-27.

Entrance into the kingdom age was not based on natural birth. Like every other nation on earth Israel had failed because of sin, and required a spiritual renewal before it could come into promised blessing. The application is obvious. If Israel must be born again to enter the future kingdom of righteousness and peace to be established by the Lord Jesus at His second coming, Gentile sinners today must be born again to receive the benefits of spiritual salvation in Christ.

We can rejoice that the Lord used the plural pronoun 'ye', not 'we'. Israel and all men need new birth, but He was entirely different, being the sinless Man, the spotless Lamb of God.

Christ and

John 3. 22-36   May 6th

The overlapping ministry of John the Baptist and the Lord Jesus Christ meant that there was a brief period in Israel's history when both were baptizing simultaneously. Not surprisingly, some of John's disciples, concerned for the declining popularity of their master, raised the matter.

John thus faced a serious **test**, vv. 22-26. Would he be tempted to disappointment (like Elijah, whose testimony to Israel was spurned), resentment (like Jonah, who took umbrage at Nineveh's repentance), or self-advertisement (like Moses, who pushed himself into the limelight, Num. 20. 10)? Would he lose sight of the truth that service is designed to glorify God, not the servant?

John passed the test with flying colours, his **triumph** recorded in the remainder of the chapter, vv. 27-36. Firstly, he affirmed his own lowly servanthood, vv. 27-30. As Messiah's forerunner he was merely the herald, whose very purpose was to fade out in the brighter presence of the Lord Jesus. But this was no occasion for regret. Rather, it brought him deep and satisfying joy to accept no more and no less than the whole of God's perfect will for him, cp. Rom. 12. 1-2. Secondly, he emphasized Christ's supremacy, vv. 31-36. In western weddings the bride is normally the focus of attention, but here the bride is as yet unmentioned, while the spotlight falls exclusively on the divine Bridegroom, a metaphor for Christ which foregrounds tender love, practical care, and earnest expectation. He is the unique One who 'cometh from heaven', v. 31, because it takes a heavenly person to disclose heavenly things. But best of all, He is the beloved Son into whose hands the Father has entrusted absolutely everything, v. 35. This statement is astonishingly comprehensive. All God's purposes of grace and judgement, His eternal programme for Israel, the Gentiles, and the church, are to be effected by the Lord Jesus, for the Son is the unfailing executor of the Father's will.

For such a One to be magnified, John was glad to diminish himself. To place the exaltation of Christ before the advancement of self is still the recipe for lasting contentment of soul.

He must increase, but I must decrease

His Apostles

May 7th   **John 4. 1-30**

Come, see a man

But of course the Lord Jesus was so much more than 'a man'. The Samaritan woman received a personal lesson in Christology and witness so that, having come into the blessing of knowing the Lord Jesus, she might tell others, v. 29.

What did she learn about Him? His **sovereignty** was demonstrated in His choice of route to Galilee. 'He must needs go through Samaria', v. 4, not because it was the shortest way (devout Jews often by-passed such despised territory) but because it was His will to meet and bless a needy soul. His **authority** was immediately apparent in His words. Though He spoke to a member of the Samaritan people this was no inter-faith dialogue about the common ground between religions but an uncompromising revelation of truth, vv. 22-24. And yet He was marked by **humility**, for while John's Gospel highlights His deity it does not deny His real manhood. He was tired and solicited a drink. His was a sinless but not a super humanity exempted from the sufferings of life on earth. Indeed, to the woman He seemed initially just a travel-wearied Jewish rabbi, v. 6. With gracious **courtesy** He initiated the conversation, honouring her by making a request, ensuring all was done in privacy (to preserve her from embarrassment), and allowing her time to reply. Personal evangelism is not the same as sermonizing. And He communicated with **clarity**, gently leading His listener from the known (literal water) to the unknown (eternal spiritual satisfaction found freely in Him).

But, crucially, He exposed her personal sinfulness. Religious she might be; righteous she was not, vv. 18, 20. It was this supernatural revelation of her stained lifestyle that made such an impact, 'Come, see a man, who told me all things that ever I did: can this be the Christ?' v. 29 ASV. And who was this Man? He was 'the gift of God', v. 10, 'greater than our father Jacob', v. 12, the provider of eternal life, v. 14, an infallible prophet, v. 19, the true object of faith, v. 21, and the fulfilment of all Old Testament longings, vv. 25-26. Not the devout Nicodemus but an anonymous Samaritan woman was privileged to hear an unambiguous assertion of the Lord's messianic identity.

Christ and

John 4. 31-54 — May 8th

This stunning second sign miracle testifies to the Lord's sovereign ability to cure without attendance, without examination, without medicine, and without convalescence. Equally importantly, it records the growth of faith in a man who encountered the Saviour. John's is particularly the Gospel of personal interviews and conversations, with the Lord Jesus ministering to the needs of various individuals.

The nobleman initially demonstrated faith in the Saviour's ability to work **wonders**, vv. 46-48, a confidence focused primarily upon what He could do. This was like the miracle-based faith seen earlier in Jerusalem where 'many believed in his name, when they saw the miracles which he did. But Jesus did not commit himself unto them, because he knew all men, and needed not that any should testify of man: for he knew what was in man', 2. 23-25. A faith grounded in miracles dies with the cessation of miracles. Simon the sorcerer is proof of its insufficiency. Though he is said to have 'believed', marvelling at Philip's 'miracles and signs', Acts 8. 13, Peter's stern language clearly disposes of any notion that he was genuine, 'Thy money perish with thee . . . for thy heart is not right in the sight of God', vv. 20-21. Hankering after the supernatural and spectacular is not the same as being saved.

The nobleman next rose to a confidence in the Lord's bare word, John 4. 49-50, a practical trust in what He said, which was demonstrated by implicit obedience to the command to 'go thy way'. 'The man believed the word that Jesus had spoken unto him, and he went his way'. How simple and yet how sturdy was this trust! He was content to rest in the divine promise, 'Thy son liveth', just as the faith that saves 'cometh by hearing, and hearing by the word of God', Rom. 10. 17. Yet it is only by obedience that we show outwardly we believe God's word.

Finally, discovering the accuracy of the Lord's announcement, he and his whole family came to rest satisfyingly upon the essential **worth** of the Lord Jesus, vv. 51-54. May we too attain that deep delight of soul which comes as we are more and more taken up with the greatness of His Person.

His Apostles

May 9th   John 5. 1-23

Thou art made whole: sin no more

The miracle at the Pool of Bethesda is a memorable illustration of man's problem and God's provision.

The **problem** is graphically spelled out in that 'great multitude of impotent folk, of blind, halt, withered', v. 3. Here were people marked by the absence of all that makes for real and healthy life. They were without strength, sick, and impotent, just as the sinner is congenitally unable to please God, Rom. 5. 6; 8. 8. They were without sight, blind to the things of God, 2 Cor. 4. 4; John 3. 3. They were without freedom of movement, unable to walk worthy of God, Eph. 4. 1. They were without vigour of life, withered, dried up, and separated from the vitality of God, Eph. 4. 18. All this describes man's natural condition, for sin never gives; it only takes away.

The individual to whom the Lord addressed Himself was perhaps even more miserable, for he had been sick thirty-eight years. Worse, he was tragically alone, with no one to give him a hand: so near the healing pool, yet so far. The very water which offered relief from his infirmity required that he overcome his infirmity to reach it. Like the law of Moses it held out blessings to which no man could attain, Rom. 7. 14; 8. 3.

But the Lord Jesus is God's **provision** for sinful, helpless man. He graciously took the initiative, demonstrating intuitive divine knowledge of the man's condition, and exercising His sovereign power by completely by-passing the pool in which the poor man rested all his hopes. Once again, the Lord's bare word was enough, 'Jesus saith unto him, Rise, take up thy bed, and walk. And immediately the man was made whole, and took up his bed, and walked', John 5. 8-9. Like the gospel message, the cure was instantaneous, complete, and free of charge. And there is also practical encouragement for believers: whatever the Lord commands us to do, He enables us to do.

But the Lord had not finished with the man. Even more important than his physical was his spiritual need, 'Thou art made whole: sin no more', v. 14. All the physical miracles were but pointers to the Lord's power to deal with the root problem – sin. And those saved by God's grace should live for God's glory.

Christ and

John 5. 24-47 — May 10th

The Father himself . . . hath borne witness

The Lord Jesus here made the most astonishing claims. Prefacing His words with a solemn, 'Verily, verily', v. 19, He asserted first of all that unity of action characterized Father and Son. That is to say, everything the Father does the Son does. 'Though Man, He was so wholly and perfectly and altogether in the unity of the Godhead that it was impossible for Him to act apart from the Father', F. B. HOLE. But He went further, insisting upon an unchangeable unity of affection, v. 20. Seven times in John we read of the Father's love for the Son, 3. 35; 5. 20; 10. 17; 15. 9; 17. 23, 24, 26, and each time the word is *agapao* – except here, where it is *phileo*, 'to love fondly and affectionately'. No one loves the Son like the Father.

These claims find specific expression in the Saviour's unique ability to perform divine actions – He has the right to raise and quicken the dead, 5. 21, and to judge all mankind, v. 22. All this gives the Lord Jesus equality of honour with the Father, v. 23. But words alone can be cheap. What evidences did He have for such startling claims? The Old Testament demanded a plurality of testimony for judicial certainty: 'at the mouth of two witnesses, or at the mouth of three witnesses, shall the matter be stablished', Deut. 19. 15, and the Lord graciously submitted to His own law. His first witness was John the Baptist, John 5. 33-35, that brightly shining lamp whose purpose was to draw attention to Christ. Second, there were His miraculous works, v. 36. Peter's argument at Pentecost was that the Lord Jesus was 'a man approved of God among you by miracles and wonders and signs, which God did by him in the midst of you', Acts 2. 22. The signs were His messianic and divine credentials. Finally and conclusively, the Father testified through the scriptures, John 5. 37-47, for the written word points insistently to the Living Word.

But the Lord Himself simultaneously bore testimony to the Pentateuch, validating its authorship ('Moses'), authority ('his writings . . . my words') and theme ('me'), vv. 46-47. Let us make sure that, unlike the Jews, we do not search the scriptures and yet fail to see in them the Saviour.

His Apostles

May 11th

John 6. 1-21

The miracle of the loaves and fishes, the only one recorded in all four Gospels, marks a turning point in John's narrative, as a simple comparison between verses 2 and 66 demonstrates. From now onwards public opposition to the Saviour's ministry would increase.

This specific sign identified the Lord Jesus as Israel's Messiah, the promised prophet, v. 14, and the expected king, v. 15. The evidence was His ability to provide food freely and abundantly. Bread was a vital part of God's provision for His people, and Old Testament kingdom promises frequently cite a sufficiency of corn and wine as a characteristic of the millennium, Joel 2. 19; Zech. 9. 17. The Saviour had already made wine; now He multiplies loaves.

Uniquely among the evangelists, John notes that the Lord Jesus used the current emergency to test the Twelve's growth in grace, John 6. 5-6. After all, they had already seen Him at work in Cana and Jerusalem, witnessing numerous exhibitions of His divine power, v. 2. But did they live in the good of what they had seen? God tests our spiritual memory to find how much we have learned from our study of His word, and how far we are able to apply the truths we have read to the circumstances of daily life. Philip thought the need was too great, v. 7: considering the huge numbers, 200 days' wages, Matt. 20. 2, would not be sufficient. Andrew felt the resources were too small, John 6. 9, for those five barley loaves were only tiny bread rolls. But John the narrator saw that the Lord Jesus was enough, v. 10. Everything depends on the direction in which we look. If, in the crisis, we focus on circumstances, saints, or self, we shall despair. Rather, we must look to a Saviour who cannot fail.

Is it not remarkable that, instead of creating food from scratch, the Creator condescended to employ what He had already made? He used a small boy's lunch, which consisted of the cheapest bread, for barley was grown primarily for horses and asses. Our God specializes in taking the nonentities of this world and making something of them to His glory, 1 Cor. 1. 27-29. If you can be nothing else, be a barley cake for God.

He himself knew what he would do

Christ and

John 6. 22-40   May 12th

In the expectation of further material benefits a miracle-hungry multitude pursued the Lord Jesus to the other side of Galilee. There the Lord exposed their carnal motivation, 'Ye seek me, not because ye saw the miracles, but because ye did eat of the loaves, and were filled', v. 26. His comment makes the paradoxical point that it was possible to witness a miracle without truly seeing it. The Jewish throng had not only beheld His supernatural ability to multiply food but also had actually eaten it and felt pleasantly satiated, for what the Lord Jesus provides is always of the best. But what they overlooked was that the Lord's miracles were far more than acts of benevolence; they were designed to draw attention to and foster confidence in His Person. It is no accident that John consistently refers to the Saviour's displays of power as 'signs'. They pointed to Israel's Messiah, God manifest in the flesh.

Although the crowd were thinking merely in earthly terms, the Saviour ratcheted up the discourse to the highest level when He announced, 'I came down from heaven, not to do mine own will, but the will of him that sent me', v. 38.

Of course, God spoke in time past to the fathers by the prophets, but no prophet in Israel's distinguished history would ever have dared to talk like this. Judges, kings, and prophets were raised up, Judg. 2. 16; 2 Sam. 23. 1; Amos 2. 11, but the Son uniquely came down. Elsewhere, speaking alone to the disciples, He would say, 'I came out from God', and 'I came forth from the Father', John 16. 27-28. Such language, simple yet authoritative, signalled the presence on earth of a divine Person. He 'came' because He acted voluntarily; He was 'sent' because, as the unfailing executor of God's will, He was the only one who could by His obedience bring the Father unalloyed delight. Just as the burnt offering was wholly for God, so was the Lord Jesus. His perfection highlights man's failure, while magnifying His grace, for by His atoning death He has redeemed a people for Himself. He came down that He might lift sinners up! Of each individual believer the Son promises, 'I will raise him up at the last day', 6. 54.

I came down from heaven

His Apostles

May 13th — John 6. 41-71

I am that bread of life

One of the great lessons of John is that the Lord Jesus is not only the divine provider of blessing but is Himself the very provision man needs. He is the Giver and the Gift, both God's final Messenger and God's final Message.

In the discourse that followed the miracle of the multiplied bread and fishes, we learn about Christ's centrality in both Testaments, 6. 30-33. As 'the true bread', v. 32, He was the ultimate **reality** of which the manna was but a picture. Whereas manna dropped from the sky for forty years to sustain physical life among the Israelites, the true bread voluntarily came down from God's dwelling place to provide everlasting life for the world. All God's purposes find their fulfilment in Him.

The expression 'the bread of God', v. 33, testifies to His **deity**. In the Old Testament this language describes the offerings as sacrificial gifts which brought God pleasure, Lev. 21. 6, 8, 17, 22, and perhaps makes us think particularly of the shewbread on the table in the holy place of the tabernacle, Exod. 25. 30. But animal sacrifices and cereal offerings in themselves could never truly delight a holy God. Only the Son as the bread of God brought glad contentment to the Father's heart, for it takes a divine Person fully to satisfy a divine Person. As the loaves on the golden table first of all pleased God and then became the priests' food, so today believers find their spiritual sustenance in the same One who brings joy to God.

His **sufficiency**, as far as sinful man is concerned, is established in the phrase, 'the bread of life', John 6. 35, 48, for He is the Giver of eternal life to all that the Father has given Him, 17. 2. There can be no blessing outside of Christ.

But those who are blessed must never forget the intrinsic excellence of the Blesser. As 'the living bread', 6. 51, He is possessed of divine **vitality**, having in Himself all life, essentially and eternally. It is no surprise that Peter rose to his grand concluding confession. Many had departed and there was much the remaining disciples could not grasp, but this they knew, 'Thou hast the words of eternal life. And we believe and are sure that thou art that Christ, the Son of the living God', vv. 68, 69.

John 7. 1-30 — May 14th

Today's passage is framed by time: 'my time is not yet come', v. 6, and 'his hour was not yet come', v. 30. In a Gospel packed with evidences (supernatural knowledge, sign miracles, fulfilment of scripture), His unfailing movement according to an eternal divine timetable is yet another testimony to the deity of Christ.

Of course the God whose name is I AM has no problems with time, being infinitely above and beyond it. And yet, 'when the fulness of the time was come, God sent forth his Son', Gal. 4. 4, so that in the miracle of incarnation the eternal Son wonderfully stooped to enter the temporal and spatial. The word 'hour' appears twenty-six times as John uniquely establishes with his careful references to the Jewish feasts a time sequence for the earthly ministry of Christ, 5. 1; 6. 4; 7. 2; 10. 22; 11. 55. His book ranges from brief time spans (thirty-eight years, three days, the tenth hour) to the vastness of eternity itself. It begins with an echo of Genesis chapter 1 verse 1, and ends with an anticipation of Revelation chapter 22 verse 20 ('till I come'). Indeed, in chapter 11 the Lord Jesus demonstrates His deity by fast forwarding an advance preview of the 'last day' in the selective resurrection of Lazarus, John 11. 24-25.

In John chapter 7 reference to the hour is a reminder that with God there can be no accidents, no hastes, and no delays. Like the Lord's unbelieving step-brothers, man always wants to rush ahead: 'your time is alway ready', 7. 6. But God's steady programme is inviolable. The Lord Jesus is our model, gladly submitting Himself to the Father's timing, v. 8. Even sinful men with no awareness of the divine purpose behind history found themselves, without any violation of their human responsibility, having to surrender to a pre-written calendar of events: 'they sought to take him: but no man laid hands on him, because his hour was not yet come', v. 30. The Son rested in the Father's plan and so can we. Every believer can confidently say, 'My times are in thy hand', Ps. 31. 15, for, as C. H. SPURGEON reminds us, 'We are not waifs and strays upon the ocean of fate, but are steered by infinite wisdom. Providence is a soft pillow for anxious heads'. Our God is always in control.

His Apostles

May 15th   *John 7. 31-53*

There was a division among the people

The Lord Jesus divided and continues to divide people by His words. In this section He uttered two cryptic predictions which found their historical fulfilment in the Acts, demonstrating that He was everything He claimed to be.

Firstly, He announced His ascension, 'I go unto him that sent me', v. 33. The One who had in grace descended from above would return whence He came, to receive from the Father 'the glory which I had with thee before the world was', 17. 5. This in itself was God's irrefutable vindication of His Son, setting the divine seal of approval on His perfect life and finished work. It happened forty days after the resurrection in the presence of witnesses who observed the Saviour ascend slow-motion into heaven so that they would be left in no doubt as to where He had gone: 'while they beheld, he was taken up . . . they looked stedfastly toward heaven as he went up', Acts 1. 9-10. Before the crucifixion the Lord could look beyond the cross, the grave, and the resurrection to His glad return home.

Secondly, in His amazing claim to be able to satisfy man's spiritual thirst, He anticipated the arrival of the Holy Spirit to indwell and energize believers, 'This spake he of the Spirit, which they that believe on him should receive: for the Holy Ghost was not yet given; because that Jesus was not yet glorified', John 7. 39. This was fulfilled on the Day of Pentecost in direct consequence of the ascension. As Peter explained to the crowd, 'Being by the right hand of God exalted, and having received of the Father the promise of the Holy Ghost, he hath shed forth this, which ye now see and hear', Acts 2. 33. The supernatural phenomena of Pentecost – rushing wind, tongues of fire, Galilean disciples speaking in languages they had never learned – were external evidences of the glorification of Christ. Therefore Israel was guilty of rejecting, not an imposter, but the Messiah who was Jehovah Himself, Acts 2. 36.

Only a divine Person can ascend in His own right into heaven. Only a divine Person can satisfy the soul by bestowing on men another divine Person. No wonder the officers reported back, 'Never man spake like this man', John 7. 46.

Christ and

John 8. 1-30   **May 16th**

Neither do I condemn thee

The primary thrust of the first coming of the Lord Jesus to this earth was to provide undeserved blessing for men. That is why He went about doing good, healing, and proclaiming pardon for sinners, for 'God sent not his Son into the world to condemn the world; but that the world through him might be saved', 3. 17. But this did not mean that He closed His eyes to the wickedness of man or remained silent in the face of iniquity. On the contrary, the same Saviour who spoke so graciously to the needy solemnly indicted the Pharisees for hypocrisy. There was in the Lord Jesus the perfect marriage of grace and truth, grace which bestowed favour on the unworthy and truth which unflinchingly denounced error.

The case of the woman taken in the act of adultery was, of course, stage-managed by Israel's religious establishment who hoped to trap the Lord in His words, 8. 6. If He condemned her to death where was His claim to be a Saviour? If He dismissed the case where was His respect for God's law? His response was to turn the spotlight onto the double standards of the nation's leaders, and then to grant the guilty woman (He never denied her sin) a free pardon which required a change of life. The righteous basis for that pardon was yet to be laid in His atoning death, for it was only there that God could be shown to be 'just, and the justifier of him which believeth in Jesus', Rom. 3. 26. Nevertheless, in advance of Calvary the Saviour applied its benefits to one who merited the death penalty.

It is noteworthy that the Lord Jesus by no means condoned sin against the marriage bond. After all, had He not taught that 'whosoever looketh on a woman to lust after her hath committed adultery with her already in his heart', Matt. 5. 28? Far from relaxing the law He actually intensified it, so that it assessed thoughts as well as outward actions. But He who spelled out the real demands of the law also pronounced forgiveness, speaking as the ultimate authority, 'Neither do I condemn thee: go, and sin no more'. Saved sinners today are expected to live in a manner worthy of God's grace, for we have been delivered from our sins that we might no longer continue in them.

His Apostles

May 17th — John 8. 31-59

I proceeded forth and came from God

It cannot be denied that the Lord Jesus made the most astounding claims. In this section of John's Gospel it all comes to a grand climax when the incensed Jewish crowd pick up stones to stone Him, v. 59. What caused their anger? Just consider some of the clear self-disclosures Christ made in the face of this hostile gathering. He was eternal in His being, v. 35, He was the Giver of true freedom, v. 36, He was able to read His enemies' murderous thoughts, v. 37, He was indisputably sinless, v. 46, and those who kept His words would be placed beyond the domain of death, v. 51. This last brought things to a head: 'Now we know that thou hast a devil. Abraham is dead, and the prophets; and thou sayest, If a man keep my saying, he shall never taste of death. Art thou greater than our father Abraham, which is dead? and the prophets are dead: whom makest thou thyself?', vv. 52-53.

And that's the key question, 'Whom makest thou thyself?' The charge would shortly be levelled against Him that 'Thou, being a man, makest thyself God', 10. 33. But of course this was the exact reverse of the truth. Rather, He, being the eternal God, graciously condescended to take upon Himself sinless manhood without in any sense compromising His deity, for 'the Word was made flesh, and dwelt among us, (and we beheld his glory, the glory as of the only begotten of the Father)', 1. 14.

While false cults desperately try to minimize His claims to absolute deity the Lord Jesus made every effort to maximize them, identifying Himself as Israel's great I AM, 8. 58. The crowd had no doubt about His meaning, nor did He correct them. Nevertheless they missed the point about His relationship to Abraham. When the Lord said, 'Your father Abraham rejoiced to see my day', they responded, 'Thou art not yet fifty years old, and hast thou seen Abraham?', 8. 56-57. But it was not that He had seen Abraham; rather, Abraham had seen Him. As J. G. BELLETT beautifully puts it, 'He was making Himself the great Object from the beginning, the One who had been filling the thoughts, engaging the hopes, and answering the needs of all the elect of God in all ages'. How good to know Him!

Christ and

John 9. 1-17   May 18th

How were thine eyes opened?

In this Gospel John aims to give his readers credible evidence to the claim that Jesus Christ is the Son of God and to invite them to believe in Him. Evidence is drawn from three different sources: the miracles He did, the words He spoke, and the testimony of witnesses who knew Him. He has already given us the witness of John the Baptist, Nicodemus, the Samaritan woman, and Peter. Now it is the turn of the man born blind.

John's selection of this miracle over many others that he could have chosen was no doubt because it illustrated perfectly what the Lord Jesus meant when He called Himself the 'Light of the world'. For all his life this beggar had sat in both physical and spiritual darkness.

The setting provided the perfect backdrop to the miracle. Every day the religious leaders of the Jews must have walked past him and were unable and likely unwilling to help him. They claimed to be the source of spiritual light to the nation and yet they were impotent. It is even likely that the disciples themselves would have passed the man without any thought for him, but not so the Lord Jesus.

Unlike other occasions when people called out to the Lord Jesus for mercy, this time it was the Lord that took the initiative. Although the man could not see, he could hear and was able to obey the words that he heard. What a lovely picture he is of the conversion of a soul! Sitting in darkness he hears the words of the Lord, by faith he obeys, and then into his heart floods the light of the knowledge of the glory of God in the face of Jesus Christ.

His response to the neighbours and Pharisees showed that true conversion attributes all the glory to the Giver. Notice the way he puts it: he 'made clay', he 'anointed mine eyes', he 'said unto me, "Go"', and 'I went', and 'I received'.

> When free grace awoke me, by light from on high,
> Then legal fears shook me, I trembled to die,
> No refuge or safety in self could I see –
> "Jehovah Tsidkenu" my Saviour must be.
>
> R. MURRAY MCCHEYNE

His Apostles

May 19th   John 9. 18-41

Lord, I believe

No doubt we have all at some time told an unbeliever that in order to be saved they must believe in the Lord Jesus Christ. But what specifically does someone have to believe in order to be saved?

Throughout this chapter the key point of controversy surrounds the identity of the Lord Jesus. It is not so much a question of what He did but rather who He *is*. In the first half of the chapter the question is, 'How did He do it?' In the second half of the chapter the key question is 'Who is He?'

In order to get to the bottom of this mystery the Pharisees call the man to appear before them and demand that he gives God the glory for what happened, rather than the Lord Jesus. The obvious inference is that they did not acknowledge His deity and therefore would not allow the man to attribute to Him a miracle that they felt only God could do.

This refusal to believe that He was the Son of God is the darkness or blindness that the Lord Jesus refers to at the end of the chapter. The Pharisees were men that claimed that they could see. They claimed to know the scriptures and to be God's ordained teachers, and yet they were only 'blind leaders of the blind'.

On the other hand the blind man was willing to receive without reservation who the Lord Jesus was. It is interesting to note the progressive nature of the illumination he had as to the identity of the Lord Jesus. The man knew that He was 'a man . . . called Jesus', v. 11, 'a prophet', v. 17, and a man 'of God', v. 33, but he still needed to learn that He is 'the Son of God', v. 35. The recognition of who the Lord Jesus really was produced a sense of worship, v. 38, and an acknowledgement of the necessity of following Him, v. 27.

We should be careful of any profession of faith that comes short of acknowledging the true deity of the Lord Jesus. An open confession of faith in Him as the Son of God will no doubt be matched in our lives by surrender to His will, obedience to His words, and a heart full of worship for Him.

Christ and

John 10. 1-21 — May 20th

The good shepherd

In the Old Testament, God through the prophets Jeremiah and Ezekiel announced severe judgements on the Jewish leaders, whom He accused of being false shepherds. They had misled the people of God and caused them to worship idols. But amidst those dark days He gave them the promise of the coming of a faithful Shepherd who would minister to the flock, Ezek. 34. 11-16. But how would they recognize Him and be sure that He wasn't an imposter and that His intentions were honourable?

In this section the Lord Jesus is still addressing the crowd that had witnessed the miracle of the healing of the blind man in chapter 9, including the Pharisees whom He had implied were themselves spiritually blind. These men had usurped the role of being the spiritual leaders of the nation but were in fact false shepherds demanding that people follow them. They were also deliberately trying to lead the people away from Christ.

The Lord now invites the people to consider the evidence that He really was the true Shepherd. He had come to the fold of Israel in the way that God had revealed in the Old Testament. His birth, ministry, miracles, and the way He would be presented to the nation via a forerunner were all foretold. In this way, He had come through the door in an open presentation of Himself, and not via some obscure, mischievous route, v. 2.

He then called His own sheep by name and led them out, v. 3. By this parable the Lord showed that He would not operate within the confines of Judaism and under the authority of Pharisees and Sadducees, but would be leading them out into something new. In doing so, He would not take them by force or drive them out. They would willingly follow Him wherever He went.

In leaving Judaism, the people that followed Him were not abandoning safety for danger, or fullness for barrenness. In fact the opposite was true. The Good Shepherd would bring them into pastures of abundant life, v. 10. And He would do it by giving His life for them. This gift of life would extend beyond Israel to 'other sheep . . . not of this fold'. How grateful we are that the door was opened to Gentiles as well! This was the true and good Shepherd that God had promised.

His Apostles

May 21st

John 10. 22-42

My sheep hear my voice

In chapter 9, one of the key characteristics of believers is that they can *see*, and in particular they can see who the Lord Jesus is. In this section we will find that true believers can also *hear*, and as a result they follow Him. These two spiritual faculties are key components of eternal life which is given to all who are His sheep.

Although the subject matter of this section (i.e., sheep and a Shepherd) appears to follow directly from the first half of the chapter, there is actually a three month break between the two sections. The events recorded in the second half occur during a visit the Lord made to Jerusalem for the Feast of Dedication.

While walking in the temple confines, He was again confronted by the Jews who asked Him a question, 'How long dost thou make us to doubt? If thou be the Christ, tell us plainly', v. 24. In effect, they were accusing Him of deliberately hiding His identity and misleading them. But, as He goes on to show them, the fault did not lie with Him but with them.

The reason for their unbelief was not that they had not had clear statements regarding His identity, but because they were not His sheep and had failed to hear Him. They were completely deaf to His claims of being the Messiah. On the other hand, the thing that characterizes those He calls 'my sheep' is that they hear His voice, and by faith they follow Him, v. 27.

His sheep are intimately known by Him, v. 27, are given eternal life, and are eternally secure, v. 28. Our eternal security does not rest on our merits or efforts, but is dependent on the ability of the Father and the Son to keep us and the fact that we possess the same life as They do. The believer is held in the hand of the Son and His hand is secure in the Father's, v. 29. Our relationship with the Son is as indissoluble as His relationship with the Father, because we all share one thing in common – eternal life.

In claiming oneness with the Father, the Jews accused Him of blasphemy and took up stones to stone Him. So this period of our Lord's ministry ends in open hostility, with the Jews desiring to have Him stoned as He escapes out of their grasp.

Christ and

John 11. 1-29 — May 22nd

Our friend Lazarus sleepeth

So often when trials and tragedy come our way we are inclined to wonder why. We cannot understand why the Lord seems to delay in coming to our need, and what the purpose of the suffering is. In the raising of Lazarus John gives us a vivid answer to these perplexing questions.

Due to the attempts on His life, 10. 39, the Lord had withdrawn Himself to Perea on the east side of the Jordan. At this time a tragedy falls on a home in Bethany, well known to Him, the home of Mary, Martha, and Lazarus. Lazarus had become seriously ill and in their desperation the sisters turn to the Lord for help.

It is interesting to see that in their message to Him they make no specific request. They simply bring the *problem* to Him and leave it there, 'Behold, he whom thou lovest is sick'. In their words they seem to imply that He was morally bound to act since this was someone whom He loved. He would, of course, act, but not in the way they expected.

The sisters were not the only ones that were confused by His actions; the disciples were as well, v. 8. If the sisters thought He was taking too long, the disciples thought that He was far too hasty in returning to Judea, as it would likely endanger their lives. They could not understand why He would want to return to the area where the Pharisees wanted to kill Him. His response to them was emphatic. As long as He was walking in the light He was doing the will of God, and whatever His enemies might have been plotting, the will of God could not be thwarted.

In the ensuing discussion with the disciples, He explains the real reason behind Lazarus' illness and the subsequent miracle that would be performed. It would be primarily for their benefit, that they might believe, v. 15. As the story progresses it would also be for the benefit of the sisters and the many others who witnessed the miracle.

Here lies an important lesson for us all. Things may happen to us for no apparent reason. Yet, our trials might be the means through which God blesses others as well as ourselves.

His Apostles

May 23rd

John 11. 30-57

He that was dead came forth

The restoration of Lazarus to life sent shock waves through the many inhabitants of Judea. Here was a miracle that undoubtedly proved the Messianic claims of the Lord Jesus. It would bolster the faith of His disciples in the face of His imminent death, and at the same time send such fear into the hearts of the Pharisees and Sadducees that they would determine to have Him put to death.

By the time the Lord arrived at Bethany, Lazarus had been in the tomb for four days. Many mourners had gathered to share the grief of Martha and Mary. As the Lord approached Bethany, first Martha went out to meet Him, and then Mary. Their words seemed to convey a reprimand. They both told the Lord that if only He had come earlier Lazarus would not have died. Although there was an evident sense of fear and frustration in their words they still expressed confidence in His ability to do something.

As the Lord draws near to the tomb, He begins to weep. Many have speculated over the reason why He wept, but it would seem at the very least it was a response to the grief He saw in the faces of Mary and Martha. His tears not only prove the reality of His manhood, but also His ability to enter into and feel the depths of sorrow of His own sheep.

In the raising of Lazarus He not only demonstrated His authority as He commanded that the stone be rolled away, and for Lazarus to come forth, but also He showed His dependence on the Father. Before raising Lazarus, He lifted up his voice in prayer to His Father to ensure that all around would know where this power had come from.

To those of us who are saved, it is a wonderful reminder that some day, even perhaps today, the Lord might come and with a shout will raise the dead in Christ. Unlike Lazarus, they will be raised to die no more.

The Pharisees and the chief rulers on the other hand were incensed. This sense of envy would now drive them on to the awful deed to be carried out at Calvary in a week's time.

Christ and

John 12. 1-26 — May 24th

In this section, John is interested in showing us the nature of true and false devotion to the Lord Jesus, and what it really means to serve and follow Him.

The most obvious contrast stands between Mary and Judas. From the outside it might have appeared that both were followers of the Lord Jesus, but their actions at the beginning of chapter 12 will highlight the true state of their hearts. If being a follower of the Lord is demonstrated by how much we are willing to give up in this life, then it is clear which one of the two is the true follower, and which is the false.

Mary took a pound of ointment of spikenard and anointed both the head and the feet of the Lord Jesus. It was the costliest anointing oil of its day and was usually purchased only by the wealthy for special guests. That she had 'kept it against the day of [his] burying', v. 7, highlights her faith and devotion. The decisive hour had come, and in love she poured out all she had on Him. Had she held some back, or waited for another opportunity, this act would never have made it into the record of scripture.

By contrast, Judas' reaction showed what motivated him. He desired to see some material benefits come from his association with Christ; this act of love by Mary seemed to him to be a tremendous waste. In recording this contrast, John seems to be highlighting the fact that faith in Christ must be accompanied by devotion and surrender, if it is to be true and genuine.

The next morning, the Lord made His triumphal entry into Jerusalem. Riding an unbroken colt, and thus demonstrating His authority as Creator, He now presents Himself to Israel as the King that the prophets had long been waiting for, Isa. 62. 11; Zech. 9. 9. It also coincided with the day that the Jews would be selecting their lambs in anticipation of the upcoming Feast of Passover. How tragic that the nation that had acclaimed Him as their King were about to reject Him and crucify Him!

With this in mind perhaps, John reminds us of a group of Gentiles who desired to 'see Jesus'. This is a picture of a future day when having been rejected by His own people He will be accepted by the Gentiles.

Sir, we would see Jesus

His Apostles

May 25th   John 12. 27-50

Yet they believed not on him

This chapter marks the culmination of the first half of John's Gospel. So far John has been selecting material to demonstrate the veracity of the claims of Christ as the Son of God. Whether it was His words, His works, the Father's witness, or the witness of those that met Him, they all attested to the truth of who He is. The astonishing thing is that despite all the light they had been given the nation remained in darkness.

As the Lord contemplated His impending death, a surge of emotion overcame Him and drove Him to His Father in prayer, v. 27. This again illustrates the complete dependence He had on the Father. He did not pray that He should be spared from death, but rather that the Father's Name would be glorified. It seems a paradox that the shame and darkness associated with Calvary could bring any glory to the Father, but in actual fact no event has ever brought so much glory to God. His life of obedience had already glorified the Father's Name, v. 28, and so too would His death. How many countless millions of people have been brought to know the Father through the lifting up of the Son of God, v. 32!

The crowd struggled to reconcile His predictions of His death with their understanding of the unending kingdom of Messiah. They could not see how He could die and also reign forever. Rather than trying to explain how both could be true and the truths concerning His resurrection and second coming, the Lord just exhorts them to receive the light that He had already given them, v. 35. It was imperative for them to receive the light before it was withdrawn, v. 36.

The remaining verses are solemn indeed. Because they wilfully continued in a state of unbelief, v. 37, God judicially blinded them, v. 40. This was something that had been foretold long before, Isa. 6. 10, and although it was a condemnation on the Jews, it would result in the ultimate blessing of the Gentiles. However, as Paul makes clear in Romans chapter 11, this blinding of the nation would be only temporary, and one day, at the second coming of Christ, they will finally acknowledge His claims.

Christ and

John 13. 1-30　　　　　　　　　　　　　　　May 26th

Before the Lord Jesus began His final teachings to His disciples He left them an example that they would never forget. On the surface it was an act of lowliness and humility that would remind them of the One who came not to be ministered unto but to minister, and to give His life a ransom for many. Beneath the surface of course lay a deeper spiritual lesson that the disciples would need to learn if they were to make progress in God's school of holiness.

In case there was any wonder in their minds why the Lord Jesus was going to leave these men behind, John reminds us that it wasn't because He had lost hope in them, or grown discouraged with their lack of progress. He still loved them and He would love them unto the end, v. 1. In a world where love is so flippantly spoken of, He demonstrated it, not only in His willingness to take the servant's place and wash their feet, but also in His willingness to lay down His life for them.

In the parabolic act of the feet washing the Lord Jesus was showing His disciples that in order for them to live lives that would be pleasing to God there was a need for a two-fold washing. The first washing was a once-and-for-all bathing all over. This symbolized what would later be called by Paul the 'washing of regeneration' and is effected by the Holy Spirit, the moment we are saved. This new birth places within us the desire and power to live a life of holiness through the indwelling Holy Spirit. In the second, the Lord Jesus spoke of a need for perpetual rinsing of the hands and the feet. This symbolized the ongoing need for the washing of the word of God. As we read the word of God, it acts as a mirror, which highlights our defilement, and causes us to acknowledge our sin before God and seek His forgiveness.

The Lord Jesus made it clear that not all the men sitting around the table were 'clean'. As the deliberations continued Judas revealed his true character in betraying the Lord, and fittingly left the room to go out into the night. It is a stark reminder of what worldliness is. At its core, it is to live as though this world is everything and that the eternal doesn't matter. He lost what was eternal in order to gain a few pieces of silver.

I have given you an example

His Apostles

May 27th   **John 13. 31 – 14. 14**

If the ultimate goal in the ministry of the Lord Jesus was to bring these men to the Father, then humanly speaking His tactics seemed destined to fail. Most political leaders usually gain loyalty from their subjects by flexing their military muscles and perpetuating a sense of fear amongst the people. The Lord Jesus' tactics were remarkable in that He would gain loyalty by first of all being lifted up on a cross, and then secondly by leaving these men alone in the world.

His going to the cross was first and foremost for the glory of God, vv. 31-32. It was the ultimate vindication of the character of God. In this way His righteousness and mercy could be displayed without compromise. It was also the vindication of Christ's claims that He was the Son of God. When God raised Him from the dead and seated Him at His own right hand it upheld the claims of Christ.

Peter's response was true to form. Although his willingness to follow the Lord was not in question, his ability to carry it out was. The problem was, as so often is the case with us, his devotion to the Lord was not matched by dependence on the Lord. Although the Lord warned him about his impending failure, He did not stop him. Of course, his failure wasn't final, and the Lord graciously restored him.

Perhaps sensing the disciples' apprehension at the recent events of Judas' exit and Peter's rebuke, the Lord now seeks to calm their fears by telling them why He had to go away. The first reason He gives is that He was going to prepare a place for them in the Father's house. This promise must have been a tremendous comfort to them over the next day or so. For when they had all forsaken Him and fled, and the devil would likely have insinuated that the Lord would never want them back, they would remember that their eternal destiny was secure.

In verse 6, the Lord Jesus reminds them that the ultimate goal of salvation is not simply the Father's *house* but coming to the Father *Himself*, and that the way to the Father was through the Son. Our primary means of getting to know the Father is through the revelation that the Son has given.

John 14. 14-31 — May 28th

As the disciples listened to the Lord's promise of His going to prepare a place for them in the Father's house and then His returning for them at His coming, they must have wondered how they would survive in the intervening period without Him.

For three-and-a-half years the Lord had provided for them, taught them, been on hand to answer their questions, and even consoled them in their times of sorrow. How could His going away be anything other than a disaster? As we read through this chapter it becomes apparent that His going away would actually be to their *advantage*.

The reason for this is that upon arrival at the Father's right hand the Lord promised that He would ask the Father and He would send another Comforter, the Spirit of truth. The Greek word here for 'another' means 'another of the same kind'. The Spirit of God would be to them all that the Lord Jesus had been, and in some senses even more, as He would be *in* them. This all came to fruition on the Day of Pentecost when the Lord fulfilled His promise, and the Father sent the Spirit of God. He has now taken up residence within the church and is the divine representative on earth. This experience is unique to the church age.

In His current ministry, the Spirit of God facilitates our relationship with the Son and the Father. He teaches us by reminding us of all that the Son said and did, v. 26, and in this way makes our relationship a living one, v. 19, and not merely the study of some historical person. In fact the Lord promises to manifest Himself to His own, v. 21. This means more than just the manifestations between His resurrection and the ascension. It means the ongoing reality that the Lord is speaking to us as we read the scriptures and that He is with us in the daily experiences of life. In no way would this new relationship be inferior to anything that the disciples had enjoyed to date.

Before they go out into the night, He leaves them with an assurance that they have no need to be afraid. Victory over the devil will be won; He will demonstrate how much He loves the Father, and so would fill us with a similar peace and confidence that the Father will bless us if we remain faithful to Him.

I will not leave you comfortless

His Apostles

May 29th   John 15. 1-17

God's master plan for witness in this world did not end at the return of His Son to heaven! In fact, His going away would actually enhance this worldwide witness. Instead of being constrained to one geographical area, the Lord could now direct His servants to reach every part of the globe. The key to it all was the ability of His disciples to replicate the wonderful graces and virtues that they had seen in their Master. But how could they do it, and what provision had God made for them?

Rather than feeling that this monumental task would fall completely on their shoulders, the Lord Jesus begins by reminding them that He is the True Vine and they are the branches. He is the ultimate source of the fruit of the Spirit and they are just the channels through which this fruit can be displayed to the world.

God's provision goes beyond simply placing us in the Vine, He also takes it upon Himself to act as the heavenly Vinedresser. Just as a farmer looks to ensure that his crops produce to their full potential, so does God. He cleanses and prunes to remove what is unproductive in our lives and ensure that fruit, and not mere foliage, is produced.

There is a difficulty in this section and it is understanding what the Lord meant when He said that some branches would be taken away if they failed to produce any fruit, v. 2. Some suggest that it means to 'lift up' rather than 'take away'. Just as the Lord did with Peter when he failed and was later restored to usefulness. However, it seems from the context (Judas has just left the room) and from other portions in John's Gospel where false profession is mentioned, that this is referring to one who claims to be in Christ and yet their lives prove that this claim is false. Judas is a prime example.

In particular, the Lord mentions certain fruits that would be expected to be seen in every Christian's life such as love, joy, and obedience. In case they were in any doubt as to what it meant to love one another He puts the ultimate standard before them: 'greater love hath no man than this, that a man lay down his life for his friends', v. 13.

Fruit . . . more fruit . . . much fruit

Christ and

John 15. 18 – 16. 11 — May 30th

In the preceding sections the Lord Jesus has been telling His disciples about the provisions that would be made for their preservation and growth in His absence. At first sight, it appears that success is almost guaranteed. The great problem, of course, as the Lord Jesus goes on to explain in these verses, is the world. Although the Lord had chosen them out of the world it did not mean that they would be allowed the comfort of growing spiritual fruit in some cosy circumstances. In fact, the opposite was the case. The Lord was going to deliberately leave them in the world, with all its hostility and opposition, as witnesses for Him.

He explains that the root cause of this opposition lay in their association with Him. Since they were no longer 'of this world', the world would see them as a threat. It is still the same today. Anything that is different from the current world-view comes under attack until it is either removed or forced to toe the line. But the Lord goes on to explain that the hatred they would face is more deep-seated than mere prejudice. The world's hatred stems from their hatred of Christ and their ignorance of the Father, v. 21. Even Paul had to admit that this was the underlying cause of his persecution of the church, 'I did it ignorantly in unbelief', 1 Tim. 1. 13.

However, this ignorance does not mean the world is blameless. They had had His words, John 15. 22-23, and His works, v. 24, yet flatly refused them both. And yet God's response was not to wipe out man as one might have expected, but rather that He would send the Spirit of truth to bear witness to who the Lord Jesus is. What a comfort it is to know that the chief responsibility of witnessing in this world has not been left to us, but to the Holy Spirit Himself!

The purpose of the Holy Spirit's ministry is threefold. Firstly, it is to convict the world of sin, and in particular, the sin of unbelief. Secondly, to vindicate the claims of Christ. When God raised Him from the dead He showed that Christ was right. And thirdly, His message is one of victory. Christ has defeated the arch-enemy, the devil.

His Apostles

I have chosen you out of the world

May 31st John 16. 12-33

Your sorrow shall be turned into joy

This chapter marks the end of Christ's teaching to the Eleven. How then would He conclude His teachings and what final lessons would He impress upon them?

The first lesson in this section, vv. 12-15, is a further elaboration on the future work of the Holy Spirit once the Lord had ascended back to heaven. It was clear that the disciples were struggling to understand the full meaning of His lessons, but the Lord assured them that some day they would. The Lord explains to them that the Holy Spirit would specifically teach them the words of the Lord Jesus. He would not originate the message, but rather would pass on to them the words that He had heard from the Son. And as the Lord Jesus had previously taught, 14. 10, His words had come from the Father. What a marvellous provision God has made in order that we might come to know Him!

The next lesson, vv. 16-24, concerns the unavoidable sorrow that they were about to experience as they witnessed the Lord being taken and led away to Calvary. He would liken the whole event to a woman giving birth. There would be indescribable pain and sorrow, but it would soon be replaced by unrivalled joy. The resurrection of Christ would forever remind them that no matter how great the sufferings of this life might be, the joy that awaited them is infinitely greater. Death had lost its sting and the grave had been defeated.

The final lesson, vv. 25-33, is really a summary of the whole of the Upper Room ministry. He admitted that much of His teaching to date had been hidden from their understanding. Over the course of the three years that He had been with them He had gradually, through His words and works, showed them who He was. It was gradual to allow them time to take it in, but now the time for the complete revelation of God had come. The cross, more than any other single event, revealed not only to these disciples, but also to us, exactly who the Lord Jesus was and what His purpose in coming was. Everything would become clear to them.

Christ and

John 17. 1-26 — June 1st

That they all may be one

This chapter has often been referred to as the High Priestly prayer of the Lord Jesus. His time of teaching was finished. He had been speaking to His disciples about the Father; now He turns and speaks to the Father about His disciples. The chapter can be divided into three: His prayer for Himself, vv. 1-8, His prayer for His disciples, vv. 9-19, and His prayer for us, vv. 20-26.

His request for the Father to glorify Him, v. 5, is not motivated by pride as it might be if we were asking for the same, but rather it is a request for His loyalty to the Father to be vindicated. He had come to manifest the Father's name, v. 6, but essentially the world had rejected His witness. The cross would be the ultimate test of the validity of His claim to be the Son of God. His prayer therefore is that in raising Him from the dead and seating Him at His own right hand, the Father would show the world that their verdict was wrong.

The Lord then turns His attention to the disciples that He was going to leave behind. Up until this point He had kept them, v. 12, and now He is going to leave them in the care of His Father, v. 11. As the next few hours would show, this does not mean that they would never let the Lord down, but that their faith would not give way under the tremendous pressure of the world. Peter is a case in point. Shortly, he would deny that he even knew the Lord, but as the final chapters of this Gospel show, his faith did not completely crumble. This was not to Peter's credit but proof that the Lord's prayer had been answered, for his faith had not failed.

The Lord finally turns His attention to those who would be the fruit of the worldwide witness that these men would commence. The results of the preaching of the apostles and many preachers of the gospel have never been in doubt. The Lord foresaw a people that the Father would give Him. Eventually, those people would be brought to the Lord Himself so that they might behold His glory. And in doing so they will for all eternity see how much the Father loves the Son, and how much the Son delights to reveal the Father to them.

His Apostles

June 2nd — John 18. 1-27

Over the brook Cedron

The Brook Cedron had been the place of many memorable events. In particular it was where King David was betrayed, 2 Sam. 15. 23, when he was forced out of the city by his son Absalom. Now another King was about to cross that same brook, and He too would be betrayed and thrust out of the city. But rather than a scene of defeat it would be the scene of an unforgettable victory.

As we contemplate the events of this chapter the darkness can almost be felt. The devil had his men and their mission was straightforward: extinguish the Light of the world. By this time Satan had entered Judas, and he came with the intention of betraying the Lord. At first glimpse we might wonder how a man who had such knowledge of the Lord could act so callously. And yet it is no different from the reaction of the world to the offer of mercy that God extends to it today. Worldliness is still the same. It is simply to want the gifts without the Giver. Judas showed that he was always after what he could get out of his relationship with the Lord, and had no true love for the Giver.

Peter's denial of the Lord, on the other hand, was not the same as Judas' betrayal. Peter's was not denying who Christ was but rather it was a denial of his association with Him. Peter's failure sprang from a lack of understanding of his own weakness. In chapter 13 he boasted about his willingness to go into death with the Lord and now he won't even stand with Him. So often we fall the same way. We fail to recognize our weaknesses and to seek the Lord's help when the trial comes.

The Lord's reaction to the betrayal of Judas and the arrival of the soldiers demonstrated the power that He possessed as the Son of God. His power did not come from a show of force with staves, swords, and shields, but was derived from who He was, the great 'I am'. If His earlier miracles displayed His power over creation, disease, and death, His submission to His enemies displayed His self-control. He could have called more than twelve legions of angels. He could have wiped these men off the face of the earth. And yet He willingly took the cup that the Father had given Him.

Christ and

John 18. 28 – 19. 13

June 3rd

Behold the man!

Due to Roman law at the time, the Jewish leaders did not have jurisdiction to put anyone to death. Later, that right would be given back to them, Acts 7. 57-60, but for now they would have to bring the matter before Pilate, the Roman governor. We can see the wisdom of God behind the decisions of men. If Christ was going to fulfil scripture then He had to be *crucified* (the Roman method of execution) rather than being stoned (the Jewish method).

In the actions of the Jewish leaders and Pilate we see the worst of human nature. At the outset, John 18. 28, they were more concerned about ceremonial uncleanness than the innocent blood of the man they were seeking to kill. This is so often the case with unregenerate religion. It is pre-occupied with the outward and with rules and regulations at the expense of truth and spirituality. The Jewish leaders tried to prove that the Lord and His disciples were anti-Rome and would be a political threat to Rome's leadership. When you read through the final chapters of the book of the Acts you will find that they tried to do the same thing with Paul. It is also dangerous when religion and politics mix.

Pilate, on the other hand, was driven by selfish motives. His indecision was evidence that all he wanted to do was protect his job and the interests of Rome. On three occasions He pronounced the innocence of Christ, and yet He still didn't release Him, in the hope that the Jews themselves would make the decision for him. What a coward!

Pilate's interrogations revolved around four questions: 'What accusation bring ye against this man?' vv. 28-32; 'Art thou the King of the Jews?' vv. 33-38; 'Shall I release the King of the Jews?' 18. 39 – 19. 7; and 'Whence art thou?' 19. 8-16. All of the answers that the Lord gave showed that He was innocent of the charges that had been laid against Him. He was not a political threat, nor seeking to oppose the Roman Empire.

The cry of the crowd completed the abject picture of the human heart. They would rather have the harsh and tyrannous rule of Caesar than the rightful King of the Jews.

His Apostles

June 4th

John 19. 14-42

He bearing his cross went forth

Recorded here is the fulfilment of the task for which our Lord was sent – to do His Father's will and to finish His work, John 4. 34. It is ironic that the perfect Man went forth bearing *His* cross to take away *our* sin! But by doing so, He was responding to the voice from heaven and glorifying God's Name again, not only in His life but also now in His death, 12. 28. The plan of salvation and the path that it took was now drawing to its final hour through a series of 'places' that would highlight the hand of God in accomplishing the work of redemption.

Little did Pilate realize his part in that work as he brought the Lord to the 'place' called Gabbatha. What a paradox to see man sitting in judgement of the One who was God in the flesh. Mockingly he proclaimed, 'Behold your King!' Previously, he had declared in the same manner, 'Behold the man!' v. 5. Both statements were true, though he did not comprehend the real meaning behind his words. But God in His sovereignty was directing the events and using the wrath of man to praise Him. The whole scene revealed the hearts of people in general who reject this King in favour of another. It proves once again the accuracy of the scripture 'that his own received him not'.

As the Lord went forth bearing His cross, He came to yet another 'place' – the place called Golgotha, v. 17. It is reminiscent of another scene, the same 'place' that Abraham saw generations before. It was the place 'afar off' to which both he and his son had walked together, Gen. 22. 4. There, his beloved son also willingly offered himself, after bearing the wood that he would be placed upon. But in contrast, this only Son was not spared and despite the sordid scene, did not come down because He was doing 'a great work', see Neh. 6. 3.

There was still another 'place' to note – a garden, next to where He was crucified, John 19. 41. Fittingly, He was receiving the burial of a king with Joseph providing the new tomb and Nicodemus, the spices. 'Behold your King' indeed! From glory to Galilee, to Gethsemane, to Gabbatha, to Golgotha, to a garden, and eventually back to glory. It was the lonely path trodden by One who endured the cross and despised the shame – for us.

Christ and

John 20 — June 5th

Woman, why weepest thou?

This question asked twice of Mary, vv. 13, 15, underscored the great load of sorrow and grief that weighed upon this devoted but forlorn follower of the Lord. Sadly, she had come to the tomb to acknowledge the events that had occurred three days earlier. But to her surprise, when she arrived she found the stone had been taken away and the sepulchre emptied of its occupant. Not piecing together all the facts on that resurrection morning, she ran to Peter and John with the message that He had been 'taken away', v. 2. Yet, before long, her despair would dissipate as quickly as the morning darkness. The first one to the tomb became the first one to herald the glorious news that He had risen from the dead in the power of an endless life. Shrouded in grief one moment; bursting forth in radiant joy the next, v. 18. What caused her to turn so quickly?

Having been delivered from the realm of darkness, it is very understandable why she rushed to the tomb, Luke 8. 2. She had been dramatically transformed by a Man who had demonstrated compassion for her like no other. Gratefully, she ministered to Him of her substance. However, this great change in her life was temporarily obscured by the current circumstances that seemed contrary to all that He had said and done. Miracles abounded wherever He went and nothing ever seemed too hard for Him. There was no obstacle too great that He could not overcome. Yet, now overcome by grief, she had somehow forgotten these things as we often do when looking at circumstances and not to Him. When she had 'turned herself back' and saw Him standing, it was the beginning of another turning, both in her emotions and in her perspective. It reached a culmination when the voice of the Stranger pointedly called her by name, John 20. 16. The result was that she 'turned herself' to acknowledge Him. Not only had she turned in her posture, but also in her understanding. Thus will be the change with us, when we listen for the Voice which speaks the same comforting words: firstly perhaps with a probing question and then with calming words of reassurance, sure to turn our night to day.

His Apostles

June 6th — John 21

Lord, thou knowest all things

This response by Peter to the Lord's thrice-repeated question, 'Lovest thou me?' reflected a reluctance in this once-confident and outspoken leader of the apostles. Unlike previously, he was now hesitant to enthusiastically declare his undying devotion, in the light of his recent failures. His perfunctory response seemed to dutifully acknowledge the implications of the question. Yes, he was aware of the gravity of his offence as he warmed himself by the opposition's fire. And yes, he was grateful that he had been forgiven, both privately, 1 Cor. 15. 5, and now publicly in the presence of his brethren. Certainly, these were some of the 'things' that he understood the Lord knew. But the soul-piercing questions, repeated for emphasis, made him uneasy and left him uncomfortable. He was now being made to think through the issue. His past failures did not excuse or exempt him from responding to the call to full commitment, despite his own personal misgivings. It should not for us either.

As with Mary at the tomb, His questions were diagnostic, designed by the Good Shepherd to stir up Peter's conscience and provoke divinely-appointed responsibilities. Previously, he had boasted self-assuredly, 'Though all men shall be offended because of thee, yet will I never be offended', Matt. 26. 33. He would soon learn the anguish of acting in the strength of self-confidence. His answer to each of the Lord's questions, 'Lord, thou knowest that I love thee' was correct, but weak, John 21. 15, 16, and simply accentuated his own personal doubt and reservation. But the gifts and calling of God are without repentance and Peter was learning the magnitude and extent of that calling. It is the process which is begun by the One who called us by His own glory and virtue, who will continue to manifest those qualities working in us what is well-pleasing in His sight, Heb. 13. 20-21. Peter had been in desperate need of restoration. He was now in need of a fresh revelation – a revelation that extended beyond salvation and personal restoration to a renewed motivation for faithful service. It was not based on personal strength and self-resolve, but on the gentle but strengthening hand of the Bishop and Overseer of our souls.

Christ and

Introduction to the Acts of the Apostles

The book of Acts picks up the narrative where Luke's Gospel leaves off. It serves as a connecting bridge between the Gospels and the Epistles. Luke's former account concludes with the finished work of Christ, the Head; the latter chronicles His ongoing work through the church, His body. Likewise, the closing charge of our Lord to the disciples, Luke 24. 47, 'that repentance and remission of sins should be preached in his name among all nations' paves the way for the main thrust of Acts.

The author, Luke, penned both volumes and has the distinction of being the most prolific by volume of the rest of the New Testament writers. He is known as the 'beloved physician', Col. 4. 14, and as such he writes with an eye to detail about the miraculous work of the Great Physician through the signs and wonders wrought by the apostles. His personal attendance on Paul's missionary journeys lends credence to his authorship, and the well-documented 'we' and 'us' passages found in chapters 16, 17, 27, and 28 substantiate the claim.

The Acts of the Apostles covers approximately the first thirty years of the history of the church. It begins with the ascension and finishes with the house imprisonment of Paul. The book mainly focuses on the ministry of Peter, Acts 1-12, and of Paul, Acts 13-28. It is Peter with the 'keys of the kingdom', Matt. 16. 19, who opens the door of faith to the Jews in Acts chapter 2, and to the Gentiles in Acts chapter 10. Paul is the one who carries the gospel to regions beyond. Acts chapter 1 verse 8 lays out the plan of the book, 'And ye shall be witnesses unto me both in Jerusalem, and in all Judaea, and in Samaria, and unto the uttermost part of the earth', see Acts 2, 4, 8, 13. Throughout, the emphasis is more on the **practice** of the early church, but there is plenty that relates to the **principles** that actuated it, later expanded upon in the Epistles. The **persecution** of the church is an overriding theme, Stephen and James being two notable examples. Time and again the infant church is attacked by outward forces that sought to destroy it; yet the church emerges strengthened as it overcomes. As a result, there was **power** in the church and in the **propagation** of the gospel. What a challenge!

His Apostles

June 7th — Acts 1

Ye shall be witnesses unto me

The Lord's words to His disciples came on the heels of their question, 'Lord wilt thou restore again at this time the kingdom to Israel?' v. 6. They understood that literal promises had been made to Abraham and to David through the Old Testament prophets who spoke of the future restoration and glory of God's earthly people. He did not correct or rebuke them for wrong theology; their understanding of these ancient covenants was quite accurate. Instead, the Lord was unveiling a new strategy for a new dispensation for what soon would become a new people, the church. It did not abrogate past promises made to His ancient people. It did not include date setting or a strategy for political and social improvement. In contrast, it laid out what would be the focus of the church for this age before He returns to restore all things. It was both singular and centred on Him, 'Ye shall be witnesses unto *me*'.

Luke had written in his previous volume that the validation for his writing came as a result of being with others who were 'eyewitnesses and ministers of the word', Luke 1. 2. This is itself an adequate description of the standard placed upon the church. Firstly, there must be a personal apprehension of the Person and work of Christ. In the words of John, it is that which has been 'heard', 'seen', 'looked upon', and 'our hands have handled of the word of life', 1 John 1. 1. This is the first stage in the life of a witness – a dynamic encounter with the risen, living Word. The second is the application of that experience. Through the appropriation of spiritual resources and empowerment by the Holy Spirit, that witness is then translated into effectual service. The outcome is that the witness becomes an able minister of the word. It is clearly exemplified by the statement of Peter and John, who boldly and fearlessly declared before the Sanhedrin, 'For we cannot but speak the things which we have seen and heard', Acts 4. 20.

As we witness for Him and tell of His wonderful work in the lives of His people, we are doing what He has called us to do, and showing that we are ready to give an answer to anyone who asks about the hope that lies within us, 1 Pet. 3. 15.

Christ and

Acts 2. 1-36 — June 8th

By the right hand of God exalted

Peter's sermon bore abundant testimony to the accuracy of the prophetic scriptures. In it he cites the prophet Joel and King David; the former originated during the period of the divided kingdom, the latter, when the kingdom was united. One dealt with the restoration by the Spirit poured out upon all flesh, the other the resurrection of the Son in His conquest over the grave. Both had an initial fulfilment and yet still have a future, ultimate fulfilment. It will be when the King and His kingdom will be over all. He will occupy a literal throne upon the earth and reign for a literal thousand years, Rev. 20. 6.

The Lord has always occupied the honoured place with the Father. In eternity past, we see Him daily His delight and rejoicing always before Him, Prov. 8. 30. In His earthly ministry, both at the beginning and throughout, the voice from heaven confirmed that honoured place with the words, 'This is my beloved Son, in whom I am well pleased', Matt. 17. 5. He, the perfect Man, was the untainted, blessed Man of Psalm 1 who always did the Father's will, always set the Lord before His face, and always did those things that pleased Him, John 8. 29. All the way to the cross, He was in constant communion with the Father, working with Him as He approached the place of sacrifice, 5. 17. Hebrews chapter 1 verse 3 reminds us that after enduring the cross and despising the shame, He ascended to the right hand of the Majesty on High where He now *sits* by virtue of His finished work, having purged our sins. It is the place where He also *stands* to strengthen us in our witness for Him, Acts 7. 55; where He *intercedes* for us in our need, Rom. 8. 34; and where He *waits* until His enemies be made His footstool. It is also the place which proves that angels and principalities have been made subject unto Him, 1 Pet. 3. 22, and where believers ought to focus their affections, Col. 3. 1.

The One who was made sin for us is also the One who has been made both Lord and Christ, Acts 2. 36. Through His humiliation came His exaltation and the Name which is above every name, 'by the right hand of God exalted'.

His Apostles

June 9th

Acts 2. 37-47

Men and brethren, what shall we do?

Today's question is typical of those who have been cut to the heart through Spirit-empowered, convicting ministry. Peter, the same man who wavered before a young maid outside Pilate's judgement hall is seen here truly living up to his name. He is inflamed with power from on high, the power the Lord promised once the Holy Spirit came upon him and upon the other apostles in Jerusalem, 1. 8. That time had arrived and the man of cowardice was transformed into a man of courage. 'Who is a pardoning God like thee? And who has grace so rich and free?' SAMUEL DAVIES. Everyone who has ever failed the Lord should be greatly encouraged by Peter's restoration and his persuasive oratory as an unlettered fisherman, 4. 13.

Not only should we be encouraged with the Lord's grace toward Peter, but also His offer of forgiveness to the undeserving crowd. Without question, Peter was opening the door of faith by using the keys of the kingdom for those to whom he had been commissioned, Gal. 2. 7; Matt. 16. 19. The first turn of the key – and always the first – is the call to repentance. It is the same priority that Paul emphasized to the Ephesian elders, Acts 20. 21. The next turn of the key is a call for baptism, the step of identification to demonstrate reality and safeguard against false profession. It confirms the actions of the heart and verifies that sins have been remitted and the Holy Spirit received, 2. 38.

The words of verse 39 are also very intriguing, 'For the promise is to you and to your children, and to all who are afar off', NKJV. It corresponds to the words of a similar group of people who only recently stood before Pilate and defiantly declared, 'His blood be on us and on our children', Matt. 27. 25. They were in essence raising their fists to heaven and shouting, 'We will not have this man to reign over us', Luke 19. 14. To the nation who had collectively jeered at Him who suffered in their stead came the free offer of salvation through Peter to 'you and your children and to all who are afar off'. This is 'love divine, all loves excelling', and a wonderful example of His amazing grace!

Christ and

Acts 3 — June 10th

Walking, and leaping, and praising God

In this episode in the ministry of the apostles, it has been pointed out that the lame man in this chapter, after asking for alms, got legs instead. Indeed, he did! He was surprised by joy and his spiritual enlightenment and the abounding joy serve as a prototype of every conversion to Christ. It reminds us of the way that God can use us in the salvation of precious souls, Mark 16. 20.

Firstly, as another has noted, there was **lameness**. Here was a man in desperate need, whose condition was keenly felt and clearly seen. Poor fellow! He was a forty-year old beggar who had been that way for a long time, with no resources or relatives to give him aid, Acts 4. 22. His lameness only highlighted his helplessness and pictures the spiritual inability of all mankind to walk in the ways of God. The persistency of his condition underscores the impotence of organized religion and any effort apart from Christ to meet that need.

With the sense of need however, came a **look**. Peter, fixing his eyes on him, with John replied, 'Look on us', v. 4. The two were not indifferent to the need that was within their reach. The man, expecting to receive some monetary gift, looked back. Like the woman at the well, his focus was on the material plane. But these servants' focus was on the spiritual. Just as Israel felt her need through the venom of a serpent, Num. 21, requiring a look to be healed, so this man's healing began with a look.

Next, we see something very indicative of this dispensation of grace. Reaching down, Peter took him by the right hand and gave him a **lift**. It is the work of grace in the life of a Christian, seeking to help another soul in need. The command given is to 'rise up and walk', but the means by which this comes is through the hand that reaches down to help, following the pattern of *the* Hand that reached down to us in grace, Titus 3. 4-5.

The **leap** along with the walking and praising was simply the outcome of an encounter with God. For him, it was the joyful, public, and audible testimony of a life that had once been bound but was now loosed and set free by God's grace.

His Apostles

June 11th   Acts 4. 1-31

Proof of the power of Peter and John's ministry for the Lord was irrefutable. Before the liberal but highly influential Sanhedrin stood a man who had been lame. His jubilant and emotional outburst had been seen by everyone. After all, he had been released from his personal prison of forty years through their words, and his joy could hardly be contained. There was no disputing this fact, v. 14. Yet it did not sit well with the seventy men that made up Israel's ruling elite. They were hard-pressed but determined to keep the news of the miracle from spreading any further. They now focused their angry threats upon these two pillars of the church. The fact that Peter and John were 'unlearned and ignorant men' did not prevent these stalwarts from speaking the things which they had but 'seen and heard', v. 20. The redeemed of the Lord should always say so in good times and bad, despite the prospect of persecution. Their boldness in speaking against this intimidating council truly did substantiate that 'they had been with Jesus', v. 13. The more we spend time with Jesus, the greater and grander will be our testimony for Him.

The cornerstone of the disciples' message was the truth of the resurrection. It was this truth and the fact that the people were being taught the word of God that greatly infuriated the priests and Sadducees, v. 2. Typically, they stood on opposite sides regarding the matter of resurrection. Yet now they were united in their opposition to Christ. Later, the disciples would quote David's prophecy from Psalm 2 as an example of this, v. 26. Like Pilate and Herod, enemies become friends in their hatred of the Lord and His Anointed, Luke 23. 12.

Despite the cacophony of vicious words against them, the disciples were released. They would not allow this attempt to intimidate or silence their testimony or curtail their activity. The persecution led to praise and rather than asking to have this trial removed, they requested a greater measure of boldness, Acts 4. 29. Such are the ways of God. In the midst of persecution will come praise and a further opportunity to proclaim His glory and grace in defence of the gospel.

Acts 4. 32 – 5. 11 — June 12th

This portion shows how the early church was characterized by rapid growth, corporate unity, and loving concern for one another. The efforts of the Jews to quash this new movement which boldly claimed that its leader, Jesus of Nazareth, had risen from the dead, were thwarted. They met an impasse as the disciples were emboldened by the Spirit and grace of God to fearlessly preach the resurrection. They courageously rose to the challenge before them. Now there was a multitude who were of 'one heart and soul', v. 32. This indicated both growth and unity. The one hundred and twenty disciples in the upper room prior to Pentecost had now mushroomed to at least five thousand souls. No one lacked as each member of the body looked not upon their own interests, but on the interests and needs of others, Phil. 2. 4. As a result, the church flourished, as it always will when abiding by the word and the Spirit of God. 'Church growth' experts who want to apply the world's business strategies for success in the ways of the Lord should take heed: God's work should be done in God's way.

But this phenomenal growth and obvious blessing will not be without challenges from within. Fightings without are accompanied by fears within, 2 Cor. 7. 5, the daily cares of the churches that Paul expressed much concern about, 2 Cor. 11. 28. Whether it was savage wolves seeking entrance, or men of perverse minds rising from within, Acts 20. 29-30; false brethren creeping in, Jude 4; or being brought in, Gal. 2. 4; the purity of the church will always be assailed, one way or another. The challenge this time would come from Ananias and Sapphira, a husband and wife team who kept back part of the proceeds of the sale of their property, but pretended to give the whole to the apostles. But a half truth is still a half lie, and goes against the One who said, 'I am the way, the truth and the life'. 'God is light, and in him is no darkness at all', and the need for purity in the early church had to be reinforced to set the standard for future generations. Is there a need to re-examine this principle in the light of present conditions, Rev. 2. 5? Let us not forget that 'holiness becometh thine house, O Lord, forever', Ps. 93. 5.

His Apostles

June 13th   Acts 5. 12-42

Ye have filled Jerusalem with your doctrine

Despite the intimidation received by the authorities, the apostles continued their steadfast testimony regarding the things which they had both seen and heard, 4. 20. Often, the greater the persecution, the greater the power as we are cast upon the Lord. The boldness they had prayed for, v. 29, was indeed granted, bringing about a great influx into the church. Consequently, believers were increasingly added to the Lord, 5. 14. This success in evangelism did not stand upon the merit of a carefully-crafted strategy nor by accommodating or courting the unsaved, but rather through the principle of separation. 'And of the rest durst no man join himself to them', v. 13. No man dared join company with them, though many did. The call of the Lord is always captivating and productive when preached with power and exalting the Saviour. Let's not forget the truth that God's word will never return void, Isa. 55. 11.

After being thrown in the common prison, an angel released the disciples that night, charging them to speak in the temple on the morrow. Prompt obedience ensued as they taught the people the following morning. They were directed by the Lord to go back to the place where they had ministered previously to openly declare the message they had been commissioned to proclaim. God wanted them (and us!) to know of His protection and provision in working for Him. When Jacob arose to go back to Bethel, God saw to it that he was protected from the nations around him as he did so, Gen. 35. 5. 'We are indestructible until our lifework is done'. Let's not forget this truth as well.

The charge levelled against the disciples was disregarding the edicts and 'filling Jerusalem' with their doctrine, Acts 5. 28. What a testimony that even the enemies of the Lord acknowledged their thoroughness in propagating the gospel! Would to God that every city were so blessed! They repudiated the intention to bring 'this man's blood upon us', yet it was what they had already declared nationally, Matt. 27. 25. Like so many, little did they realize that what they despised is actually what they needed – the doctrine of God, and to be sheltered under the blood.

Christ and

Acts 6. 1-15

June 14th

What a standard for all of God's people – honesty, and filled with the Spirit. These traits are indicative of those 'who have renounced the hidden things of shame', 2 Cor. 4. 2 NKJV, and who 'provide things honest in the sight of all men', Rom. 12. 17. It is worthy of the One who said, 'I am . . . the truth' and an imperative for useful service, knowing that 'all things are naked and opened before the eyes of Him with whom we have to do', Heb. 4. 13. Yielding to the Spirit of God as seen in this portion, dissension will be overcome, disciples will be strengthened, and discouragement will be averted.

As the number of disciples multiplied, so did the problems in the early church. Growing pains were as much a problem then as they are now. With the increase in numbers, came an increase in complaints. In this case, they centred on the care of widows, some of whom were neglected in the daily distribution. The Hellenists were bothered by the apparent oversight by the Hebrews of their widows, Acts 6. 1. Age, gender, and racial tension marked the assembly in Jerusalem.

How were problems dealt with then, and how should they be dealt with now? Certainly not in the way that they were addressed in Numbers chapter 11! The complaining congregation in the wilderness resorted to their own carnal appetites and allowed the 'mixed multitude' to dictate the agenda, Num. 11. 1, 4. The outcome was futile as the effort expended to remedy the situation proved fruitless – despite the presence of melons!

Fortunately, carnal methods did not prevail in this conflict. Through the godly wisdom of the Twelve, the congregation was presented with the challenge to identify seven men of good report and full of the Holy Spirit to lead in the practical concerns of the assembly. They were selected and brought before the Twelve who prayed and commissioned them for the task, Acts 6. 6. Among them was Stephen who epitomized the very qualities that God extols for this service. May these credentials always be present in dealing with any issue that potentially threatens the harmony of the assembly.

Men of honest report, full of the Holy Ghost

His Apostles

June 15th — Acts 7. 1-29

Men, brethren, and fathers, hearken

Stephen's prompt response must have surely caught the attention of the high priest who had asked the question, 'Are these things so?' v. 1. The false witnesses who were suborned to bring a false report against Stephen charged him with speaking blasphemous words against Moses and God, and against the holy place and the law, 6. 11, 13. They actually gave him an audience and opportunity that he might not have had otherwise. What they meant for evil God meant for good, and Stephen was intent on turning it to the glory of God. Philip was quick to open his mouth to testify to the eunuch in the desert, 8. 35. Peter did the same in the house of Cornelius, 10. 34. Stephen also opened his mouth to speak a word of testimony for his Master. Let us not be ashamed of the gospel of our salvation, for in the furnace of affliction the Son of God will manifest His presence to us as well. He enlarges us in our distress, Ps. 4. 1, while the Holy Spirit teaches us in the same hour what we ought to say, Luke 12. 12. Stephen was not intimidated by their accusations and neither should we when facing the opposition.

Stephen began his discourse with a detailed account of the history of the nation and the fathers, from Abraham to Moses; to David and Solomon. It was a glowing report of the faithfulness of God, the faith and leadership of Abraham and Moses, and the importance of the holy place and law. It contradicted the baseless accusation that Stephen had spoken against these very things, but it came from the one whose face appeared as a face of an angel. Intertwined with the account was the common thread that the actions of the leaders to whom he was speaking paralleled the fathers of the past. Despite God's work for them and the testimony of the patriarchs, they rejected His law and 'thrust him from them, and in their hearts turned back again into Egypt', Acts 7. 39. The connection between those fathers and these was undeniable. They too had proven to be stubborn and self-willed. Driving home the point, Stephen exclaimed, 'Ye do always resist the Holy Ghost; as your fathers did, so do ye', v. 51. The words were blunt but necessary to convict the heart and faithfully deliver the message.

Christ and

Acts 7. 30 – 8. 4 — June 16th

Stephen's sermon achieved its desired effect upon his hearers – conviction from God's word. He had reminded them that, as Israel's past fathers were self-willed and stiff-necked, so they were, 7. 51. It would be up to them whether they would repent and believe, or resist and turn from the offer of life and peace. The same sun that hardens the clay melts the butter, and how the message is dealt with is what determines the destiny. For this new generation of fathers, the testimony was refused as in the past, resulting in the persecution of His prophet, v. 52.

As they rushed with one accord against this faithful witness, the heavens opened to reveal the Lord standing at God's right hand ready to receive His choice servant, vv. 55, 56. The Lord who sat down at the right hand of the Majesty on high when He finished His work, Heb. 1. 3, was now standing in His office as High Priest. It represents His ongoing work on behalf of the heirs of salvation, and is an early example in the New Testament of the unchangeable priesthood of the One who ever lives to make intercession for His own, Heb. 7. 24-25.

The depth of Stephen's commitment to Christ is also seen in His response to His persecutors. How like the Saviour in his words and his actions! Crying out, 'Lord receive my spirit', echoes the Lord's words at Calvary, 'Father, into thy hands I commend my spirit', Luke 23. 46. The words, 'Lord, lay not this sin to their charge', Acts 7. 60, harks back to the Lord's request for those at the cross, 'Father, forgive them, for they know not what they do', Luke 23. 34. Stephen had become like His Saviour, exemplifying the purpose of God and the goal of every believer – conformity to Christ, Phil. 1. 6. 'And is it so, I shall be like thy Son?' J. N. DARBY.

Present among these persecutors was a young man whose name was Saul, Acts 7. 58. Respected by his peers, he was intent on making havoc of the church, 8. 3. He persecuted it beyond measure, more exceedingly zealous of the tradition of his fathers, Gal. 1. 13-14. It was this rising luminary that the eye of God was now focused upon, as He would begin His work in the life of this future trophy of grace.

His Apostles

June 17th — Acts 8. 5-40

Go . . . unto Gaza, which is desert

The widespread persecution at the hand of Saul seemed to be devastating to the infant church. Believers were imprisoned as the level of persecution was intensified. The vicious fury gave furtherance to the gospel as its seed was sown farther afield: the disciples went everywhere preaching the word. The church's trial of faith which occurred here on a massive scale was working a far more exceeding and eternal weight of glory in the plan and purposes of God, 2 Cor. 4. 17.

Philip, directed by the Spirit to Samaria, preached Christ to the people. Whenever this is done, spiritual fruit will be realized. God's word never returns to Him void, Isa. 55. 11. Multitudes believed, Acts 8. 6; people were healed, v. 7; joy abounded, v. 8, and lives were changed as God was glorified. Why would anyone want to prevent the preaching of the gospel? Yet even this success was not without distraction as Simon the sorcerer foolishly sought to purchase the gift of God to increase his power and influence, vv. 18-20. His 'descendants' continue to this day. His profession of faith seemed but a sham, and he was rebuked for the thought of his heart, v. 22.

Despite the progress of the gospel in the north, Philip was directed by an angel to go to Gaza, a desolate, desert region to the south. Angels certainly could have done the work, but the Great Commission has been given for men to act upon. Philip's charge was to fulfil a divine appointment to meet a man of great authority on his homeward journey from Jerusalem. It underscores the **worth of a soul** that the Lord would direct Philip's steps to leave a fruitful ministry to attend to the spiritual needs of just one person. God's ways are not ours, and His strategy to reach the lost is under His control. The **witness of the servant** is evidenced as Philip promptly acted to intercept the inquiring soul who held the scriptures in his hands but not his heart. He had been unmoved by his religious activities. The **work of salvation** is obvious when the eunuch requests baptism and the **way of the Spirit** is seen as He went on his way rejoicing, forgiven, and filled with joy, v. 39. One moment, this man was a traveller on the road to Gaza; the next, travelling to glory!

Christ and

Acts 9. 1-25 — June 18th

Brother Saul

These words from Ananias must have been reassuring to Saul who needed to be affirmed in his new found faith, v. 17. This infuriated zealot who had been breathing out threatenings and slaughter against the disciples of the Lord had been instantaneously translated into the kingdom of light, Col. 1. 13, and that in dramatic fashion, Acts 9. 3. Struck down on the road to Damascus, his conversion contrasts sharply with that of the eunuch in the previous chapter and with Cornelius in chapter 10. With the Ethiopian, the deliverance came through the **personal** work of Philip; with Cornelius through the **public** preaching of the word. Saul's conversion was without human instrumentality, an example of the **providence** of God in salvation.

The Voice from heaven enquired, 'Saul, Saul, why persecutest thou me?' v. 4. The words are identified as those of the Lord Jesus, v. 5. It was an explicit statement directed to Saul that revealed His care for the church. Never before did the Lord call out when He suffered, 'Why persecutest thou me'? But now as His bride was suffering, His pearl of great price, He comes quickly to her aid.

Ananias is summoned as the first one to meet the newly transformed convert. At first he is reluctant, having heard of the harm that he had done to the saints, v. 14. Even today, believers are often incredulous as to the genuineness of conversions at this level. But Saul was now a brother in the Lord as Ananias substantiated, and he was demonstrating all the salient features of new life in Christ. Firstly, Ananias is told that Saul was *'praying'*, v. 11. Ritualistic and formal prayer had been the regimen of the religious and of the unenlightened Saul of old. Now he was truly communing with the God of heaven. Secondly, after the scales fell from his eyes, he arose and was *baptized*, v. 18. Like the eunuch, he chose to immediately verify his profession of faith. Thirdly, he spent time with the disciples, and in Damascus of all places, v. 19! *Fellowship* with the Lord's people is another mark of genuine faith. Finally, Paul was unashamed of his new faith as he *preached* Christ in the synagogues, v. 20. Old things had truly passed away, for all things had become new!

His Apostles

June 19th — Acts 9. 26-43

Then had the churches rest

The dramatic conversion of Saul of Tarsus not only affected him personally but also it had an immediate impact on the circumstances of God's people over a wide geographical area. The once 'exceedingly mad' persecutor, who compelled many of the saints to blaspheme, now shunned his former companions and sought to join himself to the church at Jerusalem. Once they had been assured of the reality of his conversion, Saul was received by the believers and he engaged fully in all their activities, for 'he was with them coming in and going out at Jerusalem', v. 28.

Freed from the distractions of Saul's persecutions the church throughout all Judaea, Galilee, and Samaria enjoyed rest, but this did not cause the saints to become idle. There was a continuous spiritual development evident which resulted in a deepening awe and reverence of the Lord, and a conscious experience of the comfort of the Holy Spirit. In these spiritually vibrant conditions it is not surprising that Luke informs us that the church was multiplied, and maybe there is a simple lesson in this for us. If we want to see days of numerical multiplication we need to emulate the spiritual progress that characterized those early saints. Revival always relates to the impact of the word of God on the people of God, but its outcomes will be felt by the world.

The next section of the chapter is taken up with the recovery of a palsied man who had been ill for eight years. Unlike Saul, who had travelled far and wide opposed to Christianity, Aeneas had been bedridden and helpless. However, like Saul, the change in his life was instant and spectacular, and the change also resulted in many turning to the Lord.

The final verses bring before us the raising of Dorcas, a woman 'full of good works and almsdeeds'. This godly sister was not a preacher, but she certainly does give us a pattern of Christian service. The close of verse 39 is very striking, 'which Dorcas made, *while she was with them*', indicating that she did what she could, when she could. This principle is echoed by C. T. STUDD who wrote, 'Only one life, 'twill soon be passed, only what's done for Christ will last'.

Christ and

Acts 10. 1-23 — June 20th

The prospect of Gentiles being blessed by God was a fact with which Peter, and all the apostles, would have been very familiar for reference is made to it throughout the Old Testament. Even at the time Jehovah promised to make of Abram a great nation He said, 'I will bless those who bless you, and I will curse him who curses you; and in you all the families of the earth shall be blessed.' Gen. 12. 3 NKJV. However, although Peter would have been aware of these things there was a vital issue he had not appreciated, and it is in this chapter that his education relative to this matter is completed.

Cornelius, a Roman soldier of distinction in charge of a hundred fighting men, is one of four centurions favourably referred to in the New Testament. Despite his military background he was a devout man who feared God with all his house, which gave much alms to the people, and who prayed to God always, Acts 10. 2. By means of a vision he was instructed by an angel of God to send men to Joppa to request Simon Peter to come to him.

Two days later, Peter, unaware of God's intervention in the life of this Gentile centurion, and the impending arrival of three of his men, fell into a trance. He saw something that resembled a great sheet containing a menagerie of beasts, fowls, and creeping things, and was instructed, 'Rise, Peter; kill, and eat', v. 13. Being a thoroughbred Jew, Peter recoiled at the prospect of eating animals that were specifically forbidden under the law and responded, 'Not so, Lord', thus demonstrating that his Jewish orthodoxy outweighed his spiritual discernment.

In verse 15 Peter has to be instructed, 'What God has cleansed . . .', and corrected, 'You must not call common'. However, although this was repeated three times the apostle did not grasp immediately the significance of what was happening. His initial reaction was to doubt 'in himself what this vision which he had seen should mean'. It would be a further two days, when he arrived at the home of Cornelius, that the spiritual significance of his trance would become apparent to him.

His Apostles

June 21st — Acts 10. 24-48

Thy prayer is heard

We noted in yesterday's meditation that God was preparing Peter for the event to be considered in today's reading. What he failed to grasp at the time of his trance in the house of Simon the tanner a couple of days earlier was going to become very apparent to him, as events unfolded in the home of Cornelius. Although Paul refers to the gospel of the circumcision being committed to Peter (i.e., Peter's sphere of service was to those of his own nation), he is going to be used by the Lord to be the preacher on the occasion of the first recorded conversion of a Gentile.

Over twelve months prior to this momentous incident the Lord said to Peter, 'I will give unto thee the keys of the kingdom of heaven', Matt. 16. 19, and by means of his preaching on the Day of Pentecost the door to that kingdom was opened to the Jews. Now in Caesarea, Peter was going to use those keys to open the door for Gentiles to enter in. No longer was Israel the primary object of God's favour, Gentiles were on an equal footing with them. The centuries-old disparity between Jew and Gentile was over and 'the middle wall of partition' was broken down. Through the work of Christ converted Jews and Gentiles 'both have access by one Spirit unto the Father', Eph. 2. 18. Thus the object lesson of the sheet containing unclean animals (symbolizing the Gentiles) was learned by the entrenched apostle, therefore he could say, 'God hath shewed me that I should not call any man common or unclean', Acts 10. 28.

Despite the fact that he was a devout man, one that feared God and prayed to God always, we discover from Peter's words in chapter 11 that Cornelius was not a *saved* man. Nevertheless he had been assured by the angel that 'thy prayer is heard', v. 31. His religious observances and the alms deeds which he did had not saved him, he needed to appreciate that 'whoever believes in him will receive remission of sins', v. 43 NKJV. How thrilling it is to observe that the chapter that opens with a devout man closes with a converted man upon whom the Holy Spirit fell! This blessing was not limited to Cornelius but was also true of those with him. Later that day they were all baptized.

Christ and

Acts 11. 1-18 — June 22nd

The Holy Ghost fell on them, as on us

The eleventh chapter of Acts is a pivotal point in Luke's narrative of the early days of Christianity because it introduces a sea change of emphasis. Up to this point the primary location has been Jerusalem and the principal character has been Peter. From now on, the geographical focus broadens out to encompass many areas of the Roman Empire, and Paul replaces Peter as the key worker. However, in the previous couple of chapters the ground was prepared for this transfer of prominence as we read of the conversion of Saul of Tarsus, and of Cornelius the first Gentile Christian.

It is difficult for us to appreciate the challenge faced by the Jewish believers of the first century to come to terms with the reality that they no longer held a special place in God's dealings with mankind. For 1500 years Judaism had been the only divinely appointed religion and throughout that era the Gentiles were 'aliens from the commonwealth of Israel, and strangers from the covenants of promise', Eph. 2. 12. This explains why a group within the church at Jerusalem contended with Peter when he arrived back from Caesarea, Acts 11. 2-3. Diligently, the apostle explained to them from the beginning all that transpired in the house of Cornelius. This factual 'missionary report' resulted in a change of attitude by those of the circumcision for on hearing these things 'they became silent; and they glorified God, saying, Then God has also granted to the Gentiles repentance to life', v. 18 NKJV.

The irrefutable evidence that this was a divine work was that the Holy Spirit fell on those Gentiles, just as He had on the apostles in Jerusalem at Pentecost. In verse 15 Peter speaks about a 'beginning' and he is casting his mind back to what happened on the Day of Pentecost. On that memorable occasion God began something new, for the baptism in the Holy Spirit resulted in the formation of the church as a body incorporating converted Jews and Gentiles. This church is not an extension of Judaism; it is distinct from it, and did not come into being until Pentecost. Writing to the Ephesians Paul describes it as being a 'new man' and John refers to it as 'new Jerusalem', Eph. 2. 15; Rev. 21. 2.

His Apostles

June 23rd Acts 11. 19-30

Called Christians first in Antioch

Satan's objective in persecuting the church in Jerusalem was to eradicate Christianity at its outset, and one of his principal agents was Saul of Tarsus. It was Saul who stood and watched as the stones battered Stephen's body to death. It was the same young man who 'made havoc of the church, entering every house, and dragging off men and women, committing them to prison', Acts 8. 3 NKJV. However, God in His sovereignty used this satanic harassment for the furtherance of the gospel and, far from nipping Christianity in its bud, it resulted in the spread of the gospel.

Antioch was a large prestigious city located about 300 miles from Jerusalem and although the gospel was initially preached to the Jews, v. 19, afterwards it was proclaimed to the Gentiles, v. 20. With the Lord at work, 'the hand of the Lord was with them', and by means of the preaching of the gospel a great number were converted; thus it always is. Our responsibility is to preach, but the power to convert rests with the Lord.

Barnabas was linguistically, culturally, and spiritually the ideal person to be sent from Jerusalem to Antioch. He spoke Greek, came from Cyprus, v. 20, and 'he was a good man, and full of the Holy Ghost and of faith', v. 24. He was also a gracious man who recognized his own limitations, for he was willing to bring in Saul to help in the teaching of the newly-formed assembly.

It is hardly surprising that the believers in Antioch were the first to be called Christians, for they were a Christ-centred church. He was the subject of the message they believed, v. 20; it was to Him they turned for salvation, v. 21; and they were exhorted to cleave to Him, v. 23. In addition the 'much people' who were added to the church, v. 24, attended the year-long teaching meetings conducted by Saul and Barnabas, v. 26. Through the life-changing power of the gospel and the systematic teaching of scripture these believers relinquished their links to the ritualism of Judaism or their bondage to Gentile idolatry and became so taken up with Christ that they became known as 'Christians'. What a glorious testimony to have!

Christ and

Acts 12. 1-25   June 24th

The opening words of the chapter place this remarkable incident in the life of Peter within a particular time setting. In order to appreciate that setting we need to review what has happened in the previous chapter. The first Gentile has been converted, the message of Christ has radiated out from Jerusalem, and a spiritually vibrant church has been established in Antioch . . . 'now about *that* time'.

This was a time of blessing and spiritual prosperity, and it was then that the devil attacked, using Herod as the instrument of his opposition. How often in the Bible, and within our own experience, we discover that when things are gaining spiritual momentum Satan seeks to disrupt and discourage! It is during seasons of revival or growth that we need to be most vigilant.

The opening verses of the chapter also present to us the sovereignty of God in the lives of His servants. Why He should allow James, the brother of John, to be martyred and yet allow Peter to be miraculously delivered might seem strange at first. However Peter's work was not yet finished, for he had been informed by the Lord in John chapter 21 that he would die as an old man. He would no longer hold centre stage in respect of preaching – that responsibility would pass to Paul – but he had a duty to strengthen his brethren, and this in part was fulfilled in the writing of his two Epistles. We are not told that the believers were praying for Peter's release, but they were incredulous when Rhoda told them he was outside the house and assumed it was his spirit.

Although the chapter opens with Herod and Peter in close proximity it closes with them being separated forever. Both men met the angel of the Lord, but the angel spares the captive and slays the king. We are informed that Peter 'departed, and went into another place', but we are not told where this other place was. It's probable he went somewhere for his personal security, out of the reach of Herod. Herod also went to another place but we can be quite specific as to where this was. Far from being a place of security, it was a place of unending torment.

His Apostles

It is his angel

June 25th — Acts 13. 1-25

Sent forth by the Holy Ghost

Right at the start of this book, Luke presents to us the divine plan for the propagation of the gospel. Just as He was about to leave this world and return to heaven the Lord said to the disciples, 'You shall receive power when the Holy Spirit has come upon you; and you shall be witnesses to Me in Jerusalem, and in all Judea and Samaria, and to the end of the earth', 1. 8 NKJV. It is from chapter 13 onwards that we see the commencement of the global spread of this message.

Although Jerusalem was the centre from which Christianity emanated, Antioch became a strategic location in this process. It was the first Gentile church, it was here that believers were first called Christians, and it was from here that Paul started each of his three missionary journeys, the first of which begins in this chapter. We have already thought about the spiritual vitality of the church in Antioch, but today we do well to note the abundance of spiritual gift that was there and the sensitivity of those prophets and teachers to the promptings of the Holy Spirit.

As they ministered to the Lord the Holy Spirit instructs them to separate Barnabas and Saul for a specific work: 'the work whereunto I have called them'. In following the sequence of events in verses 2 to 4 we observe that Barnabas and Saul were called, separated, let go by the church, and sent forth by the Holy Spirit. In chapter 14 verse 26 we are also informed that before leaving Antioch they 'had been recommended to the grace of God for the work'. It's therefore not a surprise to discover that the consequence of this first missionary journey, which lasted approximately two years, was that a number of new churches were formed.

Had these two servants moved into this sphere of service at the dictate of the flesh there is no doubt that they would never have completed it. They encountered verbal opposition, suffered physical assault, and at Lystra Paul was stoned so badly the disciples thought that he had died. Whilst we may never face such severe hostility it is imperative that we also are sensitive to the leading of the Holy Spirit in our service for the Lord.

Christ and

Acts 13. 26-52 — June 26th

Lo, we turn to the Gentiles

Having set out from Antioch, Paul and Barnabas arrive at a town of identical name located in modern-day Turkey. Antioch in Pisidia was a Roman colony containing a synagogue for the Jewish inhabitants who had been brought there by the Romans. It also boasted a temple dedicated to Augustus and this became the focal point of the city. This important city was to be the location of the first recorded preaching by Paul, his message being set out in verses 16 to 41.

Paul's custom on arriving at a new city was to begin his preaching in the synagogue and this is what he did in Antioch. At first he outlined the gracious dealings of God with the nation of Israel from the patriarchs through to the reign of David, vv. 16-23, but from that he turned their attention to the seed of David, Jesus. The core of his message was that this Jesus, whom the Jews rejected and desired Pilate to crucify, was raised to life by God and 'that through this man is preached unto you the forgiveness of sins; and by him all that believe are justified from all things, from which ye could not be justified by the law of Moses', vv. 38-39.

As was often the case, and still is, opposition to the gospel did not come from those who were heathen but from the religious fundamentalists. Motivated by envy the Jews contradicted Paul and, railing against him, they rejected the very message that could have brought them everlasting life. At that point he and Barnabas made the solemn pronouncement, 'Lo, we turn to the Gentiles', v. 46.

Paul was a spiritually intelligent preacher. As to his **method** he preached the gospel, stipulated by the Lord at the end of Mark's Gospel. In respect of his **message** it was God-honouring, Christ-centred, and directly relevant to the congregation he was addressing. In reading the opening verse of Romans chapter 10 we discover what **motivated** him: it was a heart's desire to see people saved. We can't all be preachers, but we ought all to be witnesses and show an interest in the spiritual need of those around us. May we emulate Paul's example and present Christ to a world that desperately needs Him.

His Apostles

June 27th Acts 14. 1-28

The work which they fulfilled

The events recorded in this chapter bring to a conclusion Paul's first missionary journey. In respect of distance covered and the time taken this was the shortest of his three missions, but valuable lessons can be learned from the example of the man who said on one occasion, 'Be ye followers of me', 1 Cor. 4. 16.

Although the apostle firmly believed in the truth of election and the sovereignty of God he never used this doctrine to reduce evangelistic zeal. Writing to the Corinthians he stated, 'For necessity is laid upon me; yea, woe is unto me, if I preach not the gospel', 9. 16. Something of that compulsion is clearly evident in today's chapter, as there are numerous references to Paul preaching or speaking. Whilst we have access to resources and technologies that were not available in the first century, we must remember that the primary duty of the evangelist is to communicate the gospel by word of mouth.

Paul also recognized that the message was far more important than the messenger, and that attention was not to be focussed on the preacher but on God. We live in days where there is much emphasis on personalities, and even amongst Christians there is often the exaltation of well-known speakers. Barnabas and Paul deplored this practice and when the people of Lystra would have venerated them they said, 'Sirs, why do ye these things? We also are men of like passions with you', Acts 14. 15.

No one could doubt that the apostle longed for souls to be saved, but he was equally ardent in his desire to see those who were saved maturing in the ways of the Lord. He took seriously the Lord's instruction to go and 'make disciples of all the nations . . . teaching them to observe all things that I have commanded you', Matt. 28. 19-20 NKJV. Having reached Derbe the apostles then returned to where they had preached, 'confirming the souls of the disciples, and exhorting them to continue in the faith', Acts 14. 22.

The work to which Barnabas and Paul had been called and commended they also completed; what an example they are to us! May we also abound in the work of the Lord, knowing that our 'labour is not in vain in the Lord', 1 Cor. 15. 58.

Christ and

Acts 15. 1-21 — June 28th

No small dissension

The most pernicious form of wrong doctrine is that which has a semblance of truth about it; teaching which appears to be based on the word of God but is really a misappropriation of the scriptures. This doctrinal corruption is even more plausible if the teachers come from somewhere generally accepted as being important or prominent.

Such was the situation facing the church at Antioch, for men had come down from Jerusalem bringing a message based on Old Testament scripture. These men were not teaching that Gentiles could not be saved, nor did they suggest that the gospel should not be preached. What they were saying was that in addition to believing the gospel the Gentiles would also need to be circumcised. This was not some petty issue, it was undermining the very fundamentals of the Christian gospel, and to resolve matters the church at Antioch sent Paul and Barnabas to Jerusalem to meet with the apostles.

In following the narrative from verse 7 onwards we do well to observe the spiritual wisdom shown in resolving this problem. Very appropriately Peter speaks first, for he was the one who had preached the gospel when the first Gentiles had been converted. Barnabas and Paul then followed and they were able to prove that the salvation of the Gentiles without circumcision had been endorsed by God through the miracles and wonders He had wrought among them. James brought matters to a conclusion by showing from the Old Testament prophets that in a future day Gentiles would be blessed without bowing to Jewish rituals. In so doing he demonstrated that what was happening currently was in harmony with the word of God.

All agreed with the two stipulations James presented. Firstly, it should not be expected that the Gentile would subscribe to Jewish rites. Secondly, the Gentiles should show consideration for their Jewish brethren in what they eat and how they behaved. Thus through the spiritual wisdom of these men, that which had the potential to divide God's people was resolved amicably and scripturally. How much we need men of like ability today, men with wisdom and spiritual discernment!

His Apostles

June 29th Acts 15. 22-35

Whilst the conference in Jerusalem was confined to the apostles and elders, they did not communicate their decision back to Antioch until they had discussed it with the whole church. This is an important point and one that should be followed in all assemblies. There will be occasions when elders will be privy to information that cannot be shared with others, but where decisions are made that affect everyone those matters ought to be made known to all in fellowship. This openness of communication enabled the church at Jerusalem to extend greetings to their Gentile brethren, thereby helping to eradicate the problem that had occurred at the start of the chapter.

In verses 23 to 31 we have the details of the letter that was written to the brethren in Antioch and elsewhere, and although it is not a letter of commendation there are a number of principles in it that would equally apply to such letters. The letter says all it needs to, and yet it is succinct. It came from all at Jerusalem and was read to all at Antioch. It begins with a greeting and it concludes with a wish for the spiritual wellbeing of the recipients. Details are given of the spiritual worth and work of the brethren named in the letter. The result of it being read was that they 'rejoiced over its encouragement', v. 31 NKJV.

It needs to be borne in mind that when this incident occurred Christianity was still in a state of transition, moving from Jewish customs to the implementation of New Testament church practices. It would be a few more years before Paul wrote his first letter to the church at Corinth in which he does not mandate that as a principle they should abstain from meats offered to idols. However, he does remind the Corinthians that they should not use such liberty as a means of causing others to stumble.

In detailing what needed to be abstained from, the brethren in Jerusalem were not imposing man-made regulations on the Gentile Christians; they were following the dictate of the Holy Spirit. Similarly, all our practices must be verified in principle or precept by the word of God, and not the legislation of men.

Acts 15. 36 – 16. 15 June 30th

Although the issues are very different, it is sad to observe that chapter 15 ends on a similar note to where it began, for it closes with division. Who would have imagined that two brethren who had preached and taught together, and who had laboured and suffered together for many years would fall out to the extent that 'the contention became so sharp that they parted from one another'? v. 39 NKJV.

A man who had displayed such gracious humility in bringing Saul of Tarsus to Antioch in the early days of the Lord's work there now acts on fleshly impulse. Allowing family ties to cloud his spiritual discernment, Barnabas leaves Antioch without commendation; taking his nephew John Mark with him, he returns to his homeland of Cyprus. What a salutary lesson this is for each of us! We must not allow natural relationships to prejudice our decisions relative to spiritual matters.

Having been commended to the grace of God, Paul sets out from Antioch on his second missionary journey, taking Silas with him. Soon they reach Derbe and Lystra, places where Paul had been some years before. On that former occasion Timothy had been converted through the apostle's preaching, and in the intervening years he had developed spiritually. Being well reported by the assemblies in that region, Timothy was requested by Paul to join with him, and so began a long companionship. Such was the affinity between them that, writing to the church at Philippi, Paul stated, 'I have no man likeminded', Phil. 2. 20.

Working in unison with Timothy, and implementing the prudent measures which had resolved the doctrinal conflict at Antioch, Paul had the joy of seeing the Christians in various cities progressing spiritually such that they were 'established in the faith'. Coupled with that spiritual progress there was a numerical increase on a daily basis. What a thrill it would be to recapture such times of blessing in our day!

Sensitive to the Holy Spirit's guidance, Paul abandoned his attempts to go to Bithynia and moved westwards into Macedonia eventually reaching Philippi. How thankful we should be that he did so, as this is the first time we read of the gospel coming to Europe!

His Apostles

July 1st   Acts 16. 16-40

Sirs, what must I do to be saved?

Immediately prior to His ascension the Lord Jesus gave His disciples a commission in which He stipulated that the gospel was to be preached *everywhere*, 'Go into all the world', and to *everyone*, 'to every creature', Mark 16. 15 NKJV. No one and nowhere was to be exempt; racial and social barriers were to be overcome because 'there is no difference: for all have sinned, and come short of the glory of God', Rom. 3. 22-23.

The establishment of a church in Philippi began with the conversions of three people who were very different socially and religiously. Lydia was an affluent merchant who worshipped God, and her conversion was unspectacular. Luke simply states, 'Whose heart the Lord opened', v. 14. In contrast, the second convert was an afflicted medium, a young slave girl who was demon-possessed. Unlike Lydia, she didn't sit passively listening to Paul but, influenced by the evil spirit, she heckled him day after day. However, the power that graciously opened the heart of a religious woman was equally able to liberate a demonized reprobate; overcome by the authority of the Name of Jesus Christ the spirit left her instantly.

The third convert was neither religious nor demon possessed; he was a callous uncompromising jailer. Whereas Lydia responded to the gospel as softly as a flower opens its petals to the sun, God used an earthquake to get this brutal man to realize his desperate need of salvation. Not only did the doors become unhinged but so did he, for he quivered as much as the foundations of the prison. Awakened from sleep to the consciousness of his dire need, he cried, 'Sirs, what must I do to be saved', v. 30. The response was simple, succinct, and sufficient, 'Believe on the Lord Jesus Christ'.

Over a thousand years before these conversions David said of the sword of Goliath that there was 'none like that', 1 Sam. 21. 9. Those words may be applied to the gospel of God; there is no message like that. It is the power of God unto salvation; it is for all people in all nations. It met the need of a wealthy lady, a wretched slave, and a wicked jailer and, if you are not saved, it can meet your need right now.

Acts 17. 1-15 — July 2nd

A study of Paul's missionary journeys will show that he was not haphazard in his evangelistic work, but he operated very strategically. On leaving Philippi the apostle, together with Silas, continued his journey westward passing through a couple of cities *en route* to Thessalonica. His aim was to reach this thriving metropolis, located on a major transport route, and see a new church commence. The new assembly could then evangelize the surrounding areas and also reach further out by witnessing to those who were passing through.

In one of the readings last week we noted that Paul was an intelligent preacher, for whilst he never attempted to appease his audience, he always presented the gospel in a manner appropriate to those he addressed. Look at the wise way he reasoned with the Jews in verse 3, both his method and message were ideally suited to that specific audience. The consequence of this effort was twofold: there were those who believed and joined Paul, and there were those who believed not. This is how it always will be wherever the preacher of the gospel goes, hence Paul writes, 'To the one we are the savour of death unto death; and to the other the savour of life unto life', 2 Cor. 2. 16.

Due to the uproar caused by the unbelieving Jews, Paul was forced to leave Thessalonica at night and travel to Berea. As usual he looked for the synagogue, for he had a deep yearning for his own nation, which he expressed in his letter to the church in Rome, 'Brethren, my heart's desire and prayer to God for Israel is, that they might be saved', Rom. 10. 1. How receptive these Bereans were, for 'they received the word with all readiness of mind'! v. 11. However, they were not gullible: everything Paul preached they verified from the scriptures. No wonder they are deemed more noble than those in Thessalonica!

Our reading today presents to us two examples that we would benefit from imitating. As churches, we ought, like Paul, to have a definite plan as to how we evangelize within our locality rather than being *ad hoc*. As individuals, we should test all that we hear against the truth of the word of God.

His Apostles

July 3rd   Acts 17. 16-34

His spirit was stirred in him

Whilst waiting for Silas and Timothy to join him at Athens, Paul did not spend his time admiring the grandeur of the heathen temples. Instead, he saw the spiritual blindness that engulfed the city and 'his spirit was stirred in him', v. 16.

Athens was the cultural centre of the world; its citizens spent their time in propounding or listening to the latest philosophy. Sadly, they had not appreciated that 'the fear of the Lord is the beginning of wisdom, Ps. 111. 10, and their vaunted knowledge left them spiritually as dark as night. Despite the city being very religious and revering deities of all kinds, Paul discovered an altar 'TO AN UNKNOWN GOD' and he used that inscription as the starting point for his message.

He began by asserting that God is the creator and as such He is transcendently greater than all creation, and cannot be contained in temples made by men. God intended that man should seek after Him, and His handiwork is an eloquent testimony to His existence, and a revelation of His attributes. He has not left Himself without witness in that 'he did good, and gave us rain from heaven, and fruitful seasons', Acts 14. 17, and in that sense He is 'not far from every one of us', 17. 27. Alas, sin blinded the minds of those it held in bondage and instead of men worshiping God they produced gods of their own imagination, fashioning them out of gold, silver, or stone.

Until Christ came, God dealt patiently with such ignorance and generally He did not move in judgement on idol worshippers. However, following the full revelation of Himself in Christ, man's ignorance is no longer excusable. In contrast to the past, God now 'commands all men everywhere to repent', v. 30 NKJV, because there is coming a time of judgement and the Judge has already been appointed. Men may have crucified Jesus, but this will not prevent Him being the Judge, because God overturned men's actions in raising Him from the dead.

How thankful we should be that the goodness of God led us to repentance, turning us from darkness to light! For us the day of judgement holds no terror, for 'there is therefore now no condemnation to them which are in Christ Jesus', Rom. 8. 1.

Christ and

Acts 18. 1-23 — July 4th

I have much people in this city

Corinth was a distinguished place for it was the principal city in Achaia with a large population. It was located on a major trade route and hosted the Isthmian Games. The city was also divided religiously, for within its boundary there was a Jewish synagogue and several heathen temples. As might be expected from a thriving seaport, Corinth was also debauched; the immorality of the citizens became a byword throughout the region.

From the standpoint of human logic both the message and the messenger were eminently unsuited to effect any change within this huge metropolis. Here was a city that prided itself in its wisdom, so to them the gospel would have seemed utter foolishness. However, writing to the church there some time later the apostle stated, 'It pleased God by the foolishness of preaching to save them that believe', 1 Cor. 1. 21. In relation to the messenger Paul appeared as a very poor specimen of masculinity in comparison to the well-honed athletes that came to the games. He could say of himself, 'I was with you in weakness, and in fear, and in much trembling' 2. 3.

Humanly speaking therefore, Paul's visit to Corinth was bound to fail, but it didn't. Despite his initial trepidation, the Lord promised to keep Paul safe and, assured by the knowledge of divine protection, he remained preaching and teaching in the city for almost two years. The result of this labour was that 'many of the Corinthians hearing believed and were baptized', Acts 18. 8. When Paul eventually moved on he left behind something that had not been there before, something that was distinct from the Jewish synagogue, and from heathen temples: 'the church of God which is at Corinth', 1 Cor. 1. 2.

Paul had moved into this conurbation facing the unknown, being unaware of the reception he would get, and uncertain as to what the outcome would be. However, before he started preaching to the Gentiles God had His eye on Corinth and could say, 'I have much people in this city', Acts 18. 10. Long before we heard the sweet strains of the gospel God also had his eye on us: with wonder we can reflect on the fact that we were chosen in Christ 'before the foundation of the world', Eph. 1. 4.

His Apostles

July 5th — Acts 18. 24 – 19. 20

All they which dwelt in Asia heard the word of the Lord

The case of Apollos and the 'certain disciples' in Ephesus brings before us believers who were acting in accordance with the light that they had received, but whose appreciation of divine truth was defective. It may be asked how they had missed Christ? How had Apollos come under the influence of John's preaching, yet had missed the One of whom he spoke? How had these disciples, when there was an assembly in Ephesus, cp. 18. 27, failed to hear about the Lord Jesus? We cannot answer such questions. All we know is that God in His grace did not leave them in their ignorance but in His time brought them into contact with those who could enlighten them. It is interesting to see that this is not at the same time, nor does God use the same servants: in His wisdom with Apollos, who would be a great preacher, He uses Aquila and Priscilla, whilst with the other disciples He uses the apostle Paul. We might have been tempted to do it the other way round.

Apollos is testimony to the accuracy and detail of the Old Testament scriptures and to the faithful witness of John for, being ignorant of the Lord Jesus, yet he spoke accurately the things of the Lord', v. 25 NKJV, cp. Luke 24. 27, 45-46. For Apollos, then, it was a natural step when Aquila and Priscilla expounded the way 'more accurately', v. 26 NKJV. How thankful he must have been for the time that this godly couple were willing to invest, and what fruit came from it, vv. 27-28!

In chapter 19 we find that the indwelling presence of the Holy Spirit is a characteristic feature of the church age, enjoyed by every true believer in the Lord Jesus. The question, 'Have ye . . . since?' in verse 2 should be better rendered 'Did you . . . when?', that is, on believing, not subsequent to it. On accepting 'Christ Jesus', v. 4, as 'Lord', v. 5 the indwelling of the Spirit was then confirmed to them, v. 6.

When Paul 'spake boldly' in the synagogue, v. 8, cp. 18. 26, there were those who were hardened. Sadly, prolonged exposure to the gospel will not always result in conversion, yet the opposition led to the word being heard throughout all the province of Asia. How often that was the case then, and still is now!

Christ and

Acts 19. 21-41 — July 6th

Great is Diana of the Ephesians

Once again in this passage we see that where the word of God grows mightily, v. 20, the enemy is also active. Here the opposition is not primarily religious nor theological, but financial. The phrases 'no small gain', v. 24, and 'wealth', v. 25, show how much was at stake for Demetrius and his colleagues. Yet, in verse 19, there had been many in Ephesus who had been prepared to burn books of great monetary value because they had gained something far greater – they had found Christ. What a contrast! How tragic that these men could not see it!

The words of Demetrius bear tremendous testimony to the effect of the gospel in that area. Already Luke has commented on this in verse 10 of this chapter, but now Demetrius also acknowledges that the gospel has spread 'almost throughout all Asia', and that 'much people' has been 'turned away', v. 26. First and foremost, this would have a disastrous effect on his livelihood, but he also fears that the great temple of Artemis, one of the seven wonders of the ancient world, would fall into disuse, v. 27. What a contrast with the God of heaven, whose magnificence does not depend on the size or prosperity of His temples, nor upon the number of His followers!

His impassioned speech to his colleagues leads to confusion in the whole city. An impromptu and illegal assembly is formed in the theatre and eventually the slogan taken up first by Demetrius' companions is taken up mindlessly by the whole crowd – 'Great is Artemis of the Ephesians', ESV. Here we have a classic example of crowd mentality. It is senseless, purposeless, and unreasonable. Most of them did not even know why they were there, yet they had joined in anyway. The advice that Paul received from his friends not to venture into the theatre was good. As the preacher of old said, there is 'a time to keep silence,' Eccles. 3. 7. There is a great need for wisdom at such times.

Despite the efforts of Demetrius and his friends the temple of Artemis now lies in ruins. Her magnificence has been destroyed. She is no longer an object of worship. In contrast the gospel is still being preached, souls are still being saved and lives transformed by the power of the risen Christ.

His Apostles

July 7th — Acts 20. 1-16

The disciples came together to break bread

Much is passed over in the first three verses of this chapter. However, once again we see Paul engaged in a ministry of 'much exhortation', v. 2, and facing renewed opposition from the Jews, v. 3. The dangers and trials of this particular stage of his journeys are passed over. Having sent on ahead certain of his companions he sails from Philippi to Troas, once again accompanied by Luke, who now remains with him until the end of the book of Acts, and beyond.

It is interesting to note that although Paul was working to a tight schedule – he wanted to be in Jerusalem at Pentecost, v. 16, less than six weeks away, cp. v. 6 – he was prepared to wait at Troas until the believers met 'to break bread', v. 7. A number of points can be inferred from this. Firstly, the importance of the breaking of bread: Paul did not want to miss it more often than he could help. Secondly, it was the focal point of the gathering: it is the reason given for their coming together, that is, it was not Paul's preaching that drew them, with the breaking of bread tagged on as an extra. Thirdly, it was observed only on the first day of the week: the day was not changed simply because Paul was there and was in a hurry. Fourthly, although the day itself was fixed it was conducted at a time that was convenient for the believers: it is evident that they came together in the evening which was presumably the first opportunity that they had for doing so.

Note the dedication of these believers. They gathered at the end of, for some of them (Eutychus probably to be included), a hard day's work. Then they were prepared to listen to Paul until midnight initially, then 'even till break of day', v. 11, thence to go back to another hard day's work on the Monday. How many of us consider an hour's ministry meeting to be long enough? How much do we appreciate the fellowship of saints and the nourishment of the word of God?

We cannot be too hard on Eutychus. How many of us in similar circumstances would have done the same? Perhaps he wanted the cooler air from the open window to help him to stay awake? At any rate, in the mercy of God tragedy was averted.

Christ and

Acts 20. 17-38

July 8th

This section gives a number of insights: firstly, into the experience of the apostle Paul; secondly, into the role and function of elders in an assembly. Note regarding elders that: (1) there is a plurality of them and that they are a distinct and recognized group within the assembly, v. 17; (2) they are to be spiritually mature, denoted by the term 'elders'; (3) they are appointed by the Holy Spirit and are responsible to Him, remembering that it is God's assembly, v. 28. They also have a responsibility to the assembly as overseers and shepherds, v. 28 – note the terms 'flock', to 'take heed', 'to feed', to 'watch', and to 'remember', vv. 28, 31. In the fulfilling of their responsibilities Paul points them to his own example, vv. 26-27, 33-35 and commends them to God and to His word, the importance of which he stresses in verse 32.

In relation to Paul we see his tears in this chapter: tears arising from afflictions and opposition, v. 19, and tears that fell as he sought to warn the believers persistently of the dangers that they would face from false teachers, v. 31. We are reminded that the Lord Jesus, too, shed tears. Paul is not ashamed to speak of them as, perhaps, many of us would be. We understand, therefore, that the work of a true shepherd or of a preacher will involve many tears.

Notice, too, his faithfulness in declaring the word of God, vv. 20-21. His preaching was comprehensive: he 'kept back nothing'. It was 'profitable'. It was varied: he both 'shewed' or 'announced' and 'taught', that is, he declared the truth of God whether or not people would listen, and taught it to those who would, with a view to their increase in understanding. He was consistent: what he said publicly was the same as what he said 'from house to house'. He did not confine his activities to 'the platform' but also sought to instruct believers privately. Finally it was universal: 'both to the Jews, and also to the Greeks'. As a result he had confidence before God that he was 'pure from the blood of all men', v. 26, for he had 'not shunned to declare . . . all the counsel of God'. How many of us could say the same?

No wonder the believers 'wept sore' at the thought that they would not see him again, v. 37.

His Apostles

July 9th

Acts 21. 1-17

I am ready not to be bound only

The journey continues in this section, taking Paul and those with him from Miletus to Jerusalem. When they arrived in Tyre, they 'found', or better, 'sought out and found' the believers. This was not a chance encounter but a deliberate seeking out. Surely this is what we should do if we travel anywhere. As a result they were able to enjoy fellowship with one another for the week and when it was time to move on the believers all came out to see them off, v. 5. Note, too, the natural place that prayer has in their experience, cp. 20. 36. It is a wonderful privilege to have fellowship with believers in different places and we miss out on a lot if we do not take advantage of it.

Yet there is not only fellowship here. The believers also bring Paul a warning, 21. 4. In the previous chapter Paul told the Ephesian elders that 'in every city' he was being told what he was to expect at Jerusalem, 20. 22-23. In today's passage, too, Agabus comes to tell him the same thing, 21. 11. As a result the believers urge him not to go to Jerusalem, vv. 4, 12. Paul's response is essentially the same as in chapter 20: that is, that he is ready to die for the name of the Lord Jesus, if need be, and that his desire is that he might finish his course with joy and fulfil the ministry that he has received, cp. 20. 24. These, then, are the reasons that he gives for not avoiding Jerusalem, as many of us might have done in similar circumstances. Yet, we may ask whether he was right to do so? Why did the Lord tell him what was going to happen if He did not want him to take evasive action? Would it not have been better had he remained at liberty? However, the Lord may rather have been preparing Paul for what would take place. Had He not done so, it may well have been perplexing and demoralizing for Paul to endure imprisonment. And what would liberty have been worth if it was not the Lord's will for him? When we consider what has resulted from Paul's imprisonment we may be thankful that he, like the Lord Jesus, was unmoved by such knowledge! Whilst we do not know what trials lie ahead may we, too, be resolved to do the Lord's will, and to stand up for the name of the Lord Jesus, whatever the personal cost.

Christ and

Acts 21. 18-40 — July 10th

Bound with two chains

It must have been wonderful to hear Paul's detailed account of his missionary journeys, of which we only have a small part recorded for us. It is no wonder that those who heard it 'glorified the Lord', v. 20. Notice what Paul declares: it is 'what things God had wrought', v. 19 – Paul ascribes all the glory to Him. What a privilege to be workers together with God! Yet, we must always remember that it is *His* work.

The section that follows illustrates the difficulty that many Jewish believers had with leaving behind the trappings of Judaism on conversion to Christ. Yet, Paul does not argue with them over their request. As he teaches elsewhere, he is prepared to submit to them to avoid stumbling others or causing disunity amongst the believers. It is ironic, therefore, that it is as he is seeking to demonstrate his adherence to the law that he is accused by the Jews of doing the opposite, v. 28. Note that it is not the Jews of Jerusalem who cause trouble for him, but the Jews of Asia. Note, too, that the accusation that seems to have stirred up the Jews most, namely that he had brought Gentiles into the temple, thus polluting it, v. 28, was not true but merely a supposition. How often it is the case, that unfounded rumours or mere suppositions cause the most trouble and heartache for the people of God! Such is the ensuing tumult that Paul is beaten and would have been killed had the chief captain not stepped in and saved him. We see, then, the sovereign hand of God, who yet had work for Paul to do. Luke graphically describes the scene, and we can picture it as the soldiers run down into the crowd and bind him with two chains, cp. v. 11, the chief captain questions the people, and the soldiers then carry Paul up the stairs to the fortress, being harried by the riotous crowd. All this we can picture, but we cannot imagine what it must have been like for Paul to be in the middle of it, for his body to be bruised and battered, to see the savagery on the faces of the people crowding around him, trying to reach him, baying for his blood.

Would we have done what he does next? Would we have requested to speak to the people or would we have taken shelter? Yet what an opportunity is now afforded to him!

His Apostles

July 11th   Acts 22. 1-21

So, Paul starts his defence before the people. How does he do it? Does he justify himself? Does he protest his innocence? Does he harangue them for making unfounded accusations? No! He tells his testimony. It must have been an amazing event to witness. Luke records that there was a 'great silence', 21. 40, and then comments that, when they heard him speak to them in Hebrew, the local language, they 'kept the more silence', 22. 2. What a contrast to the tumult only moments before!

Notice the respect and courtesy with which he addresses the people, v. 1. He stresses the orthodoxy of his upbringing, mentioning the well-respected Rabbi Gamaliel as his mentor. He speaks of his zeal toward God, v. 3, and acknowledges that they too shared it, though 'not according to knowledge' as he will say in Romans chapter 10 verse 2. He calls the high priest and the elders to witness to his pre-conversion manner of life, v. 5, that he had been a persecutor of believers in Christ. Here was not a man who was easily convinced or gullible, but a man who had been stopped in his tracks by a direct revelation from heaven of the risen Christ. Truly, the conversion of Saul of Tarsus is one of the great evidences for the truth of the resurrection. Note that there is not one voice raised in dissent; they knew the truth of what he was saying.

He then recounts the details of what took place on the Damascus road and Ananias' subsequent visit to him. Note that Paul makes it absolutely clear which 'Jesus' spoke to him, v. 8 – it is 'Jesus of Nazareth'.

He finally returns in thought to Jerusalem and to the temple itself where he receives, first of all, a divine warning that the Jews would seek his life, cp. 9. 29. In response Paul reaffirms his previous manner of life, which the Jews all knew. How, then, could they fail to accept the testimony of one who had known such a radical change? Yet, as a nation, they had rejected the Lord Jesus and the subsequent testimony of Stephen. Now they would reject Paul's testimony, too. Paul then relates how that in the temple he received the divine commission to go to the Gentiles. How would the Jews respond?

Christ and

Acts 22. 22 – 23. 11   July 12th

The Jews' response is to hear him up to this point but no further. In Luke chapter 4 it was the Lord's reference to God's gracious dealings with Gentiles that provoked the people to try to cast Him over the brow of the hill. So, too, here it is the divine commission to the Gentiles that is one step too far for the Jews. Yet, how we rejoice that the grace of God is not limited to one nation, nor to one level of society, nor to a specific type of person, but that salvation is offered to the 'whosoever'. Sad indeed if we, in our thinking, should exclude any from God's universal invitation!

For the second time, a riot arises on account of Paul, and the chief captain understandably desires to discover what Paul has done and so commands him to be scourged. Whilst on many occasions Paul is prepared to endure beatings, cp. 2 Cor. 11, this time he makes it known to the centurion that he is a Roman citizen. The reason for this, I judge, is that this was more than simply a question of Paul's personal rights. This had to do with justice: the chief captain was supposedly an upholder of law and order on behalf of the Roman government and yet was prepared to torture a man who was not only uncondemned but innocent. Paul was able to use his status as a Roman citizen to bring the man under conviction, with the result that the situation was radically and rapidly altered, Acts 22. 29.

The next day, therefore, the captain does what he should have done initially and brings Paul before the religious leaders to find out what he is accused of. Paul's fearlessness as he stands before them, 23. 1-3, his graciousness, v. 5, and his wisdom to discern his audience, vv. 6-9, are all displayed.

For the third time, then, a riot arises and Paul is rescued by the soldiers. We can only imagine what Paul must have been feeling by this time, despite having known that it would take place. However, in verse 11 we read that 'the Lord stood by him'. Not only so, but He gave Paul a promise that he would testify for Him in Rome. What a comfort and encouragement this must have been both at the time and in the dark days of imprisonment, and the shipwreck that lay ahead. The One who stood by him then would stand by him all the way.

His Apostles

July 13th

Acts 23. 12-35

Nothing laid to his charge worthy of death

Hard on the heels of the Lord's promise to Paul comes another attempt on his life. We are reminded that the enemy is constantly active in trying to thwart the purposes of God. In this instance he has more than forty willing accomplices. Like Paul in unconverted days, they are fanatical in their opposition to the gospel, and will go to any lengths to eradicate it. Their plan was simple and, humanly speaking, fool-proof, for there would be no reason for the captain to mistrust their intention.

However, the Lord who had guaranteed safe passage to Rome to His servant would not fail him now. The plan was overheard and made known to the captain, and steps were taken to move Paul safely to Caesarea in high security and secrecy, v. 23. May we never lose sight of the fact that the Lord has His hand upon us at all times. He is in control of all our circumstances, and His will and His promises cannot be thwarted.

The letter that the captain sends to Felix the governor is interesting. We note with irony how he makes much of his own heroism and patriotism in saving a Roman citizen from death at the hands of the Jews, remembering that the reality was somewhat different. Yet, amongst it all, he writes that there was 'nothing laid to his charge worthy of death or of bonds', v. 29. This is to be a recurring theme over the next chapters, testified by various individuals, but still Paul remains bound. Why? Simply put, because it was the Lord's will. Many times in life we cannot understand the workings of God, reasons for events that take place, or why certain trials are not lifted when we want or expect them to be, but we may be sure that He has a purpose in it all, as He had for Paul. If we submit ourselves to Him that purpose will be worked out for His glory.

Under cover of night they bring Paul to Antipatris, just over half way to Caesarea as the crow flies and, the most dangerous part of the journey now lying behind them, the soldiers head back to Jerusalem and the rest of the party carry on to Caesarea. Paul's background evidently made some impression on Felix, v. 34, reminding us again of the Lord's hand in all things. In addition, he was to be kept in the praetorium – the officers' quarters.

Christ and

Acts 24. 1-27 — July 14th

When I have a convenient season

Over the next three chapters Paul has the opportunity to bring the gospel to three high-profile individuals: Felix, Festus, and King Agrippa. Each of them represents a different but equally tragic response to the gospel message. None of them, as far as we know, made the vital decision to bow to the Lordship of Christ.

When the Jews arrived in Caesarea they hired an orator by the name of Tertullus to accuse Paul. He comes with eloquence and flattery, and with flagrant distortion of the truth, in order to accomplish his ends. By way of contrast, Paul clearly and simply rebuffs the charges laid against him. Was Felix in any doubt about the matter? The answer is, 'No'. The way in which Paul was treated in verse 23 suggests that Felix knew he was innocent.

So what kind of a man was Felix? The picture painted by Tertullus is of a kind, benevolent ruler who had brought peace and stability to the region. However, historians tell us otherwise. Apparently Felix was a licentious and cruel man, under whose governorship crime, feuding, and looting rocketed which, because he profited from it, he initially allowed to continue, but was then caused to take drastic measures to bring under control. In verse 26 of our passage, we learn that he was also corrupt, looking for a bribe from Paul in order to release him. This and his lack of concern for justice are also seen in that when he left office he also left Paul in prison.

It is no wonder, then, that when Paul reasoned with him of 'righteousness, temperance, and judgment to come', v. 25, he trembled, for he had much on his conscience. What did he know of justice or of self-control? Well might he tremble at the thought of coming judgement! What an opportunity he had, as he heard of 'faith in Christ', v. 24, and yet we hear the tragic words 'when I have a convenient season'. Here we have the solemn reminder that fear is not faith. Despite further conversations with Paul, as far as we know he was never converted. Drusilla, his wife, perished in the eruption of Mount Vesuvius. How salutary the lesson to us that we do not know what a day may bring forth, and that 'now is the day of salvation'! 2 Cor. 6. 2.

His Apostles

July 15th   Acts 25. 1-22

I stand at Caesar's judgment seat

Felix's successor was Porcius Festus, an altogether different character. Whereas Felix had been susceptible to bribes and flattery, Festus appears to have been confident in his authority and concerned with doing things properly. Thus, he does not accede to their request to bring Paul up to Jerusalem but exercises that authority in making the Jews come to Caesarea, in order that Paul might have a fair trial in accordance with Roman law. However, he is not beyond making political decisions at the expense of justice for, when Paul's accusers come and bring their unfounded accusations against him, the case should have been dismissed then. Festus, though, prolongs the issue, wanting to strengthen his own position by granting the Jews a favour, v. 9. At the same time it is clear that he was ignorant of Jewish religion and had never heard of the Lord Jesus, and may have genuinely wanted to get to the bottom of the matter.

Paul therefore appeals to Caesar. It was his right as a Roman citizen, but was he right to do so? Paul knew the hearts of his fellow countrymen, that they were set on murdering him whatever it took. After his appeal and its being granted Jewish opposition was silenced, and he does not face it again in Luke's account. Yet, as Agrippa later says, he could have been set at liberty had he not appealed, 26. 32. Could not the Lord have preserved him before the Jews? The answer is, of course, 'Yes'. The Lord had promised that Paul would testify for Him in Rome and so he would. Yet, in this appeal we surely see the Lord's hand. Remaining bound Paul had the opportunity to preach to both Festus and Agrippa, which he would not have had otherwise, he was conducted to Rome at Roman expense, Malta was reached with the gospel on the way and, once in Rome, he would potentially have the opportunity to stand before Caesar himself. How important it is to be sensitive to the leading of the Lord, to know when to speak and when to remain silent, to know when to assert our rights as citizens of an earthly country, knowing as believers we have nothing to fear from justice, Rom. 13. 3-4, and when simply to submit to earthly authority as ordained by God! May the Lord give us such wisdom.

Christ and

Acts 25. 23 – 26. 11   July 16th

What a scene is depicted for us at the beginning of our passage! Agrippa and his sister, Bernice, arrive with great ceremony and the great and the good of Caesarea are all gathered together. Festus explains his predicament to them: Paul has appealed to Caesar and yet there are no legitimate crimes that can be laid against him. What should he write? How can he justify sending him to be heard by the emperor? It is good when our testimony is such that the world can find nothing whatever against us. We are to be 'blameless and harmless . . . without rebuke', Phil. 2. 15. Such was Paul's testimony. Such, now was Paul's opportunity. What would he say before such an august company? What would we say if given the opportunity to speak to royalty? Before Felix he had reasoned of 'righteousness, temperance, and judgment to come', Acts 24. 25; here he once again tells his testimony. We may recall his determination when he came to Corinth, a place where great oratory was prized, 'not to know any thing among you, save Jesus Christ, and him crucified', 1 Cor. 2. 2.

When given permission by Agrippa to speak, Paul says that he counts himself 'happy', literally 'blessed', v. 2, to be able to offer his defence before him. In contrast to Festus who knew nothing of Jewish customs and laws, and Felix who, because of his length of time in office, would have been aware of some of them, he knows that Agrippa is an 'expert', v. 3. Here there was a starting point, a common ground on which to build. He could speak freely without fear of losing his audience. It seems to be increasingly rare in the day in which we live to find those who have any knowledge of the scriptures at all. Indeed, it is safer in our gospel preaching to assume no knowledge rather than risk losing our audience.

To Agrippa he speaks of the 'hope of the promise made of God', v. 6, that is, the resurrection of the dead. The nation of Israel and Paul before he was converted were dedicated in their pursuit of that hope, not apprehending that it cannot be earned, but is obtained by faith, and that, in Christ. Let us pray for the nation of Israel that their eyes may be opened.

Thou art permitted to speak for thyself

His Apostles

July 17th Acts 26. 12-32

Paul goes into more detail here regarding his previous manner of life than anywhere else, leaving his hearers in no doubt as to the dramatic nature of the transformation that took place. We see the grace of God in all its glory as it is extended to a man who was so diametrically opposed to the gospel.

Paradoxically, the light that blinded him physically was the means of opening his eyes spiritually, for in it was revealed to him the Man in the glory, 'Jesus whom thou persecutest', v. 15. Having had his own eyes opened he was then commissioned to do the same for others, in particular the Gentiles, v. 17. Having been given such a commission he is diligent to fulfil it. We too have been commissioned, Mark 16. 15 – do we show the same diligence or are we disobedient?

It is interesting to notice Paul's method of preaching in these verses. At this point he makes clear the requirements of the gospel, Acts 26. 20, without bringing a direct challenge to his hearers, outlining the blessings that accompany salvation without presenting an invitation for them to experience them for themselves. The challenge and personal application come later.

There are two responses to Paul's testimony. The first, from Festus, is of derision, 'You are mad', he says. Paul addresses this heckling and answers it but does not dwell on it. In Festus' intervention we can see an attempt of the evil one to distract attention. But Paul is not to be distracted for he directs his remarks once again to Agrippa and brings to him the challenge of what he has been saying. 'Believest thou the prophets?' If so, the inference is clear: he has a responsibility to place faith in the One of whom they spoke.

'Almost thou persuadest me', v. 28. Whether in sarcasm or sincerity the response rings with indecision, a failure to act. So near, and yet so far! Small comfort the verdict that Agrippa gives, that Paul could have been set free had he not appealed to Caesar, v. 32, if his own soul remained bound in sin and darkness. There is no doubting the sincerity with which Paul says, 'I would to God . . . not only almost . . .', v. 29. 'Sad, sad that bitter wail – "*almost* – but lost!"' PHILIP P. BLISS.

Acts 27. 1-26   July 18th

When the time came for Paul to be sent to Italy, Luke went with him – note the 'we' in verse 1. It is not certain how many of his companions went with him, although Aristarchus is mentioned by name, v. 2. This must have been of great comfort to Paul as he took his journey. Also, Luke appears to have been his constant companion until the end of his life. Even when others forsook him, Luke, the 'beloved physician', was there, so that Paul says, 'Only Luke is with me', 2 Tim. 4. 11.

Paul was delivered into the custody of a centurion named Julius. There are a number of centurions mentioned in scripture who appear to have been good men, e.g., Luke 7; Acts 10. This one is no exception, for he seems to have treated Paul well and to have given him a fair amount of liberty, Acts 27. 3. We can see the goodness of God in this choice from Paul's point of view. Yet, what a privilege was that of the centurion to be in close proximity to Paul! Whilst there is no written account of Paul preaching to him, he was able to observe his manner of life and demeanour, especially during the storm, and to observe his confidence in God. Indeed, although we do not read of his conversion we can see a marked change in his attitude towards Paul and the things he said over the course of the chapter. So should it be with us. As those in the world observe our lives, whilst they may not like us or agree with us, we should earn their respect, and glory will be brought to the God whom we serve.

The centurion had a great responsibility. Though the ship's master was in charge of sailing the ship, it was the centurion who had the final say, v. 11. God graciously gave them a warning; if they had heeded it, the ship and its cargo would have been saved, not just the people on board, v. 10. They chose to ignore it and suffered the consequences. Once they had exhausted their resources and with all hope gone Paul later reminds them of this, yet at the same time he brings them a wonderful promise from God that their lives would be saved. 'I believe God', he says, v. 25, and that this faith was not misplaced would soon be demonstrated to all.

His Apostles

July 19th   *Acts 27. 27 – 28. 6*

They escaped all safe to land

Faith trusts despite the storm. The fourteenth night had come and still there was no prospect of salvation. Yet, whilst it is clear that the others on board did not have the confidence that Paul had he continued to rest upon the promise of God. We notice the cowardly actions of the shipmen who sought to escape by stealth, leaving the rest to perish without their expertise. We are not surprised, for it is the way of the flesh to act in self-preservation. However, their actions cannot escape the all-seeing eye of God; their presence on board was necessary to secure the safety of the rest.

Despite Paul's earlier reassurance, those on board had not eaten for fourteen days. He now shows them publicly that his faith is not just theoretical: by eating in front of them, and encouraging them to do the same. Note how he also gives thanks publicly. What do we do in trying circumstances? Does anxiety consume us or are we able to rest in the One who holds us in His almighty hand? Do we, as Paul, 'in every thing give thanks', *1 Thess. 5. 18*? Is it clear to all that our confidence is in God?

The reason why the shipmen had to remain on board is now made manifest: there were a number of procedures that had to be carried out that only they would have known how to do. Again we see the overriding wisdom and control of God, who organizes events and people in accordance with His purpose.

The next potential problem that arises to prevent the fulfilment of this purpose is the counsel of the soldiers to kill the prisoners. Yet here the centurion steps in, 'willing to save Paul', *Acts 27. 43*. And so the divine promise is kept: all 276 souls reach land safely, an evidence of divine grace and miraculous preservation! Even those who could not swim reached land safely. How these events must have spoken to all involved!

We may note that all were saved because of one man. To Paul it was said, 'God hath given thee all them that sail with thee', *v. 24*. Does this mean that all were eventually saved in a spiritual, as well as a physical sense? It may well do – they would certainly have been without excuse! Did initial failure to listen, though causing trial, actually result in greater blessing?

Christ and

Acts 28. 7-31   July 20th

Not long after they arrive on shore there is a further attack of the enemy: a viper comes out of the heat of the fire and strikes Paul on the hand. Over these past few chapters we have seen so many attacks on Paul's life, as the enemy would seek to thwart God's purpose. It is hard to imagine how Paul must have felt with such sustained pressure against him. However, once again we see that our God is far greater than the enemy. As so often, what starts out as an attack of the enemy turns instead to the glory of God. The islanders' conclusion that Paul was a god gave him an attentive audience to which he could explain the truth. The healing of Publius' father, and, subsequently, of many others on the island, would also have given authority to the message that he brought to them, as pagans, who knew nothing of God.

And so the gospel came to Malta. Yet, it came by way of a shipwreck. Had they taken Paul's advice they would have bypassed the island altogether, yet all was under the controlling hand of the Almighty. Often, when we are passing through difficult circumstances, it is easy to forget this, but, as we have seen already, the result that the Lord has in mind is far greater than we could imagine. Let us, then, take encouragement from this.

Whether verse 10 refers to the whole company, or just Paul and his companions, it is clear that others benefitted from the actions and testimony of the apostle. How often it is the case that one person standing for the Lord will bring blessing on those around, even the ungodly!

So Paul arrives in Italy. Note the change that has taken place, v. 14. Although Paul is still technically a prisoner he is now much more than that. The brethren at Puteoli desire them to stay for a week and there is no voice raised against it. The journey to Rome is one of joy and fellowship as the believers come out to meet him. What an encouragement it was to Paul to see them, v. 15. It wasn't much that they did, but it meant a lot to him! In Rome, no doubt on the centurion's recommendation, he was permitted to stay in his own hired house and to continue 'preaching . . . and teaching . . . no man forbidding him', v. 31.

So we went toward Rome

His Apostles

Introduction to Romans

The Epistle to the Romans is a wonderful setting forth of the gospel of God. It describes how God has provided the means whereby the guilty, through grace, may be the sharers of His glory. It explains in cogent argument that though 'he that justifieth the wicked, and he that condemneth the just, even they both are abomination to the Lord', Prov. 17. 15, it is, in fact, a just God who justifies the ungodly 'which believeth in Jesus', Rom. 3. 26.

To have a grasp of the truth of Romans is essential for all believers. It establishes one in the 'word of the truth of the gospel', Col. 1. 5, thereby giving assurance in the matter of the soul's salvation and, at the same time, furnishing one with that which is vital for witnessing to the guilty about their standing before God. It has often been said that 'a true Roman can go anywhere'.

It is generally recognized that this letter falls into three parts. The opening eight chapters expound the doctrine of the gospel, with particular emphasis on a righteousness which God has provided, and which is available to all, through the work of Calvary. Two matters prevent a person from having a clear standing before God. They are: (1) what he has done in practice, his sins; and (2) what he is by nature, a sinner. The answer lies in the blood and death of God's Son. The next three chapters, nine to eleven, deal with questions arising from the first section in relation to the nation of Israel. There is present gospel blessing available to Israelites (even though God is not now dealing with them nationally and the gospel is also going out to Gentiles) and in the future there will be national blessing, in accordance with the ancient promises of God to the nation of Israel, 'for the gifts and calling of God are without repentance', Rom. 11. 29. The final five chapters demonstrate that the gospel makes reasonable demands upon believers to be yielded to God in daily living, in view of His mercies toward them. Behavioural change is demanded by the gospel and is evidence of the reality of conversion.

Romans is not the easiest book to understand, but its truth is both establishing and liberating for the believer.

Romans 1. 1-17   July 21st

At the beginning of the first chapter of Romans and at the end of the last chapter reference is made to the fact that the gospel is made known to all nations for 'the obedience of faith'. These two references stand, as it were, as two great columns on which the whole tapestry of the Epistle is hung. They inform us, firstly, that the gospel offer spreads beyond the nation of Israel (to whom the law was given) to all nations, and, secondly, that the proper response to the message is one where a person yields in faith to its claims. This is not just an intellectual or emotional assent to its truth, but a yielding of the will to Christ.

Paul was particularly the 'apostle of the Gentiles', 11. 13 and as such had a great desire that he might go to Rome that the believers might be established, 1. 11, and that he might have fruit among them, v. 13. Three statements tell us of the apostle's mind as he thinks of making the arduous journey to Rome. **'I am debtor'**, v. 14, indicates that he considered that he owed it to God to preach the gospel to all kinds of people. In view of this he tells them, **'I am ready'**, v. 15, to pay that debt at Rome. This would not be out of a mere sense of duty, but he served God in his spirit, v. 9. Although there would have been many competing philosophies and ideologies at Rome, the centre of the empire, Paul indicates, **'I am not ashamed'** of the gospel, v. 16, and then proceeds to state his reasons.

Perhaps the most important word in the Roman Epistle is 'righteousness'. In God's courtroom, man needs a right standing before the Judge. The Judge is righteous, and a person can stand before Him only in a righteousness as perfect as His own. The apostle will demonstrate that the law made all kinds of demands but was powerless to produce for man the righteousness that it demanded. However, the gospel fully reveals a righteousness which God has provided which is not on the basis of man's works, as every other religious message in the world insists it must be, but on the basis of the work of Christ at Calvary. That righteousness is, in the gospel, offered to faith, and is unfailingly reckoned by God to every believer in Jesus. Truly, 'The just shall live by faith', v. 17.

The gospel of God . . . concerning his Son

His Apostles

July 22nd

Romans 1. 18-32

God gave them up

From this point until chapter 3 verse 19 the apostle brings forward three main witnesses 'that every mouth may be stopped, and all the world may become guilty before God'. He looks back to world history before Calvary and sees that man's need of a righteousness from God is demonstrated by the fact that man consistently acted against the light that God gave him.

The first of the witnesses Paul calls in God's courtroom is the creation. Creation reveals to man the eternal existence and power of God. This is not mere intelligent design but God showing to man things that are eternally true of Him by means of that which He made. This is one reason why creation is in the form it is; and it should have resulted in man glorifying God and being thankful, v. 21, and worshipping and serving Him, v. 25. Such is the evidential power of creation that man is without excuse and the fact that he acts contrary to that evidence, by becoming vain in his imagination and dark in his heart, shows that however wise man professes himself to be he is, in fact, a fool to suppress that knowledge of God that He has revealed.

It should be noted that this passage is not teaching that if man had believed in the eternal existence and power of God he would have been saved. Rather, it teaches that the guilt of man is established by the fact that man acted contrary to the clear evidence that creation gave him.

The deliberate exclusion of the eternally existing and powerful God from the mind and heart of man leads, inevitably, to corruption and perversion. Where there is no absolute reference point for morality there is no right and wrong; all is mere opinion. The morally squalid history of the world shows this and gives evidence for God's judgement on man by 'giving him up' to 'uncleanness', 'vile affections', and 'a reprobate mind'. Man practised that which is unclean and dishonourable, v. 24; vile and unnatural, v. 26; unseemly and erroneous, v. 27. Modern man, too, with all his boasts of being progressive and diverse, is no better morally than ancient man. He glories in his shame, given up to a mind that cannot determine that which is right and wrong, and filled with every kind of sin.

Christ and

Romans 2. 1-29 — July 23rd

Thou art inexcusable, O man

The next witness to man's inexcusable guilt before God is conscience. There were those who did not have the law of God as the nation of Israel had it, 'written with the finger of God' on tables of stone, Exod. 31. 18. Nevertheless, they had shown 'the work of the law written in their hearts', Rom. 2. 15, by acting at times according to a conscience of what is right. However, they also acted against the conscience God had given them and were thus guilty before Him; their guilt exacerbated by the fact that they condemned others for committing the sins of chapter 1 whilst doing the same thing themselves, 1. 29-32. In contrast, 'the judgment of God is according to truth against them which commit such things', 2. 2, and God's judgement is inescapable.

When God judges He will do so fairly. If a person were to seek for glory, honour, and immortality by unfailingly continuing in well doing he would be rewarded with eternal life by the just Judge, v. 7, for that would be perfect law keeping, but in fact 'there is none that doeth good, no, not one', 3. 12. Equally just is the judgement of God that will visit indignation, wrath, tribulation, and anguish on all who, rather than obeying the truth, obey unrighteousness and do evil. What a day it will be when the secrets of the heart are exposed, and all is judged according to absolute righteousness.

Another irrefutable witness is introduced into the courtroom from verse 17 of chapter 2 onwards. The evidence is particularly directed against that nation which had received the law of God at Sinai: a law which set out the righteous standards of God for human behaviour towards God and man. Addressing the Jew, Paul reminds him of the fact that he rested in the law as the foundation for his life, and boasted in God. In fact, the Jews had despised those nations which had no such revelation of God's will, guiding the blind, instructing the foolish, and teaching the babes, but at the same time continually breaking the very law in which they boasted. That in which they rejoiced actually condemned them. They are, therefore, without excuse, along with the Gentiles, and stand guilty before God, with nothing to say in their defence. These witnesses show the need for a righteousness *from God*.

His Apostles

July 24th   Romans 3. 1-31

God's verdict on mankind is written in stark terms. Both Jew and Gentile are proved to be 'all under sin', v. 9, and the whole world has 'become guilty before God', v. 19. There is 'none righteous', 'none that understandeth', 'none that seeketh after God', 'none that doeth good'. Indeed, their throat, their tongues, their lips, their mouth, their feet, and their eyes are used in the service of sin.

The law served to set out the righteous standards of God for man but it also demonstrated the complete incapacity of man to produce righteousness for himself by adherence to that law. If a person is to have a right standing before God it will not therefore be one brought about by his own efforts. God will need to provide that righteousness which we require, and in wondrous grace He has done so. 'All have sinned', but a righteousness from God is offered 'unto all' without exception, and it is 'upon all them that believe', vv. 22-23.

For a just God to justify those who believe in Jesus it is absolutely essential that the claims of His righteous throne be met with regard to the question of sins. An unrighteous God would not be worthy of trust. The glory of the gospel lies in the fact that God Himself has acted so that a person is justified freely, without meritorious cause in himself, through the redemption that is in Christ Jesus. This redemption is altogether impossible apart from His shed blood. God has set Him forth to view – 'a propitiation through faith in his blood', v. 25.

We owe everything to the blood of Christ which He shed sacrificially at Calvary. On the Day of Atonement, the shed blood of a sin offering was sprinkled on, and before, the mercy seat. In picture, divine justice was satisfied and man had a righteous standing in the presence of God. The picture is of Calvary. There, satisfaction was rendered to God by the Lord Jesus Christ in the blood which He shed, and an infinite provision was made by the infinite worth of the sacrifice made by God's infinite Son. All are guilty, but in divine grace all are offered a righteousness from God, to be received by faith in His Son now seated at the right hand of God.

Christ and

Romans 4. 1-22 — July 25th

Faith is counted for righteousness

In chapters 1 to 3 it has been established that man stands in need of righteousness and that he cannot provide it for himself. The glory of the gospel is seen in that God has provided that which man needs and has done so freely. In the first chapter we learn that a righteousness from God is revealed in the gospel of Christ, and that it is a righteousness to be received by faith. In chapter 3 reference is made to a righteousness from God 'which is by faith', v. 22; it is 'upon all them that believe', v. 22b; the benefits of the propitiation in His blood are enjoyed 'through faith', v. 25; and God is 'the justifier of him which believeth in Jesus', v. 26.

In the fourth chapter the apostle enlarges upon the subject of faith and shows that, as the means by which divine blessing is appropriated, faith is deeply rooted in the Old Testament. At the start of the chapter reference is made to Genesis chapter 15 verse 6, a pivotal verse in relation to the subject of saving faith, and Psalm 32. In Genesis, Abraham was justified through faith, and he who believed the promise of God was accordingly reckoned righteous. David, who after great failure knew the mercy of God, also enjoyed the blessings of the justified man, for he describes 'the blessedness of the man, unto whom God imputeth righteousness without works', Rom. 4. 6.

The nature of Abraham's faith was that he believed God, who would fulfil His promise to him that he would be the heir of the world. This necessitated the birth of a son to Abraham and Sarah at a time in their lives when faith would need to disregard the deadness both of Abraham's body and of Sarah's womb. If God's promise were to be fulfilled it would be in no part due to any power of Abraham and Sarah; it would completely depend on the power of God, who is clearly presented here as the God of resurrection. Abraham was fully persuaded that what God had promised He was able also to perform, and because of this faith he was reckoned righteous by God. Faith is not righteousness, nor is it in the place of righteousness, as if it were meritorious, but it is 'unto righteousness': it was because he exercised faith that God put righteousness to his account.

His Apostles

July 26th — Romans 4. 23 – 5. 11

Justified by faith

The narrative of Abraham's faith and the fact that it was imputed unto him for righteousness was written so that we might have the same kind of faith as he did, and similarly know what it is to be reckoned righteous. As Abraham believed the God of resurrection, so do those who believe 'on him that raised up Jesus our Lord from the dead', v. 24. When our Lord was delivered up for our offences He accomplished everything that was necessary for our justification. Thereafter, He was raised again by God and those who believe are justified in that risen Man.

The happy results are varied and abundant. No longer is the believer under judgement, for he has *peace* with God. All guilt has been removed, for God has acquitted the believer and has declared him to be *righteous* before Him. Further, he has a standing in *grace* and rejoices as he considers that the *hope* lying before him embraces all that is connected with the glory of God. This impacts upon his daily life as he rejoices in the midst of tribulations, because their outcome will be patience, experience, and hope. We have the Holy Spirit given unto us and He has shed abroad in our hearts the love of God.

What love is this! When we were *without strength* Christ died for the ungodly, v. 6. When we were *sinners* Christ died for us, v. 8. When we were *enemies* we were reconciled to God by the death of His Son, v. 10. His love surpasses human love, for whereas a man might dare to die for a good man and, with difficulty, for a righteous man, who but Christ has died for the ungodly, for sinners, and for those who were enemies?

Accordingly, we are justified by His blood, reconciled by His death, and saved by His present risen life, vv. 9-10. His blood has met the claims of the righteous throne of God; in His death He has dealt with the man He represented there, in all his offensiveness before God, so that God may now reconcile him to Himself; and in His life we are saved from everything that would rob us of what we have.

What grace we have known! Our guilt has been removed; our present standing is in grace; our future hope is the glory of God.

Christ and

Romans 5. 12-21 — July 27th

The first verse of our passage marks a turning point in this first section of Romans. Up to this point there has been an emphasis on guilt because of sins, and of God's answer founded upon the blood of Christ. The emphasis from now until the end of chapter 8 is more on what we were, rather than what we had done, and the answer for that is found in the death of Christ.

Our passage presents two men, each of whom is the head of a race of men. The first man, Adam, is the fallen head of a fallen race. By his offence, v. 15, sin, v. 16, disobedience, v. 19, and transgression of the one law God had given him, v. 14, sin and death were introduced into the world. The results for his race were devastating. By a principle of headship that was operating, the race sinned in Adam, v. 12; death reigned, even over those who lived between Adam and Moses who had not received any direct law from God, v. 14; there was judgement to condemnation, v. 16; death reigned, v. 17. There is truly no hope for man apart from the intervention of God, in Christ.

We thank God, however, that there was another Man, the second Man, the Lord out of heaven. Everything about Him is in contrast to Adam. In contrast to Adam's disobedience in Eden our Lord's one act of obedience, v. 19, at Calvary produced righteousness for His people. This is a gift of God's grace, v. 15, despite their many offences, v. 16, with the effect that they shall reign, in the future, in the full enjoyment of eternal life, v. 17. From the moment of conversion they are no longer linked to Adam and all the baneful effects of his failure, but to Christ and all the glorious effects of His finished work.

Grace is magnificent. When the law entered the offence abounded. The law of Sinai showed sin in its true character as an offence against God, and it abounded in the heart of man, which was rebellious to the revealed will of God for man, and in the actions of man. Yet, where sin abounded grace super-abounded, with the result that though sin had reigned unto death, grace now reigns through righteousness unto eternal life by Jesus Christ our Lord, v. 21.

July 28th — Romans 6. 1-14

Newness of life

The apostle now anticipates that some objectors to what he has just taught will suggest that because grace super-abounds where sin abounds recipients of that grace might well continue in sin, for to do so would magnify grace. Such things are still suggested by many who insist that salvation is by works, and not by grace.

The answer to this objection is, in this chapter, linked to the fact that believers have died with Christ to sin. By that association with Him in His death they have been delivered from that old master to walk in newness of life, serving the new Master, God. Just as a master cannot demand obedience from a dead slave, no more can sin demand service from the believer who by death has been delivered from its mastery. The believer's death to sin occurred, from the divine standpoint, at Calvary, v. 8. When Christ died, the believer died. This was made good to them at conversion and it was symbolized in their 'baptism into death', v. 4.

The old man, that Adamic order to which we once belonged (and not to be confused with 'the flesh'), was utterly judged by God at the cross when 'our old man was crucified with him', v. 6. We owe the old man nothing. Adamic man was given every opportunity in the Old Testament to prove himself, but all that God could do with man in Adam was to bring him under judgement. 'I am crucified with Christ', Gal. 2. 20, is true of every believer, whose body is now not the territory where sin reigns but the vehicle through which God is to be glorified.

All of this is not an aspiration for the believer to achieve, but solid fact for faith to apprehend. It is continually to be reckoned, v. 11, or counted as true, by the believer that he has died unto the old master, sin, and is alive unto the new master, God. When temptation to sin comes along, the believer is to look back to Calvary and remember this great fact, not letting sin reign in his mortal body, nor yielding its members as instruments of unrighteousness unto sin. Rather, he is to yield himself unto God as being alive from the dead and the members of his body as instruments of righteousness unto Him.

Christ and

Romans 6. 15 – 7. 6 — July 29th

Servants of righteousness

In answer to the question raised in verse 1, 'Shall we continue in sin, that grace may abound?', the apostle brought before us the fact that we have actually been delivered from sin by our identification with Christ in His death and resurrection. Here, in verse 15, another question is raised, but in answering it the apostle refers us to that motivation and disposition of heart that we are to have as believers. Recognizing the wonder of divine grace, the child of God is to yield to, and obey, righteousness.

In fact, at conversion we 'obeyed from the heart that form of doctrine' that was delivered to us. This is the obedience of faith, cp. 1. 5; 16. 26. What the apostle now points out is that if obedience marked us at the beginning of our lives as believers, it should be true of us every day. We are 'servants *of* righteousness' now, v. 18, and are therefore to be 'servants *to* righteousness', v. 19, yielding to righteousness with holiness in view. Indeed, we are now 'servants to *God*', v. 22, with our fruit being holiness, and the ultimate goal being the full enjoyment of eternal life.

In chapters 6 and 7 Paul deals with two matters arising from the truth at the end of chapter 5. We have seen that the believer's relationship to sin is examined in chapter 6, but in chapter 7 it is the believer's relationship with the law. In the opening verses it is established that the law has dominion over a person only while he is alive. This is illustrated by reference to the law of marriage. For so long as the husband is living, that law binds a wife to her husband, so that if while he lives she becomes attached to another she is an adulteress. However, the death of her husband releases her from that law and sets her free to marry another man.

If in chapter 6 the believer is delivered from the dominion of sin by identification with Christ in His death and resurrection, in chapter 7 he is, by that same means, delivered from the dominion of the law. It is no longer the principle by which he lives. It provides neither justification nor sanctification. He has died to it and is now married to Christ risen from the dead, in order that he might bring forth fruit unto God.

His Apostles

July 30th   Romans 7. 7-25

O wretched man that I am!

A lot of confusion has surrounded the proper understanding of this chapter, and it has to be said that it is not the easiest. A couple of basic things might help us. Firstly, we should distinguish it from Galatians chapter 5. There the conflict is in the believer and is between the Spirit and the flesh. The believer is indwelt by the Holy Spirit but still has the flesh to contend with, an evil principle within each person which never gets any better, and which he has until he knows sonship in all its fullness, conformity to the image of God's Son. In Romans chapter 7, however, the conflict is not between the flesh and the Spirit but between the flesh and the law.

Secondly, whereas only the believer knows the conflict between the flesh and the Spirit, any person could have known the conflict between the flesh and the law. The main question in this chapter is not, therefore, whether it has a believer or unbeliever in view, but rather the dynamic between the law and the flesh.

In verse 5 the statement is made that the passions of sins, 'which were by the law', worked in the members of our bodies in unconverted days to bring forth fruit unto death. This gives rise to two questions which are answered in our passage. 'Is the law sin?', v. 7, is the first question. No, the commandment is holy, just and good, v. 12. There is nothing wrong with the law, but when it is applied, sin fills the mind and heart with what it forbids. Whereas adherence to the law would have brought life, it did, in fact, bring a curse. 'Was then that which is good made death unto me?', v. 13, is the second question. That thought is immediately to be dismissed from the mind. The reality is that sin works death in the individual by that which is good, and thereby shows itself to be exceeding sinful. The flesh has no power in respect of the law of God, either to do what it commands, or to abstain from what it forbids, for in it no good thing dwells. How blessed then to know that the believer has been delivered from the dominion of the law, by death and resurrection with Christ, to walk after the Spirit and to know all the privileges and blessings of sonship revealed in chapter 8!

Christ and

Romans 8. 1-17 — July 31st

The effect of Adam's one offence, Rom. 5. 19, was that all in his race were threatened with eternal condemnation. But in Christ Jesus that threat is gloriously lifted in its entirety, and for ever. The person who is in Christ, who characteristically lives his life after the Spirit, has by the law of the Spirit, which is life in Christ Jesus, been made free from the law of sin and death. The law was powerless to bring life because of the flesh, as we saw in chapter 7, but God's own Son, by His flesh given in death, has condemned sin, with the effect that the righteous requirement of the law has been fulfilled in the case of those who are in Christ Jesus.

This could not possibly be true for those who are still not saved, those who are in the flesh. They are dominated by, and absorbed in, the mind of the flesh. This mind is enmity against God because it is not, and cannot, be subject to the law of God. Accordingly, such cannot please God. Believers, however, are no longer 'in the flesh' but 'in the Spirit'. They are taken up with the things of the Spirit as the bent of their life, and the Spirit of God dwells in them to replicate features of Christ.

This is so important to grasp. We owe the flesh nothing. It brought only that which was evil before we were saved, and is no different now that we are saved. If a believer lives according to it he shall never enter into that kind of life which God desires that we enjoy, in fellowship and communion with Him. It is vital therefore, through the Holy Spirit, to keep the members of our bodies in the place of death, as far as sin is concerned, in order that we might live that life of bliss and peace in the enjoyment of being sons of God. It is true that we shall not enjoy sonship in all its fullness until we are 'conformed to the image of his Son', 8. 29. But led by the Spirit of God, we may know now the joy of sonship, involving intimacy with the Father who delights to share His heart, His mind, His purpose, and His life with us. Not only are we *sons* of God, with all the dignity that that bestows, but we have known generative change, and are now also the *children* of God and heirs of God, the Holy Spirit bearing joint witness to this with our spirits.

His Apostles

August 1st — Romans 8. 18-39

The reference in verse 17 to being 'glorified together' and in verse 18 to 'the glory which shall be revealed in us' leads the apostle to think of that which lies ahead. The gospel brings us from guilt, by grace, to glory.

Creation itself will share in the glorious future. At present it groans and travails in pain, having been made subject to vanity as a result of man's fall, but it waits for the manifestation of the sons of God. Then it shall be delivered from the bondage of corruption into the glorious liberty of the children of God. This looks on to the millennial kingdom, in which there will be a profuse outpouring of the Spirit of God, which we have already anticipated as having the 'firstfruits of the Spirit', v. 23. At present, even though we have the Holy Spirit indwelling us, we also groan as we live amid a groaning creation in an unredeemed body. We groan as we wait for sonship in all its fullness. The interim is marked by infirmity, and often by ignorance in which we are helped by the Spirit as we wait in hope.

As we are in such a state there is something that God has revealed to us which fills us with cheer. We are 'called ones', according to God's purpose that His Son will have a people for Himself and, in our being made like Him, have greater glory. To that end He has foreknown us, predestinated us, called us, justified us, and glorified us. All of this is seen from the divine standpoint: to Him to whom all things are as present, it is already done. From our perspective we await its full accomplishment, resting in the inviolability of divine purpose. Though we have many enemies none can be successful against those who are called according to His purpose, for God is *for* them. To secure all this for us He did not spare His own Son from the unmitigated suffering of Calvary. It is God who has justified His elect ones; they are kept from condemnation by the One who died and rose again and now intercedes for them at God's right hand. From His love they can never be severed. That love, seen in all its fullness at Calvary, is the same today, and no matter the height and depth of hostility directed towards us we are more than conquerors through Him that loved us.

If God be for us, who can be against us?

Christ and

Romans 9. 1-29 — August 2nd

Chapter 9 begins a new section of the epistle. The apostle now deals with questions arising with regard to the status of the nation of Israel, and God's dealings with that nation as a result of the gospel offer being made to Gentiles as well as Jews. Will God renege on His gifts and calling in respect of that nation? In answering such issues Paul speaks in chapter 9 about Israel in the past, in chapter 10 regarding the present, and in chapter 11 regarding the future that the nation has, for indeed the gifts and calling of God are without repentance 11. 29.

Although at the end of chapter 8 the apostle has spoken of the inviolability of the believer's salvation and the impossibility of being separated from the love of God, he immediately states in chapter 9, as he thinks of his 'kinsmen according to the flesh', v. 3, that he would wish himself 'accursed from Christ', if it would result in their conversion. A proper view of the sovereignty of God, to which Paul has alluded in chapter 8 and now in chapter 9, never diminishes a desire for the salvation of the lost. Indeed, it can only enhance it.

Israel had been in a wonderful position of privilege in God's dealings with man. Chief among them, though at that time disregarded by them, was the fact that Christ, who is God over all, blessed for ever, came from Israel, according to the flesh. The only reason why they had such privileges, Paul argues, is because of divine sovereignty. In His sovereignty God chose Isaac and his children, the children of promise, above Ishmael and his children, the children of the flesh. Additionally, when two sons were in Rebecca's womb it was said that the elder, Esau, would serve the younger. Neither had done good or evil, but God called the one and not the other that the purpose of God according to election might stand. There was no ground for boasting. God will have mercy on whom He will have mercy, so that it is altogether not of man but of God when a person receives divine blessing. For this reason Israel could have no argument against God bringing Gentiles into blessing, making known the riches of His glory on vessels of mercy, whom He has afore prepared unto glory, both Jews and Gentiles who believe on His Son.

His Apostles

August 3rd Romans 9. 30 – 10. 21

A zeal of God, but not according to knowledge

Turning from the nation of Israel in the past, and their having been favoured as a matter of divine sovereignty, the apostle now thinks of that nation in the present in connection with the subject of divine righteousness. As Paul writes he is mindful that though Israel had a zeal for God it was 'not according to knowledge' because they were ignorant of that righteousness from God which is revealed in the gospel. This showed itself in that they went about to establish their own righteousness by means of law-keeping. The righteousness of the law is described by Moses, v. 5, as being one that is obtained by unfailing and continual adherence to the law, something that is impossible as chapter 3 has already shown. However, the righteousness which is of God, and declared in 'the word of faith', v. 8, is not secured by anything that man can do. Rather, all the work has been done by One who died and rose again, and heart belief in Him is 'unto righteousness', and confession is 'unto salvation'.

In this there is no distinction between Jew and Gentile, vv. 11-13. Just as 'there is no difference: for all have sinned', 3. 22-23, so 'there is no difference' in terms of the offer of righteousness, 'for the same Lord over all is rich unto all that call upon him'. The gospel may be freely preached to all, without exception, 'for whosoever shall call upon the name of the Lord shall be saved'.

To this end the gospel is universally preached and necessarily so, vv. 14-21. People cannot call on Him in whom they have not believed, or believe in Him of whom they have not heard. They cannot hear if nobody preaches to them, and no one can preach except he is sent. Who would not delight in making known that word? It is the 'gospel of peace' and 'glad tidings of good things'. This is the 'word of faith' and the 'word of God', v. 17, which people must obey with the obedience of faith. Having quoted from the law in verse 5, and from the prophets in verse 11, Paul now quotes from Psalm 19. Indeed, the sound of the gospel has gone into all the earth, and it is the responsibility of each of us to continue its proclamation in our day.

Christ and

Romans 11. 1-21 — August 4th

Hath God cast away his people? God forbid

This chapter concludes the section that has considered the setting aside of Israel. In it Paul seeks to show that there is a remnant, a spiritual Israel, and that they will be restored through the grace of God.

In the simplest response to the question that forms the title to this meditation, Paul points to the fact of his own salvation. His lineage establishes his credentials as an Israelite, yet he has been saved. God has not cast away His people! However, Paul seeks to draw a distinction between the physical nation and God's spiritual people. He calls upon the testimony of scripture to substantiate his case. The parallels with Elijah's day show that election is a divine work and God does not choose on the basis of merit. But, if a remnant has been chosen, what of the rest of the nation?

In verses 11 to 36, a second question is considered and answered, 'Have they stumbled that they should fall?' v. 11. Paul shows that the 'fall', or 'trespass' (RV margin), is a temporary rather than a permanent state. In the purposes of God, Israel's setting aside 'has opened the treasures of divine mercy to the world', A. PRIDHAM. Equally, when they are restored nationally they will become the channel of God's blessing to all mankind, v. 12, cp. Ps. 67. 1-2. But bringing the gospel to the Gentiles was 'to provoke them (the Jews) to jealousy', vv. 11 and 14. Whilst the salvation offered was not national but individual, it was certainly Paul's desire that his preaching to the Gentiles might bring about the salvation of Jews also. Is it ours?

By way of illustration, Paul uses the example of the olive tree as a picture of the nation of Israel. This would be physical Israel, Abraham's natural progeny, rather than spiritual Israel, possessed of Abraham-like faith. Over the course of time some branches become dead – some, once faithful tribes, become marked by unbelief. The dead branches are broken off and the parts of the wild olive tree are grafted in, v. 17. But this should not be the cause of a proud or haughty attitude. Gentiles were not to be 'highminded', v. 20, for the gospel came to them originally as a consequence of Jewish believers, cp. John 4. 22!

His Apostles

August 5th   **Romans 11. 22-36**

The wisdom and knowledge of God!

It is worth examining these verses for what they tell us of God. We are told of the goodness of God, v. 22, seen in the blessings enjoyed by the believer. Verse 22 also tells us of the severity of God: He is unbending and will not compromise His principles; unbelief will be judged wherever it may be found. In verse 23 we read, 'God is able'. He is capable of acting contrary to the natural order in grafting in the Gentile; He is able to restore the Jews also; Jewish 'blindness' is only temporary! Also, it is only 'in part'. As verse 1 shows, it is not total but partial, here it is not eternal but temporary, v. 25. When the Deliverer comes, 'all Israel shall be saved'. What a title for the Lord! It is worth noting that the use of the present participle indicates the permanence of this title and character, and the use of the definite article teaches the uniqueness of His claim.

The work of the Deliverer is twofold: He will turn away ungodliness, v. 26, and take away their sins, v. 27. It is worth dwelling upon the permanence of that work – sins are removed. God will also establish His covenant with them, a covenant that emanates from, and depends upon, God alone. Whilst the Jewish nation is excluded from God's favour by unbelief, v. 28, His promises to them have not been retracted, v. 29. There is assurance here, because God is consistent in His actions to all generations. God has brought all men to the same level. Due to unbelief marked by their resistance of the divine will, the Jews have lost their position of privilege. But, as PRIDHAM comments, 'This was to bring them (the Jews), as a nation, within the effectual reach and operation of that mercy which, in Christ, could alone be the means of the national blessing'.

Considering such a revelation of God's grace it is appropriate that this section of the book should close with an ascription of praise, v. 33. There is an unfathomable depth to the riches of His grace that cannot be computed, and of His knowledge and wisdom that cannot be comprehended. We can acknowledge only that God is the first cause of all things, is responsible for their subsistence and government, and His glory is their ultimate goal, v. 36. Give Him the glory today, and every day!

Christ and

Romans 12. 1-21 — August 6th

Your reasonable service

This chapter commences the section of the book that is intensely practical. It takes the truth taught in chapters 1 to 8 as the basis for a life of sacrifice and devotion. One of its keywords is service, vv. 1, 7 (ministry), and verse 11.

It is important to see chapter 12 against the background of chapter 8. Think of what God has wrought in Christ. Think of the conditions from which we have been rescued. Such a work demands our complete separation from the world and conformity to Christ, v. 2. See the extent of the sacrifice: 'present your bodies'. God does not entertain half-measures! God does not want only a part: He wants all! The world should no longer shape our thinking and govern our actions.

In verses 3 to 13, Paul shows how the exhortation of the first two verses is to be worked out in the Christian life. There are three key thoughts in the section: humility, diversity, and unity. 'God has dealt to every man', v. 3. This truth emphasizes the sovereign activity of God. He has given the gifts, dispelling any thought of pride in the servant. The power that God gives is to be seen in the exercise of the gifts given. Seven gifts are mentioned, ranging from the public and prominent gifts to the private and personal. It is emphasized again that all are 'according to the grace that is given to us', v. 6. Note too that the exercise of these gifts is described by the present participle – this should be habitual!

For any gift to be a benefit to the saints it must be exercised by Christ-like people. The marks of such a person are listed in these verses: (1) love, practically demonstrated, v. 9 RV; (2) separation from evil; (3) 'sticking fast' to that which is good, v. 9; (4) full of tenderness, v. 10; (5) unflagging zeal, v. 11; (6) heavenly vision and steadfast prayer, v. 12; (7) fellowship with saints in genuine need, v. 13; and (8) hospitality, v. 13.

Finally, vv. 14 to 21, the apostle considers how we relate to the world. He acknowledges difficulties that will confront us. He says, 'If it be possible', v. 18. It is not always possible to be at peace with all men. However, as H. C. G. MOULE puts it, 'Let the peace, if broken, be broken on the other side'!

His Apostles

August 7th — Romans 13. 1-14

The powers that be are ordained of God

In this chapter Paul asks every believer to consider his responsibility to the structures within society rather than, as in chapter 12, to individuals within that society.

The Principle stated, vv. 1-2: subjection. Rome was given its power in the will of God, for only God can establish or overthrow kingdoms. Therefore, the believer is to be subject to those governmental authorities that owe their existence to God.

The Power vested, vv. 3-4: the ministers of God. Paul puts into context the purpose for which rulers are instituted. Their duty is to maintain and enforce right and to punish wrong, v. 3. These rulers also have a duty to maintain the welfare of their subjects, v. 4. They are to mete out justice on behalf of God to those who practise evil.

The Purpose stated, vv. 5-7: for conscience sake. We maintain an attitude of subjection by paying our taxes or customs, vv. 6-7. We show appropriate respect, v. 7. We acknowledge those upon whom the state has conferred distinction, v. 7.

The Prohibition given, vv. 8-10: avoid debt. Be no man's debtor, v. 8, except in love. The extent of the prohibition is interesting – 'no man' and 'anything'. It is what H. C. G. MOULE describes as 'a watchful avoidance of the state of debt'. Love should be the only debt that is always owing. A. T. ROBERTSON describes the thought, 'This debt can never be paid off, but we should keep the interest paid up'!

The Promise of His Coming, vv. 11-14: this life of obedience should be moulded by the fact that the Lord is coming! Although we do not know the exact timing of the event, we should regard it as imminent, v. 11. The night of spiritual and moral darkness is drawing to its close; the daybreak is at hand, v. 12. As in a normal day, we are assured that the night will end and the day will come; we can wait upon the Lord's return with equal certainty. As Christianity is not a moral and spiritual void, we should take off the clothing associated with the night, and put on the armour of light. Finally, 'Let us walk honestly', or, as K. WUEST translates, 'Let us order our behaviour after a seemly fashion', v. 13. Do we?

Christ and

Romans 14. 1-18 — August 8th

Our reading today focuses upon the theme of relationships between fellow believers. The prevailing thought is the Lordship of Christ, which is mentioned implicitly, vv. 4 and 7, and explicitly, vv. 6, 8, 9.

Paul clearly shows that there are brethren who have certain scruples that those of greater understanding and Christian experience have discarded. One can imagine that the convert from Judaism might find it difficult to discard those aspects of Jewish ritual pertaining to meats and days. Similarly, those saved from the midst of Gentile idolatry may be extremely careful of meats and drinks, because of their knowledge of their use within the idolatrous systems. Paul is careful not to pass judgement upon either view. What he enjoins upon his readers is **cordiality**, v. 1. Those that are weak in the faith should be received with warmth and interest. He encourages **communion**, v. 3. The strong should not hold the weak in contempt, and the weak should not condemn the strong – there should be no real barriers to fellowship. As Paul teaches, God has received both at conversion without conditions. He would encourage individual **conviction**, v. 5. In matters of food as in matters of days, 'Let every man be fully persuaded in his own mind'. In such matters of indifference, it is appropriate for the individual conscience to be the guide. Paul teaches **consideration**, vv. 6-7. It must be remembered that both weak and strong live their lives 'unto the Lord'.

It has often been said that we are saved to serve. But service does not cease with death for 'whether we die, we die unto the Lord', v. 8. We were purchased for a purpose, and, as MOULE states, 'When we die, we do not pass out of His bondservice, but only into another mode of it'. Emphasizing the Lordship of Christ teaches us that we have a responsibility to Him and He will review the outcomes of our service. Paul clearly states, 'We shall all stand before the judgement seat of God', v. 10 RV and JND. The 'all' is strongly emphatic, showing that none is exempt, but we must remember that our account is of ourselves, v. 12. We are answerable for our own service; not that of others!

Who art thou that judgest another man's servant?

His Apostles

August 9th
Romans 14. 19 – 15. 13

In our reading today Paul concentrates on what should be the aim of our service. We should 'earnestly and eagerly seek after peace', 14. 19 K. WUEST. These peace seekers will be: characterized by a desire and effort to build up the saints, vv. 19-20, and willing to sacrifice personal liberty to protect a weaker brother, v. 21. It is to God that we are accountable. Hence, blessed is the one who does not need to pass an adverse judgement upon himself, whose conscience is at ease.

If we wish to please God then we will 'bear the infirmities of the weak'. This is not an occasional thing but is a matter of conviction and habit of life. Paul is quick to bind this practice upon himself, 'We that are strong', 15. 1. Similarly, v. 2, those that seek to please God will promote the spiritual growth of their fellow believer. Bearing the infirmities of the weak does not mean that we allow them to remain weak! The believer should also remember that 'even Christ pleased not Himself', v. 3. He who had the authority and right to please Himself sought to please the Father, at supreme cost to Himself. With such an example before us we should expect to meet man's hostility and opposition, but we should not allow it to deflect us from pleasing God. The believer has the hope of glory in Christ, v. 4.

There should be an affectionate unanimity amongst believers, united by the example of Christ, v. 6. This chapter contains much of the character of God and this section reveals Him as the God of patience and consolation, the source of all patience and consolation. Paul's prayer is that He would grant a true union of affection amongst the believers. Those from different cultural backgrounds should not be treated differently – Christ has received those who were once strangers and enemies, v. 7.

Verses 8 to 12 deal with millennial conditions. These events 'relate to the future effects upon the nations of the world, of the reign of Immanuel, as the true Son of David, the anointed King of Israel', PRIDHAM. This truth is contained in Psalms 18 and 117, and Isaiah 11. In that day, the rejoicing will involve all, both Jew and Gentile, in a continuous exercise, vv. 10-11.

Follow after the things which make for peace

Christ and

Romans 15. 14-33 — August 10th

We move now to the closing remarks of the book. Here, Paul commends the believers for: their goodness, in manifesting the fruits of the Spirit, their knowledge of spiritual truth, and their use of that spiritual truth in admonishing one another.

Paul employs one aspect of admonition – 'as putting you in mind', v. 15. There is validity in reminding the saints of what they already know, and we should not despise ministry on a well-known subject. The apostle's desire was to see the Gentiles saved, and their lives devoted to the service of the Lord. The language of verse 16 is priestly and sacrificial, linking with Paul's opening words to this section of the book, 'ye present your bodies a living sacrifice', 12. 1. Such a sacrifice, sanctified by the Holy Spirit, will be acceptable.

Conscious of what had already been wrought amongst the Gentiles, Paul is quick to acknowledge that such fruit was as a consequence of the work of Christ in him, 'which Christ hath . . . wrought by me', v. 18. Those 'signs' accompanying the spread of the gospel he attributes to 'the power of the Spirit of God', v. 19. Here is a picture of Paul's ministry – 'I strived to preach the gospel', v. 20. So far, he had reached almost unto Illyricium. He now proposes to go further, to Rome and beyond into Spain.

Feeling that the mission in his present location is complete, his desire is to come first to Rome, v. 23. He tells the Romans what he plans to do, leaving the timing as well as the destination to God, 'Whensoever I take my journey', v. 24. However, there is a more immediate task to fulfil. He had a gift to deliver to the saints in Jerusalem, v. 25. The Macedonian believers, together with those in Achaia, had made a contribution to the needy saints in Jerusalem. The importance of the gift necessitated Paul's own involvement: it was convincing evidence of the faith of the Gentiles who had sent it. Such a mission was crucial for the development of the infant church, bringing, as it did, Jew and Gentile, together. Finally, he sought their prayers that the work of God might flourish. What a lesson! Do we have the same passion for the lost, and prayerful care for the saints?

The minister of Jesus Christ to the Gentiles

His Apostles

August 11th — Romans 16. 1-27

The churches of Christ salute you

This chapter is one of salutations, as the apostle recounts fellow believers who had an interest in the assembly at Rome. Some of the long list would have been well known for their work of the Lord. They demonstrated: **(1) Commitment.** It is obvious from what is said that Phoebe, Priscilla, and Aquila were particularly well known or worthy of note. Of Phoebe it can be said that she ably fulfilled the ministry of a sister, 'a succourer of many', v. 2. For such an industrious servant of the Lord there should be a welcome from the assembly and appropriate assistance in her work. From Priscilla and Aquila we see the support given to the Lord's work and the Lord's workers and the value of it in an individual as well as assembly sense, v. 4. **(2) Consistency.** Of Epaenetus we are told he was continuing in divine things. Of Mary, v. 6, we see commitment and consistency to the point of exhaustion. Of Andronicus and Junia, v. 7, though imprisoned for Christ, they remained faithful to their Lord and to the Lord's people. Of Amplias, v. 8, it can be said that he was 'beloved in the bonds of Christian service', H. ALFORD. **(3) Community.** The apostle has emphasized the community of believers bringing together Jew and Gentile in Christ. Andronicus, Junia, and Herodion are stated to be Jews. Others are Gentiles, but involved in the work of the Lord and in support of the apostle's labours. As well as of different *national* background, there are those of different *gender*. Phoebe, Priscilla, Mary, Junia (although gender is unclear), Tryphena, Tryphosa, and Persis were all women, playing a considerable part in the work of the Lord yet in their proper sphere of service. Finally, there are those of different *social* background brought together: prisoners for Christ, and slaves alongside those of greater social standing and position, such as Priscilla, Aquila, Phoebe, and Erastus, v. 23.

The closing verses are a tribute to the God of the gospel, the theme of the book. Paul tells us of God's power, v. 25. He describes God as the revealer of secrets, v. 25, the God of eternity, v. 26, and yet also the God of all grace. Finally, He is God only wise, v. 27. As this epistle displays that particular truth so fully and so ably, here is its most fitting close.

Christ and

Although many aspects of this book reflect the low spiritual state of the church at Corinth, it also provides us with much of the church truth that forms the basis of our mode of gathering. It addresses errors which are practical, moral, doctrinal, and spiritual. It handles questions relating to human relationships, things offered to idols, spiritual gifts, and collecting for the saints. Equally, even though we know from Acts chapter 18 verse 11 that Paul spent eighteen months in Corinth, it is clear that they were still ignorant of important truths such as those covered in chapters 3, 5, 6, and 9.

One of the keys to this epistle is revealed to us within the first ten verses of the book. While it is written to 'the church of God which is at Corinth', 1. 2, it also provides some defining characteristics of the church of God in a local setting. Such a church belongs to God, is composed of 'them that are sanctified in Christ Jesus', v. 2, owns the Lordship of Christ, exercises the gifts bestowed by the grace of God for the edification of His people, enjoying the fellowship of divine persons, v. 9, while waiting for the coming of the Lord, v. 7. What a dignity has been bestowed by the grace of God!

In our reading of this book we may think that the issues it covers were important only in first-century Corinth. However, from the very outset of the book Paul makes it clear that the truths of which he wrote had a far wider application than the assembly at Corinth – 'as I teach everywhere in every church', 4. 17. Thus, in the 21st century, this book is as relevant to church life for today as it was for the time in which it was written.

1 Corinthians seeks to address many different matters. Reading some of the chapters that deal with their moral turpitude, and serious doctrinal error, we might expect a very robust approach to dealing with these failing Christians. Yet one of the things that is remarkable is the apostle's remembrance of his spiritual relationship to the believers that formed this church. He describes them as 'my brethren', 1. 11; 11. 33, 'my beloved brethren', 15. 58, 'my beloved sons', 4. 14, and 'my dearly beloved', 10. 14. There is a genuine affection for these saints and, although initially there may be things that he would have to rectify, he constantly expresses his desire to visit them.

His Apostles

August 12th — 1 Corinthians 1. 1-31

Ye come behind in no gift

In Paul's introduction to this Epistle, covering the first three verses, he stresses his apostolic authority and its application. His calling as an apostle was a realization of the will of God and the Corinthian believers were evidence of that work of God. This is the basis of this letter.

At the outset Paul emphasizes the Lordship of Christ, vv. 2, 3, 7, 8, 9, 10. The gifts that God has bestowed upon this young church are many – they 'come behind in no gift', v. 7 – but those gifts must be exercised under the control of Christ alone. They are gifts of divine grace and not for the exaltation of any servant.

Sadly, the first issue that needs to be resolved by the apostle is the exaltation of servants. The Corinthians were forming party allegiances and withdrawing from aspects of fellowship as a result. Petty differences were leading to division and a gradual dismantling of the assembly. How sad! Yet the apostle's approach does not exacerbate the situation, He beseeches them in love, reminding them twice that they were his 'brethren', vv. 10, 11. He also stresses his specific ministry – 'to preach the gospel', v. 17.

In the remainder of the chapter Paul gives us a clear outline of that gospel. It is 'the preaching of the cross', and 'the power of God', v. 18. It confounds the wisdom of this world through the 'foolishness of preaching', v. 21. It brings salvation to those that believe. While it is a stumbling block to the Jew and folly to the Gentile, it is a demonstration of the wisdom and power of God. Finally, it is the means that God uses to call those He has chosen to salvation and blessing, in order that all the glory might be His.

What should be the response of the believer to such a salvation? As those who are 'in Christ Jesus', v. 30, we find in Him 'wisdom, and righteousness, and sanctification, and redemption'. What tremendous provision is found in Christ! We have contributed nothing. Hence, 'He that glorieth, let him glory in the Lord', v. 31. When we think of the gifts that God has bestowed, and the salvation that He conceived and completed, can there be any other response than praise and worship?

Christ and

1 Corinthians 2. 1-16 — August 13th

The wisdom of God

If the close of chapter 1 deals with the message of the gospel, in the opening of chapter 2 Paul looks at his own preaching when in Corinth. It is very personal: four times he mentions 'I' and twice 'my', in the first four verses. He wishes to emphasize that his preaching of the gospel fitted with the nature of the message. He used **simplicity** of speech, v. 1. Natural eloquence has no place in conveying a divine message. His subject? 'Jesus Christ and him crucified', v. 2. He conveyed the **solemnity** of the message, v. 3. He came to them 'in fear, and in much trembling', conscious of his responsibility. He preached with **sincerity**, v. 4. He did not rely upon natural wisdom or persuasive techniques, but wholly upon the Spirit of God. What a challenge to every gospel preacher!

There is a strange paradox in the gospel. Those who might be expected to know, by their own knowledge or that of their advisers, actually know nothing. In reality, it was the 'princes of this world' that 'crucified the Lord of glory', v. 8. It is the despised believer, part of the foolish things of this world, who speaks 'the wisdom of God in a mystery'!

Having started with the gospel Paul desires the progress and growth of believers. The last section of this chapter deals with this theme. **The principle is established**, vv. 9-10. Revelation is by the Spirit of God and this holds true from Old Testament times through to the present. 'The natural man receiveth not the things of the Spirit of God', v. 14. **The principle is exemplified**, v. 11. If we are in any doubt then nature furnishes us with an example. We can only really get to know someone in the measure they allow us. Equally, our knowledge of God is divinely revealed through the operation of the Spirit of God. **The principle is experienced**, v. 12. Throughout this section it is worth underlining the use of the emphatic 'we'. '*We* have received . . . the Spirit which is of God', v. 12. '*We* have the mind of Christ', v. 16. In closing this meditation perhaps we ought to pause and consider the enormity of the blessings bestowed upon us. God wants us to know 'the things which God hath prepared for them that love him', and He has given us the means! Amazing!

His Apostles

August 14th

1 Corinthians 3. 1-23

Against the background of the closing verses of our previous meditation, it is sad to read of the carnality of these Christians. But what is carnality? It is evident in **dwarfism**, v. 1. There was no growth at Corinth. They had not progressed. They were still babes. There is evidence of **deadness**, v. 2. These believers seemed to have no appetite for divine truth. When they should have moved on to meat they were still content with milk. There is also evidence of **division**, v. 3. Petty jealousies had led to strife and strife had resulted in division. Rather than building up they were pulling down. **Distortion**, v. 4. The focus of the message is not the preacher! Carnality distorts our view of what is important and what is not!

To counter the problem of carnality Paul reminds the Corinthians of some vital facts. (1) God gives the resources, v. 5. It is not a matter of Paul or Apollos. They are merely servants, gifted of God. Equally, God gives the increase, v. 7. The results of the preaching are not simply a consequence of the actions or words of the preacher. (2) God expects unity, v. 8. This means unity amongst the workers and a subjection to the overall purposes of the God with whom we are 'fellow-workmen' v. 9 JND. (3) God provides regulation, v. 9. The emphasis is upon the fact that 'ye are God's'. We work to His command and to His plan!

In the latter half of this chapter Paul teaches the truth of accountability, 'every man's work shall be made manifest', v. 13. Hence, how important it is to build in an appropriate way! **The manner of the building** is important. The foundation is given, v. 11. What is built upon must be in keeping with the one who is the foundation of the building. This requires discernment and examination. We must also think about **the materials for the building**, v. 12. As with the manner in which we build, so it is with the materials. The intrinsic worth of the Person who forms the foundation is undisputed. Let us look to use materials of spiritual value. After all, the building is God's, v. 17! But how amazing that there is **merit in building**, vv. 14-15! What receives reward? That which abides! Let us build that which will abide and bring God the glory.

1 Corinthians 4. 1-21

August 15th

Stewards of the mysteries of God

The main subject of this chapter is that described by the title of our meditation – stewardship. Using himself and Apollos as the basis of his teaching the apostle covers some of the characteristics of the faithful steward.

In a general sense a steward was one to whom household affairs were entrusted. In spiritual terms it was one to whom spiritual affairs were entrusted. As such Paul emphasizes **dependence**, v. 1. Every servant of the Lord is a minister of Christ. The word for minister means 'under rower' and suggests subordination in service to Christ. Equally, a steward must be **devoted**, v. 2. Faithfulness is a requirement, not an option! As God has given us the responsibility so we answer to Him, 'he that judgeth me is the Lord', v. 4. A steward must also be **disciplined**, v. 3. We do not answer to human judgement nor do we operate in the light of 'man's day', the present. The disciplined steward serves in the light of the day when he will answer to the Lord. He will 'bring to light the hidden things of darkness, and will make manifest the counsels of the heart', v. 5.

Against that background the apostle explores the service of the Corinthians. What a contrast! They were marked by **pride**, v. 7. They were 'puffed up'. Rather than appreciating that their gift was divinely bestowed they regarded it as a mark of honour. They were also distinguished by **prosperity**, v. 8. This is not a condemnation of wealth but a criticism of the value they placed upon the temporal rather than the eternal, and how their wealth had become all-consuming. They set themselves up as **prudent**, v. 10. Solomon said, 'Be not wise in thine own eyes', Prov. 3. 7, and yet this was their folly. They claimed **power**, v. 10. This was not spiritual strength but human strength. Finally, they sought **position**, v. 10. The glory and honour that might be bestowed by their fellow men was what motivated their service.

We can see that the Corinthian believers had much to learn about stewardship. However, Paul not only reminds them of what he had taught them but provided them with two examples – his own life and that of Timothy! What a challenge to be able to say, 'Be ye followers of me', v. 16!

His Apostles

August 16th

1 Corinthians 5. 1-13

Ye are puffed up, and have not rather mourned

What a sad chapter this is! The sin that was present in the church at Corinth was catastrophic. Not only to the corruption of the fellowship internally but also to the testimony externally, as it was an issue 'not so much as named among the Gentiles', v. 1. What is so remarkable is the complacency of the believers in tolerating such a sin in their midst!

So often the focus of a chapter like this is upon the perpetrator of the evil. 'He that has done this deed', v. 2, needs to face church discipline as a consequence of his actions. This discipline should be administered in the authority of the name, and with the power of 'our Lord Jesus Christ', v. 4. It should be administered by the whole company, 'when ye are gathered together'. Such are the principles taught here. The outcome is 'to deliver such an one unto Satan', v. 5. What he had chosen to be morally he would become physically – part of the world.

The reason for the discipline outlined here is twofold. Firstly, the local church must be free from moral evil. If it is to function for God it must be a sanctified company. On that basis the 'old leaven' must be purged out, a thorough cleaning instituted, and this is accomplished, in part, by the excommunication of the offender. Secondly, once the offender is put out there is a work that can be done upon him – 'the destruction of the flesh', v. 5. The strong will and the proud heart need to be broken and an appreciation of the gravity of the sin established. If there is going to be restoration to fellowship, it can only be on the basis of true repentance. To be outside of the assembly is to be in the sphere where 'God judgeth', v. 13.

However, the title that forms the basis of our meditation bids us to consider ourselves – 'ye . . . have not rather mourned', v. 2. Mourning feels the loss of the individual, as well as the damage done to the whole. If an offence of this nature occurs in any assembly, should we not ask why? Why didn't we see the danger, and seek to stop it happening? Was our spiritual state so low that we didn't notice such wickedness? Have we taught moral standards so that all know such behaviour is unacceptable?

Christ and

1 Corinthians 6. 1-20   August 17th

The theme of this chapter is in contrast to chapter 5. In a company that seemed so complacent about moral issues of such gravity, they were prepared to go to law over matters of relative triviality. What a challenge! How important to put things into the right perspective!

Paul seeks to teach these believers something of the dignity of their calling. 'Saints shall judge the world', v. 2. 'We shall judge angels', v. 3. 'Ye are washed . . . sanctified . . . justified', v. 11. Should they not think of what they once were and what God had made them in Christ? When we think of the honour bestowed upon us in the purposes of God, why is it that we cannot 'judge between . . . brethren?' v. 5.

The latter section of the chapter is of significance when facing issues for which there is no direct divine revelation. In a society where 'anything goes', and the rights of the individual seem paramount, the scripture offers guidance for the believer. There are three guides: (1) **expediency** – what do I stand to gain spiritually? Is this activity for my spiritual profit? (2) **enslavement** – will it endanger my spiritual liberty? Will I 'be brought under the power of any', v. 12? (3) **expectation** – will it hinder my service for God? 'The body is . . . for the Lord', v. 13.

On the basis of these principles we should be able to appreciate that immorality is completely out of character with the confession we have made. Seen against the background of the immorality of the city of Corinth, it was important to state clearly that any association with harlots was wrong. But as well as the statement of the negative, Paul also stresses what positive action we can take to preserve our character and testimony, 'Flee fornication', v. 18. We are indwelt by the Holy Spirit of God. Our body is the inner temple, or holy place, of the Holy Spirit. We should bear the character of the One who indwells us. Equally, the indwelling Holy Spirit tells us that we are no longer our own – we have been 'bought with a price', v. 20. Well might we pause to consider that awful price that was paid and, consequently, the debt of gratitude that we owe! Do we glorify God in our every word and deed? Could we start today?

Such were some of you

His Apostles

August 18th 1 Corinthians 7. 1-40

One of the most complex matters in any spiritual life is that of relationships. First century Corinth had many parallels with practices in our own society and Paul knew it was important to address the issue. What blessing could be brought to Christian marriage through a careful consideration of this chapter!

In the previous chapter Paul has emphasized the need to flee fornication. One way to achieve that objective might be to marry, but let us appreciate what Christian marriage requires. We are to 'render . . . due benevolence', v. 3. This is expected of both partners – there is an equality of responsibility between the sexes. Rather than exercise our personal rights we defer to the other. What we do within the marriage relationship should be governed by mutual consent, for a specified time, and for a defined spiritual purpose, v. 5.

Sadly, there may come a time where there is a breakdown in a Christian marriage. That separation may be temporary or it may become permanent. In this situation the apostle is clear, 'Let . . . [them] remain unmarried', v. 11. However, there is the matter where one of the couple is a believer and the other is not, and scripture offers help here. Overall, the believer should seek to maintain the relationship in the hope that actions towards the unbelieving partner might be the means of bringing them to salvation. Sometimes the maintenance of the relationship is not possible, but, if all attempts have been made, then believers should not blame themselves for the failure; they are 'not under bondage in such cases', v. 15.

In the closing section of the chapter the apostle seeks to summarize his spiritual advice. Single people should consider remaining in that state – having an ability to care 'for the things that belong to the Lord', v. 32. Single people may wish to marry, and this is acceptable provided it is 'only in the Lord', v. 39. It is acceptable that one who has lost a marriage partner may remarry, provided, again, that they marry a believer.

In a world where relationships are entered into so casually, let us teach these biblical principles to every believer!

As the Lord hath called every one, so let him walk

Christ and

1 Corinthians 8. 1-13 — August 19th

Things offered unto idols

We might summarize the teaching of this chapter as: liberty exercised with responsibility. In considering things offered unto idols, Paul is dealing with a matter that was of little interest to some believers and yet of profound importance to others. The concern of the apostle was that the liberty of one group should not become an occasion of stumbling to other.

To those who 'had knowledge' Paul says, 'We know that an idol is nothing in the world', v. 4. The images and icons created by man's devices were empty. The suggested structures and ranks within the realms of pagan deities were also unfounded. In reality, Paul says, 'To us there is but one God, the Father', v. 6. And what a God He is! Wholly unique, He is the Creator of the universe, the One who created man for His purpose and pleasure. But, remarkably, He is the One who can be known as 'Father'! What a privilege!

However, the liberty that might be enjoyed by those with knowledge might not be shared by everyone. Such believers were aware that meat presented before them had been offered first as a sacrifice to an idol. This they felt to be wrong – the conscience was troubled. But, because of the example of others, they ate of the meat and their conscience was defiled.

The importance of this matter is given at the close of the chapter: 'the weak brother shall perish', v. 11. Although he may be weak, the apostle emphasizes that he is a 'brother'. He is one 'for whom Christ died'! As a fellow believer, he deserves our thought and consideration. But what does it mean when the apostle says 'shall perish'? This relates to the spiritual usefulness of the brother. The spiritual prosperity of younger saints may be in our hands. How do we respond to the responsibility?

As this chapter closes we might apply the principle to our own lives. In many cases, younger believers will be noting our lives as carefully as they listen to our words. It may not be a matter of meat, but are we prepared to put aside our own liberty for the sake of the spiritual development of others? The apostle stresses that to sin against one brother is to sin against all. Worse still, it is to 'sin against *Christ*', v. 12!

His Apostles

August 20th   1 Corinthians 9. 1-23

They which minister about holy things

Paul's activities were strictly governed by divine principles. His God-ordained apostleship was no mere occupation, because his service entailed 'holy things', v. 13. Although he was not motivated by money, the scriptures clearly gave precedence for servants like him to receive financial support from other believers, 'But I have used none of these things', says the faithful missionary, v. 15. Rather than send the wrong message to new and potential converts in Corinth, he ministered without any pecuniary requirement towards his hearers. Elsewhere, he declares that he did not use the gospel as 'a cloak of covetousness', 1 Thess. 2. 5. Sadly, many false teachers still use holy things for material advantage, giving Christian workers a bad name.

Like the high priests who ate some of the offerings, Paul had scriptural warrant for living 'of the gospel', 9. 13-14. He gave up his right to remuneration in order to maintain an irreproachable testimony in a region where wandering philosophers and teachers frequently fleeced their gullible followers. The Lord's things are holy and must not be profaned. Any service for Him must be conducted in accordance with His word. There are also times when legitimate personal desires must take a backseat to what benefits others spiritually and glorifies the Almighty.

Ministry in holy things functions according to different principles from the world. Like the God they serve, Christians must count it a privilege to put themselves last for the blessing of others. Paul considered it his reward, v. 18, to present the gospel free of charge, even though it meant that it 'cost' him financially. He not only placed others' interests before his own, he also reckoned it a great recompense for his labours. Indeed, his heart was so captivated by the sacred good news that was committed to his trust that he pronounced woe upon himself if he failed to proclaim it, v. 16. He laid aside personal considerations such as culture, diet, and dress, in pursuit of the greater purpose of winning people to Christ. Personal pride was shelved in favour of humbly sitting where one's hearers sit, dispensing with anything that might distract from God's truth.

Christ and

1 Corinthians 9. 24 – 10. 14 — August 21st

These things were our examples

The Old Testament events of which Paul writes are meant to convey truth by example to the Corinthian church, as well as to all believers everywhere from the first century to the present day, 1 Cor. 1. 2. Of course, examples may be good or bad. The same word is used to describe the outstanding witnessing example of the Thessalonians, 1 Thess. 1. 7. In 1 Corinthians chapter 10 it is the decidedly *evil* example of the Israelites in the wilderness during Moses' day that is in view.

Despite the spiritual advantages that the Almighty gave to the Israelites, vv. 1-4, their wicked behaviour included idolatry, v. 7, immorality, v. 8, and irreverently testing God, v. 9. Each of these are base and egregious disloyalties to the Creator and Redeemer. The first error substitutes false, impotent deities, Ps. 115. 1-11, in place of the only true and living God. He is uniquely glorious, all-powerful, and wise, Isa. 42. 8. What is more, He has a proven record of providential kindness towards His creatures, Acts 14. 17; Rom. 2. 4. The second sin – often linked with the first, as in the case of the veneration of Baal Peor, Num. 25. 1-9 – still plagues the church in many different places. The third is perhaps the most common of the three iniquities among professing Christians. Where the King James Version has 'tempt' others render it 'put to the test' ESV. The temerity of these wayward Israelites was unbounded. They were unthankful to the Lord who delivered them out of Egypt and fed them throughout their desert journey. Each of these things brought swift and severe judgement upon them.

Israel's lamentable sins stemmed from lack of true spiritual life and its attendant self-control. Paul's example – or 'type' as the word literally is, 1 Cor. 10. 6 – is much more spiritually salutary. Using athletic imagery from the race course and the boxing ring, he says, 'But I discipline my body and bring it into subjection, lest, when I have preached to others, I myself should become disqualified', 9. 27 NKJV. He wants to compete according to God's rules and gain the crown. Believers today must restrain themselves from lust and be temperate, Gal. 5. 23.

His Apostles

August 22nd   1 Corinthians 10. 15 – 11. 1

Give none offence

Much like the contemporary scene, the ancient world was a pluralistic society; multitudes of belief systems coexisted throughout the Roman empire. Spiritual issues pervaded the culture to the extent that it influenced everyday life in numerous ways. In the face of this rampant idolatry Paul told the Corinthian believers to 'flee' it, 1 Cor. 10. 14. He goes on to explain that they could not fellowship at the Lord's table and at the demons' table, vv. 18-21. As befits their 'set apart' status, the saints must remain loyal to the Lord and His people, and not compromise with evil.

Verse 17 says that believers are one body, symbolized by the one loaf; thus, they have a responsibility towards each other not to defile the fellowship. There is freedom in Christ, but it is not licence to do whatever one pleases. The Almighty desires us to build each other up and not discourage one another by our actions. The principle is expressed in this way, 'All things are lawful for me, but all things are not expedient: all things are lawful for me, but all things edify not', v. 23.

Participating in overt idolatrous ceremonies or in feasts at the pagan temples was forbidden, v. 20. But private situations might still lead to problems in the church. 'The earth is the Lord's and the fullness thereof', Ps. 24. 1, gave justification for the enjoyment of freedom when purchasing meat in the ancient equivalent of the grocery store. Instead of scrupulously asking the butcher concerning the meat's provenance the believer could eat it with a clear conscience, unaware as to whether it originated on a farm, or came from a temple. But when eating with unbelieving friends, if they remark that the food was first offered to Zeus (or one's ancestors' spirits, or another deity), then the saint must abstain – for 'the earth is the Lord's', v. 28. Saints must not wound the weak conscience of a fellow-believer sitting nearby, nor can they allow the unbeliever to think that they are indifferent to idolatry. Their actions must not give unnecessary offence to 'the Jew, the Gentile, or the church of God', v. 32. We must always bear in mind the effect that our words and deeds will have on someone for eternity.

Christ and

1 Corinthians 11. 2-34 — August 23rd

Keep the ordinances

The word 'ordinances' is often rendered 'traditions' in the Bible. The Lord Jesus used the term to rebuke the self-righteous Pharisees for their elevation of human opinions to the same level as scripture, Matt. 15. 3, 6. It signifies something handed down or delivered to someone else. Its cognate verb is used of the people who 'handed Christ over' to be crucified, Matt. 26. 24. Thus it pictures something passed on to someone else.

Traditions are not inherently bad; it depends upon what kind they are. Some traditions are innocuous, such as having a set time for a church meeting. That habit only becomes spiritually counterproductive if it is insisted upon as a commandment of the Lord. Other types obscure the gospel and therefore are more destructive. Paul affirmed that he was passionate about his ancestral traditions, but they led him to try to establish his own righteousness before God by his own adherence to ancient human opinions, Gal. 1. 14; Phil. 3. 4-6. Any tradition that negates God's word is wicked and must be swiftly rejected.

Christianity originates from the teachings of the risen Christ through His apostles, John 16. 13-15; Acts 2. 42. Its truths are meant to be handed down, as Paul charged Timothy, 'The things that thou hast heard of me among many witnesses, the same commit thou to faithful men, who shall be able to teach others also', 2 Tim. 2. 2. The ordinances, or traditions of the apostles, come from the Lord and must be obeyed, even though many of these things are controversial. They are cross-cultural, trans-generational, and reflect the Lord's character and will.

Ironically, the ordinances of 1 Corinthians chapter 11 are frequently forgotten in Christian circles. Nonetheless, the symbols of the uncovered head of the man and covered head of the woman are powerful reminders of the truths of divine headship and the necessity of giving God the glory. By the same token, the Lord's supper is an indispensable memorial of the Christ who died, rose again, and is coming again. In the freshness of the early church's first love for her Lord, the saints delighted in meeting to remember their Beloved. May we also do the same on the first day of the week!

His Apostles

August 24th — 1 Corinthians 12

The body is one, and hath many members

Modern leaders spend large amounts of time and money trying to bring divergent people together. Racism, tribalism, unbridled nationalism, and class distinction all divide man from his fellow man. Education is touted as the answer, until it is discovered that the educated are still deeply prejudiced, and even embittered, against individuals from outside their preferred circle. Peace treaties are regularly signed and regularly broken. Human philosophy, religion, politics, business, and academia are all plagued by persistent and entrenched schisms.

Sadly, Christians sometimes fall prey to the same forces of disunity, and evidence similar divisive attitudes as their secular counterparts. As James puts it, 'From whence come wars and fightings among you? come they not hence, even of your lusts that war in your members'? Jas. 4. 1. Even among the Corinthians Paul could speak of 'contentions' among them, 1 Cor. 1. 11. This ought not to be, for believers comprise a spiritual body with Christ Himself serving as the head, 12. 27; Col. 1. 18. Thankfully, this spiritual body has never ceased from the earth. People from every kindred, tribe, and tongue continue to be added to this living organism to which they will belong for eternity.

The passage in today's reading focuses on the way the one body functions in spiritual service. It is one in essence, but it is composed of many members. What is more, these individuals have different roles and diverse spiritual gifts. This should not diminish the unity, for physical bodies also have different parts to accomplish varying tasks. The foot does not go on strike because it is not a hand, 1 Cor. 12. 15; nor does the eye tell the hand that it is redundant, v. 21. Rather these divergent parts harmoniously coexist and work together for the general good of the entire body. The many are one under their all-wise head, who governs their behaviour. Although they have different personalities, talents, and spiritual gifts, believers share a common life in Christ's spiritual body. They must use their differences to complement and serve one another. They must also be unified in their attitude and ambitions under the guidance of their Head.

Christ and

1 Corinthians 13 — August 25th

Charity never faileth

Modern people use the word 'love' so flippantly. Today it frequently denotes a temporary preference, a passing emotional feeling, or worst of all, lust, euphemistically described by another name. The Bible tells of a real love which transcends meagre human notions that are rooted in irrational subjectivism. Biblical love is sacrificial, and spends itself for the enrichment of its object. It loves the unlovely, undeserving, and is closely allied with God's grace and goodness. That is to say, it is grace in action: unmerited favour and altruism that stretch from heaven to earth and eternity to eternity. It is best demonstrated in the working of God the Father through His Son the Lord Jesus Christ. As Romans chapter 5 verse 8 famously puts it, 'But God demonstrates His own love toward us, in that while we were still sinners, Christ died for us' NKJV. Love is rooted in the divine nature, for 'God is love', 1 John 4. 7-8.

The Corinthians demonstrated many symptoms of an incipient preoccupation with themselves. Their gifts were employed for fleshly exhibitionism, rather than to edify their fellow Christians. They boasted in gifted men, and relegated Christ to a background position in the practical outworking of their meetings. In short, they behaved in a selfish manner that was inconsistent with God's love.

In view of this, Paul directs our minds back to the most important thing, saying, 'Love never faileth', v. 8. Chapters 12 and 14, which deal with spiritual gifts and their proper exercise, are held together by chapter 13, which explains the absolute necessity of true, God-centred love. Spiritual gifts are important. Without love, however, they lose their effectiveness and the God-glorifying purpose for which they were given. As dramatic as they may be, gifts will one day cease; indeed some have already passed off the scene. Nevertheless, love will abide as 'the bond of perfectness', Col. 3. 14, that undergirds the moral characteristics that the Lord wants the saints to manifest. 'When years of time shall pass away, and earthly thrones and kingdoms fall . . . God's love so sure, shall still endure, all measureless and strong', (F. M. LEHMAN *The Love of God*).

His Apostles

August 26th   1 Corinthians 14

Be not children in understanding

Christians are sometimes stereotyped as anti-intellectual. Sadly, this accusation fits some untaught believers. Nevertheless, the Lord expects the saints to love the Lord with their *minds*, Mark 12. 30, and to become practised in using their grey matter for the advancement of His church. Spiritual cogitation that leads to an understanding of how to properly deal with complex situations among believers ought to be the norm. When one is born again, God does not say, 'Leave your brain at the door'; rather, mature biblically-informed thinking is to be the hallmark of godly Christians. They are not to be 'children in understanding', 1 Cor. 14. 20, abusing the gifts and privileges of life in God's church.

If Christians should have any area of ignorance it ought to be in the realm of evil, v. 20. Let them be untaught and inexperienced in immorality and doctrinal falsehood. Unfortunately, it is often the reverse; professing believers are sometimes well-schooled in worldly thinking to the detriment of their spiritual understanding. For example, the Corinthians were well-acquainted with incest, 5. 1, illicit business practices, 6. 8, and idolatry, 8. 10; yet they were novices in conducting a God-honouring and spiritually edifying meeting of the assembly. They liked man-centred spectacles, misusing their God-given abilities for their own aggrandizement. Personal gratification trumped edification of their brothers and sisters. Glorifying the Lord took a backseat to ego-boosting theatrics, manifested in the unbridled misuse of the gifts of tongues and prophecy.

'Let all things be done unto edifying', 14. 26, is the operative principle of the gathering of the local church. To spend one's energy and gifts upon oneself is short-sighted and immature. Service must be performed with eternity and the judgement seat of Christ in mind, as opposed to momentary subjective highs and the acclaim of fellow human beings. That type of thinking is truly worldly and hinders the proper function of the assembly. Believers should think in obedience to God's word, and be unsophisticated as regards frivolous, wicked things.

Christ and

1 Corinthians 15. 1-34 — August 27th

The nineteenth-century Christian theologian and apologist JAMES ORR wrote that 'the resurrection of Jesus stands fast as a fact, unaffected by the boastful waves of scepticism that ceaselessly through the ages beat themselves against it; retains its significance as a cornerstone in the edifice of human redemption, and holds within it the vastest hope for time and for eternity that humanity can ever know'. Despite the impressively detailed historicity of the first-century accounts of this dramatic fulfilment of prophecy, Ps. 16. 10, many in Corinth doubted the possibility of physical resurrection. Probably they did so on naturalistic grounds, reasoning that since they had never seen anyone rise from the dead, then it must be impossible. Nevertheless, Paul unashamedly asserted that Christ did just that, and in so doing He laid a rock-solid foundation for the Christian faith.

If the Lord Jesus had remained in the tomb, His claims would be declared false. The apostles would be labelled perjurers, and the faith itself would have collapsed as a groundless fairytale. The gospel would be emptied of saving content, for there would be no factual basis for believing it. To put it succinctly, Christianity stands or falls with the bodily resurrection of the Son of God.

Thankfully, verse 20 confidently declares, 'But now is Christ risen from the dead, and become the firstfruits of them that slept'. This vindicates everything. Rather than being a charlatan or a deluded terrorist, Christ is powerfully declared to be the Son of God, Rom. 1. 4, and His word is verified, John 10. 17-18. The apostles are set forth as trustworthy witnesses of the greatest miracle in world history. Best of all, the promise of eternal life triumphing over sin, the grave, and death itself is assuredly demonstrated. Christ was the first to rise from the dead never to die again, but He shall not be the last. There remains a great harvest, when the spectacular fact of Christ, the resurrection's firstfruits, is shown to be the leader of a race of resurrected and glorified men and women. All who trust in Him for salvation will share in this future resurrection.

His Apostles

August 28th   1 Corinthians 15. 35-58

This mortal must put on immortality

Decay and death are ubiquitous realities in this fallen world. Hospitals are not in danger of becoming obsolete anytime soon, nor are funeral homes facing an uncertain future. Humanly speaking, the future of this planet – and of mankind itself – looks extremely bleak. The frequently used term 'mortal' comes from the Latin word for 'death', reinforcing the harsh nature of life in the post-fall world.

The Lord Jesus' resurrection completely alters the picture. Since He has triumphed over the grave, sin, hell, and death there is resounding hope for those who place their faith in Him. Crucifixion was a brutal death – one that made an example of the victim and inspired fear in the eyewitnesses. Not only was this execution excruciatingly painful, it also was calculated to inflict maximum humiliation upon the sufferer. Additionally, 'the Lord . . . laid on him the iniquity of us all', Isa. 53. 6, making Christ as the Lamb endure God's wrath against sin. Surely after such an ordeal He would never be heard from again, His enemies undoubtedly reasoned. But the resurrection proved that under divine power no sorrow is insurmountable, and evil has been vanquished (although it has yet to be totally eradicated from the earth).

Christ, as the resurrection's firstfruits, ensures that 'this mortal must put on immortality', 1 Cor. 15. 53. The believers' current bodies – so afflicted by the effects of life in a sinful world – will one day be transformed into glorious bodies fit for the presence of the glorified Lord throughout eternity. Our 'body of humiliation', Phil. 3. 21 JND, will give way to a version suited for dwelling in the Father's house, John 14. 2-3. Disease, pain, weakness, and exhaustion will be banished from our members, as we are finally liberated from the consequences of the fall. The limitations of our present mortal frames will be history, as the saints are freed to worship and serve the Lord without distraction. Death and its effects will be artefacts of the past when the Sun of righteousness arises 'with healing in His wings', Mal. 4. 2. The power of His resurrection will be the governing principle of the new heavens and new earth.

Christ and

1 Corinthians 16

August 29th

Let all your things be done with charity

Some people suppose that Paul was melancholy, austere, and uncaring – a stoic despot who chauvinistically imposed his personality on the early Christian church with unrelenting egotism. This could not be further from the truth. His Epistles exude a warm, genuine love towards saints in multiple and different situations. After all, the Holy Spirit used him to pen one of the greatest paeans to love in literature's annals, 1 Cor. 13. Even when he dealt with problems in the churches he was motivated by paternal love for his children in the faith, 1 Cor. 4. 15. He combined sagacity and strength with warmness of heart towards God's people, leaving them an outstanding example of the balanced life that ought to characterize believers and their congregations.

Whereas other men might be driven to bitterness or cynicism by dealing with recalcitrant converts and insidious false teachers, the apostle maintains an affectionate attitude towards the Corinthians. Instead of closing with a barrage of complaints against their persistent spiritual immaturity, he ends with an exhortation that all things should 'be done with love', 16. 14 NKJV. He was not jaded by his doctrinal or disciplinary conflicts with them. Even when they erred, his correction was motivated by genuine interest in their well-being. His instruction followed his call for them to 'stand fast in the faith' and be brave, v. 13, showing that he saw no inconsistency between strength and tender feeling. Power must be wielded in conjunction with love. In turn, he expected them to behave consistently with the same ethos.

Church discipline, the exercise of spiritual gifts, receiving fellow-saints, the proper usage of Christian liberty, and other relevant issues to the Corinthians could all be correctly resolved by acting in a loving manner. Today, love is spoken of a great deal, but the practice of it among believers is less frequent. Nevertheless, Bible teaching, fellowship, service, worship, and every other activity must be done in keeping with true Christ-like love. Only by imitating Christ the supreme Lover under the guidance of the Spirit can we live in this way, Gal. 5. 22.

His Apostles

Introduction to 2 Corinthians

Author & Date: Paul, c. A.D. 56.

Structure: The book broadly breaks down into three sections: (1) chapters 1-7: The apostleship and service of Paul explained in his defence (how to suffer and serve in holiness); (2) chapters 8-9: Instruction regarding the Corinthian saints' obligation in the collection for the poor (principles of giving); (3) chapters 10-13: Response to Paul's adversaries in Corinth (spiritual authority contrasted with the false equivalent).

Key Themes: 2 Corinthians' personal tone is the result of Paul's defence of his position and service. This offers several interesting autobiographical references within the book, and nearly every chapter mentions the apostle and his conduct towards the believers. What is more, his sufferings are explicitly detailed, e.g., 1. 5-10; 4. 7-18; 11. 22-28. Beyond mere historical documentation, however, Paul explains that his sufferings are for the benefit of the saints, 1. 6, and they are nothing in comparison with the eternal glory that is prepared for him by the Lord, 4. 17. Mortality will be replaced by immortality as Christ's resurrection power transforms him into a form fit for dwelling with God in glory, 5. 1-8. Among the many trials that he endures, 'the thorn in the flesh' becomes the means of keeping the apostle from pride, which would destroy his effectiveness; furthermore, it makes him more dependent upon the Lord's all-sufficient grace, 12. 7-11. The book also majors upon the superiority of the new covenant (with its eternal glory) to the old covenant, which false teachers often tried to foist on the early church, see chapters 3 and 4 in particular. The importance of giving in the light of God's grace and faithfulness to His promises is an important theme. The Lord generously gave us His riches entirely apart from any worth of ours. We in turn are to give to His people and Him. Comfort in trials recurs in the Epistle from the time we meet 'the Father of mercies and God of all comfort' on the first page, 1. 3-5, until the closing doxology, 13. 14. God's righteousness, reconciliation, and holiness are also important concepts at key points in the book. The proper restoration of a repentant brother, formerly put out of the assembly under discipline, is also discussed, 2. 5-11. The Epistle shows what love ought to be among the saints from beginning to end.

Christ and

2 Corinthians 1 — August 30th

The God of all comfort

Because of sin and its effects, the world is a dangerous place. There are innumerable trials and sorrowful situations that plague mankind. Christians are not exempt from the ordinary problems of life in a fallen world. What is more, they face other struggles that their unbelieving counterparts do not share. For instance, the unregenerate do not experience persecution, because they do not identify with the Christ who was crucified. In contrast, 2 Timothy chapter 3 verse 12 promises, 'Yea, and all that will live godly in Christ Jesus shall suffer persecution'. Likewise, Paul informed his converts of the difficulties along the saints' pilgrimage, and spent his time 'confirming the souls of the disciples, and exhorting them to continue in the faith, and that we must through much tribulation enter into the kingdom of God', Acts 14. 22.

Along with the natural and diabolical hardships that Christians encounter, they have 'the God of all comfort', 2 Cor. 1. 3, ministering to them throughout their sufferings. He consoles, encourages, and strengthens them in their strivings against sin and the evil one, with a view to equipping them to comfort others who are similarly afflicted. A believer who has been tested by opposition and hardship, yet has found God to be his encouragement, is uniquely outfitted to come alongside other beleaguered saints. He can assure them that the Almighty is in control, and that He 'works all things after the counsel of his own will', Eph. 1. 11. The tried and victorious Christian can testify that 'all things work together for good to them that love God, to them who are the called according to his purpose', Rom. 8. 28. The sovereignty of God and His immutable love are not theoretical truths to such saints, but are treasured facts borne out in their own scarred and battle-hardened frames.

No wound is beyond the Lord's ability to bind up. No sorrow is too deep for His ministry of consolation to assuage the pain. God the Son was 'a man of sorrows and acquainted with grief', Isa. 53. 3, and so is able to perfectly comfort the downtrodden. In the future He will 'wipe away all tears' and usher in a new creation where pain is permanently exiled, Rev. 21. 4.

His Apostles

## August 31st						2 Corinthians 2

Confirm your love toward him

Due to the inconsistent actions of human beings, local church discipline is sometimes fraught with difficulties. At times, believers are too lax and tolerate grievous sin that demands serious action, as in the case of the immorality dealt with in 1 Corinthians chapter 5. On other occasions, they react harshly and do not carry out correction in a truly loving spirit that reflects Christ's ways. Like many failings of the church the answer lies in the middle, for biblical truth is always balanced. The Lord Jesus Christ was 'full of grace and truth', John 1. 14. He knew when to be severe, as with the Pharisees who were obscuring God's word through their traditions, Mark 7. 6-13. But He also understood when to be merciful, as with the Syro-Phoenician woman, Mark 7. 24-29. He pronounced judgement on some, Matt. 11. 21, and mercy on others, John 8. 1-11.

In 2 Corinthians chapter 2 the mood of the local assembly tilted towards severity. Someone who was previously put out of the fellowship under discipline had repented, but they were unwilling, or at least reluctant, to restore him to their gathering. It was likely the man who is mentioned in 1 Corinthians chapter 5. Given their earlier lackadaisical attitude towards the immorality, and the apostle's stern command to excommunicate the offender, 1 Cor. 5. 3-5, it is no wonder that they overreacted in the opposite direction! It is a human weakness to fly from one extreme to another! that is why our thinking and activities must be guided by God's word.

Now Paul urges them to 'confirm your love towards him', 2 Cor. 2. 8. This meant that they were to reaffirm their wholehearted affection for the corrected brother. Unbounded Christian love must flow towards him again, assuring him that what God had pardoned, they too forgave. Otherwise, this man might despair and be permanently impaired in his walk with the Lord. Believers need to welcome and reiterate their love towards those who were judicially separated, but have now been biblically restored. Formerly disciplined believers must not be held at arm's length indefinitely. When they repent the assembly should restore them with assurances of love.

Christ and

2 Corinthians 3. 1 – 4. 6

September 1st

Important tasks are normally entrusted to trustworthy and capable individuals who faithfully discharge their service. In setting forth the nature of his ministry as a servant of the new covenant, Paul confessed that his sufficiency was divine in origin, 3. 5, and therefore did not emanate from within himself. His ability was dependent on the Lord's preparation of him for the work he was called to perform. Furthermore, his work did not set aside the old covenant on his personal initiative, but instead, was conducted under the authority of the God who gave the new covenant. Accordingly, his competence in this new era of blessed promises stemmed from the Lord equipping him for this labour. As BARNES comments, 'There is no assertion . . . that they were men of talents, or peculiar ability, but only that God had qualified them for their work, and made them by his grace sufficient to meet the toils and responsibilities of this arduous office', *Notes On The New Testament*.

The new covenant provides unparalleled access to the glory of God, v. 18, and its message must be presented clearly without any sort of deception, 4. 2. It is the good news that tells how God reveals Himself by shining His light upon those who are blinded by Satan. This diabolical enemy is the usurper of this age, whom men adore instead of their actual Creator, the rightful Lord of the universe. Today, Christians must continue to hold forth the word of life in an upright fashion.

Like the apostles, their trust must be in God and in the preparation that He provides for His service. No human knowledge, eloquence, or technology can replace divine training for the ministry of the gospel. Likewise, the service of the assembly is undertaken with conscious dependence on the Head of the church for His wisdom, strength, and mercy. In addition, believers ought to imitate Paul in proclaiming Christ, rather than themselves. The modern church is in danger of preaching about lesser things such as programmes, politics, culture, and social ills. The phenomenon of the celebrity preacher must also be rejected, for the church is to proclaim and adhere to *Christ*.

His Apostles

September 2nd

2 Corinthians 4. 7 – 5. 10

Earthen vessels

The world thrives on brash, assertive personalities who take what they want. Captains of finance and business are popularly dubbed 'masters of the universe', and athletes are praised in proportion to their muscular self-aggrandizing displays of power and physical grace. Fictional heroes in novels and films are almost always those who refuse to suffer abuse, and manage to enact their revenge by the end of the story. In contrast, Paul describes himself as a lowly clay jar – a self-effacing metaphor, to say the least. Beyond merely abasing himself, however, the apostle simultaneously refers back to a singular triumph under the judge Gideon. This historical reference aptly depicts the principles by which evangelism is to be conducted.

Gideon's forces for the battle against the Midianites first numbered 32,000, but at God's instruction they were reduced to 300, so that He could receive the glory for the triumph, Judg. 7. 1-8. In a three-sided guerrilla assault, his men sent their enemy into a wild panic by using the unconventional weapons of lamps within earthen vessels. The combination of a surprise attack at night with sensory duplicity – torches, shouting, and trumpets in multiple directions – utterly routed the hapless Midianites. Significantly, the clay jars were broken so that the light could shine forth.

In similar fashion, Paul often suffered so that the gospel could illuminate those lost in darkness, 2 Cor. 4. 8-11. As he says elsewhere, 'But God hath chosen the foolish things of the world to confound the wise; and God hath chosen the weak things of the world to confound the things which are mighty . . . that, according as it is written, He that glorieth, let him glory in the Lord', 1 Cor. 1. 27, 31. The vessel delivering the treasure of the gospel is meant to be ordinary, so that attention may be focused on God and His grace as shown in the Lord Jesus Christ. Therefore, the preacher must not exalt himself or draw attention to his gifts and attainments. 'Not I but Christ' must be the motto of the witnessing Christian. Moreover, whatever trials and persecution we endure, we can receive these as the means whereby the vessel is broken to let the light shine out.

Christ and

2 Corinthians 5. 11 – 6. 10 — September 3rd

Ambassadors for Christ

Ambassadors represent something larger than themselves – something that demands the subjection of personal interests to the greater task of advancing their government's interests. Diplomats must remember that they are the face of their homeland and stand for their nation's interests. Their treatment by the host country is also a good indicator of the reception that their sending nation's leaders would receive. In each of these ways this metaphor well describes the nature of Christian testimony in this world.

As Christ's emissaries, believers are to implore lost ones to be brought into harmony with God through His Son, whose sacrifice undergirds this reconciliation, 5. 20-21. Their lives in this world are representative of God and the new life that He freely provides through the gospel. Consequently, misrepresentations of the divine character may be conveyed through careless or sinful behaviour. On the contrary, a life sweetened by fellowship with God spreads forth the fragrant odour of eternal love and grace. The business practices of such Christians, their academic integrity, and their personal work ethic loudly say to the world, 'We are part of a new creation; our lives proclaim the glory of the Lord who saved us, and demonstrate the changes He has made in us'.

Because of sin, humanity is in a state of warfare against their Creator. Human minds are alienated and hearts are darkened against God. Yet He offers a way for minds to be enlightened and hearts to be cleansed, that they might be brought into a state of agreement and love with the Almighty. Only Christ's sacrificial death could remove such enmity from mankind – as well as satisfy the just demands of the holy Judge of the earth. Now the enemy is pacified and purified – declared righteous through the justifying blood of the Lord Jesus, v. 21. Redeemed sinners are remade as new creatures, v. 17, with new attitudes and aspirations to please the Lord who purchased them at such a price. In turn, these vanquished enemies, now turned to servants of the King of kings, go back to the spiritually dead world as ambassadors proclaiming the true and living God.

His Apostles

September 4th   2 Corinthians 6. 11 – 7. 16

Our passage begins with Paul underlining his affection for his spiritual children. Just as his heart was open to them, he desired that they would open their hearts to him. He then appeals to them to avoid close associations with unsaved people. They must not take on an unequal yoke. The picture is one of an ox and a donkey yoked together. Intimate relationships between a Christian and a non-Christian are equally incongruous. There are fundamental differences between them. Paul shows that by posing five searching rhetorical questions. The answer to each of them can only be 'No'. Paul's concern is that God's people should preserve their radical distinctiveness. The apostle's challenge is not merely negative. God makes a special promise to those who take Paul's plea to heart. He welcomes and receives all who reject the embrace of the world. They will experience His presence as members of His family. What an incentive to cleanse ourselves from all that defiles body and spirit and to advance in holiness in the fear of God!

Paul now recounts his experience in Macedonia when he was afflicted by outward opposition and inward anxiety. That included concern about how Titus had been received on a visit to Corinth as his representative. It was relieved by the comfort God supplied when Titus arrived, bringing his report. He recounted the reaction of the church in Corinth to Paul's first letter. It had produced godly grief and sincere repentance. Paul rejoiced. He would have preferred not to have grieved the Corinthians but their earnest change of heart encouraged him.

Their repentance had been radical. They had implemented church discipline against an unrepentant sinner and had put themselves in the clear after their earlier indifference to his sin. Thus, the purpose of *1 Corinthians* had been fulfilled. The church had been restored to loyalty to its spiritual father.

Their altered attitude had also encouraged Titus. His difficult task had been successful. They had reverently submitted themselves to his ministry and he had responded with deep affection to them. Paul's boasting in them had proved to be true.

2 Corinthians 8 — September 5th

The theme of chapters 8 and 9 is Paul's encouragement of the Corinthians to participate fully in the collection being raised among the Gentile churches for the impoverished saints in Jerusalem. This was a project very dear to Paul's heart. It was a practical display of the truth of the one body, Jew and Gentile – one in Christ. Titus was on his way to Corinth to collect their contribution. Paul wanted a good response.

He begins by telling the Corinthians about the Macedonians. Out of deep poverty and affliction, they had displayed a wealth of generosity. They had given beyond their means and had begged to be allowed to share enthusiastically in the gift for Jerusalem. The dedication of their means reflected their self-consecration to God. Paul holds them up as an example. He urges the Corinthians to excel in the gift of giving just as they excelled in so many other areas of Christian living.

Sharing in the collection would not be the result of compulsion. It would be a response of love. By far the greatest incentive to generous giving to the needs of others is the supreme example of the Lord Jesus. He was rich beyond all telling, yet voluntarily He became poor. He stooped to be born in the manger. He humbled Himself to labour at the carpenter's bench. In His ministry He depended on the gifts of loyal supporters. At last He descended into the abject impoverishment of the cross. His self-abnegation was to enrich us beyond our wildest dreams. Let the Corinthians rise to the challenge. They had planned to participate; now let them put their desire into effect by giving proportionately to their resources. Let their willingness be proved by their actual contribution. After all, their abundance would supply the deep needs of their brothers. One day the roles might be reversed and others would meet theirs.

In planning the collection Paul had taken the utmost care to make it clear that everything was utterly above board. The highest standards of probity were being maintained. Titus and two unnamed exemplary brothers were coming to receive Corinth's offering. Let the Corinthians prove by their generosity that Paul's boasting about them was true.

If there be first a willing mind

His Apostles

September 6th

2 Corinthians 9

God loveth a cheerful giver

Paul continues to exhort the Corinthians to contribute to the relief fund for Jerusalem. He reminds them of their readiness to commit themselves to involvement. He had boasted to the Macedonians about Corinth's plan to play its part. That boasting had stirred them to contribute as lavishly as they did. Now the time had come for the Corinthians to fulfil their promises. Would their actions live up to their words? If they did not, Paul, to say nothing of the Corinthians, would be humiliated. Paul trusts that when the messengers arrived his converts in Corinth would justify his confidence in them by contributing willingly and 'not as a grudging obligation', v. 5 NKJV.

To encourage their generosity, Paul now states a general principle. To sow in a niggardly way leads to a niggardly harvest but to sow bountifully produces a bountiful harvest. This certainly applies to financial giving. Each individual should give as a free expression of personal commitment. There must be no grim sense of obligation, far less the grudging attitude that grieves at our loss of what we have given. Genuine giving is a cheerful experience. God delights in His people when they give to Him with delight in their hearts. What counts in giving is the glad spirit of sacrifice behind it.

Giving will certainly not impoverish us. God promises His people that He will lavishly supply our every need. He could not be more generous in His bounty. He will liberally provide us with the resources to be liberal givers. Generosity to others not only meets their needs, it produces thanksgiving to God. As the believers in Judaea received the bounty of their Gentile brothers, they would glorify God because the contribution from them established the reality of their confession of faith in the gospel of Christ. By their giving the Gentiles showed they had a faith which worked in everyday life. Further, bonds of affection and fellowship in prayer would result from the handing over of the Gentile offering to the needy Jewish Christians.

The chapter ends with praise to God for His gift above all others, the Lord Jesus. The Son of God is heaven's supreme gift, utterly beyond human language to express or explain.

Christ and

2 Corinthians 10

September 7th

Our chapter begins with Paul appealing to the Corinthians by the example of the meek and gentle character of Christ to respect his personal integrity and apostolic authority. Some of them were insinuating that he was totally inconsistent. He was craven when present and courageous when absent. Paul asserts that he would indeed act with boldness against those who levelled such charges when he came to Corinth. He did not want to have to do so, hence his plea to abandon the slurs against him.

His detractors suspected that Paul led his life by fleshly standards. He makes it clear that although he lived in a body of flesh and blood he was waging a spiritual warfare by spiritual values. In his conflict for God he used spiritual weapons. God's panoply is divinely mighty in the hands of His warriors to demolish the strongholds of Satan. Paul knew that the key battle is fought for the minds of men and women. He destroyed the bulwarks proud intellectualism had erected against the knowledge of God, and took every thought captive to obey Christ. As part of that conflict, he desired to see the loyal obedience of the Corinthians when he came to them. He was then prepared to punish all who continued to defy his message and authority.

That authority was delegated. It had been given to Paul by the exalted Lord with the aim of upbuilding the Corinthians. Paul's critics needed to realize that his actions and his written words would match. Paul present and Paul on paper were consistent.

However, Paul realized that God had assigned him an 'area of influence', v. 13 ESV. He would glory only in what had been achieved in that sphere. His area of service definitely included Corinth where he had brought the gospel and planted the church. False teachers had trespassed into the sphere marked out for the apostle, claiming credit for the labour of others. Paul never did. Nor did he intend to. His hope was that the growing maturity in faith of the Corinthian assembly would free him for evangelistic labours where Christ was still unknown. Paul never lost his bright vision to evangelize the Gentiles, nor his fervent desire to gain the commendation of the Lord.

We will not boast of things without our measure

His Apostles

September 8th

2 Corinthians 11

I speak as concerning reproach

Paul writes highly ironically in this passage. He feels that he has to defend the authenticity of his apostleship against an attack from Jewish teachers who had arrived in Corinth. They made tremendous claims, asserting that they were 'super-apostles', v. 5 ESV. Actually, they were false apostles, human emissaries of Satan masquerading as apostles of Christ. Their ruthless aim was to enslave and dominate the Corinthian Christians. The message they brought was a false gospel. They spoke about a Jesus, but their Jesus was not the risen and exalted Lord of apostolic testimony. Paul was jealous for the pure devotion of the Corinthians to the Saviour and feared that the incomers would lead them astray, even as the serpent had deceived Eve.

One charge the intruders laid against Paul was that he had not taken financial support in Corinth. They argued that this proved his dubious status. Surely, the better the teacher the greater would be his fee. In truth, Paul had waived his right to receive support from the Corinthians. This was to make it crystal clear that his preaching was 'free of charge', v. 7 ESV. Paul's policy proclaimed the utter freeness of the gospel. It also destroyed the claim of the incomers to have the same level of ministry as his. They greedily sought monetary gain. Paul never did. Who then was the true apostle of Christ?

Triumphalistic bombast was the stock-in-trade of these religious bullies. Paul cringes as he stoops to their level and answers their boasting in kind. Yet boast he must. The Corinthians were willing to kowtow to these overbearing men. Paul must dislodge their grip. The apostle asserts all their claims and more for himself. His was actually the better pedigree by far.

Yet, paradoxically, what Paul really boasted in was his weakness, not his strength. Massive suffering in the service of Christ was the hallmark of an authentic apostle. It was his autobiography. Paul silences the boasters by cataloguing his reproaches and reverses, his humiliations and hardships. Above all, he underlines his wearing anxiety for every church and his deep emotional involvement with each weak, stumbling Christian. These are the true credentials of a leader of God's people.

Christ and

2 Corinthians 12.1-13

September 9th

A thorn in the flesh

Forced by his opponents' attack on his apostleship to continue to use their tactics of boasting, Paul moves on to his experiences of visions and revelations of the Lord. Specifically, he narrates the most wonderful of those divine disclosures. He does so with reticence. He describes himself as 'a man in Christ' rather than making too personal a claim to such a lofty privilege. Paul had been caught up into Paradise, the third heaven. He had entered the immediate presence of God. There he had received verbal communications which he had never disclosed on earth. The words he had heard were too sacred for repetition. He was not permitted to communicate them. Paul refrains from further boasting about any other spiritual mountain tops. He was concerned about anyone thinking too much of him. Most of us are concerned about people thinking too little of us!

Paul is eager to emphasize his infirmities. God had permitted him to be harassed by a 'thorn in the flesh'. From one point of view, this perplexing problem was a messenger from Satan which he was using to try to thwart Paul's effectiveness. More significantly, God was using it to prevent His servant from becoming carried away with pride and over-elated by the transcendent glory of the wonderful revelations he had been privileged to receive. The Holy Spirit did not inspire Paul to specify the thorn. Probably it was an embarrassing and humiliating physical disability. We should be thankful for Paul's reserve. It enables each of us to identify with his experience whatever distressing problem afflicts us.

The thorn was so severe in its effects that Paul had pleaded with the Lord for its removal on three separate occasions. Those prayers were not unheeded. They were answered in an unexpected way. The Lord's response was not to take away the thorn. Rather, He assured His servant that His grace was all sufficient. The purpose of Paul's painful problem was to highlight that wonderful promise. God's aim in our trials is to teach us to lean on His divine power in our human frailty. Paul gladly welcomed the Lord's answer. He gloried in his weaknesses because through them Christ's strength was displayed.

His Apostles

September 10th — 2 Corinthians 12. 14 – 13. 14

As he concludes, Paul turns to a planned visit to Corinth. He stresses that he had no intention of changing his stance on finance. He would continue to waive his right to support from the Corinthians. Paul did not want their money. He desired their personal affection and their devotion to Christ. He was willing to spend his time and energy on them unstintingly. However, he was wounded by a wicked slander that he was extracting finance from them by guile, using his associates like Titus as front men. Paul answers by appealing to the integrity of Titus. Could they really imagine him taking advantage of them?

Nor could they really believe that of Paul. His goal was their spiritual upbuilding, not his own gain. His fear was that he would encounter gross disharmony and flagrant sexual sin on his visit. Let his readers be aware that he would use severe discipline if serious sins were proved. In doing so, he would be acting in the power of the risen Christ. That would be the proof some of the Corinthians were demanding that he was Christ's authentic and authoritative spokesman.

If they were so keen to put Paul's apostolic claims to the test, why did they not test themselves, to discover by self-examination whether they had really received Christ? If they did so, a consequence ensued. Paul would be the last man for them to criticize since he had led them to faith in the Saviour.

Paul prays that his readers may be preserved from sin and do what was right. That was his great concern, not his apostolic reputation. His aim was to bring the Corinthians to a mature, robust faith. His energies were wholly focussed on their spiritual well-being. His hope was that the letter would produce obedience, repentance, and restoration. That would remove the need for stern measures when he arrived in Corinth.

The epistle ends with an appeal to rejoice, to aim for maturity, mutual encouragement and harmony, and an assurance of the presence of the God of love and peace. Paul prays for the Corinthians to experience the grace of the Lord Jesus Christ, the love of God the Father, and the fellowship of the Holy Spirit in his final words of Trinitarian benediction.

We do all things . . . for your edifying

Christ and

Galatians has never been attributed to anyone but Paul, even by the most radical critics. Indeed, it is such an intensely personal and passionate document that it bears the authentic stamp of the great apostle in verse after verse.

The identity of the readers is debated. One view holds that they were ethnic Galatians, people of Celtic heritage, living in North Galatia, an ancient kingdom conquered by the Romans. The alternative position is that they lived in the southern area of the Roman province of Galatia, which had wider boundaries than the old Celtic kingdom, and were of varying racial backgrounds. Put simply, they were the people converted to Christ in Pisidian Antioch, Iconium, Lystra and Derbe, now in central Turkey, Acts 13-14. This view gives a better life setting for the letter than its rival. If it is correct, then Galatians dates from the early 50s AD and may be Paul's first Epistle.

The key to Galatians is the spiritual crisis facing these young churches. These new Gentile Christians, delivered from idolatry, were being swayed by eloquent Jewish preachers who were telling them that they had to submit to circumcision and keep the law of Moses to be saved, Acts 15. 1. With insight, Paul realized that legalism undermined the foundations of the gospel. With passion, he wrote to defend its truth.

The intruders were using three arguments. The six chapters fall into three sections, each of two chapters, designed to refute them. The false teachers said that Paul was not a fully-fledged apostle. He replies that his calling was by God and Christ, yet recognized by the Twelve. They asserted that circumcision was necessary to be part of Abraham's family. Paul shows that it is faith in Christ which makes men and women Abraham's seed. They insinuated that salvation by grace led to immoral living. Paul emphasizes that it is God's Spirit who produces true holiness. This can never result from adherence to law.

Positively, this polemical epistle emphasizes that salvation is bestowed by grace alone, is received by faith alone, and is in Christ alone. Thus, it is to the glory of God alone. It rests entirely on the all-sufficient sacrifice of the Lord Jesus. Nothing can be added to His saving work. Christ supplemented is Christ supplanted. That is the abiding message of Galatians.

His Apostles

September 11th

Galatians 1

Another gospel: which is not another

Paul confronts the issues raised by the false teaching head-on at the start of his letter. His apostleship was a divine appointment. Its source was in the risen Lord Jesus and God the Father. They had bestowed it on him directly. No human agent had been involved, neither Ananias nor any of the Twelve. On the Damascus road Paul had witnessed the resurrection glory of Christ. The exalted Lord had commissioned and sent him as His representative, Acts 26. 15-18. The apostles were invested with the full authority of Christ Himself, John 13. 20. They had a unique foundational role. We have no apostles today. Their authority is enshrined in the writings of the New Testament. We cannot dismiss apostolic teaching as just good advice or merely an expression of personal opinion. Rather, we must recognize it as the commandments of the Lord, 1 Cor. 14. 37.

Paul also emphasizes that Christ's death was a divine achievement. Galatians is the only Epistle where he includes a reference to the cross in the opening paragraph. The false teaching threatened the unique value of the saving work of Calvary. There, Christ gave Himself for our sins so that they might be forgiven, and rescued us from the domination and doom of the present evil age. In carrying out this great deliverance, the Lord Jesus fulfilled God's will and brought His Father infinite glory. To add to His work on the cross is to detract from that glory.

The apostle stresses that the gospel of Christ is a divine announcement. He had received it from God, not from men, by revelation not instruction. The message being presented to the Galatians was a different gospel. It was no gospel at all. It could not bring salvation. There is only one gospel. The gospel of Christ is the only saving message just as He is the only Saviour. The teaching which was swaying the readers had fundamentally changed the gospel from the inside out by adding human merit. Solemnly, Paul affirms that to preach it or any substitute gospel is to incur God's eternal judgement. What matters is the truth of the message, not the prestige of the messenger. Because the gospel of God's grace is exclusively His good news we must take every opportunity to proclaim it boldly to all.

Christ and

Galatians 2 — September 12th

Justified by the faith of Christ

In our chapter Paul uses a phrase twice, in verse 5 and again in verse 14, which is the keynote of the whole letter. The phrase 'the truth of the gospel' embodies the message of Galatians. That is what Galatians is all about. The key element in 'the truth of the gospel' is that salvation from sin is received 'by faith in Jesus Christ', v. 16 NKJV, plus absolutely nothing else. Personal trust in Christ without any works of merit secures complete forgiveness. Verse 16 is a remarkable text. It asserts positively, no less than three times in one verse, that faith in the Lord Jesus is the way, and indeed the only way by which anyone, Jew or Gentile, can be justified by God. Justification is a legal term, borrowed from the law courts. It means 'to be declared to be in the right'. It is the verdict of 'not guilty' pronounced by the Supreme Judge of all the earth. That verdict can never be set aside. It is final. God fully acquits everyone who places their faith in the risen Saviour. Verse 16 asserts, again three times, negatively that justification does not come through moral performance or spiritual achievement. 'The works of the law' will never justify any human being. How different is biblical Christianity from all man-made religions! We must recall every day that we are saved by grace alone, through faith alone. We must constantly preach the gospel to ourselves.

Paul asserts these great truths as he records a distressing confrontation with Peter. Peter had happily enjoyed fellowship with Gentile Christians. He had shared meals with them without any problem. However, under pressure, he had reverted to eating only with Jews. Sadly, his example was followed by all the Jewish Christians in Antioch, even Barnabas. Paul declared that Peter's behaviour was hypocritical and out of line with 'the truth of the gospel'. To impose a kosher diet on Gentiles denied the truth that there was only one way of salvation. There are no second-class Christians. Every believer is justified before God 'in Christ', v. 17 ESV, and in Christ alone. None of us has any special claim on God. He accepts us because of the merits of His Son. Faith brings us into living union with Him. Faith means 'Forsaking All I Trust Him'.

His Apostles

September 13th — Galatians 3. 1-14

The just shall live by faith

There are two opposing approaches to securing God's favour: believing and doing. The false teachers presented the way of works. Paul demonstrates that it is the way of faith which alone can bring us into God's blessing.

He shows this, firstly, from the experience of the Galatians. Paul challenges them with a series of rhetorical questions. They could not deny that they had already received God's greatest gift, the Holy Spirit. They had not received Him by doing, but by hearing and believing the message of a crucified Saviour. How foolish of them to think that having started their Christian life in the Spirit they could be brought to spiritual maturity by human effort! The grace and power of God's Spirit was constantly supplied to them by faith and not by works. We must realize that all of our Christian life depends on daily trust in Christ and reliance on the Holy Spirit.

Secondly, the experience of the readers exactly matched the classic example of Abraham. He was counted righteous before God when he believed God and His promise, Gen. 15. 6. It is those who trust Christ who are Abraham's true descendants. Circumcision was unnecessary. God always planned to bless all the nations through Abraham. Men and women of faith of every background share Abraham's blessing of justification.

Thirdly, the rest of the Old Testament supports the apostle's argument. Relying on the works of the law leads to cursing, not blessing. Every commandment must be kept all the time. All who break even one commandment stand under God's curse, Deut. 27. 26. Doing never justifies. Believing justifies. The just shall live by faith, Hab. 2. 4. How can we escape the curse of the broken law? Another passage pronounces a curse on all hanged on a tree, Deut. 21. 23. On the cross, the Lord Jesus experienced the full execution of that dreadful curse. It is the great exchange. He came under God's curse as our substitute, not for Himself, because He never sinned. By enduring it in our place He liberated us from it. Now, instead of experiencing God's cursing we enjoy His blessing in Christ. Through faith, we receive the Holy Spirit, the crown of salvation.

Christ and

Galatians 3. 15-29 — September 14th

The argument of this passage is complex and challenging. Firstly, Paul shows that the law of Moses cannot set aside God's covenant with Abraham, fulfilled in the gospel. The law was given 430 years after the final confirmation of the Abrahamic covenant. In everyday life, when a will has come into effect it cannot be set aside. So the law could not supersede God's promise to Abraham, centred on Christ, his Seed. The precision of the language is important. The promise was made to Christ, one Seed, not many descendants.

Secondly, Paul emphasizes that God's covenant with Abraham was a *promise*, not a contract. God took all its obligations on Himself. In a promise, everything depends on the reliability of the person who makes it. In contrast, the law was like a contract. It was a two-party arrangement made between angels, representing God, and Moses, representing Israel. The nation placed themselves under a duty to obey God's commands. Their blessings depended on them fulfilling that obligation. The key note of promise is God's 'I will'. The key note of the law is His 'Thou shalt'. Our relationship with God rests entirely on His faithfulness. He can never break His promises.

Thirdly, Paul shows the true function of the law. It could never give a right standing before God because it never gave the power for its obligations to be fulfilled. Thus it could never save. Its purpose was to demonstrate that men and women are transgressors, showing that they persistently break God's commands. Its role was temporary. God's people were only under it until Christ came. The law was like a prison warder. In Christ, men and women are liberated. The law was like the slave who strictly supervised the master's children. In Christ, men and women are adults. Why renounce freedom and maturity to go back to bondage and childhood?

By faith, we are brought into living union with Christ, pictured in baptism. In Him, we are Abraham's seed, heirs of God's promises. These wonderful spiritual privileges are equally shared by every Christian irrespective of race, status, or gender. One with Him, we are one with each other.

All one in Christ Jesus

His Apostles

September 15th   Galatians 4. 1-18

No more a servant, but a son

Paul continues to contrast the era of the law and the age of the gospel. Remember that the false teachers were seeking to put the Galatian Christians back under law. He uses the illustration of an heir to an estate. Until he reaches his majority, he is little different from a slave. A steward looks after his property. A guardian controls his personal life. Only when he becomes an adult does he enter into the enjoyment of his privileges as son and heir. So under the law God's people were in minority. They were enslaved to the ABCs of religion until Christ came.

The Father sent His Son into the world at the exact time He had appointed. In His providence, He had prepared the ancient world for the coming of the Lord Jesus. One language, Greek, was widely spoken around the Mediterranean. The scriptures had been translated into it. Synagogues had spread far beyond Israel. Many earnest Gentiles disillusioned with idolatry attended them. These 'God fearers' would respond in large numbers to the gospel. The Roman peace prevailed. The seas had been cleared of pirates. Paved roads linked the empire. Built for the legions, they would be used by evangelists. A faithful remnant in Israel consciously waited for Messiah. Among the nations many unconsciously yearned for a divine Deliverer.

The Son came as a real man, the son of Mary. His mission was to liberate from the law's bondage by paying the infinite price on Calvary. Thus, God's people were brought to their full sonship. God has also sent the Spirit of His Son into the heart of every Christian to assure us of our status as God's sons, by bringing us into conscious intimacy with our dear Father. Paul addresses each reader personally. Every single one of them was no longer a slave but now stood in the closest possible relationship with God – His son by grace, and His heir through Christ.

Before their conversion the Galatians had experienced the bondage of paganism. Now, under the zealous influence of the false teachers, they were on the very brink of submitting to weak and worthless legalism. It brought no spiritual power and offered no spiritual wealth, only a new enslavement. What a poor exchange for true freedom in Christ alone!

Christ and

Galatians 4. 19-31 — September 16th

Two sons

The passage starts with Paul expressing the deepest possible pastoral concern for the Galatians, his little children in Christ. God had used him to lead them to faith. Now he tells them that he is enduring the spiritual equivalent of childbirth once again. This time it was to see them brought to Christ-likeness, real spiritual maturity. That cost him a deep expenditure of time and emotional energy in earnest intercession and the writing of this mighty Epistle. Are we willing to spend and be spent for the blessing of others?

Ideally, Paul would have loved to have come alongside the Galatians to appeal to them face to face to remain faithful to the gospel. Instead, he relies on the challenging exhortation of the Spirit-inspired words of his letter.

The apostle presents an allegory, a symbol of spiritual truth from history. He draws attention to the story of Hagar and Sarah and the sons each bore to Abraham: Ishmael and Isaac. The two mothers and their sons embodied the conflict in Galatia. The point of the argument is that legal bondage and evangelical freedom cannot co-exist. They stand in deadly opposition.

Hagar was a slave. Sarah was free. Ishmael was born by the operation of the flesh. Isaac was born in fulfilment of God's promise. Hagar represented Mount Sinai. That stern mountain symbolized the system of legalistic bondage with its headquarters in earthly Jerusalem. In contrast, the heavenly Jerusalem is the mother city of the true people of God, the citadel of spiritual freedom. Isaac corresponds to all Christians, God's freeborn sons by His Spirit. Ishmael sneered at Isaac. So the followers of the law persecuted those who relied on the gospel. Ishmael's taunts led Sarah to demand the casting out of the slave woman and her son. She knew that Ishmael would always be a threat to Isaac. Abraham could only have one heir, not two.

Legalism endangered the spiritual inheritance of the Galatians. They had to make up their minds. Which covenant would they follow, the Old or the New? They must grasp that spiritually they were the children of Sarah. They were born to be free. Liberty in Christ was their birthright. It is ours.

His Apostles

September 17th — Galatians 5

Be led of the Spirit

Christians are called to liberty. We must firmly stand in our God-given freedom, purchased for us by the Lord Jesus the great Emancipator, resisting all attempts to bring us under legalistic bondage. However, it is a common misconception that liberty equals licence. Actually, they stand in contrast. Liberty is not giving free rein to our flesh, our fallen self-centred nature. It is not doing whatever we like. Rather it is being the men and women God wants us to be, and doing what He wants us to do. Christian freedom is freedom from sin to serve God. That involves commitment to the loving, practical service of our fellow believers. Paradoxically, it is in serving God and others that we are most truly free.

Such a lifestyle is impossible naturally. It is only possible by the supernatural power of the Holy Spirit. He is the dynamic of holiness. We are exhorted in our chapter to live empowered by Him, to submit to His gracious leading and to keep in step with Him. Walking in the Spirit demands reality. It means seeking to forsake sin and to obey God's commands. It means feeding on God's word and praying, drawing on His grace and power. It is living as a Christian with all our heart.

However, full perfection will never be achieved on earth. We all have a 'fifth columnist' within, our flesh. The flesh and the Spirit are locked in deadly conflict. Only by reliance on the Spirit will we be freed from gratifying the desires of the flesh. Even then, the continuing battle prevents the full fulfilment of our aspirations for God and holiness.

The flesh manifests itself in an ugly catalogue of vices, all involving self-gratification. These works are varied. They are sexual, idolatrous, anti-social, and intemperate. In contrast, the Spirit produces a beautiful cluster of fruit. The nine-fold fruit of the Spirit essentially means being like Christ. His life perfectly manifested these virtues. The Holy Spirit is at work reproducing Christ's character and conduct in His people. Are the features of love, joy, peace, longsuffering, kindness, goodness, faithfulness, meekness, and self-control apparent in my daily life? Only the grace of the Spirit can produce them as I submit to Him.

Galatians 6

September 18th

This chapter spells out what life in the Spirit actually means. Galatians, above almost every other book in the Bible, has strongly stressed that salvation does not issue from good works. As Paul ends, he emphasizes equally strongly that salvation manifests itself in good works. Free from the law's bondage, we are nonetheless called to fulfil the law of Christ, to obey what He commanded and to live the way He lived. That means living for the blessing of others. We are exhorted to carry the burdens of our fellow Christians, to help them in their weaknesses and problems, and to share their difficulties and sufferings. That includes gently seeking to restore brothers and sisters overtaken by sin. We must do so free from all moral superiority, conscious of our own tendency to fall. We are called to support financially those who enrich us spiritually by their teaching of God's word. In everything, we must sow to the Spirit, not the flesh, looking to reap an eternal harvest of resurrection glory.

That glorious future is sure but it demands present perseverance. It is our task to do good without giving up. Wherever there is human pain and distress, the Christian should be at hand to help with his time, his talent, and his treasure. In our global village, over-exposure to the news of wars and earthquakes, famines and tidal waves, disasters of every kind often leads to 'compassion fatigue'. We should resist that temptation. We must not become weary in well doing. Whether in distant lands or in our own communities, we must be eager to provide practical aid and spiritual help to all in need, following in the steps of our Master. However, we must pay special attention to the needs of all those with whom we share a Father in heaven, the fellow members of the worldwide family of faith. Our brothers and sisters in Christ have the primary claim on our aid. Opportunities to do good abound. Let us seize them.

Paul takes up the pen from the scribe to conclude the Epistle in his own handwriting. With bold letters, he brings us to the cross of Christ. The world disdains it. The Christian glories in it. It is our only source of eternal salvation and endless exultation. Let us never cease to glory in our Saviour's death for us.

Do good unto all men

His Apostles

Introduction to Ephesians

Ephesians is one of Paul's prison letters, written from Rome, around AD 61. The lack of personal references suggests that it was from the outset intended for wide circulation, and may well be 'the epistle from Laodicea' which the Colossians were bidden to read, Col. 4. 16. We see the wisdom of God, detaining His servant in order that the church could be permanently enriched by this writing.

If Romans is the exposition of the gospel *par excellence,* then Ephesians is correspondingly pre-eminent in setting forth the truth of the **universal church** which is Christ's body. It stands as the supreme revelation of the eternal purpose of God from before the foundation of the world, 1. 4, and extending 'throughout all generations forever and ever', 3. 21 ESV.

The letter divides into two parts. Firstly, chapters 1 to 3 unfold the purpose of God to reconcile all things unto Himself, heading them up in Christ. This reconciliation begins by uniting in one redeemed community – the universal church – men and women of every nation. Paul is the steward of this special revelation. Language is taken to its limits to spell out the sheer **wealth** of God's power exerted in the resurrection of Christ, and His grace in the salvation of believers.

Chapters 4 to 6 set out the present provision for the practical outworking of this great purpose, and calls for a worthy response on the part of the redeemed, both in personal conduct (**'walk'**) and collectively. **Warfare** must be waged, ch. 6, against the devil and his hosts, who constantly oppose the believers' enjoyment of their unique blessings in Christ.

In richly expressive metaphors, the church is seen to be: (1) a sacred **building**, a temple indwelt by God; (2) a **body** of diverse members, growing towards the stature of its Head, and, by implication (3) a **bride**, the object of Christ's sacrificial love and constant care. This corporate emphasis in the letter is very important, and reminds us that God's plans include *all* of His people, and their relations one with another forged by grace. *'Love'* is the essential unifying bond, with over twenty references. Above all, the letter is radiant with the glory and grace of the Triune God; the harmonious activities of Father, Son, and Spirit are seen throughout in a series of triadic patterns.

Ephesians 1. 1-14 — September 19th

Accepted in the beloved

In these opening verses each Person of the Trinity co-ordinates in love to secure the blessing of the believer. In language vibrant with adoration, Paul writes of the sovereign **will** of the Father, the redemptive **work** of the Son, and the confirmatory **witness** of the Holy Spirit. Verses 3 to 14 form a single sentence, showing that the glorious truths unfolded form a unified purpose of grace. The goal at every point is not simply human blessing, but the praise of the glory of God, vv. 6, 12, 14.

The **source** of our blessings lies in the will of God. The location of our blessings is not earth but 'the heavenlies' and 'in Christ'. The Epistle emphasizes that believers are eternally united with Christ, and hence with one another. We are 'in Christ' and Christ is in us. The electing and predestinating purposes of God reach back before the world's foundation. But mark the objective: 'that we should be holy and without blame before Him'. Costly love, not merit, was the sole basis of such an amazing objective, cp. Deut. 7. 7-8. Throughout, the sovereign will of God is stressed, vv. 5b, 9a; what He has purposed, He will bring to pass. What assurance this conveys!

Yet, these sublime purposes depended absolutely on the **sacrificial obedience** of 'the Beloved'. How could guilty rebels and captive sinners find acceptance in the Beloved? We have 'redemption through his blood'. In the work of Christ, all the wealth of God's grace has been lavished on us, v. 7, and abounds towards us, v. 8.

Moreover, the grand divine plan is ultimately to 'unite all things' in Christ, v. 10 ESV, which here implies 'the entire harmony of the universe, which shall no longer contain alien and discordant elements, but of which all the elements shall find their centre and bond of union in Christ' (J. B. Lightfoot). In pursuance of this, even the Gentiles ('ye also') have been admitted in Christ to the holy fellowship of the people of God, cp. Deut. 32. 9. What an inheritance is ours!

The Spirit's seal upon those who believe denotes ownership, security, and authority, 2 Tim. 2. 19; Matt. 27. 66; Esther 8. 8. The indwelling Spirit is the witness and guarantee of our inheritance!

His Apostles

September 20th — Ephesians 1. 15-2. 10

By grace are ye saved through faith

'For this cause', v. 15 RV, i.e., in view of the mighty truths already unfolded, Paul prays for spiritual wisdom and illumination for his readers. His prayer is marked by thanksgiving, intercession, and reverence, recognizing their faith, love, and progress. It is full of the majesty, glory, and power of God exercised for the realization of His purposes for Christ and His people. He prays that they might understand what is 'the hope of his calling', not least that they participate in 'the riches of the glory of his inheritance in the saints'.

If the classic Old Testament demonstration of God's power is the deliverance of Israel at the Red Sea, the resurrection and exaltation of Christ is a far greater miracle. Paul desires that no less a power may operate in the experience of the believers. Its limitless potential is seen in the raising of Christ to the highest heights of glory, 'far above all principality and power . . . and every name'. Everything is under His sovereignty, cp. Col. 2. 10. Here we have the additional disclosure that He is given as Head over all things *to the church which is His body*. Such is the heavenly calling and destiny of the church that she is the 'body' (through whom the will of the Head is realized) and the 'fullness of Him (Christ) that filleth all in all'. She is indissolubly united to the supreme Lord of the universe.

And it is that same resurrection power that has been active in the salvation of the individual believer, 2. 1, 5. The helpless and hopeless condition of both Jew and Gentile is sketched, vv. 1-3. *But God* in infinite mercy met our dire need in love, power, and grace. Note our *identification with Christ,* vv. 5, 6 (twice), 7. Throughout the coming ages this will be the abiding monument to the glory of God's grace, for salvation is the *gift* of God, and the church is the *masterpiece* of His new creation.

It is typical of Paul to stress the ethical objective of all this grace, cp. Titus 3. 5-8. In a context which is crystal clear that salvation is not the result *of* works, we are reminded that we are saved *for* good works.

> 'Teach me, Lord, on earth to show,
> By my love, how much I owe'.

R. M. McCheyne

Christ and

Ephesians 2. 11-22 — September 21st

Israel in the Old Testament was ordered by God to be a people separated from the moral and spiritual pollutions of the heathen world. He hedged them about, and many of the precepts of the law (e.g., food laws) were designed to make social intercourse with Gentiles difficult. The 'middle wall of partition', 2. 14, separated Jew from Gentile, just as there was a literal wall in the Jerusalem temple barring the Gentile under pain of death.

The Gentiles were 'separate from Christ', v. 12a NASB, having no part or lot in the Messianic people, Rom. 9. 5. Like Ruth the Moabitess, they were all strangers to the covenants of promise. 'Having no hope and without God' in the world accurately describes the prevailing moral conditions of the ancient pagan world.

But now what a glorious transformation has been brought about by the death of Christ, and realized in *union* with Christ, v. 13a! The vast redemption price is expressed by references to His blood, and His cross. A new entity – the church – has thus been brought into being, by including the Gentiles on *an equal footing with the Jews*: a body (with a common life), a city (with equal citizen privileges), a family (with no poor relations), and a magnificent spiritual temple (integrated together with diverse living stones), vv. 16, 19, 21. Old barriers and enmities have been swept away, for Christ has *made* peace, *preached* peace, and indeed *He is* our peace. The church is thus uniquely the vehicle and display of God's reconciling power, the effects of which will one day be seen to be universal.

The world is broken at every level; alienation and conflict make life misery for millions. How tragic, too, is the injury to the cause of Christ caused by the endless rifts between Christians! Nevertheless, throughout the earth God's reconciling grace through the gospel is seen, and, unheralded, the church still grows unto that holy temple in the Lord. The outcome is not in doubt, for the blessed Trinity is ever active to that same end, 'In [Christ] ye also are builded together for an habitation of God through the Spirit', v. 22. Even now 'through [Christ] we both have access by one Spirit unto the Father', v. 18.

He is our peace, who hath made both one

His Apostles

September 22nd — Ephesians 3

The manifold wisdom of God

In this chapter, Paul resumes his prayer for the saints. He digresses to unfold 'the mystery of Christ', vv. 2-7, and his faithful stewardship of it, vv. 8-13. The prayer, vv. 14-19, in view of the sheer magnificence of the truths expressed, fittingly concludes with a doxology.

Paul indicates that the 'mystery of Christ' has been committed to him. A mystery in the New Testament is something undiscoverable by human reason, but now revealed by God. In essence, this mystery is that believing Gentiles participate in all the promises and privileges in Christ on exactly the same basis as the believing Jews, something previously hidden, but now revealed by the Spirit, vv. 5, 9. The terms of inclusion in this holy fellowship are such that 'the Gentiles are *fellow*-heirs, and *fellow*-members of the body, and *fellow*-partakers of the promise in Christ Jesus', v. 6 RV. Paul's special mission is to make this known to all men – something that bows his heart in humility and wonder as he considers his past.

The church, however, is not simply for the benefit of the redeemed, but (according to the outworking of the eternal purpose of God) for the display of the 'multi-faceted' wisdom of God to spirit beings in the heavenly realms, cp. 1 Pet. 1. 12c. Since the outworking of God's purpose centres in Christ, faith in Him opens direct access to the Father's presence with boldness and confidence.

The conclusion of the prayer aligns with Paul's earlier prayer, Eph. 1. 15-22, but reaches fresh heights of adoring worship and petition. Again, Paul's focus is fully Trinitarian. Our enablement lies in the *Father's* riches of glory, v. 16; the power resides in the indwelling *Spirit*; his desire is that *Christ* might make His home in our hearts by faith and that we might know His love, cp. John 14. 23. The grand objective is to enter into all the dimensions of divine purpose, cp. Job 11. 7-9, not as isolated individuals, but 'with all the saints'. His final plea is that saints might come to be all that God wants them to be, before he closes in a paean of praise to the Triune God who has the limitless resources to respond beyond even an apostle's thought.

Christ and

Ephesians 4. 1-16 — September 23rd

Chapter 4 begins the second part of the Epistle. The sublime truths of chapters 1 to 3 place weighty practical and ethical obligations on the church's members. What would constitute a worthy response in view of such a heavenly calling?

Significantly, Paul calls for humility, meekness, and longsuffering – qualities despised rather than admired in the ancient world. The church is not yet perfect, therefore the unity established by the Spirit of God must be diligently maintained, v. 3.

The apostle then identifies a seven-fold uniqueness uniting Christian faith and life: (1) one body (of Christ), i.e., the church; (2) one Spirit; (3) one hope (to share the glory of Christ); (4) one Lord; (5) one faith (in the Lord Jesus); (6) one baptism (in water); (7) one God and Father of all. These considerations are central to the shared life of the church.

But there is also diversity. Upon His exaltation, the conquering Lord received gifts for men, and shed them forth upon His church. Some gifts were foundational in their exercise – apostles and prophets, 2. 20. The essential truths revealed through them are permanently recorded in the writings of the New Testament. The gifts of evangelist and pastor-teacher have to do respectively with bringing men *to* Christ, and thereafter instructing them *in* Christ and looking after them *for* Christ. These gifts will continue to be graciously supplied until the church is complete. Not that these gifts monopolize the church's ministry; rather, they are 'for the perfecting of the saints' enabling them in turn to develop their particular gifts 'unto the work of ministering, unto the building up of the body of Christ', v. 12 RV.

The objectives of this corporate growth are stated, vv. 13-16. Saints will be preserved from the instability caused by wily false teachers. More positively, the body will grow up to approach the fullness which is resident in the Head, Christ. This collective growth must be sought and experienced by local assemblies today. If Christ is to be truly represented and proclaimed, we need to develop in Christ, not simply as individuals, but in relation to one another. Love is indispensible, if the body of Christ is to grow and be built up, cp. vv. 2b, 16.

Walk worthy

His Apostles

September 24th — Ephesians 4. 17-32

Be renewed in the spirit of your mind

This portion continues Paul's directions for the walk (practical conduct) of the believer. It is well for every Christian to recognize plainly that there are past pursuits, behaviours, and associations which no longer have any place in the holy life of a member of the body of Christ.

Firstly, they are not to behave as the Gentiles do, vv. 17-24. In language reminiscent of Romans chapter 1, Paul describes the spiritual condition and resultant lifestyle which characterized the pagan world: darkened, cut off from the life of God, hardened in heart, conscience calloused, with the result that sinful desires are indulged.

In complete contrast to the ignorance of pagan society, the Christian has *learned* Christ through the gospel. Indeed, Christ Himself is his teacher even though apostolic lips may have been instrumental. The earthly life of Jesus shows us God's ideal for human behaviour. Thus we should discard the ways of the old man and put on those of the new. The 'old man' expresses what we once were in Adam; we must always remember that God has terminated that old solidarity. The 'new man' is Christ, whom we must 'put on', Rom. 13. 14, the present tenses indicating that this is to be realized afresh in daily experience. Significantly, the *thinking* of the believer is pivotal, 'be renewed in the spirit of your mind', cp. 12. 2. The resultant righteousness and holiness is God's new creation in the believer.

Paul then supplies precepts to direct the new social life of the believer, Eph. 4. 25-32. In this section two considerations are to regulate his living: (1) give no place to the devil, and (2) grieve not 'the Holy Spirit of God', where the full and expressive title adds solemnity to the appeal. The devil is adept at exploiting any openings, and those who nurse grievances provide him an easy opportunity. 'Out of the abundance of the heart the mouth speaketh', and here Paul indicates that our words are to be wholesome and edifying, conveying grace to the hearer, vv. 29, 31. Ever mindful that our *many* sins have been forgiven, 'Be ye kind one to another, tender-hearted, forgiving one another, even as God for Christ's sake hath forgiven you'.

Christ and

Ephesians 5. 1-21 — September 25th

Walk as children of light

Today's passage continues the focus on the *conduct* of the believer: walk in love . . . as children of light . . . circumspectly, vv. 2, 8, 15. We follow the example of the Lord, who gave Himself for us, and, by implication, there will be fragrance from lives where there was formerly a stench. The contrast is emphatic between our former state of darkness and our new situation in the *light* of God, vv. 8, 9 RV, 13. In verse 14 the exhortation is to abandon the darkness of the spiritually *dead* and embrace the light of Christ. The moral battles to escape the pollutions of the world are every bit as real today, as they were in the 1st century. As MARTIN LUTHER put it, 'We can't stop the birds flying overhead, but we can stop them building a nest in our hair'.

Paul's words are plain, vv. 3-7; we dare not fool ourselves or be misled by sophisticated falsehood. Those who engage in the sins described here have no place in the kingdom of Christ and God. The apostle traces the wickedness to its source, covetousness, a subtle sin which can also take respectable forms, cp. Rom 7. 7f.; Col. 3. 5. We cannot be 'partakers' in iniquity, and at the same time 'fellow-partakers' in the body of Christ, Eph. 3. 6.

Spiritual wisdom and alertness to every passing opportunity should mark the believer, 5. 15-17. Instead of social drinking with its intoxicating effects, saints are to 'be filled in the Spirit', v. 18 YLT, i.e., be fully controlled by the Holy Spirit. A result of such blessing will be a readiness to sing praises to God, the outflow of thankful hearts. The terms 'psalms, hymns and spiritual songs' include both the canonical psalms and edifying sacred songs of human composition. The songs of Zachariah, Mary, and Simeon illustrate the close connection between the Spirit's fullness and praise to God, Luke 1. 46ff., 68ff.; 2. 29ff.

Paul mentions two further things. Firstly, thanksgiving to God at all times for all things is easier to talk about than practise, but Paul could genuinely embrace all his experiences as furthering God's purposes for him, cp. Rom. 8. 28. Secondly, be subject to one another, motivated by reverence for Christ – the antidote to many domestic and assembly problems today.

His Apostles

September 26th — Ephesians 5. 22 – 6. 9

If the former section had to do with counsel to believers in general, the apostle now focuses on the Christian household and specific relationships within it. Today, Satan is relentlessly attacking the family and seeking to undermine scripture's teaching associated with it. On the positive side, it is instructive to observe how the matchless love of Christ for His church supplies both the model and inspiration for the mutual responsibilities of husbands and wives – a fine example of how teaching and practice must interact in authentic Christian living.

The Christian wife is to be *subject* to her own husband, as unto the Lord. This recognizes the Creator's design for harmony within the family based on the acknowledged headship of the husband, v. 23. That Christ is Saviour of His body suggests that the husband is to be the defender and protector of his wife.

The husband is further directed to *love* his wife, as Christ also loved the church. And how did He do so? Firstly, His love was utterly *sacrificial*. Secondly, His love and care is *constant,* and *purposeful*: cleansing and preparing the church with the great day of presentation in view. The deep 'one flesh' relationship forged by marriage reflects the eternal union between Christ and His people, so that 'he that loveth his wife loveth himself'.

Children are to be brought up in 'the discipline and instruction of the Lord', 6. 4 ESV; they are to *obey* and *honour* their parents. The fifth commandment is distinguished as the only one which carries a promise. On the other hand, parents have an obligation to their family to act in a Christ-honouring manner, and always with a view to their salvation, 2 Tim. 3. 15.

Slavery was a major feature of Ephesian society, yet the gospel tended to draw the sting from this institution, and curb its excesses. Slaves and masters *alike* have a Master in heaven, so *both* have a powerful incentive to serve the Lord Christ. On the other hand, slaves must not belittle or short-change their earthly masters on that account.

What a powerful testimony and force for good is the well-ordered Christian household! Cp. 1 Tim 3. 4-5.

Christ also loved the church, and gave himself for it

Ephesians 6. 10-24 — September 27th

Put on the whole armour of God

Finally, the apostle issues a call to warfare. Just as Canaan was robustly defended by heathen armies and walled cities, there are hordes of wicked spirits intent on denying saints the enjoyment of their inheritance in the heavenlies. All Christians are inevitably involved in spiritual conflict.

The key imperative is to *'stand'*, vv. 11, 13, 14. It is not a question of seeking to possess new ground, but rather to stand foursquare in the enjoyment of blessings secured for us by Christ's victory over all the powers of darkness, cp. Col. 2. 15. We must never underestimate the foe; yet, conversely, the power available in God is superior, so we must continually seek His strengthening, Eph. 3. 16. Satan will typically attack on the 'evil day', a day of trial, cp. Job 1. 6, 13. As surprise is one of his core tactics we must be prepared at all times, Eph. 6. 18.

In scripture, clothing is a metaphor for character, commitment, and equipment for a task, and the 'whole armour of God' pictures the protection of a heavily-armed Roman soldier. As the conflict is spiritual, only spiritual defences will work.

The girdle of truth and the breastplate of righteousness recall the garments of God Himself, Isa. 59. 17, hence practical righteousness, faithfulness, and truth are in view. We need to fight in the strength of personal integrity. Readiness to share the gospel at all times will be a preservative to ourselves, as well as a blessing to others. The shield of faith recalls the large shield preferred by the Romans, and points to steadfast faith in God as the means of quenching the fiery darts of Satan, cp. Dan. 3. 17-18. The head is vital, the seat of thought and sight, so the hope and assurance of salvation as a helmet serves as essential protection. The Lord Jesus in His wilderness temptations showed masterful dexterity with the sword of the Spirit which is the word of God, quoting, 'It is written . . .', Matt. 4. 4-10.

Fittingly, this great Epistle ends in *prayer*. Paul has prayed fervently for the Ephesians, but now he humbly solicits their perseverance in vigilance and prayers, not for his personal freedom or prosperity, but that the gospel might be effectively communicated by him.

His Apostles

Introduction to Philippians

The Philippian assembly had its origin in the labours and sufferings of Paul and Silas, Acts 16. After those difficult and costly experiences, they had become an outstanding Christian assembly, dear to Paul's heart and characterized by sacrificial service and giving; see 2 Cor. 8. 1-5.

Paul spent two years imprisoned in his own hired house in Rome, Acts 28. 16, and it is most likely that his letter to the Philippians was sent from there.

Paul's purpose in writing is fourfold. Firstly, he is writing a **thank you letter**, acknowledging a recent substantial gift from the assembly. Christians should be quick to acknowledge the sacrifice of others. 'Fellowship' is a key word in the letter, and the Philippians' gift was a very practical and timely expression of their fellowship with Paul and the work of the gospel.

Secondly, it is a letter of **commendation**. This is a courtesy too. Fellow servants Timothy and Epaphroditus are warmly commended. As we read the glowing statements about Epaphroditus, 2. 25-30, we might well each ask, 'What could Paul have written about me?'

Thirdly, he writes to **reassure** them as to his current situation. So we have Paul the *prisoner* exhorting and encouraging those who are at liberty! What is the secret of such rare joy and contentment? His life is *Christ-centred*; Christ is his whole reason for living. His passion is for Christ's gospel, and he rejoices that, despite the faulty motives of some, Christ is preached, and that converts have been won even in 'Caesar's household'.

Finally, and most importantly, he writes to exhort the saints to **unity and harmony**. Paul is concerned lest a difference between two sisters in the Lord would escalate and mar **the saints'** harmony and effectiveness. The antidote to disunity is for each to share the **mind** of Christ – this is a recurrent and vital emphasis in the Epistle. Christ is the purpose, pattern, prize and power for living. Far from showing favouritism, Paul goes out of his way to emphasize his love for *all* the saints; note the frequent reference to 'all'.

Let us learn from Paul to pursue the truly joyful Christ-centred life, share his passion for the gospel, and seek the unity and fellowship of all God's children.

Christ and

Philippians 1. 1-20 — September 28th

Today's reading focuses first of all on the affairs of the Philippians, and then those of Paul.

A unique bond exists between the soul-winner and his converts. As Paul writes to his beloved Philippians his heart is overflowing with thanksgiving vv. 3-11. He gives praise for their fellowship in the furtherance of the gospel, vv. 3-5; that even in his bonds they are partakers with him of grace. He prays that their love may abound and that they may be free from offence until the 'day of Christ', vv. 6, 10. This is the first of several references in the letter to the future consummation of Christ's purpose for the believer. The day of Christ is ushered in by the coming of Christ for His people. We should focus on this goal as a stimulus to faithfulness and purity. Verse 6 is wonderfully comforting: what God has graciously begun in our lives He will complete to His everlasting glory.

Paul next expresses a real passion for their friendship, vv. 7-8. His desire was heartfelt. How church life would be revolutionized if we each took a leaf out of his book!

Paul then prays for their fruitfulness, vv. 9-11. Whilst they bring him much joy, he is not complacent; he wants their love to abound, yet also to be knowledgeable and discerning, in view of spiritual dangers identified later in the letter. A section which begins with thanksgiving thus climaxes with the desire that they should be to the glory and praise of God.

Paul's love for his converts leads him to update the Philippians regarding his personal situation. He speaks frankly of his imprisonment, and he alludes later to sorrow, 2. 27, but what is the secret of his irrepressibly joyful mindset? It is that Christ is the centre and substance of his living. See how he rejoices that Christ is preached, 1. 14, 15, 16, 18, even by those whose motives were dubious. He has faithfully and fruitfully witnessed to the élite soldiers of the 'praetorian guard', v. 13 RV. The only thing that ultimately matters is that 'Christ shall be magnified in my body, whether it be by life, or by death'. Our circumstances may not always be to our liking, but Paul surely points the way to Christ being glorified whatever our experience.

His Apostles

I have you in my heart

September 29th   Philippians 1. 21 – 2. 11

We live in a selfish age. The 'me first' culture dominates the godless world around us. Yet this letter shows that authentic Christian living both (1) has *Christ* as its centre and passion, and (2) places the needs of *others* ahead of our own, 2. 3. Thus, Paul's concern for the spiritual welfare of the Philippians outweighs even his longing to be in Christ's immediate presence which would be 'far better'.

The apostle faces uncertainty as to the outcome of his imprisonment. Whatever happens, however, it is important that the Philippians' lives match their profession – that they conduct themselves in a manner worthy of the gospel: by boldness, 1. 26; by being a colony of heaven, v. 27, just as the city of Philippi gloried in being a colony of Rome. Paul is concerned about their *corporate* experience, not simply individual progress. He appeals for complete unity both in defence and attack. Focus on the gospel always strengthens and unites the church.

The beginning of chapter 2 presents an impassioned appeal to unity and steadfastness. The ground of the appeal in verse 1 consists of the wonderful blessings which saints have received from Christ, the Father, and the Spirit, cp. 2 Cor. 13. 14, and the tender affections enjoyed between Paul and his converts. The mind, or thinking, of the believer is seen to be critically important: 'likeminded'; 'lowliness of mind'; 'let this mind be in you', Phil. 2. 3-5. We need to *think* and act as Christ did.

The mindset that looks not on its own interests but, sacrificially, thinks first about the needs of others is seen in the sublime example of the Christ Himself. Subsisting in the 'form of God', such was His concern for the needs of others that He made Himself nothing, assuming the form of a servant. In the pathway of absolute obedience, further humiliation is seen in His enduring the death of the cross. Such selflessness has resulted in His exaltation and the award of 'the name which is above every name', v. 9 RV. All rational beings will one day acknowledge Him throughout the regions celestial, terrestrial, and infernal, and in so doing *glorify God*. 'It is the way the Master went; should not the servant tread it still?' H. Bonar.

Philippians 2. 12-30 — September 30th

If in chapter 1 we have 'Christ the passion of a devoted life', in chapter 2, we have 'Christ the pattern of a selfless life', W. Trew. The Lord Jesus is in fact the first of four such examples, the others being Paul himself, Timothy, and Epaphroditus.

But first, Paul appeals to the believers to 'work out [their] own salvation with fear and trembling', adding, 'For it is God which worketh in you both to will and to do of his good pleasure' – a most reassuring truth, v. 13. His appeal is corporate and not merely individual, as the particular threat posed to the church was that of disunity. Note the reference to 'murmurings', and to its fruit, 'disputings', something that proved highly destructive to Israel in the wilderness. Addressing such dangers they will together be a bright witness to the world, and a joy to Paul when he renders account at the judgement seat of Christ, v. 16.

Paul's humility, and his estimate of the Philippians is seen in likening himself to a drink offering, v. 17 NKJV, associated with their (to him, much more significant) sacrifice and service. In his reference to his personal *sacrifice* as a drink offering there is a clear implication of the costly pouring out of his life in devotion to the Lord and his people.

Paul then commends **Timothy**, whom he plans to send to assess conditions in the church. He focuses on Timothy's outstanding credentials as a servant, for Timothy truly exhibits single-minded concern for the glory of Christ and the blessing of His people. What could Paul have written about me?

As the fourth example of selfless devotion to others, he writes to allay their fear regarding their envoy **Epaphroditus**, whom they had heard had fallen ill. In so doing he commends this faithful *soldier* of Jesus Christ. This dear brother had devotedly laboured, and indeed hazarded his own life, to ensure that the gift sent by the church reached Paul safely, v. 30.

This Epistle shows no demarcation between doctrine and practice; they intermingle. The self-abasement and exaltation of Christ carry the greatest possible implications for our behaviour. In a self-centred age, let us display the mind of Christ so nobly demonstrated in these His servants.

His Apostles

October 1st   Philippians 3

That I may know him

This chapter, rich in athletic metaphors, presents Christ as Paul's *pursuit* and goal. Accordingly, we are exhorted to 'rejoice in the Lord', a healthy discipline for the believer. There are those whom Paul warns about who could thwart progress in the Christian race, vv. 2, 3. In the first instance there are Judaizers, legalists who relentlessly sought to bring Paul's converts into bondage. Their modern counterparts abound.

In fact Paul was once a prime example of just such a person. We have first of all what Paul once was in Judaism, vv. 4-7, then what he aspires to be as a Christian, vv. 8-11. As a Jew he had unrivalled credentials racially, religiously, and in zeal as a defender of his ancestral faith. But the Damascus Road experience changed all that, and forced a radical reassessment of his priorities. In his 'profit and loss account', vv. 7-8, he confesses that every glittering prize once held dear came to nothing in the light of Christ and His cross. Christ is now his unqualified gain, his righteousness, and pursuit. He has an insatiable desire to 'know him, and the power of his resurrection, and the fellowship of his sufferings, being made conformable unto his death'. Paul longs to know Christ in a progressive and constantly enriched experience – the power of the risen Lord realized in his daily life and service. Not that death can have the final word: the path of perseverance in suffering with Christ has resurrection as its ultimate goal and eternal reward, cp. 2 Tim. 2. 11, 12.

Paul presents himself here as an ardent spiritual athlete untroubled by 'those things which are behind'. 'Reaching forth' means stretching out his head and body towards the *goal*. His total focus is the prize, the crown, glory everlasting, by contrast with the fading earthly victor's wreaths. The upward calling of God in Christ 'is a heavenly calling in origin, operation, and final issue', H. C. G. MOULE. May we each run with endurance the race for which we are entered, Heb. 12. 1.

The final appeal is to our status and destiny as colony people whose 'citizenship is in heaven', Phil. 3. 20. Thence we await the coming Saviour who will then complete His work in us – conforming our bodies of humiliation to His body of glory.

Christ and

Philippians 4

October 2nd

In this chapter the apostle appeals in turn to two hard-working sisters, Euodias and Syntyche, to 'be of the same mind in the Lord'. His appeal is prefaced by words of great tenderness and affection, and is bracketed by the words 'in the Lord'. As we each submit to the lordship of Christ differences can be resolved. Sometimes the assistance of a third party is helpful, hence the words to the 'true yokefellow', v. 3. Here is further cause for thanksgiving as Paul recalls those 'whose names are in the book of life', cp. Luke 10. 20.

The following verses, Phil. 4. 4-7, point the way to personal tranquillity and collective harmony. Far from asserting our rights, we can afford to be gentle and forbearing, knowing that 'the Lord is at hand', both currently and prophetically. Further, the antidote to anxiety is prayer and gratitude to God. As a direct consequence, 'the peace of God, which surpasses all understanding, will guard your hearts and your minds in Christ Jesus', v. 7 ESV. Once again the Christian's mind is pivotal, and disciplined thinking is seen to be central to the believer's experience of the God of peace. Literally 'reflect on these things', v. 8; the focus is on the *character* of our thoughts: wholesome, pure, and commendable.

In a most valuable paragraph, vv. 10-19, Paul supplies the secret of Christian contentment: it is fellowship with Christ, 'I can do all things through Christ which strengtheneth me', v. 13. He has been initiated into the secret of how to be humbled and how to abound, how to be filled and how to be hungry. Yet the Philippians have done well to remember him in his bonds, v. 14, continuing their previous generosity. Referring to their substantial gift, Paul sees it as a true burnt offering to God, v. 16, employing language akin to that used to describe the sacrifice of the Lord Jesus Himself, Eph. 5. 2! Moreover, the Lord is no man's debtor, v. 19.

How different the sensitive and spiritual approach of the apostle from the crass commercialism of the world's fund-raising! Their sacrificial gift had brought Paul the prisoner great joy; now it moves him to a concluding doxology.

The God of peace shall be with you

His Apostles

Introduction to Colossians

This is a prison Epistle by Paul, written evidently about the same time as Ephesians, and dealing with the relationship between the church and the Lord. Ephesians deals with the church as the body of Christ and its functioning; Colossians, with the headship of Christ and His glory as supreme Lord. Colossians also has links with Philemon, who lived in Colossae.

The supremacy of Christ is directly relevant to the problems which were assailing the assembly at Colossae. These included false ideas about the power of angels, and the alleged spiritual benefits to be sought through ecstatic experiences. Such teachings robbed believers of their intimacy with Christ as their Lord and hope, while stirring up a search for hidden 'knowledge'. Paul writes of Christ as Lord of the cosmos as well as of the church, insisting that His redemptive work includes the cosmic dimension.

References such as 'in him dwelleth all the fulness of the Godhead bodily', 2. 9, are aimed at correcting ideas which were being proposed by false teachers. They taught that all matter is evil, including the material universe. This was a common idea in ancient heathen Greece. It led to a denial that God created the world. Paul writes of Christ as Creator and Sustainer of all things, including angels. He declares that we are 'complete in him', v. 10, needing no other source of 'fulness'.

Paul declares that all Christians can have confidence and hope in Christ as our all. This is his answer to the suggestion that we should seek superior status over other believers through visions and ascetic rigour. He claims that there is completeness of satisfaction for all believers because their satisfaction is found in Christ – Christ is our life, His word is our guide.

As being 'risen with Christ' we can 'seek the things which are above', 3. 4. We can put off what speaks of the old, barren life of the flesh and put on Christ. The word of Christ and the peace of Christ must rule. All believers, not just an initiated élite group, can have a rich experience by the means open to all. In daily work we all, even if slaves, can know that we 'serve the Lord Christ', v. 24.

Colossians 1. 1-19 — October 3rd

The image of the invisible God

Paul recalls how the Colossian Christians had been saved when they responded to the gospel. They had received the grace of God, as Epaphras reported, and had entered into the enjoyment of salvation. Paul prays that they may develop in their experience of God, in practical holiness and the knowledge of God's will. He reminds them that God's grace gives them access to the firm hope of a spiritual inheritance, free from the powers of darkness, safely in the kingdom of the Son of His love.

All of this blessing is theirs because of the place which Christ occupies in the divine purpose, as well as in their own experience. Christ is the key to all Christian experience. He is supreme Lord over all creation and over the church. In Him the Father is visibly expressed, for the Son is divine, exactly as the Father is.

Christ is supreme over all creation because He is its Creator and all exists for His glory. Angels are included in this creation. He also maintains all creation. When Isaiah in chapter 6 saw the glory of Jehovah, it was, in fact, the glory of Christ which he saw, John 12. 41. Christ is also Lord over the church, the Firstborn, the supreme Lord, as raised from the dead. Our link with Him is as the crucified, risen and glorified Head of the church.

Christ is Head of the church, His body. This closeness helps us to take it in that we are 'meet to be partakers of the inheritance of the saints in light', Col. 1. 12. We should not feel that we need an intermediary angel or priest as we come to Him. Coming near to us in truly human flesh, He went to the cross, and we are now 'complete' in Him, accepted because of our link with Him.

He lost none of His eternal glory in becoming man; rather, He raised His own redeemed to hitherto unimaginable privilege. Israel's high priest went into the inner sanctuary once a year on behalf of his people. We are bidden to draw near through our divine Forerunner and glorious Lord, Heb. 6. 20; 10. 19.

'Within the holiest of all, cleansed by His precious blood, Before Thy throne Thy children fall, and worship Thee, our God', J. G. DECK.

His Apostles

October 4th — Colossians 1. 20 – 2. 7

Christ in you, the hope of glory

The Saviour's unique glory, invested with the 'fulness', 1. 19, as the Reconciler of all things to God, is the basis of our blessing. Our past, as enemies of God, has been removed from God's reckoning by the work of Christ 'in the body of his flesh', v. 22. We note again how Paul rejects any suggestion that Christ lost anything of His deity in His taking on humanity in a literal human body.

But our acceptance with God when we were justified is not the end of what God has in mind for us: He aims to 'make us holy, without blemish and unreprovable in his sight'. It is clear that this is not a mere theory, for Paul writes of our continuing 'in the faith, stable and steadfast, not shifting from the hope of the gospel', v. 23 ESV. These three terms are taken from the language of building, solidly constructed, and not shaken (as in an earthquake). Christian progress in the things of God is a down-to-earth practical thing, not a matter of visionary ecstasy.

Paul's ambition, pursued in his service at great physical cost (his 'flesh', v. 24), was directed towards the blessing and promoting of the body of Christ. He suffered on behalf of Christ and His church. He valued highly God's purpose to bless the Gentiles in this age of grace. So he can write to the Colossians, who had been sinners of the Gentiles, of 'Christ in you, the hope of glory', v. 27. Whether he means Christ dwelling in individual believers, or Christ 'among' Gentile believers corporately, this is a great wonder. But he goes further – he writes of 'every' person, v. 28, in the Colossian assembly being brought to maturity through the power of God working in the ministry of Paul. This is an answer to the élitist visionary aspiration of the questionable teachers whom Paul opposes.

He accepts that this goal involves struggles on his part. All this on behalf of Gentile believers whom he has never met! The goal is that they may reach 'the knowledge of God's mystery, which is Christ', 2. 2 ESV. This is open to all believers. Did they desire wisdom and knowledge? It is all in Christ, hidden from the world at large, but open to all believers – 'all the treasures of wisdom and knowledge'. This will be lived out in a steady walk, solidly founded, and gratefully enjoyed.

Christ and

Colossians 2. 8 – 3. 4 — October 5th

Since Christ Jesus is your Lord, says Paul, you need not be subject to ritual and mere human traditions. Christ is your Redeemer and your hope. He, our victorious Saviour, is exalted to the right hand of God, supreme over all angelic beings. We need not seek to gain favour with any spiritual forces, good or bad. Christ overcame all hostile spirits at His cross, exposing their helplessness to prevent His work there for us.

In circumcision the men of God in Old Testament times declared their covenant relationship with God. But our link with God depends on what Christ secured for us on the cross. He died to cancel our debt of sin, paid the debt in full, was victorious by His dying, rose to declare His victory and is at God's right hand for us.

Old Testament ritual, therefore, is superseded, for it merely gave a shadowy advance hint of Christ's work for us. The old food laws and feast days, linked to an earthly order of approaching God, have been made obsolete.

Preoccupation with seeking mystical experiences or ascetic practices will rob us of our enjoyment of the vital link we have with Christ our Head. It is in experiencing His ability to meet our daily need for spiritual strength that we, in fellowship with other believers, can become spiritually strong.

We have died with Christ, but we are also raised with Him to walk in newness of life. In accepting the reality of this link we can begin to see life's experiences from a heavenly standpoint. Thus, we value and set our hearts upon what is in keeping with our allegiance to the glorified Lord. This applies both to material things and spiritual aspirations; there is no room here for self-congratulation based on our supposed superiority.

Our life is hid with Christ in God. We must not expect that worldly people will admire our choices or understand our priorities. This hidden life is secure, but it glorifies God the Giver and seeks no human sponsor or recognition. We take the long-term view: when Christ is manifested in the future day of His glory we shall then be manifested with Him. Heaven knows only one song: Christ our Lord is to be worshipped and adored.

Let no man therefore judge you

His Apostles

October 6th   Colossians 3. 5-25

Ye have put off the old man with his deeds

Today's reading falls neatly into three sections: *putting off* what belongs to pre-conversion days, *putting on* what belongs to our new life, and learning the supreme value of *submission* in the Christian life and its relationships.

The presence of the characteristic Pauline use of 'therefore' focuses our thoughts on the implications of the foregoing doctrines on the practicalities of daily living. The new life in Christ mentioned in the earlier part of the Epistle is not just a theory. It has to be lived out. What kind of things, then, marked the old godless life? It displayed a devotion to unclean things, a grasping for self-gratification, and a violation of decent regard for others in act and word. Self is at the heart of thinking in this old way of life, and it calls down the wrath of God. This 'old man' is marked by disobedience to God. The rejection of the authority of God leads to corruption, perversion, and strife. And such, basically, were we all. Verse 11 may even suggest that our loyalties, racial, social, or religious, if followed without Christ, are a mere manifestation of our need of new birth.

But now, in Christ, all that marked us is changed, for Christ is all, and in all. This is a strong basis for the uniting of diverse characters. A first result of the change is that we consider the needs and feelings of others. We forgive, for we remember how we need forgiveness. We acknowledge that we are united with believers in one body, a basis for peace. We unite in praising God, as the 'word of Christ', v. 16, makes us conscious of the blessings which demand joyful expression. This leads to thankfulness as the atmosphere in which we conduct our daily lives. Do we recognize ourselves as we meditate on this teaching?

In contexts where authority is involved in our relationships Paul uses *submission* as a key concept. He teaches that in marriage the husband has the role of leader, the wife of follower. But there is a balance – he is not a dictator. Children are expected to obey parents, but the parents need to show them consideration. Slaves should obey masters (and in doing so serve the Lord Christ), but the masters need to remember that they are bondsmen of the Lord. Such is orderly, Christian society.

Christ and

Colossians 4. 1-18 — October 7th

Walk in wisdom toward them . . . without

What sort of impression do our values and behaviour make on people whom Paul describes as being 'without', v. 5? In other words, what do unsaved people around us think of how we treat each other, and them? The practical implications of the end of chapter 3 of this Epistle are extended in today's reading.

The Colossian Christians are exhorted here to show a prayerful interest in the gospel, reflected in their prayers for Paul in his apostolic preaching. Paul himself would seek to preach plainly, as he ought. He expects that they will also be interested to hear about the spread of the gospel.

But the Christians will also make a contribution to the cause of the gospel by their own conversations and attitudes. Charitable opinions and wholesome values expressed make a vital contribution to the spread of the truth of the gospel.

We notice here how the believers show an interest in each other. The ungodly take note of this. Paul himself, though these Colossians were not his converts, is interested in their general and, specifically, spiritual welfare.

We notice the tactful reference to Epaphras, 'one of yourselves'. Paul is anxious to give moral support to a good Christian who is known to the Colossians, indeed who probably had led them to Christ.

We notice that Paul includes other fellow-workers, Luke and Demas, men also known to the Colossians. He also sends greetings to Christians in a neighbouring assembly, and to an individual believer whose home is used as a meeting-place for the assembly. This recognition of the contribution to Christian witness made by relatively obscure believers betokens true spiritual values. The influence of such consistent but quiet believers in a district often has an impact on public perceptions of the gospel which only the judgement seat of Christ will fully reveal.

What about Archippus? We are not told what his role was in the divine plan. Paul's exhortation to him implies that Archippus knew what God expected of him. What does He expect of each of us? May we seek to fulfil what He has entrusted to us. It may not be noticed by many, but it is significant.

His Apostles

Introduction to 1 and 2 Thessalonians

The gospel had been brought to Thessalonica by Paul and Silas during Paul's second missionary journey around 49-50 AD. They had reached Thessalonica after they had preached in Philippi and been treated very violently there. Their preaching drew forth a violent reaction from the Jewish community in Thessalonica also, and Paul and Silas had to move on. Persecution against the believers continued after Paul's departure.

Unable to return to support the Thessalonian believers in person, Paul sent Timothy, 1 Thess. 3. 2, to strengthen and encourage them. Paul's First Letter to them was one of his first epistles to any assembly. It contains praise for the reputation which they were gaining for active evangelism. It also reveals the depth of mutual affection between Paul and this new assembly. It addresses an issue which was of concern to the believers concerning the place in the kingdom of those believers who had passed away. Paul had taught them about the Lord's second coming. Would their departed friends miss out on that great occasion? Paul sets out the truth of the coming of the Lord for the church, including those already with Christ.

Another matter was of concern: should believers cease daily occupations in the light of the imminent return of the Lord? More generally, how should they live as they waited for God's Son from heaven? This raises the subject of practical sanctification and the resources available to believers to this end.

The Second Epistle deals with another issue relating to the second coming: did their suffering under ever-present persecution indicate that the day of the Lord had already begun? Paul says no, and explains what events must precede the beginning of the day of the Lord with its accompanying judgements against the ungodly.

These two Epistles show the high esteem in which Paul held these believers, the bond that been formed in the early days when they had suffered together, and the confidence he had that they would continue in their faithfulness as believers should.

The atmosphere of the epistles is set in Paul's declaration: 'Ye are our glory and our joy!' 1 Thess. 2. 20.

1 Thessalonians 1. 1-10 — October 8th

The narrative in Acts 17 makes it clear that the gospel came to Thessalonica in an atmosphere of stormy contention. This was going to mark the ongoing experience of the new converts. Their steadfastness under persecution showed the genuineness of a work of God in their lives, and the power of the Holy Spirit.

But this work of God was manifested in the preachers before there were any converts. They preached with conviction and their hearers were convicted of sin by divine power. Before their conversion they had been idolaters, and when they heard the gospel preached with power they turned to God, who became to them infinitely more worthy of devoted service than the idols. The character of the preachers was also a vital influence.

Three things convinced Paul that they were true believers, truly God's elect. Firstly, they became worshippers: God replaced idols, which were now rejected. Secondly, they began to serve God, to work for Him. Their evangelistic zeal was talked of far and wide. Thirdly, they began the patient occupation of waiting for God's Son from heaven. This anticipation of the future provided a lively encouragement as they suffered persecution for the Saviour's sake. In this they followed Paul's faith.

These people had a holy joy, even in persecution. What had they gained? They had realized that Paul's God is the living and true God. They knew that they had been brought into a living relationship with the Creator, the Sustainer, and the Judge of all. Their life was not just an escape from harsh realities. God had spoken in His Son, had shown His saving grace at the cross, and had raised and glorified His Son. They knew that Jesus will reign.

We must not fail to take account of the fact that God's Son is 'our deliverer from the wrath to come'. Christian lives, whether in Paul's day or ours, are often lived under constant pressure of persecution for Christ's sake. This fact demands that we are convinced that He will put down all rule which denies His sovereign rights. He will judge His enemies and deliver His own. His wrath, 'the wrath of the Lamb', Rev. 6. 16, will be awesome when it is manifested. This is a future phase of God's dealings, and essential for the glory and honour of God's Son.

Our gospel came not . . . in word only

His Apostles

October 9th — 1 Thessalonians 2. 1-17

We were gentle among you

Those who responded to Paul's gospel preaching in Thessalonica were, humanly speaking, placing themselves in the position of sheep facing slaughter. The successful preacher needed to be a man with a fearless shepherd's heart. He must be realistic, not starry-eyed, and he must think first of their needs, not his own. Their memories of those early days were of a kind man whose life persuaded them, perhaps even before his words did. He was a man whose burning passion was to please God, not to court popularity.

Paul had worked hard, paying his own expenses while he evangelized. He followed the example of his Master, who came not to grasp but to give; not to make demands but to bring spiritual benefits; not to have servants but to be one. His instruction was such as a good father would give, his care such as a devoted mother would give. Such care is not cheap, it makes demands. In this context God worked, for it is the prerogative of God to work conviction when the gospel is preached. Power belongs to God in the matter of salvation. God was pleased to bless the efforts of His servants, and, despite the opposition, souls were saved.

The gentleness of the preacher as he fulfilled the role of shepherd is in contrast to the ferocity of the opposition. The spirit which moved the Jews to murder the Lord Jesus was at work, and Paul thought first of the needs of the 'little flock'. In this situation, he reminds them, God takes notice of such persecutors' activities. In the case of the Jews at Jerusalem 'the wrath has come upon them'.

Though absent, Paul has not forgotten the Thessalonians, but Satan has hindered him from visiting them. As he thinks of them he thinks of the future day of reward. He will rejoice to see them richly rewarded. That will be his greatest joy. When their service is accurately assessed by the Lord, Paul will be able to say, 'How well they have done!'

Can we think of those to whom we owe most as Christians and feel any confidence that they could say such things of us, or would they be embarrassed by our lives in view of that day?

Christ and

1 Thessalonians 3. 1-13

October 10th

The two themes, love and faith, together form the framework of this chapter. If we take them in that order it helps us to understand why Paul expresses his thoughts as he does.

Firstly, how striking his writing is about the impact of his separation from this, his dearly loved assembly – he 'could bear it no longer', v. 5 ESV. His love for them drove him to seek to help them, though he himself could not go to them. Indeed, his choice of Timothy to go to Thessalonica is based on his love for Timothy and confidence that Timothy will be a genuine help to them.

Then we notice how Paul's love for them was practical and realistic, for he foresaw the testing times ahead of them and forewarned them, so that they might be prepared. This was practical love, focused on suitable means of helping them.

Paul's love was the reason for his delight on receiving Timothy's encouraging report of how things were with them. He valued their love and did not take it for granted. Meanwhile, he prayed for them and looked forward to being able to give helpful teaching for their spiritual benefit. His love is marked by giving and serving rather than grasping and controlling; and such always is true spiritual love, modelled on God's love to us.

But the mutual love between Paul and the Thessalonians was manifested in the context of the great pressures under which they served God. The tempter was testing their mettle. This was not the seductive temptation which might lure us into self-indulgence and lust. Paul's concern was that the tempter might *succeed* in breaking their resolution to persevere under persecution. He was concerned that their faith should not fail.

Thus, Timothy's mission was to encourage them and strengthen their faith. In this way Paul's initial warning ministry was being reinforced by Timothy. Paul was emotionally involved in their spiritual wellbeing, 'Now we live, if ye stand fast', v. 8. He looks forward to visiting them himself to this end.

His prayer for them links the power of God and the faithful performance of the man of God's responsibility. What matters most is how our faithfulness measures up in the coming day of review, at the Lord's return. God does not fail; we often do.

His Apostles

October 11th

1 Thessalonians 4. 1-18

The first twelve verses reinforce aspects of truth already known by the Thessalonians: 'Ye know what commandments we gave you', v. 2. The principles of love as being generous, not covetous, underlie the teaching of verses 3 to 9, applying the teaching in the context of sexual morality. Specifically, Paul spells out the need for sexual restraint and respect for the marriages of other believers. Verse 6 is clearer in the RV: 'That no man transgress and wrong his brother in the matter'; that is, the matter of how one accepts that my brother's wife is his partner exclusively. Solemnly, Paul reminds his friends that failure in this matter is equivalent to rejecting (or despising) God. 'The Lord', says Paul, 'is the avenger in all these things', v. 6 RV. He reminds them also to be industrious and self-supporting.

But now Paul has vital new truth to impart, a revelation from the Lord. It touches on the anxiety of some believers about whether those believers who have been called home will miss some aspect of future glory. He explains that those of us who are alive when the Lord returns will not be glorified ahead of those who have already died. He says he has a word directly from the Lord on the matter, newly revealed, about the first phase of the Lord's return. The Lord Himself will descend. Those first affected by it will be 'the dead in Christ', v. 16, who will be raised. They will be reunited with believers who are still alive. Then, together, 'we shall be caught up in clouds' to meet the Lord in the air. 'And so shall we ever be with the Lord'.

We recall the first impact of Paul's preaching at Thessalonica: they turned to God from idols to worship, and witness, and work, and wait for God's Son from heaven. This waiting gives character to Christian living. Our hope is set on the Lord's return. This binds believers together. It gives us patience to endure. It fortifies our love for each other. It saves us from the tyranny of material prosperity. Even believers who daily face the threat of persecution to the point of martyrdom can draw strength from this hope. He is coming for us, and together we shall be caught up. When disappointment is at its bitterest we cling to this, 'So shall we ever be with the Lord'. Praise Him!

The word of the Lord

Christ and

1 Thessalonians 5. 1-28 — October 12th

Today's reading depicts society in terms of contrasts: there are people who belong to the darkness and those who belong to the light. The Christian moves in a world where there is much said and written about peace, awards are given to 'peace-makers', talks are arranged to set up 'peace initiatives'; but society as a whole lacks the fundamental element of peace and integrity of heart. That is why the Thessalonian Christians were so persecuted; hence their need of mutual encouragement and care.

What will mark the Christians who, through God's grace, belong to light and peace? They will be awake to the great realities of salvation and its accompanying uprightness. They will be temperate and sensitive to God's care, believing His promises. They will seek the good, spiritual and material, of others. They will be looking for the return of the Saviour; this is 'the hope of salvation', v. 8. When their Saviour comes He will deliver them from vilification and persecution. In that day they will 'live with him'. Among themselves they will be orderly, will respect their leaders and guides. Towards those outside their circle they will show kindliness and generosity. They will pray and rejoice and seek to know and do God's will.

The society around is very different. The persecutors will talk of peace but practise discrimination and injustice. They resent the light of God's truth being shone on them. They forget that they will one day give account to God, as if He did not exist or had not spoken. They indulge in excesses, typified in this context by drunkenness. They repay kindness by ingratitude.

The future of the godless is that they will experience the sudden intervention of God in what is here called the 'wrath' of God. As society today lurches from one crisis to the next we see the seeds of the culmination of the best that mere human ingenuity and skill can achieve; it is a nightmare scenario. The Bible calls it the rule of the Beast. Misrule will characterize worldly governments before the Lord comes to reign. Might will present itself as right, tyranny will replace the rule of law.

Do we live as those who understand the implications of this future prospect as a stimulus to simple, faithful, godly living?

Comfort . . . and edify one another

His Apostles

October 13th

2 Thessalonians 1. 1-12

He shall come to be glorified in his saints

In this Second Epistle to Thessalonica Paul writes in a way that suggests that the social setting around the assembly was even more hostile than previously. He wisely begins by acknowledging how he appreciates their faithfulness. He even tells other Christians how well the Thessalonians cope with persecution. This leads on to his message for such a situation: their faithfulness will give an indication in the future of how just God is in His judgement against the persecutors of people so undeserving of hostility. The First Epistle contrasted two ways of life and two destinies – the sons of light in contrast to the people who walk in darkness. This Epistle will expand on the contrast, especially in terms of the end which lies ahead for each group.

First, Paul reassures the Christians that God has taken note of their enemies, who will answer to God for their hatred, which in the first place is against God, then against His people. God's anger will burn fiercely against His enemies: He will 'afflict them that afflict' the Christians, v. 6 RV. Justice demands as much. He will act 'in flaming fire taking vengeance' on the enemies. They are described as those 'that know not God and obey not the gospel'. Not 'knowing' God may, in the context, mean not acknowledging God as God. They will be 'punished with everlasting destruction from the presence of the Lord, and from the glory of his power', v. 9.

By contrast, the faithful, who look for God's Son from heaven, will enjoy rest, v. 7, in the kingdom, at His manifestation. They are the believers, in contrast to the deliberate rebels who do not obey the gospel. In the day of His manifestation the Lord shall be glorified in the completion of His purpose to bring many sons to glory. A possible rendering of verse 10 would refer to His being 'glorified *among* his saints'. For those who suffer with Him, the future is glory with Him. All the glory connected with our presence there will be His, and His alone.

Verse 10 recalls how this future glory comes to be our prospect: there was a time when we believed the gospel testimony. This was by grace, the future glory with Him will be due to the same grace. And now it is grace which moulds us to His ways.

Christ and

2 Thessalonians 2. 1-17 — October 14th

Let no man deceive you

The Thessalonians had been troubled by rumours. Some of these were claimed to have come from Paul or by direct revelation from God. Rumour had it that violent opposition was an indication that the day of the Lord had begun. This rumour would indicate that the severe judgements preceding the setting up of the earthly kingdom of the Lord had already begun.

Paul explains that events will develop along different lines. There will be an uprising against the authority of God, a resentment against the very idea of God, the Judge of all. Human arrogance based on the advance of science and technology in our day is close to this spirit. The restraining influence, v. 7, may be the rule of law or the work of the Holy Spirit in the church, probably the former.

Simple people can be swayed by sensational displays of seemingly miraculous powers. Satan knows that the Lord Jesus will come with awesome power, so he will have his counterfeit in place before the Lord is manifested. Those who steadfastly refuse to accept obvious truth become a prey to spurious authority based on implausible fraud. Those who steadfastly reject the gracious authority of the Lord Jesus will follow the man of sin and end in perdition.

How refreshing, then, to trace the origin of the Christian's experience, which stands in glorious contrast to this picture of doom! God moved towards us in His grace, the Holy Spirit took specific and personal dealing with us, leading to our acceptance of salvation by grace. Paul writes of what he calls 'our gospel', but it was of course the call of God that was heard, changing everything for believers, giving us a firm hope.

In times of challenge, when the enemy of souls seems to be winning the day, we are called to stand fast, hold fast, and remember the truth which brought us light and peace. We have hope in the coming Christ, our Deliverer from coming wrath. Our future is glory, for He is coming. He is going to reign over all the earth. This should encourage and strengthen us in every good work and word. Remember the example, 'All that Jesus began both to do and teach'; *doing* comes before teaching.

His Apostles

October 15th — 2 Thessalonians 3. 1-18

Brethren, pray for us

Paul's main burden in this closing section of this Epistle is to encourage his spiritual children to live lives which display practical Christianity. It will not be as simple to achieve this as it might appear, for there are factors which could hinder them from responding as well as they might.

Leading the forces arrayed against them is the evil one himself, v. 3 NKJV. Allied to this formidable enemy are 'unreasonable and evil men', v. 2 RV, the persecutors. Unwitting helpers against the Christians are those of their own number who discourage them by idling and interfering. If the godly had been disposed to give up they would not have lacked excuses.

But over against these factors we must look at the advantages and encouragements which they received to persevere and remain faithful in work and prayer. They had the knowledge of Paul's constant prayers for them; and closely intertwined with this is his expectation and request that they should pray for him. In prayer they would be encouraged by the sure conviction that 'the Lord is faithful', v. 13: He can be depended on to remember their circumstances and their needs. He knows and cares.

An important encouragement, too, would be their memory of the example which Paul had set them by his unselfish life among them. His teaching had backed up his example – works, as is proper, preceding words. They would remember that he had suffered in Philippi that they might have the life-giving message from God. These factors would help to strengthen their will to persevere, not to grow weary in well-doing.

And the outcome of such perseverance? 'Now the Lord of peace himself give you peace always by all means. The Lord be with you all', v. 16. In effect, Paul is expressing his constant prayer for them. Parted from them, he prays for them – an encouragement to them to pray for him.

Does he, the great apostle, need the prayers of young believers? Prayer is of value, we note, not because of the greatness of the ones praying, but that of the God to whom they pray. Even we could be of use to servants of God engaged in great enterprises for Him, if we were to pray for them as we ought.

Christ and

The Epistles under consideration were written by the apostle Paul to three of his very dear and personal friends, each of whom found himself in a very difficult situation. For Timothy there were many problems in Ephesus, and particularly with those who taught wrong doctrine. Titus was in Crete with the responsibility to ordain elders in every church, and then to silence the Cretans who persisted in trying to overwhelm the saints with aspects of Judaism. Philemon had to face up to handling the delicate matter of the return of a runaway slave to the satisfaction of his family, the local church, and Paul.

Throughout the Epistles there are many repetitive themes and words but perhaps the most common is 'faith' and 'faithfulness', whether it be saving faith, the defence of the faith, or living a faithful life. In all situations faithfulness to God is paramount for those who desire to serve Him.

The Epistles were probably written in the following order: Philemon, 1 Timothy, Titus, and finally 2 Timothy. They were penned during a time when Paul was under immense pressure, imprisoned, released and then imprisoned yet again. He found that many of the Christians sought to distance themselves from him, especially during his final imprisonment when he faced imminent death. He shared with Timothy that all Asia had turned away from him. However, he could rely on the continuing friendship and faithfulness of these three, Timothy, Titus and Philemon, and of course we have that wonderful word, 'Nevertheless the Lord stood by me, and strengthened me'.

These Epistles offer advice and admonition on many subjects including elders, deacons, false teachers, prayer in the assembly, the dress and place of women, widows, relationships between masters and servants, and the perilous times that lie ahead. Reference is made to the appearing of the great God and our Saviour the Lord Jesus; indeed, here we have all things that pertain unto life and godliness.

The Pastoral Epistles are not only for pastors, preachers, and elders but for all the flock, and are required reading for saints of the 21st as well as the 1st century AD.

October 16th

1 Timothy 1

Paul immediately introduces himself, the writer, and Timothy, the recipient, of this compelling letter. He declares his apostleship in the strongest possible terms; he is commanded by both God and Christ; he is, according to A. T. Robertson, 'an apostle under orders'. Then he decribes Timothy in most affectionate terms as 'my own son in the faith'. Contextually, it is not so much that he is father in connection with Timothy's salvation but more perhaps in regard to his discipleship and godly walk. He recognized in Timothy those marks of character that were a reflection of his own personality and way of life. Timothy was a genuine son, and the strong bond between the two and the difficult circumstances Timothy would find himself in cause Paul to include in his salutation the word 'mercy' which is, apparently, only ever used by him in connection with Timothy.

It is evident that there were problems in Ephesus, and Paul is quick to detail them and explain the approach to resolving them. He charges Timothy that he in turn should charge others to beware of false teachers and their false doctrines. The aim of this charge is to produce believers who are genuine, and manifest love that is the product of three things: a pure heart, a good conscience, and sincere faith. Those who majored on law, of itself good and right, did not exhibit love but selfishness, and the destruction of individuals and perhaps assemblies as well. This swerving off into law and lust was not the anticipated outcome of the glorious gospel of the blessed God.

In the next few verses Paul describes his own journey of faith from being an arrogant and self-centred blasphemer and persecutor, through a realization of his sinnership, to his obtaining mercy. He was chief of sinners but became the chief illustration of God's grace to men. This causes him to break forth into praise to God and encouragement to Timothy to emulate him in warring a good warfare, while always remembering those like Hymeneus and Alexander who had not done so and had been delivered unto Satan for the destruction of the flesh.

We too should strive to be genuine sons marked by love, not by petty points of law which distract from godly living.

1 Timothy 2 — October 17th

Just as an individual convert, like Saul of Tarsus, feels a compelling desire to pray, so an assembly should feel a strong urge to engage together in prayer. Indeed, this should be the priority – it should be 'first of all'. Different kinds of public prayers are suggested such as supplication (regarding assembly needs), prayers (drawing near to God in worship), intercessions (seeking divine intervention) and giving of thanks (for the blessings of salvation and for answered prayer). Assembly prayer meetings need not be dull! 'Where a local church ceases to depend on prayer, God ceases to bless its ministry', W. W. Wiersbe.

The apostle proceeds to say for whom we should pray (all men); why we should pray for them (that we might lead a quiet and peaceable life in all godliness and good order); what the results of such prayers are (good for the assembly and acceptable, i.e., pleasing, to God). Prayers such as these are based on the will of God for salvation and the work of Christ in His role as Mediator. He intervenes for God's glory and the benefit of men in salvation and preservation. As to who should pray he says it is 'men', i.e., the males. It could not be put more clearly that public prayer is for men and not for women. And they should do so with clean hands and without wrath or doubting.

He now instructs the women as to their deportment and subjection. For public meetings of the church they should dress modestly and without ostentation. 'In-your-face' jewellery, large hats and inappropriate dress are not modest. They are to be silent as far as teaching and prayers are concerned and their modesty displayed by subjection to men and submission to other sisters in the practical things of assembly life. It is sad when an assembly is troubled by 'attitude' between sisters, Phil. 4. 2.

The background to this teaching goes back to Genesis where Eve took the lead, stepped over the boundary, and pulled Adam with her. He knew he was wrong while she thought she was right; she was 'thoroughly deceived', W. E. Vine. But believing women can be saved from such dangers by concentrating their efforts on the demanding circumstances of home life where they can please God and channel His blessings to the family.

I will therefore that men pray

His Apostles

October 18th — 1 Timothy 3

A good work

Some are ambitious to hold position in the assembly and such a desire is often to be commended, as here. However, it is made clear that if one anticipates that being an elder is just the holding of an office then he needs to understand that there is much more to it than that. It is work that is in view and the office-holding is very much secondary. Men who are leaders of God's people and responsible for their care need to be of strong character and have a high moral standing among the saints and before the world. Minimum standards are set out for elders and deacons, and, indeed, for the wives of both. Attempts are made to divide the qualifications into sections but the real exercise should be to try to ensure that we fulfil them all, whether we be elders, deacons, or not. May those engaged in such demanding ministries be assured that the Lord views this service as 'a good work', and if well done results in a good degree, or good standing among the saints. So, too, should the believers respond by following the lead of spiritual elders in all things, and ensuring that they themselves personally aspire to the standards required in the elders, deacons, and wives. If they do not, where will the elders and deacons of the future be found?

In the assembly itself there is a need for all to behave responsibly in the gatherings, in the understanding that this is the house of God, v. 15. It is no mere gathering together of certain people, but both the Lord and the Holy Spirit are present, thus appropriate behaviour is required at all times in the presence of the living God. The local church is the pillar and ground of the truth in that it clearly declares Christ and maintains His word and testimony in spite of opposition both from without and from within. Determination is needed to do this work well.

The mystery of godliness brings the chapter to an end. These are lovely expressions of the Person of Christ from incarnation, through His spotless life here on earth, His death, resurrection and ascension and on to His being preached to the nations and the reception by many millions around the world of His gospel message. Eventually, all will be received up in glory to eternal blessing, so today we rejoice and avidly look for His coming.

Christ and

1 Timothy 4 — October 19th

This chapter commences with a warning against apostasy, declaring prophetically that in the latter days some shall depart from the faith. These are not the apostates but those who seduced them with doctrines of devils, and consistently spoke lies in hypocrisy. Having consciences seared with a hot iron they emphatically declared 'bad' what God had said was 'good' and to be enjoyed with thanksgiving; theirs was outright denial, just the same as Satan in his conversation with Eve in the Garden of Eden so long ago. It was Timothy's responsibility to regularly remind the saints of these things and through such teaching he would himself become a good minister of Jesus Christ. Even today saints should be reminded time and time again of the dangers of wrong doctrine and poor behaviour.

There would be some who would despise Timothy and his teaching, solely on the basis that he was a young man. How young, we do not know, but certainly no novice in experience of the Lord and His people. To counter such disparaging remarks, and to support the repeated warnings he is called upon to give, Paul exhorts him to be an example of believers in what he said and how he lived. His life was to be pure, beyond reproach, and his prime characteristic was to be love in the Spirit. Such a life would invariably silence the ignorance of foolish men.

Unquestionably, Timothy had a gift for service for the Lord, but that gift had not only to be used, but maintained daily by reading and with a clear concentration on understanding doctrine. Further, he must bolster that gift by meditation on the word of God and be completely committed to the cause. Such dedication in service to his Lord and His people would be clear for all to see, and his personal 'profiting', or 'progress', would be obvious, thus ensuring that few would be so bold as to challenge him. Timothy must first take heed to himself and continue in the doctrine, because in that way he himself would be preserved, as would the assembly at Ephesus. Big challenges are here for all of us, and we should put ourselves and others in constant remembrance of the way forward in the things of God.

Put the brethren in remembrance of these things

His Apostles

October 20th   1 Timothy 5

Observe these things without . . . partiality

Partiality was the first problem that the apostles had to face in the church in Jerusalem, shortly after Pentecost, Acts 6. And here Paul reminds Timothy that partiality, or even the appearance of it, can be damaging to an individual or an assembly. It has the idea of not being favourably inclined towards one rather than another, but in our dealings with people, whether they be young women or old men, all prejudice must be eliminated. The assembly at Ephesus was likely very large and today's chapter gives us an idea of the variety of people within the fellowship. There were elders (older people), young men and young women, various kinds of widows, children and grandchildren (nephews). Partiality is destructive to those affected by prejudicial judgements and the person who is partial soon debilitates himself as well. Paul advises how Timothy can avoid falling into this trap.

Older people, men and women, should be treated with care and respect. They should not be victims of unkind words but be treated as one would treat one's own parents in an atmosphere of mutual love and a readiness to forgive. Younger men should be treated as brothers and younger women as sisters. In 'these things' a family atmosphere should prevail. Similarly, with elders (overseers), there must always be a remembrance that these are men doing a very difficult job and that they too are vulnerable to Satan's wiles and temptations. Indeed, he will, on occasion, raise up church members to accuse elders of things most foul, and maybe without a shred of evidence. Such accusations must be treated carefully and pursued only if supported by two or three witnesses – people who have seen something and not people who have just heard something, vv. 17-19! Proven sin earns a rebuke before the church so that others may fear. This charge regarding partiality is given in the sight of God and before Jesus Christ and the elect angels, thus signifying its importance.

Being a leader often takes a physical toll on people and this proved so with Timothy. He was under stress and was often ill. Paul suggests he consider taking wine as a medicine and not to restrict himself only to water. He does not suggest that Timothy should become a social drinker. Nor should we!

Christ and

1 Timothy 6 — October 21st

Our chapter today demonstrates again the variety of circumstances of the believers in Ephesus as it opens with instructions to slaves and closes with admonitions to the rich. This is a suitable backdrop for the statement that 'godliness with contentment is great gain', and this is true whether in poverty or plenty. The apostle Paul states, 'I have learned in whatsoever state I am therewith to be content'. Add to that 'godliness', and the result is 'great gain'. It would seem that there were some who suggested that slaves in Ephesus, especially if they worked in a Christian household, were entitled to be set free and should not rest until that aim was achieved. Paul gives such short shrift and reminds us all that with food and raiment we should be content, whatever our lot, whether in employment or even in slavery. To be discontent with one's lot may in turn encourage a love of money, which is described as being 'the root of all evil'. This may cause the believer to fall into and be destroyed by this particular snare cunningly set by Satan.

The believer, instead of spending time hoping for things that are just not obtainable physically or materially, should flee such things, follow after righteousness, fight the good fight and firmly grasp the spiritual benefits of eternal life. This attitude will be seen by many witnesses, in the assembly and in the world, and is an imitation of the Lord's own courage when, before Pontius Pilate, He witnessed a good confession.

We are further reminded that this approach should be maintained constantly until the appearing of our Lord Jesus Christ when, as King of kings and Lord of lords, He manifests His power and justice. At that day all wrongs will be righted and patience rewarded. The rich are to be reminded that what they have comes to them as a gift from the living God. Therefore, they should not be proud, nor reliant on these riches. Instead, they too should be content and endeavour wherever possible, and in various ways, to help the poor. In so doing they will lay up for themselves a good foundation against the time to come when they, and, of course, we, are reviewed at the judgement seat of Christ.

His Apostles

October 22nd

2 Timothy 1

Stir up the gift of God, which is in thee

This Epistle, written from prison in Rome, is thought to be the last by the apostle Paul. The recipient is his dearly beloved son Timothy. In this opening chapter Paul is writing out of a keenly felt sense of loss: loss of his freedom which, for a little while, had been so sweet; loss of Timothy's company; loss of support from Phygelles and Hermogenes; and the loss of 'all . . . in Asia'. Additionally, he is now facing the loss of his own life. So, it is rather amazing that he speaks of 'the promise of life which is in Christ Jesus'. None of these losses could extinguish, or even dampen, his enthusiasm for the promise that physical death was but the entrance to eternal life in glory.

He looks back and speaks of his own forefathers and their influence on his early life. Then he considers Timothy, and is buoyed by the remembrance of the unfeigned faith seen in the lives of his mother and grandmother. This same faith and its intensity he now sees in Timothy himself. Parents and grandparents have a huge influence on the spiritual strength of their offspring today, as well as those did in the first century AD.

Now he looks forward to the future needs of the Lord's people and reminds Timothy that he has a gift graciously given by God and recognized by Paul and the brethren. However, that gift, like all gifts, needs to be constantly encouraged, so Timothy is told to 'stir up the gift' that was in him. In other words, 'If you don't use it, you lose it'! God is gracious to enrich His people through the giving of gifts, and servants must be responsible for their appropriate use. Associated with God's call and gifts are also His purpose and particular plan for their use.

In certain circumstances the exercise of gift may involve suffering, perhaps even unto death. But God has abolished death and should it occur then Timothy could look forward with Paul to 'life and immortality . . . through the gospel'. Thus, he should not be ashamed of the message but preach it at every opportunity. Paul says, 'I am not ashamed'. Concerning Onesiphorus, 'he . . . was not ashamed', and to Timothy, 'Be not thou therefore ashamed of the testimony of our Lord'. For such selfless sacrifice there will be abundant mercy in that day!

Christ and

2 Timothy 2 — October 23rd

In this chapter Paul is writing to encourage Timothy in his very difficult ministry in Ephesus. He will need to cultivate many spiritual qualities and be strong, yet at the same time gentle and patient. Leaders of God's people have many demands upon them and leading the flock is not at all an easy undertaking. Paul draws seven word-pictures to encourage leaders by showing what they are and how they should conduct themselves.

1) A courageous son – Timothy is reminded that he is a spiritual son of the great apostle himself, and, of course, also a son of God. He should therefore be strong in the grace that is in Christ Jesus. This is a sure foundation on which to build.

2) A good soldier – Timothy was not asked if he had an interest in soldiering but told that he had been chosen to be a soldier. It is a high privilege to be chosen by the Lord. As such he will not be confined to barracks but will be in the field at the forefront of the battle. Hardness of circumstances will feature regularly and that is something, if not to be enjoyed, then to be endured as a good soldier, without complaint. Loyalty and obedience would also be necessary and, in the end, victory, while assured, is not without pain, disappointments, and tears.

3) A trained athlete – He would have to strive and to keep within the rules of engagement, lest, having run well and encouraged others, he himself should be disqualified.

4) A patient husbandman – results will not be achieved overnight, nor in one's own strength. The farmer is patient and waits for God to give the increase in connection with his labour.

5) A skilled workman – in handling the word of God he must rightly divide it so as not to be guilty of deceit.

6) A sanctified vessel – ever ready for the Master to use, and prepared unto every good work as opportunities arise.

7) A gentle servant – showing diligence and patience even with those who oppose themselves, trusting that God will give them repentance to the acknowledging of the truth.

These are encouragements, but there are also warnings to be heeded. Satan and the flesh are ever active, both for the servant and those whom he has the privilege to serve. Dangers abound.

His Apostles

October 24th
2 Timothy 3

Perilous times shall come

Timothy is warned of a great departure in 'the last days' and, while doubtless he saw many portents of this evil, surely the worst is yet to come; we should be on our guard. Verses 2 to 7 speak of the character and wickedness of these men as they are compared to the infamous Jannes and Jambres who so blatantly withstood Moses as he engaged in the struggle to lead the people of God in his day. How welcome to read the determination in verse 9, 'But they shall proceed no further'! God will eventually say that enough is enough.

These are the sorts of men who continuously opposed Paul and spoke out against him as being weak, self-exalting, and having scant regard for God's ancient chosen people. In verses 10 to 12 Paul defends himself from their fierce accusations mentioning his doctrine, manner of life, purpose, faith, longsuffering, charity, and patience. He reminds Timothy that he had, for the Lord, endured persecutions and afflictions almost beyond belief at Antioch, Iconium, and Lystra; we know of other places too where he was abused and attacked, but the great thing about this is his testimony that 'out of them all the Lord delivered me'! It seems that while godliness and persecution may go hand in hand, and affect all believers, so too, even in worsening situations, the Lord is able to deliver His people for their personal safety and for His own glory.

For a young servant of God this may seem a frightening situation, but Timothy is exhorted to 'continue', v. 14, in the faith and in his service for the Lord, and through the good word of God to be throughly furnished unto good works in an evil world. How could he have the necessary confidence to continue? Because that from a child he had known the holy scriptures and these not only initially made him wise unto the salvation of his soul but constantly and strongly assured him, and others also, of divine protection and sustenance in service.

This chapter which commenced with dire warnings closes with delightful words as to the inspiration of all scripture and to its usefulness for doctrine, reproof, correction, and instruction in righteousness. May it become our constant resource.

Christ and

2 Timothy 4   October 25th

This is the last chapter of Paul's last Epistle and records his last words to Timothy, and to us. Issues Paul felt were important for Timothy are that he should: preach the word; watch in all things; endure afflictions; do the work of an evangelist; make full proof of his ministry. Certainly, these were things Paul himself had fully pursued and accomplished and it is his burning desire that his beloved son in the faith should do likewise.

Having thus exhorted him, Paul now reflects on his own service and speaks of his readiness to depart. He views his impending death as an offering up to God of his life of sacrifice. His death will be like the pouring out of a drink offering over a sacrifice. HIEBERT declares, 'His whole life has been presented to God as a living sacrifice; now his death, comparable to the pouring out of the wine as the last act of the sacrificial ceremony, will complete the sacrifice'. Not only is he ready to die but feels that it will be soon – 'the time of my departure is at hand'. Death is a harsh word but there are some lovely ideas behind it. The Greek word used by Paul signifies the unloosing of a ship from its anchorage, or the unloosing of an ox from its harness. It suggests thoughts of freedom and rest. Paul had been attached to earth for longer than he cared for, and now he confidently looks forward to heaven and home. So, too, should we!

As to his life of service he had fought the fight, finished the course and been faithful in the ministry with which he had been entrusted by the Lord. He looks forward with confidence to the crown of righteousness which he will receive from his blessed Lord. What comfort for Timothy that his 'father' is so relaxed.

But even in his last days here in Rome he needs practical help. Not many are willing to give it now for one reason and another, but there are some on whom he can depend. Certainly, Timothy is one . . . and John Mark is another. Paul desperately wishes to have them both with him, along with Luke, to see out his last days. He needs the cloak, he would like the books, and he would really love to have the parchments from Troas. Can he have them before winter? With these and his friends, the cold will be tolerable, the end joyful, then . . . at home with the Lord!

I am now ready to be offered

His Apostles

October 26th — Titus 1

Set in order the things that are wanting

The apostle Paul looked on Titus, like Timothy, as his son in the faith. He may have led him to the Lord and he certainly was instrumental in Titus' growth and development as a Christian, evangelist, and teacher. Here, Titus is in Crete having been left there by Paul to set in order things that are wanting, and to ordain elders in every city. It appears that in those days there were many cities in Crete, so Titus had quite a job on his hands. As he read the introductory part of Paul's letter, however, Titus would have been encouraged to the task. Like Paul, he too was chosen for salvation and for coming to the knowledge of the truth, so that through preaching the gospel and teaching the believers God's plan for the island of Crete would be realized; this was 'according to the commandment of God our Saviour', v. 3.

There was opposition to Titus and to the truth in Crete, but firstly it was necessary that some structure be implemented in the assemblies by the appointment of elders in every city, which it is reasonable to equate with every assembly. The qualities of character and behaviour to be seen in those appointed to this responsibility are similar to those detailed in 1 Timothy chapter 3. The bishop, or elder, is 'the steward of God', Titus 1. 3 and as such he must be blameless, faithful to the truth taught by Paul, and have an ability to exhort and to convince the gainsayers. The Lord would have already been working in these Cretan assemblies and such men would not only be present, but coming to the fore. These Titus would formally recognize and appoint.

Only when proper order was established could the task of facing up to the false teachers, the circumcision, take place. Who were they and what were they doing? Certainly these were men of Crete, and they seemed to be insisting that the tenets of Judaism should be taught and adhered to. They were pretty insistent and fairly successful in subverting even whole households. Their motives were suspect: they were mercenary, hoping to get personal advantage from the folk they deceived and misled. Their 'mouths must be stopped!' exclaimed Paul; it was Titus' responsibility to do that, with the Lord's help of course. Today, good order and pure doctrine are still of paramount importance.

Christ and

Titus 2. 1 – 3. 15 — October 27th

Be careful to maintain good works

In the previous chapter *wrong* doctrine was denounced, and now *sound* doctrine and its effects are described. The things that adorn sound doctrine include the behaviour and manner of life of its adherents. This affects all in the congregation including aged and young men, aged and young women, and servants. A recurring theme is sobriety, which means taking great care in all areas of life not to give outsiders wrong impressions of the gospel or of the Lord's people. Whether in the home, or in the assembly, or at work, the believer must seek to demonstrate that his life in Christ is attractive and advantageous. The grace of God in Christ has appeared and should have taught all how to live in this present world: 'a peculiar people, zealous of good works', 2. 14. Also, we look forward to the blessed hope, and the glorious appearing of our Saviour to rapture His own and to reign in the world. All who associate themselves with Him and have this hope should live lives that commend Him and the doctrines they profess to believe.

During the time of waiting for His return we have a responsibility to obey those set up by God to rule over us. Before our conversion we may well have been a problem for the state, but since we have experienced the love of God our Saviour we obey magistrates and indeed hold ourselves ready to exploit every opportunity to engage in good works, without which our professed faith may be thought to be dead.

Having been made heirs of the hope of eternal life we look forward with anticipation to enjoying this life in heaven, but here and now it is necessary to show to others the blessings we have in Christ. These things are 'good and profitable unto men'. Some might seek to destroy this testimony by foolish questions and strivings about the law, but these are distractions to be avoided, as are those who peddle them.

The Epistle closes with greetings from Paul, 'Greet them that love us in the faith', and a plan that Paul should meet up with Titus, Zenas and Apollos in Nicopolis where he had decided to stay over the winter period. Great fellowship would be enjoyed no doubt; a sweet foretaste of fellowship soon in glory!

His Apostles

October 28th

Philemon

I beseech thee for my son Onesimus

Philemon and his family were wealthy, well known, and greatly loved by the apostles and saints. A church met in his home, and he was occupied in the work of the Lord as well as running his own household business. It is thought that Apphia was his wife and Archippus his son. He refreshed the saints in his life and ministry and accommodated the Lord's servants as opportunity presented itself. Recently, however, one of his slaves, Onesimus by name, had absconded and probably purloined some of his master's goods as he did so. But I think Philemon had drawn a line under that and moved on. He did not pursue him.

How surprising then to receive a letter from Paul in Rome, signed also by Timothy, with news of the runaway! More than that, Paul had personally met him, it seems, and now the man was a believer in the Lord Jesus and was on his way back home! Sent and commended by none other than Paul himself! The letter that Onesimus carried to Philemon is a masterpiece. Rightly praising Philemon and his family it asks that Onesimus be received back into their home. In case there should be grounds for objection, in that restoration should be made Paul says, 'If he hath wronged thee, or oweth thee ought, put that on mine account . . . receive him as myself', vv. 18, 17.

Paul, having introduced himself to Philemon as a prisoner, now speaks of being a partner with him, but is unwilling to take decisions that should rightly be his. He muses that perhaps Onesimus departed for a season that he should be received for ever, no longer as a servant but as a brother beloved. His confidence that Philemon will do the right thing is to say that he himself will be coming shortly and that he is sure he will be welcome – so should Onesimus.

So, what happened? The answer is that we don't know. But we do know the kind of man Philemon was, and are sure he would have received the runaway back again into his service. Perhaps even beyond that, some speculate that he may not only have received him back but sent him back again to Paul in Rome to continue to minister to the aged apostle on behalf of all the friends at Colossae. Forgiveness benefits all involved!

Christ and

This Epistle was written to Hebrew Christians who were looking back to what they had possessed in Judaism, and to some it seemed, at times, better than what they now had in Christ. They were ridiculed for adopting a religion which had no visible temple, priest, or altar, but having a leader who had died on a cross. They were charged with abandoning a religion which had been ordained by God, mediated by angels, and administered by Moses. Though they were still loyal to Christ, they were questioning in their hearts whether they were suffering loss for nothing. Was it all a mistake? What could the writer do for them in this situation? What would *we* do? We could warn them of the consequences of reverting to Judaism. There are herein short passages, parenthetical and admonitory, which contain stern warnings. We could try exhortation. The writer does this in passages marked by the phrase 'let us'. Each of these, with the exception of the first, 4. 1, is a call to a higher state of spiritual attainment, culminating in the final test of allegiance to Christ and His cross, 13. 13. Are admonition and exhortation in themselves sufficient, or is something more needed?

The writer presents Christ. He knows that if his readers could but see the glory of Christ, all their doubts would vanish. Warning and exhortation are good in their place, but we need more. The presentation of Christ is the answer to our doubts and questionings. The call is to 'consider him', 3. 1; 12. 3. So he leads us first of all to the Person of our beloved Lord, unfolding to them the glory of His Person, the wonder of His work and love, and the presentation of His personal greatness and His unique achievements. What the Hebrews and we possess in Christ is so much better than Judaism, or any other religion, offers. He is greater than the prophets, ch. 1; angels, chs. 1 and 2; Moses, ch. 3; Joshua, ch. 4; Aaron, chs. 5 to 8; the offerings, chs. 9, 10; the Old Testament worthies, ch. 11. This is 'Christ all-excelling'. There is nothing that can serve as a substitute for this. It has been well said that the consideration of our blessed Lord is not only good for us, it is *vital*. For us now, as ever, the first great message of this Epistle meets our present and necessary need – to consider Him!

His Apostles

October 29th — Hebrews 1

So much better than the angels

'Better' is a characteristic word of this Epistle. It occurs thirteen times and has the idea of superiority in dignity and worth. The old dispensation, the law, was given by the mediation of angels. If Christ is greater than angels, then His dispensation of the new covenant has to be higher than that of the law. How was He greater than angels? Because there are predicated of Him things which could be said of only God Himself. Consider the name given to Him, the Son, v. 5. The writer quotes Psalm 2 first. Though views differ here as to whether the reference is to the incarnation, or the resurrection, let us not miss the point being made that no angel was ever addressed thus. Then the writer quotes from the covenant made with David, 1 Chr. 17. 13; 2 Sam. 7. 14. The promise was made to David of a son whose kingdom God would establish for ever. Son of David, He would be as man, Matt. 1. 1, but as God He was eternally in the relationship of Son. The Son is described as 'the first begotten', Heb. 1. 6. The reference is to the second coming of the Lord, 'when He again bringeth' RV. As Firstborn He has priority to, and sovereignty over, all creation, Col. 1. 18, precedence of those who rise from the dead, and supremacy over His brethren, Rom. 8. 29. His return is accompanied by a host of angels, 2 Thess. 1. 7; Rev. 19. 11-16 who are enjoined to worship Him. If He were not the Son it would be idolatry and blasphemy to worship Him. Angels are 'ministering spirits' but He is addressed by the Father as 'O God', Heb. 1. 7, 8. To Him the Father has given a throne and a sceptre for ever, and speaks to Him as His equal from all eternity to all ages. On the fact of His essential nature as God, the Father bases the eternal character of His government. He is the Lord who carried out the original work of creation, bringing it into being. He is the unchangeable Lord amid the changing universe, for it shall perish, but He remains, v. 11. He not only laid the foundations of the earth, but He is sovereign over the changes of the universe, for 'as a vesture [He shall] fold them up', v. 12. No angel was ever invited as He has been to sit on God's throne. Service, not dominion, is the function of angels, v. 14.

Hebrews 2 — October 30th

Made like unto his brethren

That the Son of God became man is stressed in this chapter. We are told that He 'was made a little lower than the angels', v. 9. Chapter 1 has been emphasizing His superiority to angels. Here the name Jesus fixes our attention upon the Lord's humanity. The human nature which Christ assumed, He still retains. 'Made a little lower' indicates that He became man. It has in view degree rather than time, the moving from a more exalted position to a lesser one. This was that He might suffer death and 'taste death'. Tasting death has to do with the experience, Matt. 16. 28, and nothing to do with brevity. He tasted all the humiliation and bitterness of death. All that was in death was concentrated in that cup which the Lord emptied on the cross. 'Partaking of flesh and blood' signifies humanity. He partook of the same. They were sharers of flesh and blood, but He of His own free choice 'took part' in them. Human life was not His first condition. He 'took hold' of human nature, without its sin, in the incarnation. This He did that being incarnate He might die, and rising again break the power of one who had the power of death, Heb. 2. 14-16. The writer refers again to the necessity of the incarnation in verse 17. Note the force of the word 'wherefore'. 'It behoved Him', i.e., 'He was bound', has the idea of a necessary condition to achieve a desired result.

Here was a moral necessity if He was to become our Mediator. The purpose of becoming like His brethren was that He might be a merciful and faithful high priest. He had to become like men because a priest must always partake of the nature of those for whom he officiates. So He must share in the circumstances, trials, temptations, sorrows, and pain of men, and thus He was fitted to be merciful. At the same time He is faithful, in the first instance to God, though the word also has the idea of one who is absolutely to be relied upon. The purpose also was to make *propitiation*, breaking down the barrier which sin interposes between God and man, and delivering the believer from God's wrath by His own death. 'In order to die He must take on Himself our human nature. Others die because they are born; Christ was born that He might die', F. B. MEYER.

His Apostles

October 31st — Hebrews 3

A son over his own house

The Hebrews have been shown that the Lord Jesus is greater than angels, and that He became man. Is He greater than the greatest of men? To Israel, its greatest leader was Moses. Proudly, their leaders had said, 'We are Moses' disciples', John 9. 28. Was Jesus 'counted worthy of more glory than Moses'? First of all they are reminded of their relationship to the Lord. They are 'holy brethren, partakers of the heavenly calling': holy because of their standing in Him, brethren because of their oneness with Him, Heb. 2. 11-14. All true believers are holy as to their position, and they should be holy as to their practice. Their calling was heavenly, and this was distinct from Israel's under Moses, which was to an earthly inheritance. The Israelites' claim to be God's chosen people was based on the fact that they had received a divine call through Moses. The call comes now through One who is far superior to Moses, and not to an earthly inheritance, but to a heavenly kingdom. The writer invites them to consider this diligently and undistractedly. If we are ever to learn Christian truth a half-hearted glance is never enough. We must 'gird up the loins of our mind', 1 Pet. 1. 13, and concentrate our gaze upon our subject. They are to consider the One they confess, their Apostle and High Priest. Moses had been a faithful mediator, cp. 2. 17; 3. 2, 5. To be faithful is most important in a servant of God, Matt. 25. 21. God bears witness to Moses that he 'was faithful in all his house', Heb. 3. 5, cp. Num. 12. 1-8. In every department of his great work Moses obeyed the Lord totally, but he finally failed, Num. 20. 9-12. The Lord was always faithful, His work perfectly complete. The superiority of Christ to Moses is now described, Heb. 3. 3-5.

Moses was part of the house in which he served, himself one of the people of God. Christ as the builder had greater honour than the house, and its faithful servant. Moses was faithful within the house, but Christ a Son over it. Moses' work was one of preparation; it 'gave witness to' a 'coming Prophet'. Deut. 18. 15-19. The Lord is the fulfilment of all that Moses foresaw; He points to none but Himself. Moses could witness only to the ultimate authority – 'he wrote of me', John 5. 46.

Christ and

Hebrews 4. 1-13 — November 1st

A rest to the people of God

We have a promise of rest. The rest which dominates this section is God's rest, 3. 18; 4. 1-5, 10. We are told that God rested on the seventh day of creation. That rest was not made necessary by fatigue, and we are told by the Lord Jesus, 'My Father worketh hitherto, and I work', John 5. 17. He continues that upholding and governing of which creation was the beginning. Just as creation was His work, so the work on which the eternal rest is built is God's work. 'The rest is God's rest which He will enjoy in perfected glory with those who believe in Christ, who alone by His work could fit men to share it', W. KELLY. The invitation to share that rest is offered to all who will hear His voice and not harden their hearts. There were those in Israel in time past who did not enter the rest God promised. The good news of the rest was preached to them, but they did not believe it. What was the nature of the message they heard? Deliverance from Egypt was its starting point, and entering an inheritance in Canaan its destination. Reaching the promised land they refused to go in. That same gospel of deliverance to an inheritance these Hebrews had heard. They must be sure they have believed it. For the Israelites the rest was Canaan, but unbelief kept them out. We have an inheritance still future, and entry into its rest is certain one day, though we can enjoy some of the inheritance now, Eph. 2. 6. Israelites entering the land with Joshua faced conflict, and the rest they did eventually have was not the rest of God, for the offer was held out prospectively some hundreds of years later by David, Heb. 4. 7, 8, cp. Ps. 95. That rest yet remains, a Sabbath rest, God's rest, for the people of God, v. 9. Note that in verse 1 the writer refers to 'a promise being left us', that is a promise remaining yet unrealized. After salvation, we engage readily in loving service for Him. We may at times become weary *in* it, but not weary *of* it. In God's eternal rest we shall cease from our labours down here, though we shall not be inactive in heaven, Rev. 22. 3. Without fatigue and weariness we shall worship and serve Him. Unbelief and disobedience kept Israelites out. Be diligent, therefore. God's word searches the heart, and all is open before the Lord.

His Apostles

November 2nd   Hebrews 4. 14 – 5. 10

A great high priest

We now return to the subject we left at chapter 2 verse 17, the high priesthood of Christ. The sheer greatness, the absolute deity, of the Lord Jesus is stressed. He is not indebted to man for the honours which are His. He is great in His own right, in His own essential Being. He is both truly man, and truly God. Note then, the following:

What He is, 4. 14; 5. 10, a great high priest. 'We have' is emphatic and suggests that there were some Hebrews who were claiming that Christians had no priesthood like the Aaronic. The writer insists that we have a greater high priest than Aaron. There were many high priests in Israel's history, but none had been called great. The divine call honoured Aaron; it glorified Christ, 5. 4, 5. His call was based on His Sonship. None but the divine Son could have filled such an office. His priesthood was of a higher order than that of Aaron, 'saluted of God' a high priest after the order of Melchizedek. Unlike Aaron's, His priesthood is for ever.

Where He is, 4. 14. He has passed through the heavens and up to the throne of God. He has done more than Aaron prefigured. He has not passed through the veil only. His ministry takes place not in an earthly tabernacle, but in the presence of God Himself in heaven.

Who He is, 4. 14. He is Jesus, the Son of God. Jesus, the human name, gives us assurance of sympathy. One of the requirements of an earthly high priest was that he was taken from among men, 5. 1. Another was that he was compassionate, 5. 2. The phrase 'touched with the feelings of', 4. 15, is rendered 'compassion', 10. 34. He sympathizes with our infirmities, not with our sins. The name Son of God speaks of His deity, and gives confidence in His strength. As Jesus He understands our need; as Son of God He can meet our need. He was tempted in all points like as we are with this difference, 'apart from sin'. He knew no sin. There was no vulnerable point in Him, John 14. 30. Sin had nothing in Him. He was free and separate from it. In Him was no sin. He was ever the impeccable One.

Christ and

Hebrews 5. 11 – 6. 20

November 3rd

Having introduced the Melchizedek priesthood of Christ, the writer wonders whether they were able to understand such teaching. They were 'dull of hearing', 5. 11, that is, slow to understand. 'Dull ears cannot receive deep truths', John 16. 12 Believer's Bible Commentary. They were not always like that. They had reached a point and stopped there. There was lack of progress and spiritual growth. They should have been teaching others, but they still had not mastered the rudiments. At the beginning it was no disgrace to require elementary teaching, but to continue thus was deplorable. Sadly, many Christians are content to stay as they began, content with their earliest grasp of truth. They still feed on milk, not solid food, spiritual infants. Those who are mature partake of solid food. Spiritual maturity is not gained by apathy or slothfulness. It is gained by regular meditation upon the word of God, and results in spiritual discernment. So, press on, he says. He describes what these 'elementary teachings about Christ' are, Heb. 6. 1-2 NIV. The list is of things which both Jews (excluding Sadducees) and Christians accepted. There was nothing distinctly Christian about them, as for instance, the deity of Christ. From these they must progress if they are genuine believers. They must go on to perfection, to maturity. But what of those who had no desire to do so, and had fallen away, gone back to Judaism, and in effect asserted that Jesus had been justly condemned? v. 6. Were they, or had they ever been true believers? Note what is said of them and not said. They had been enlightened by the Holy Spirit to understand the message of Christ, but not born again. They had tasted of the heavenly gift, Christ, but tasting is not enough, John 6. 53. Partakers of the Holy Spirit, but not sealed; tasted of the good word of God, cp. Matt. 13. 21, but even sinful men sometimes enjoy a good sermon! They had tasted of the powers of the world to come in the signs and miracles they had seen, but so had the leaders of the people and they had not believed. Note now the change of pronouns – 'they', v. 6, and 'you', v. 9. There were others of whom the writer was persuaded better things.

Ye have need that one teach you again

His Apostles

November 4th

Hebrews 7

An unchangeable priesthood

The writer uses what the Genesis record, 14. 17-20, says and does not say of Melchizedek to demonstrate the superiority of his priesthood to that of Aaron. What is *not* said of him is anything about his birth or death, or his parentage. Birth and parentage were important in Israel, in particular in regard to the genealogy of priests; they had to be born into the family of Aaron. The writer is going to tell of a Priest who was not born into Aaron's family, just as Melchizedek who pre-dated Aaron. There is no mention of Melchizedek's death to indicate the continuity of his priesthood, for the High Priest he foreshadowed is high priest for ever. We are told that Melchizedek was a king-priest. His relations with Abraham are described in order to show his superior greatness to Abraham, and ultimately, the superiority of his priesthood to that which derived from Levi, Abraham's descendant. Abraham, the friend of God, the possessor of the promises, was blessed by Melchizedek, Heb. 7. 6, 7, and gave tithes to him as to a superior, v. 4. Because Levi and his priests derived from Abraham, he by figure paid tithes to Melchizedek. We have already learned that the Lord Jesus is a priest 'after the order of Melchizedek', 5. 6, 10; 6. 20. The Aaronic priesthood was not perfect. Priesthood and law went together 7. 11. The 'law made nothing perfect', v. 19. The law needed to be changed, and therefore also the priesthood. So Christ, born into Judah, not of Aaron's family, became priest of a completely different order, a king-priest like Melchizedek. The law, too, must change, no longer based upon carnal ordinances which had no intrinsic value, v. 10, but founded on the power of an endless life. Unlike Levi's priest, this High Priest was confirmed by an oath, v. 21. He brought in 'a better hope' whereby we draw nigh to God. Death terminated Levi's high priests. Now there is a great High Priest who will not die, and His priesthood is untransferable, inviolable, and His power of saving is complete. No one will ever draw near to God, looking to the Lord Jesus to save, and fail to find Him there, active to intervene and support even in the deepest trouble, and the most dire of circumstances.

Christ and

Hebrews 8

November 5th

Not only here does the writer refer to the terms of the new covenant, vv. 8-12, quoting from Jeremiah chapter 31 verses 31 to 34, but he does so later, Heb. 10. 16, 17. In this chapter the new covenant is to be made with the house of Israel, and with the house of Judah, vv. 8, 10, and points to a future day, cp. Rom. 11. 26, 27, whilst in chapter 10 'the Holy Ghost also is a witness unto us', vv. 15-17, cp. 1 Cor. 11. 25. There was an old covenant which offered life to those who kept the law. There God demanded, 'Thou shalt', and the promise of life could not be fulfilled unless they kept the commandments. Two parties were involved: God who gave the law, and Israel who said they would obey. The terms of the covenant told the Israelites what to do, and not to do, but did not impart the power to comply. The trouble was also with the people to whom it was given – 'finding fault with them', Heb. 8. 8. 'I took them by the hand', v. 9, the Lord says, and when their sense of divine help and power was fresh, they obeyed. However, they soon turned to revolt and turn God from them. This was their custom – 'they continued not'. The old covenant was based on *man's* promise to obey. The new covenant tells us what *God* will do. By making it an unconditional covenant of grace, God avoids any possibility of failure, since fulfilment depends upon Him alone, and He cannot fail. He assumes the entire responsibility for fulfilling its terms – 'I will', vv. 10-12. Because Christ is the Mediator of this covenant, He will unfailingly carry out its conditions. It is referred to as a 'new covenant', different in kind and quality. Because it provided in Christ's death a sacrifice which procured for sinful man redemption from sin's bondage, cleansing from its defilement, and remission from its guilt, it was calculated to succeed where the first had failed. So it is called a 'better covenant', founded upon better promises. It is a better covenant because it has a better Mediator. The mediator of the old covenant was Moses, 3. 1-6, Gal. 3. 19. The Mediator of the new covenant is Christ. He is the surety of the covenant because He is the pledge of its fulfilment. As Mediator He is the One through whom its terms are carried out.

His Apostles

November 6th

Hebrews 9. 1-14

Service and sanctuary are the first themes we meet in this chapter. For the latter we are given a description of the tabernacle, vv. 1-5, and for the first we have a description of the service of high priest and priests, vv. 6-8. The sanctuary is 'of this world', v. 1 RV in contrast with the heavenly sanctuary, v. 12. What the Jewish high priests offered is contrasted with the offering that the Lord Jesus made, as is also their entrance into the holiest. Israel's high priests offered the blood of goats and calves, v. 12, and bulls and goats, v. 13. The two examples selected in verse 13 cover the entire legal provision for removing uncleanness, whether contracted by sin, or contact with the dead. The first is found described in Leviticus chapter 16, and the second in Numbers chapter 19. The Levitical law required two remedies; the Christian gospel furnishes one for all types of defilement.

The superiority of the offering of Christ is framed in a question, vv. 13, 14. Israel's sacrifices sanctified 'to the purifying of the flesh'. They expiated ceremonial guilt, but were inadequate in regard to moral guilt. Only the blood of Christ could remove the guilt of sin and provide moral cleansing. The other contrast, that of entrance into the holiest, is marked by the word 'once', 'once every year', v. 7, and 'entered in once', v. 12. The first indicates the limitations of Israel's priesthood. Only the high priest could enter the holiest but once a year. There was no free access to God. Under law, the way was not open to the people, and the high priest's service was transitional and transitory, v. 8.

The contrast comes in verse 11. Jesus entered by His own blood, v. 12, a once-for-all entrance, the great High Priest for all who trust Him, securing for them access to and acceptance in God's presence. He did not make a double entrance like Israel's high priest, 'first for his own sins, and then for the sins of the people', 7. 27 RV. Because He was sinless the first was not necessary, neither did He need to repeat the entrance due to the finality of His sacrifice. One entrance left the way open for ever. The veil was rent. There was no longer any obstacle between worshipper and God. Redemption frees from defilement and the guilt of sin.

Christ and

Hebrews 9. 15-28 — November 7th

In this section some words occur more than once: 'once', vv. 26, 27, 28; 'often', vv. 25, 26; and 'appear', vv. 24, 26, 28. The last represents three different words in the Greek which mean: to present, v. 24; to manifest, v. 26; to be seen, v. 28. As prophet Christ was manifested, as priest He presents Himself, and as king He will be seen. His entry into heaven is dealt with first. He has entered into no man-made holy place as Israel's high priest did. He entered heaven to be presented before the face of God on our behalf, in all the efficacy of His work and all the acceptance of His Person. He entered to open the way for us, and He represents us there as our great High Priest. Note the contrast with the earthly high priest, vv. 25, 26. Once every year in Israel, atonement had to be made. It was then that Israel's high priest entered the holy place with 'blood of others', v. 25. He could not offer himself. He offered first for himself, and then for the people.

Christ appeared 'at the end of the ages' RV, when the law had clearly demonstrated man's failure and weakness. He did not have to offer Himself often. There was no necessity for Him to suffer more than once. Repetition implies imperfection. There is no trace of this in His work. His work is final because it is perfect. Only one appearance was necessary, for only one sacrifice. Israel's high priests called sins to remembrance, but could not put them away. He put away sin by the sacrifice of Himself. It was no longer an annual affair, but eternal forgiveness. To emphasize the finality of His once-for-all atonement the writer points out that what was the ordinary lot of mankind befell the Lord Jesus. He could not die often because He was truly man. He must become man by being born in order to die, but having become man He must die but once, vv. 27, 28. So He was once offered to bear the sins of many.

The last verse in the chapter records the final appearing of the passage. 'Unto them that look for Him shall He appear the second time without sin', apart from all connection with it, 'unto salvation', cp. Phil. 3. 20. 'Even so, come, Lord Jesus', Rev. 22. 20.

So Christ was once offered to bear the sins of many

His Apostles

November 8th   Hebrews 10. 1-18

A body hast thou prepared me

Having stated the finality of the sacrifice of Christ the writer reverts to the ineffectiveness of the Levitical sacrifices. Their ceaseless repetition indicated their inability to save. The offerers still were loaded with the burden of guilt and had no direct access to God's presence. So the sacrifices continued. What they did do was create a remembrance of sins, the conscience of the offerer becoming aware of the reality of sins, which called for a propitiation which annual, animal sacrifices could never provide. These sacrifices could not meet the need of sinful men, v. 4, neither did God have any pleasure in them, vv. 6, 8. The offering of insensible beasts could never furnish a foundation on which God's justice could finally find satisfaction and provide the basis for the dispensing of His mercy. God's will with regard to sacrifice would be fulfilled when Someone sinless, and thus qualified, in the freedom of His own moral choice, would appear and devote Himself to doing God's will, even to the sacrifice of Himself.

We are allowed to hear the divine counsels concerning the provision of such a sacrifice. He who speaks has come to sacrifice Himself. His coming was not with a view to His incarnation only, but to His atoning sacrifice. The thought of entire willingness to obey the will of God on the part of the Son is expanded into the preparation of a body for absolute surrender to that will. Psalm 40's 'mine ears hast thou opened', v. 6, is given as 'a body hast thou prepared me', Heb. 10. 5, following the Septuagint version. The psalm gives the thought of a listening ear, cp. Isa. 50. 5. The phrase in Isaiah 50, 'I was not rebellious, neither turned away back' strengthens the thought of willingness and obedience. The body prepared by the Father for the Son was the instrument of His self-surrender and devoted submission to the Father's will. This was no unthinking sacrifice. He saw the horror of sin as no one else: in its dark rebellion against God and its results for man. He knew what He had to do about it – He offered Himself. Majestically He proclaims, 'I come . . . to do thy will'. There was no uncertainty as to the competence of the sacrifice; there would be no doubt about the fulfilment of God's will.

Christ and

Hebrews 10. 19-39 — November 9th

A new and living way

Privileges and responsibilities are before us, vv. 19-25: privileges indicated by the participle 'having', and responsibilities by the phrase 'let us'. The first privilege is 'having boldness to enter', v. 19 NKJV. Boldness, because God has said 'their sins and iniquities will I remember no more', v. 17, and because the way is open. We enter the holiest. That which under law had been the privilege of one only, and once a year, is now the privilege of all believers at all times. This is by virtue of the blood of Jesus. The way is new, for it did not exist under the law, and living, for He who died, rose. It is through the veil, His flesh. As long as He 'tabernacled among us' in flesh, sin was not atoned for, but when that flesh was rent so that His life-blood flowed, the way into the holiest was made manifest, ct. 9. 8. The veil was done away with for ever, Matt. 27. 51. Our second privilege is we have a great High Priest, Heb. 10. 21. We enter the holiest. Who do we meet there? Our great High Priest in all the glory of His Person, the One who has opened the way for us, and made those who were far off nigh by His blood.

What about responsibilities? The first is, 'Let us draw near', v. 22. We may do so with complete confidence, with no doubt or question about our right of access, or our acceptance with God. The second response is, 'Let us hold fast', v. 23 NKJV, the confession of hope. The full enjoyment of all that God has promised us in Christ we may not appropriate now. The best is yet to be. The crowning consummation of our salvation still awaits us in the future. Because God is faithful, our confidence is no vain hope or empty delusion. Our hope is rooted in the very character of God – 'He is faithful who promised'. The third response is, 'Let us consider one another', vv. 24, 25, and this 'to provoke unto love and to good works'. To 'consider' denotes attentive continuous care, to have a practical spirit of love and concern for one another. God desires to see us stir one another up, not to anger, envy, strife, or malice, but to love and good works. One practical effect of this follows, that is 'not forsaking the assembling of ourselves together'. Note that these responses are centred on faith, v. 22, hope, v. 23, and love, v. 24.

November 10th — Hebrews 11. 1-19

Without faith it is impossible to please him

As faith is necessary to please God, we are told its characteristics. Faith covers two areas: things hoped for, and things unseen. It is equally sure of the fulfilment of the one, and of the present reality of the other. Faith is the confidence of things hoped for, the conviction of things not seen. It makes 'the future present and the unseen evident'. It makes things future as real as if we already had them, and provides unshakeable evidence that the unseen blessings are absolutely certain. It is fully necessary to believe in the existence of God, so that He becomes the repository of faith and His very word is totally accepted, and to believe that He rewards those who seek Him. How else can we have dealings with One who is unseen and whose chief rewards lie beyond this present life? Abraham's faith was in a marked way an evidence of the unseen, and a guarantee of something to be enjoyed in the future. He had the promise of an inheritance, v. 8. He believed the promise, though he did not know how it would be fulfilled. He left Ur, resting on the reality of an unseen God, not knowing what he was to receive, or where he was going. All that he knew was that the land he was going to in the end was to be his. When he reached it, he lived in it as a sojourner. The only land he possessed in it was a cave for a tomb, Gen. 23. 17. He believed his descendants would have the land and he would leave his bones there, the witness that he laid claim to it for them. It was by faith he offered up his beloved son, Isaac, Heb. 11. 17. The demand of God seemed to run counter to God's promises. If Isaac were slain, what of the promised seed? Gen. 17. 16, 19.

Abraham did not doubt the promise; the solution of the problem he left to God. The obedience of Abraham rested on his faith in the creative power of God. He had seen God bring life out of death already, Heb. 11. 11, 12. He could do it again, and father and son would come again, Gen. 22. 5. Abraham's faith extended beyond Canaan. He lived in a tent like a stranger in a foreign country. Nothing on this earth could be his main goal. He looked for an eternal city whose Builder and Maker was God. How deep are our tent pegs here?

Christ and

Hebrews 11. 20-40 — November 11th

Today's title expresses the divine estimate. The world treated them as unworthy to live in it. Actually the *world* was not worthy of *them*, though it treated them as worthless. All they had in it was the bare hillside, the desert, or a den, a cave. What are the characteristics of this world? It is *godless*, having no consciousness of things not seen; it is *hopeless*, having no conviction of things hoped for. The true wealth of the world resided in these people who were despised and suffered, yet who won through. In terms of value, the world could not compare with them.

Prominent amongst them was Moses, vv. 24-28. He gave up all earthly glory for the people of God. Do not underestimate the choice he made. On the one hand there was a servile, abject, downtrodden race, and on the other the pleasures and treasures of Pharaoh's court. He had every opportunity that a great civilisation could give. Humanly speaking there was no limit to his prospects. He calmly estimated, and he chose. He accounted, balancing things in order to come to a decision. Great was Egypt's power, its pleasures manifold, and its treasures immense, but it all was 'for a season', v. 25. He 'refused to be called the son of Pharaoh's daughter', v. 24, and forsook Egypt, looking away from its treasures and fixing his eye on the heavenly reward. He endured with tenacity of purpose, seeing the Invisible. Faith is the evidence of things not seen. He saw One whose presence dwarfed all else to its true level of insignificance.

Moses was not alone in the writer's mind. Names of some are mentioned, others are anonymous. Where their histories can be found the writer expects us to read them to see their faith in action, v. 32. God knows and rejoices in them all. In conflict with their enemies they subdued kingdoms. In ruling the people and opposing evil, they wrought righteousness. In their dealing with God, they obtained promises. Who would not think of Daniel when the lions' mouths were stopped, Dan. 6, or of his three friends who were flung into the furnace but came out unharmed, Dan. 3. So the exploits of these heroes of faith goes on. Their faith amidst extraordinary sufferings is given to strengthen ours in the ordinary.

Of whom the world was not worthy

His Apostles

November 12th — Hebrews 12. 1-17

Looking unto Jesus

Rotherham translates 'Looking away unto', v. 2 EBR. Away from what? A great cloud of witnesses found in chapter 11. They exemplified faith in certain facets, but the call now is to look off to the Author and Finisher of faith. In what way were they witnesses that surround us? Are they watching our race? How disappointed they would often be, and surely they have that which is far better to gaze on in glory! The word 'witnesses' has been interpreted to mean 'those whose lives and actions testified to the worth and effect of faith, and whose faith received witness in scripture', W. E. Vine. In what way is this so? They had their failures and we learn from their mistakes. They were men 'of like passions' as ourselves, and yet completed the race, and we should not fail. Above all, their lives witnessed to God's faithfulness to them, and 'He abideth faithful' to us also. There are encumbrances, the weights and sin, but there is also encouragement, 'looking away off to Jesus'. It is to look beyond the cloud to a form radiant and sublime, to the supreme Leader and Perfecter of faith, the Lord of the whole host of the faithful. His faith never wavered, and was characterized by a true dependence upon God. He is thus the author, the file leader, the One who takes precedence, and the Perfecter, the One who supremely reveals faith in its working. He exercised the patience of faith – He endured, as did the patriarchs, 11. 8-22. He exhibited the power of faith – He despised, 'cared nothing for the shame', Goodspeed. Faith is confidence in things hoped for, and He looked to 'the joy set before him'. There was the joy of pleasing the Father, and so 'he became obedient unto death, even the death of the cross', Phil. 2. 8. There was the joy of the Father's presence, returning there as the perfect and glorified Man, and the triumphant Messiah, Ps. 16. 10, 11. There was the joy of knowing His sufferings purchased for Him a bride, Eph. 5. 25-27. He endured, and now He is set down, enthroned. Beware of losing that single gaze. The moment we take our eyes off the Lord Jesus and fix it on others, our pace in the Christian race will slacken and our onward progress in grace decline. Let us, then, so run the race set before us.

Christ and

Hebrews 12. 18-29 — November 13th

See that ye refuse not him that speaketh

This exhortation comes at the end of a passage which one might call 'The Tale of Two Mountains'. One is Mt. Sinai, which represents the law, and the passage looks back to its being given, Exod. 19. 16ff. There are seven things said of it. It was a mount that was death to touch, Heb. 12. 20. It burned with fire, Deut. 4. 11; 5. 4-5. There was blackness and darkness and tempest. There was the trumpet of awful warning and alarm. There was that which was most human, the articulate voice, which filled the hearers with overwhelming dread. The mountain is lost in fire and smoke. It becomes a manifestation of terrible divine majesty. The effect upon Israel was terror, the awestruck fear which is afraid to look, and even to listen. The fear was felt by Moses himself, v. 21. What is represented here is the majesty of God *above* us as creatures, and the wrath of God *against* us as sinners. It expresses the state of darkness, of distance, of alienation from God and His inapproachability.

Then there is in contrast Mt. Zion. Seven things are said of it also. It is the city of God, the heavenly Jerusalem. God is its maker and builder and light. There are myriads of angels, cp. 1. 14, all God's hosts that excel in strength and do His commandments and extol the worth of His Son, Rev. 5. 11, 12. There is the general assembly and church of the firstborn ones, holy brethren, partakers of a heavenly calling, children and heirs of God, the church of God, firstborn by divine grace, among whom Christ is the firstborn among many brethren. There is God, the Judge of all, to whom we come unafraid, because Another has borne our judgement. There are the spirits of just men made perfect, Old Testament saints, as yet disembodied and awaiting the resurrection, God's purposes being otherwise complete for them. There is Jesus, the mediator of the new covenant, cp. Luke 22. 19, 20; Heb. 8. 6ff.; 10. 16, 17. Finally, there is the blood of sprinkling, Jesus' blood, speaking of pardon, not vengeance as did Abel's. 'The heaven-descended God gave the law on Sinai. The heaven-ascended Son declares glad tidings from His throne of glory. Jesus speaking from heaven is God's most perfect and loving, as well as His ultimate message' ADOLPH SAPHIR.

His Apostles

November 14th — Hebrews 13

Be not forgetful

Among the final exhortations come those to remember, vv. 3, 7, and not to forget, vv. 2, 16. 'Let brotherly love continue', he writes. Note the emphasis on *continuance*. Brotherly love will not thrive on neglect. Two ways follow in which such love may be shown: by hospitality, v. 2; and by sympathy, v. 3. Don't forget to entertain strangers, we are told. The God who we worship is a lover of strangers, Deut. 10. 18, 19. Elders are to be given to hospitality, 1 Tim. 3. 2, and so are all saints, Rom. 12. 13. Neither is it to be shown only to those in fellowship, but to *strangers*. A good exponent of this was Gaius, 3 John 5-7. Those who are prisoners and those who suffer adversity are to be remembered. Brotherly love shows itself especially with the afflicted. Sympathy is fellow-feeling. It means putting oneself in the position of the sufferer. So the law of sympathetic fellowship is pressed home, cp. 1 Cor. 12. 26.

These Hebrews were to remember their former guides, Heb. 13. 7. They were to consider carefully their teaching, their faith and the outcome of their conduct. These guides had died, but they had left a heritage, and their influence remained. Their loss would be keenly felt, as is the loss of all such believers, but they should remember God's promise never to leave them, vv. 5, 6. Further, though these had died, their Lord and Saviour not only abides forever, but remains the same, the eternal, unchangeable Christ, v. 8. There may be change and loss of believers who are beloved, but Him they could never lose. As believer-priests the duty to give to those in need, to 'communicate', v. 16, was not to be forgotten. That went along with the sacrifice of praise, placed first here as of primary importance, v. 15. Nothing is so unworthy of a Christian as a fretful spirit, a gloomy temper, or a morose look. The real element of sacrifice comes in the word 'continually', for that involves self-surrender and self-denial. Another sacrifice is 'the fruit of our lips which make confession to His Name' RV. If we love the Lord Jesus it should be natural for us to say that we do. What motive is there for such sacrifices? God is well pleased with them, v. 16. Why this repetition of remembering and not forgetting? Simply because we do just that!

Christ and

The epistle of James has suffered many attacks from critics over the years. They have highlighted what they claim is its lack of doctrine, its conflict with the teachings of Paul, and its lack of coherence. Some have even gone so far as to question its divine inspiration. It is as well that the formation of the canon of Scripture was under the sovereign hand of God, rather than the ill-informed wisdom of men. Almost certainly penned by James, the Lord's brother and one of the leaders in the early church in Jerusalem, Acts 15. 13ff.; Gal. 2. 9, this letter is as much a part of the inspired word of God as any other book. It was the first book in the New Testament to be written. Its recipients were probably Jewish believers living outside of Palestine. However, its message is applicable to believers of all generations.

During our meditations upon the letter we will, no doubt, be challenged and, at times, made to feel uncomfortable. It is easy to talk about our faith, but James constantly invites us to show that it is a genuine and living faith by what we do. He was anxious that his readers should be 'doers of the word, and not hearers only', Jas. 1. 22. He would have had no argument with Paul about the importance of justification by faith as far as our new birth is concerned; however, he complements this truth by emphasizing that 'faith, if it hath not works, is dead, being alone', 2. 17. Saving faith is more than mere profession.

Our meditations will show that James understood the great doctrinal truths of the Christian faith, including those concerning God and Christ. Indeed, his practical teaching flows out of these doctrinal truths. Far from being a disjointed letter, seemingly unrelated subjects flow seamlessly from one to the other as James prompts us to test our faith. Facing trials, dealing with temptation, confronting discrimination, controlling the tongue, ending fights and quarrels, overcoming worldliness, resisting the devil, planning our lives with God, and exercising patience are all underpinned by the requirement to show our faith by our works. There is a close correlation between the moral teachings of the Sermon on the Mount, Matt. 5-7, and this letter. Prepare to be taken out of your comfort zone as you meditate upon it!

His Apostles

November 15th — James 1

Be ye doers of the word

What part does God's word play in our hearts and lives? James reminds us that it was the divine means used in our salvation. The Father loves to give us good and perfect gifts, v. 17, and one of these is new life: 'of his own will begat he us with the word of truth', v. 18. In the light of this, James encourages us to 'be swift to hear, slow to speak, slow to wrath', v. 19. The importance of God's word does not begin and end at new birth. It is vital to our spiritual growth that we are quick to hear what God has to say to us, as this will save us from swift and unwise reactions to what we hear, e.g., anger. We cannot lose our salvation, but we need to be saved constantly from the power of sin in our lives. We can achieve this only if we strip away all forms of uncleanness and humbly receive (in a deliberate and welcoming way) the divinely implanted word of God, v. 21.

However, it is not enough to be hearers of the word; therefore, James also challenges us to be 'doers of the word', v. 22. There is a danger of us treating God's word like the man who looks into the mirror at his natural face, considers his image, goes away, fails to return, and forgets what he has seen, vv. 23-24. Unlike this man, we should spend time looking intently and repeatedly 'into the perfect law of liberty', v. 25, which will give us an accurate picture of ourselves, and reveal how God wants us to live. His law is complete, and it liberates us in such a way that we, now being free from sin, want to obey it. Such an exercise will keep us from being forgetful hearers and ensure that we are blessed in our doing of the work, v. 25.

There is a danger that we can deceive ourselves. It is possible that persons can 'seem to be religious' by the things they do, and yet not to be genuine. Such persons will betray themselves by an inability to bridle their tongues, v. 26. True 'doers of the word' will care for others and keep themselves from being polluted by the defiling world in which they live, v. 27.

If God's word is lived out practically in our lives it will regulate our attitude towards trials, vv. 1-12, and temptations, vv. 13-16. Indeed, we will be patient throughout our trials, v. 4, and know that the source of all temptation is our lust, v. 14.

Christ and

James 2 — November 16th

Today's reading challenges us as to the reality of our faith. Is it a faith that saves or is it a dead faith? True, it is faith alone that saves, Eph. 2. 8, but our faith must be more than mere profession. Indeed, it is possible for us to believe great truths, e.g., 'there is one God', Jas. 2. 19, and yet for our faith to be dead. Even demons believe this, but they are not saved. It is not words, but *actions* that prove our faith is genuine. Good works will always accompany saving faith. Are we able to say, 'I will shew thee my faith by my works', v. 18? Just as 'the body without the spirit is dead, so faith without works is dead also', v. 26.

Two contrasting Old Testament characters bring home the challenge to our hearts. It was 'when he had offered up Isaac his son upon the altar', v. 21, that Abraham witnessed to the reality of his initial faith in God. It had already been said of him, 'He believed in the Lord; and he counted it to him for righteousness', Gen. 15. 6; however, his faith was 'made perfect (complete)', Jas. 2. 22, by his works. Similarly, Rahab's faith, Josh. 2. 8-11, was seen to be genuine, 'when she had received the messengers, and had sent them out another way', Jas. 2. 25.

Are we aware of brethren and sisters who have need of the basic necessities of life, v. 15? If we are, and yet offer them only words of concern, v. 16, we prove that our faith is dead. A living faith will recognize that words alone will not suffice, but works that alleviate the suffering must accompany them.

Do we show acts of favouritism based upon people's wealth and social status, vv. 2-3? If we do, we cast doubt upon the genuineness of the faith that we say we have in 'our Lord Jesus Christ, the Lord of glory', v. 1. He did not show favouritism towards the rich at the expense of the poor. Such behaviour is serious, because it is contrary to God's choice in salvation, v. 5, glorifies the oppressors, vv. 6-7, transgresses God's royal law of love, vv. 8-9, and ignores the fact that we shall be judged by that same law that gives us freedom, but not licence to do as we please, v. 12. Showing mercy to others is proof that we have a living faith and enables us to face the judgement seat of Christ with confidence, v. 13.

Faith, if it hath not works, is dead

His Apostles

November 17th   James 3

How great a matter a little fire kindleth!

Yesterday's meditation focused upon the importance of works as an evidence of our faith. However, today we are reminded that it does matter what we say. The tongue, although a little member of our body, is powerful. It is like a spark that can set a great forest on fire, v. 5. It is so influential that if it were under control we would be able to keep our whole body in check, v. 2. However, such maturity is beyond our grasp; indeed, we all stumble in many ways, v. 2. Teachers of the scriptures carry a special responsibility for the impact their words have upon others, for which they will be held particularly accountable at the judgement seat of Christ, v. 1. This ought to prevent us from coveting such a position if we are not so gifted.

The potential of the controlled tongue to be a real power for good is seen in the bit in the horse's mouth and the rudder of a great ship, vv. 3-4. Although they are small, they control the entire horse and ship respectively. The bit secures the horse's obedience, and the rudder ensures the ship's safety through stormy seas. Similarly, a controlled tongue can produce obedience in all areas of our life and prove a blessing to those, including ourselves, who are passing through troubled times.

It is disturbing to consider the descriptions given to the uncontrolled tongue: 'a fire, a world of iniquity . . . it defileth the whole body, and setteth on fire the course of nature (i.e., our entire life) . . . an unruly evil, full of deadly poison', vv. 6, 8. The source of such a destructive fire is hell (Gehenna). We cannot therefore tame the tongue in our own strength, vv. 7-8; indeed, our inconsistent use of it, both to bless God and to curse men, is a proof of our inability so to do, vv. 9-10. Even nature does not display such inconsistency, vv. 11-12.

If we fail to control our tongues, envy and strife will mark our lives and we will display wisdom that 'is earthly, sensual, devilish', v. 15. Let us pray today that the indwelling Holy Spirit will enable us to display in our works and our words 'the wisdom that is from above', v. 17. This wisdom is pure, peace-loving, gentle, willing to listen, full of mercy and good fruits, impartial, sincere, and produces the fruit of righteousness.

Christ and

James 4 — November 18th

God resisteth the proud

Solomon reminds us that one of the things the Lord hates is 'a proud look', Prov. 6. 17. Indeed, He resists (sets Himself in battle array against) the proud, Jas. 4. 6. Pride therefore puts us into a position of open warfare with Him.

Pride can manifest itself in a variety of ways in our lives and it ruins our testimony. Sadly, it is at the heart of wars (fights – prolonged hostilities) and fights (quarrels – specific outbursts of hostility) among us, v. 1. Such behaviour ought not to be seen among the Lord's people. It damages our prayer life, vv. 2-3, and reflects our unfaithfulness to God and 'friendship (regard and affection) of the world', v. 4. A society that is alienated from God acts in this manner, but we must take care not to embrace its ways and thus put ourselves into the position of being at enmity with God. If we do, we have only ourselves to blame, because such unhealthy behaviour springs from the lusts within each one of us, v. 1.

The antidote for pride is clear, but challenging. It is via the pathway of submission to God, resisting the devil, drawing nigh to God, practical holiness, intense feelings of shame for our sins, and genuine humility before the Lord, vv. 7-9. The rewards will be worth it, because the Lord will give us grace, v. 6, draw near to us, v. 8, and lift us up, v. 10. The devil, who fell through pride and who loves to see the fights and quarrels among us, will flee in the face of those who have submitted to God and His word. The positive outcome for our brethren is that we will not speak evil of or judge them, recognizing that God alone is qualified to be their Judge, v. 12.

Pride also raises its ugly head when we speak and act as if we are in total control of our future plans, even to the point of confidently predicting successful outcomes, v. 13. By so doing, we ignore God's plans for us, our own ignorance of what tomorrow holds, and the brevity of life, v. 14. We know better than to do this; therefore, our failure to obey God's word means we are guilty of sin. The precursor, not the postscript, to all our plans ought to be, 'If the Lord will, we shall live, and do this, or that', v. 15.

His Apostles

November 19th   James 5

Be patient therefore, brethren

How easily do you lose patience with people and circumstances? James' readers could easily have done so as they faced immense pressure from their unscrupulous employers. These rich men held back their rightful wages, v. 4, and also took advantage of the fact that they did not resist them, v. 6. James made it clear that such men will reap what they sow, v. 1. Indeed, their ill-gotten wealth would be short-lived, vv. 2-3.

James' message to his beleaguered readers was clear, 'Be patient (long-suffering with people) therefore, brethren', v. 7. We might well ask whether it is possible for believers, including ourselves, to exercise patience in the midst of such hostile circumstances. James gives us the secrets that will enable us so to do. Firstly, we can be confident that we have a God, the Lord of Sabaoth (the New Testament equivalent of the Old Testament 'Lord of hosts'), who hears our cries, v. 4. He is stronger than our persecutors. Secondly, we can look beyond the dark days to the coming of the Lord that will bring to an end any injustices we might suffer now at the hands of ungodly men, vv. 7-8. Thirdly, we must live in the light of the judgement seat of Christ, where we will have to give an account of how patient we have been with each other, v. 9. Fourthly, we can gain encouragement from the patience of others in the midst of adverse circumstances, e.g., the farmers, v. 7, the prophets, v. 10, and Job, v. 11. Indeed, we will discover, like Job, 'that the Lord is very pitiful, and of tender mercy', v. 11. He always has positive ends in view for us, even if we cannot see them at the time.

Our lack of patience under pressure can lead us to succumb to the temptation of reinforcing our statements with oaths, v. 12. We should reject such speaking; our word should be sufficient.

One of the greatest tests of our patience can be when we face bodily suffering. This may be in the form of general physical suffering, v. 13, or sickness as a result of spiritual failure, vv. 14-15. In both cases recovery is to be found in patient prayer and confession, of which Elijah is a supreme example, vv. 17-18. Elders also need to exercise patience during their ministry of restoration for those who have erred, vv. 14, 19-20.

Christ and

In an upper room in Jerusalem the Lord said to Peter, 'I have prayed for thee, that thy faith fail not: and when thou art converted, strengthen thy brethren', Luke 22. 32. In a moving scene by the Sea of Tiberias the Lord restored him following his denial of Him in the high priest's palace. He said to him, 'Feed my lambs', and 'Feed my sheep', John 21. 15-17. The Lord's intercessions on behalf of His people never fail; therefore, we discover in 1 Peter that he is an elder, 1 Pet. 5. 1. Indeed, both of his Letters reveal his deep interest in, and care for, the flock of God. He wanted to strengthen his brethren so that they would not experience the failure he had known. Let us pray that this same care for the spiritual welfare of others is stimulated in our hearts as we meditate upon Peter's writings.

The Lord also revealed to Peter the manner of his death, John 21. 18-19. He knew therefore from the outset of his ministry that he faced a pathway of suffering that would end with crucifixion. Thus he was well qualified to strengthen and encourage his brethren who were facing the prospect of a 'fiery trial' from without, during the cruel reign of Nero the Roman emperor, 1 Pet. 4. 12. Indeed, suffering 'for righteousness' sake' and bearing reproach 'for the name of Christ', are dominant themes of his first Letter, 3. 14; 4. 14. Clearly, the three years that Peter spent in Christ's company had made a deep impression upon him. He never missed an opportunity to point his brethren to Him as the supreme example of how to respond to suffering. May we gain encouragement from our meditations, so that there are positive outcomes to the trials that we face in our lives.

In his Second Letter, Peter warns of the dangers that come from false teachers within the flock. He reminds his readers of the importance of the scriptures in confronting error. He also encourages them to look forward to the time when the day of the Lord, i.e., His judgement of the wicked, will come, which will lead on to the day of God when there will be 'new heavens and a new earth, wherein dwelleth righteousness', 2 Pet. 3. 10-13. His desire is that such a hope will lead his brethren to godly living, and keep them from error.

His Apostles

November 20th — 1 Peter 1. 1-12

The trial of your faith

At first reading, the term 'strangers scattered', v. 1, might give the impression that those to whom Peter wrote were insignificant, isolated and vulnerable. However, nothing could have been farther from the truth; indeed, they were the most secure people in the Roman Empire. They had a hope, v. 3, a faith, v. 7, and a love, v. 8, which others knew nothing of.

Their security rested in divine Persons acting on their behalf to bring them salvation. God the Father chose them according to His foreknowledge, the Holy Spirit sanctified (set apart) them with a view to the obedience of faith in the gospel, and they had been sprinkled with the blood of Jesus Christ, i.e., the power and value of His sacrifice had been applied, v. 2. God's 'abundant mercy', v. 3, towards them meant that they possessed a living hope that was grounded in the risen Christ, and an inheritance that was incorruptible, undefiled, and reserved in heaven for them, v. 4. Furthermore, they were being continually guarded by the power of God through faith, in anticipation of the time when they would appear with Christ at His return to reign, v. 5. We too, by grace and mercy, share with them in this living hope, and ought to take Peter's words upon our lips, 'Blessed be the God and Father of our Lord Jesus Christ', v. 3.

Although we can rejoice that we are on the pathway to glory, it does not mean an absence of trials, vv. 6-7. Trials are sometimes necessary, and they can be painful. They are varied, but limited in their duration. If we view them within the context of our salvation, we will see that God has eternal glory in mind. His desire is to refine our faith so that it 'might be found unto praise and honour and glory' when we return with Jesus Christ to reign, v. 7. We have not seen Him as yet, but we love Him, believe Him, and rejoice in Him with a joy that cannot be expressed in words, and that is full of glory, v. 8. We receive even now the goal of our faith, i.e., the joy and glory associated with the final salvation of our souls, v. 9.

Our salvation ought to thrill us! The sufferings and glory of Christ interested the Old Testament prophets, vv. 10-12. Angels also desire to look into God's dealings with mankind, v. 12.

Christ and

1 Peter 1. 13 – 2. 10 — November 21st

As he . . . is holy, so be ye holy

Today we are challenged to live holy (set apart) lives. God is holy, therefore He calls us to be holy, 1. 15-16. We will never be as holy as He is; nevertheless, we are called upon progressively to become holy in all areas of our lives. Peter reveals the mind we must cultivate in the pursuit of holiness:

A disciplined mind, v. 13. There is no room for loose thinking; therefore, we must exercise self-control and focus our minds on the hope that is before us of Christ's return to reign.

An obedient mind, vv. 14-16. As members of a family, we are called to obedience. We should not be marked by the desires that we displayed in the days when we were ignorant of God.

A reverent mind, vv. 17-21. We should not presume upon our relationship with the Father. He is impartial in His judgements and therefore we must show Him the reverence that His holiness demands. An appreciation of the cost of our redemption, i.e., 'the precious blood of Christ', v. 19, should lead us to fear the Lord. It is humbling to remember that He was marked out beforehand as the One who would be revealed, die, and be raised up, so that our 'faith and hope might be in God', v. 21.

A loving mind, 1. 22 – 2. 3. Both the Holy Sprit and the word of God were instrumental in our salvation, and one of the evidences that we are born again is our love for the brethren. It is a love that ought to be sincere and fervent. However, we must lay aside the attitudes that hinder its display, and 'as newborn babes, desire the sincere (unadulterated) milk of the word', 2. 2.

A priestly mind, 2. 4-10. The grace of God made each one of us priests at new birth, vv. 5, 9. The centre of our priesthood is Jesus Christ, who is the living stone, the chief corner stone and the head (top) stone. It is through Him that we have become living stones, a spiritual house, a holy priesthood, a chosen generation, a royal priesthood, a holy nation, a people for possession, and the people of God. As a holy priesthood we are called to offer up spiritual sacrifices, e.g., our praise, Heb. 13. 15; our bodies, Rom. 12. 1; our prayers, Ps. 141. 2; our giving, Phil. 4. 18. As a royal priesthood we should show forth the Lord's praises to others.

His Apostles

November 22nd 1 Peter 2. 11 – 3. 7

Christ ... suffered ... leaving us an example

It is only as we respond to the call to be holy that we will view our relationship to the world in the right way. We will see ourselves as 'strangers and pilgrims', 2. 11, i.e., those who are travelling home to heaven. As such, our lives ought to be distinctive; therefore, we must abstain from the strong desires of the old nature within us. Our lives should be of such a character among unbelievers that, in spite of their accusations against us, they are led to glorify God. To this end, we must display a submissive spirit.

Firstly, we must be responsible citizens by submitting 'to every ordinance (institution) of man for the Lord's sake', v. 13. It is the Lord's will that we silence our opponents by submitting to all levels of government. Our liberty in Christ must never be interpreted as a licence to do as we please. A submissive spirit will lead us to honour all men, love our fellow believers, reverence God, and honour the king.

Secondly, we must be submissive in the workplace. Our conduct as employees should be exemplary, whether our employer is just or unjust. It is one thing to suffer patiently when we deserve it, but quite another to 'endure grief, suffering wrongfully', v. 19. This is acceptable with God and glorifies Him.

Thirdly, we must be submissive in the home. Christian wives must submit to their husbands, even if they are unbelievers. It is their 'meek and quiet spirit' that will win them over, not outward appearance and words, 3. 4. Old Testament women, e.g. Sarah, displayed such a spirit. Husbands must honour their wives, recognizing the eternal spiritual relationship that links them together. If they do not, their prayer life will be hindered.

Christ has left us the perfect example. His actions were without sin and His words without deceit, yet He was reviled and suffered. He was never vindictive, but committed everything into the hands of God, the righteous Judge. His submission to suffering has given us spiritual healing. He is our Example, our Substitute, our Saviour, our Shepherd, and our Overseer. If He bore our sins on the tree, those sins ought now to be absent from our lives as we submit to the word of God.

Christ and

1 Peter 3. 8-22 — November 23rd

Suffering for righteousness' sake is an integral part of the Christian pathway. It is amazing therefore that we also read the following phrases in this context: 'inherit a blessing', v. 9; 'love life, and see good days', v. 10; 'do good . . . seek peace', v. 11; 'happy are ye . . . be not afraid . . . neither be troubled', v. 14.

Christians need each other in times of suffering. Let us pray for harmony, compassion, love, pity, and true friendliness among us, v. 8. Nothing will be gained by returning evil for evil; indeed, we must restrain our tongues from speaking evil and deceit, v. 9. We must seek and pursue peace, v. 11. We might well ask how it is possible for these things to be a reality.

Firstly, we must understand that we are called to suffering for righteousness' sake; yet, we must also be encouraged by the prospect that ultimately it will lead to blessing, v. 9.

Secondly, we can be confident that the Lord watches over us, hears our prayers, and is against evil men, v. 12. They cannot do permanent harm to us if we follow zealously what is good, v. 13; therefore, we can be happy and not afraid or troubled, v. 14.

Thirdly, we must sanctify (set apart) the Lord God (lit., 'Christ the Lord') in our hearts, v. 15. This will enable us at all times to bear testimony, with meekness and reverence, to the hope that is within us. Consciences will be clear and enemies put to shame.

Fourthly, it is encouraging to know that 'Christ also hath once suffered for sins, the just for the unjust, that he might bring us to God', v. 18. His suffering for sins was a once-for-all act that culminated in His resurrection. He was 'quickened (made alive) by the Spirit', v. 18. By the same Spirit, He preached through Noah to wicked men prior to the flood, but they despised the message. As a result their spirits are now in prison awaiting final judgement, vv. 19-20, whereas 'Jesus Christ . . . is gone into heaven, and is on the right hand of God; angels and authorities and powers being made subject unto him', vv. 21-22. Our baptism is a figure of His death and resurrection; it witnesses to us having finished with the old life and desiring to walk in newness of life. It is therefore the appeal of a good conscience towards God that we will obey Him.

His Apostles

November 24th   1 Peter 4

The end of all things is at hand

The emphasis on suffering throughout this letter reminds us that even though we are a people linked with eternity, we are also creatures of time. However, the prospect of our eternal blessings ought to have an impact upon our lives now. Today's meditation challenges us as to our attitude towards time.

'**The rest of his time**', vv. 1-2. Christ has 'suffered for us in the flesh'; therefore, this ought to inspire us to arm ourselves 'with the same mind' for the battles ahead, v. 1. Indeed, the believer who has suffered is the believer who knows what it is to have died to sin, cp. Rom. 6. In the light of Christ's sufferings we should not waste the rest of our time pandering to the flesh, but rather seeking to pursue God's will.

'**The time past of our life**', vv. 3-6. It is beneficial to look back on past times and to remind ourselves that former conduct ought to remain in the past, v. 3. Our previous associates will find it difficult to accept the change in our lives, but ultimately God will judge them, vv. 4-5. Peter encourages us by pointing to believers who have died, who had the gospel preached to them while they were here and believed. Men judged them as worthy of persecution in this life, but they are alive in heaven.

'**The end of all things**', vv. 7-11. We do not know the exact time, but we are told that it 'is at hand', v. 7. This should have an impact upon our lives in the present. We are called upon to be clear thinking, watchful, prayerful, earnest in our love toward each other, willingly hospitable, and ready to use our spiritual gifts for the benefit of others, vv. 8-10. Whether our service is in word or deed it should bring glory to God, v. 11.

'**For the time is come**', vv. 12-19. It is a sobering thought that 'the time is come that judgment must begin at the house of God', v. 17. It is not retributive, but corrective judgement; however, it ought to serve as a warning to those who disobey the gospel that God will judge them, vv. 17-18. However, as Christians we are able to view 'fiery trials' as allowed by God to purify and cleanse us. We can rejoice that we are sharers of Christ's sufferings, be happy that we are reproached for His name, and feel no shame, vv. 13-14, 16.

Christ and

1 Peter 5

November 25th

Be clothed with humility

Humility is the inward feeling of lowliness. It has been described as, 'the inner grace that once you know you have it, you have lost it'. 'Be clothed', v. 5, is a reference to the apron that was tied around a person's outer garments as they worked. Our service for the Lord ought always to be characterized by humility. There is a great incentive for us to be humble: 'God resisteth the proud, and giveth grace to the humble', v. 5. If we are 'clothed with humility':

The care of the God's flock will be right, vv. 1-4. Elders will recognize that they are among the flock, not lords over it, vv. 2, 3. They will feed the flock willingly and free from impure motives, v. 2, knowing that it belongs to God and is His heritage, v. 3. They will lead by example, v. 3, appreciating that the reward and the glory for their faithful service is future, vv. 1, 4.

We will be in subjection, vv. 5-6. Naturally speaking, subjection hurts our pride. Younger believers must submit to older believers, respecting their maturity and experience, v. 5. Indeed, we should all 'be subject one to another', v. 5. There is no room for standing on our dignity or rights. Above all, we must be subject to God, and He will exalt us at the right time, v. 6.

We will be free from anxiety, v. 7. Pride prevents us from reaching this haven of peace. Humility will lead us to trust God's word: 'Cast (as a once for all act) all your care (anxiety) upon him (God); for he careth for you'.

We will take the devil seriously, vv. 8-9. He is a defeated, yet dangerous, foe. He is our adversary the devil (accuser) and he is like a roaring lion. Pride will close my eyes to the danger, whereas humility will ensure that I am clear thinking, wide awake and resisting him 'steadfast in the faith', v. 9.

We will give all the glory to God, vv. 10-11. He allows us to suffer for a while, but as 'the God of all grace', v. 10, He uses it to complete, establish, strengthen, and settle us. It is humbling to know that He has 'called us unto his eternal glory by Christ Jesus', v. 10. It is fitting therefore that we should close our meditation today with a note of praise, 'To him be glory and dominion for ever and ever. Amen', v. 11.

His Apostles

November 26th 2 Peter 1

The prospect of his fast-approaching death by crucifixion could have made Peter inward looking, but it had the opposite effect. It spurred him on to be diligent in meeting his responsibilities towards his fellow believers, v. 12; therefore, he took up his pen to bring to their remembrance truth that they already knew, vv. 12, 13, 15. It will be beneficial for us to remind ourselves of these same truths in our meditation today.

Firstly, we 'have obtained like precious faith', v. 1, i.e., it is of equal value in the sight of God to that of any other saint, including the apostles. We did not obtain it through any merit of our own, but 'through the righteousness of God and our Saviour Jesus Christ (*not* two persons, but one)', v. 1.

Secondly, this faith is accompanied by divine power, i.e., God gives us all that we need for 'life and godliness', v. 3. There is nothing incomplete about our salvation, because it rests on 'him that hath called us to glory and virtue', v. 3, i.e., Jesus Christ.

Thirdly, God has 'given unto us great and precious promises' in His word, v. 4. We must embrace them and live in the light of them. The end product of these promises is that we have become recipients of a new nature, i.e., the divine nature, and have fled from the corrupting influence of the world, v. 4.

Fourthly, such great blessings call for a response from us. Our faith must be active if we are to grow spiritually. We must make every effort to add into our faith virtue, knowledge, temperance (self-control), patience, godliness, brotherly kindness, and charity (love), vv. 5-7. It is only as we do so that we will live fruitful lives, confirm to ourselves the truth of our election and calling by God, and ensure an *abundant* entrance into 'the everlasting kingdom of our Lord and Saviour Jesus Christ', vv. 8-11.

Fifthly, we need to be constantly reminded of the importance of the scriptures. They are a light that shines in a dark place until the day when Christ returns to dispel the darkness, v. 19. Peter, unlike us, had been an eyewitness of the coming glory, vv. 16-18; nevertheless, we have 'a more sure word of prophecy' in the scriptures. They are absolutely reliable, because the writers were 'moved (borne along) by the Holy Ghost', v. 21.

Christ and

2 Peter 2
November 27th

'Cursed children', v. 14, cp. John 8. 44 – what a contrast these people are to those who 'have obtained . . . precious faith', and have received 'exceeding great and precious promises', 2 Pet. 1. 1, 4! Let us thank God today that we, through grace, are among the latter. Although we might prefer a more positive theme to meditate upon, it is vital for us to be forewarned about the destructive activities of false teachers.

Spot the denial. All teachers stand or fall by what they say about the Person of Christ. If any deny His deity and Lordship they are false and to be shunned. Peter speaks of them 'denying the Lord ('absolute Master') that bought them', 2. 1. Christ purchased the entire field (the world), Matt. 13. 44; therefore, false teachers are bought, but they are not among the redeemed.

Sense the danger. Firstly, false teachers are often to be found among believers, i.e., they know the truth, but deliberately turn their backs upon it, 2 Pet. 2. 1. Paul's words to the elders at Ephesus are apposite, 'Also of your own selves shall men arise, speaking perverse things, to draw away disciples after them', Acts 20. 30. Secondly, they make a deliberate choice to bring in 'damnable (destructive) heresies', 2 Pet. 2. 1. Thirdly, they manage to attract a considerable following, v. 2. Fourthly, like Balaam, they are covetous and seek financial gain, vv. 3, 15-16. Fifthly, they sound impressive, but there is no truth in their teaching, v. 18. Sixthly, they target vulnerable new believers, v. 18. Seventhly, they promise freedom, but they bring their converts into greater bondage, vv. 19-20. Eighthly, they have no intention of obeying spiritual authority, v. 10. Indeed, they behave like animals, v. 12, and therefore pose a real threat to the welfare of believers.

Savour the security. It is encouraging to know that 'the Lord knoweth how to deliver the godly out of temptations', v. 9. Noah, v. 5, and Lot, v. 7, bear testimony to His keeping power. However, He also knows how 'to reserve the unjust unto the day of judgment to be punished', v. 9. Fallen angels, v. 4, and the cities of Sodom and Gomorrah, v. 6, provide us with powerful reminders of this truth. Similarly, false teachers will not prevail: they 'shall utterly perish in their own corruption', v. 12.

His Apostles

November 28th — 2 Peter 3

The day of the Lord will come

The cry of the scoffers continues to be heard in this present day of God's grace, 'Where is the promise of his coming? for since the fathers fell asleep, all things continue as they were from the beginning of the creation', v. 4. Such men and women are motivated by their own lusts, v. 3, and display their wilful ignorance of God's word.

Firstly, the scoffers are ignorant of what happened to 'the world that then was', i.e., the world before the flood in the days of Noah, vv. 5-6. Men assumed that things would continue as they were then, but they were wrong: it 'being overflowed with water, perished', v. 6. Peter had written earlier about God 'bringing in the flood upon the world of the ungodly', 2. 5.

Secondly, they are ignorant of the destiny of 'the heavens and earth, which are now'. They are being 'kept in store, reserved unto fire', 3. 7. God is restraining the potential of the elements at the present time, but ultimately He will use fire, not water as in the days of Noah, to judge ungodly men. Peter uses graphic terminology to describe the coming end of the present heavens and earth, e.g., 'great noise', 'fervent heat', 'burned up', and 'dissolved' (setting free what is bound), vv. 10-11. Unbelieving evolutionists state that the cosmos began with a big bang, but God says that it will end with a big bang!

Thirdly, they are ignorant of how God views time. He is eternal and therefore He is not limited by time. Even believers need to be reminded of this, v. 8. What often appears to be a delay in God's plans is not so from the perspective of eternity.

Fourthly, they are ignorant of His character. What they regard as slackness on His part in carrying out His promises is evidence of His 'longsuffering to us-ward, not willing that any should perish, but that all should come to repentance', v. 9.

We leave the ignorant scoffers, resting in the assurance that the day of the Lord, i.e., the day of His judgement, will suddenly overtake this godless world, v. 10. We will not pass through that day, but we look beyond it to the day of God, when there will be '(completely) new heavens and a new earth', vv. 12-13. Such a blessed hope ought to lead us to holy and godly living, v. 14.

Christ and

The three Epistles ascribed to John, like his Gospel, do not carry his name. 2 and 3 John certainly offered the first readers the identifier 'the Elder', as his Gospel described him as 'the disciple whom Jesus loved' and 'the other disciple', John 21. 20; 20. 2. Style and common themes such as love, light, and life confirm with certainty that the anonymous writer is John, the beloved disciple. His Epistles were written to 'you that believe on the name of the Son of God; that ye may know that ye have eternal life', 1 John 5. 13, a purpose perfectly aligned to that expressed at John chapter 20 verse 31, 'that ye may believe that Jesus is the Christ, the Son of God; and that believing ye might have life through his name'.

There is reason to believe that John was an old man when he penned these three Epistles. His use of the phrase 'little children' and the title 'the Elder' would suggest both seniority and genuine concern for those he loved in the Lord. Each of the letters reveals individuals under pressure in John's absence. Each need draws forth from John a tenderness that assures of his care, and a ministry that is calculated to address the particular circumstance the recipients faced. In 2 and 3 John, we can identify the initial recipient: in 2 John, a woman, probably widowed, whose children John knows. He also knows that false teachers are active in her locality and to her he offers guidance. 3 John concerns a worthy fellow-servant Gaius in whom John has great confidence. He and other good men were troubled by an overbearing man Diotrephes, a man who had rejected apostolic doctrine and whom John will deal with face to face. However, the general problem facing all saints at that time is more clearly set out in 1 John, evidently a letter for wide circulation at a time when false doctrine about Christ's Person and work was circulating and being taught by false teachers.

John's teaching in the three Epistles is Christ-centred. John addresses the family of God in its entirety and particular individuals in that family to ground them in the faith, that they might know that Christ is righteous, pure, and sinless, 1 John 2. 1; 3. 3, 5, 7, and that He is the only begotten Son of God, 4. 9, 15; 5. 5, 10, the true God and eternal life, 5. 20. John was confident that God's work in their souls would preserve them.

His Apostles

November 29th   1 John 1

Walk in the light, as he is in the light

Without needing to introduce himself, John announces his message that God is light, v. 5. Like the other apostles, John was well known among Christians. He was also singularly qualified to deliver this message, firstly because the apostles had heard and seen, and engaged mind and heart in contemplating the Eternal One who had come into time. Indeed He had come near enough for them to touch Him, vv. 1-2. Their experience was unique. Neither their contemporaries nor those who followed them were so favoured. The apostolic testimony was declared to other Christians that they might all know fellowship with the Father and His Son, Jesus Christ, vv. 3-4. John will also write of 'fellowship one with another', v. 7; which has been defined as each saint enjoying 'exactly the same blessing of grace', and so exactly the same joy, v. 4.

To those enjoying that grace John sets out his message that God is light, a message wholly consistent with the testimony of Old Testament writers. Moses' face once showed the effects of the light of God's glory, Exod. 34. 29-35. David and an unnamed psalmist associated light with God, Pss. 27. 1; 36. 9; 104. 2. Nonetheless, after the appearing of the Light of the world, John 8. 12; 9. 5, the apostle was able to write more boldly than Moses or David, that God is light. The Light of the world had identified 'the sons of light', John 12. 35-36 RV, as those who walked in the light and not in darkness.

John's message that God is light means that we cannot enjoy fellowship with Him and walk in darkness, v. 6; nor should we deceive ourselves into thinking that we have no sin and have not sinned, as some of John's opponents were suggesting. If we are to enjoy fellowship with the Father and His Son, and with one another, we need to walk in the light, the light of uncompromising purity, the light that causes us to judge all that is not holy, all that is not pure. The apostle adds, 'as he (God) is in the light', v. 7. He is fully revealed in Christ, so we immediately accept John's message and the responsibilities it brings with it, knowing the abiding efficacy of the blood and Christ our Advocate secure for us the joy of fellowship, as we walk in the light.

Christ and

1 John 2. 1-17 — November 30th

Every family has its characteristics, so too does the family of God. Those born into it have the same Father, vv. 1, 13, 15, 16; they don't habitually sin, v. 1; they love their brothers and sisters, v. 9; their sins have been forgiven, v. 12, and in the family they grow and mature, vv. 13-17. John underlines his personal interest in this family with the seven occurrences of 'I write'.

'If any man sin . . .', that sin is disruptive in the family. But says John, there is no need for the Christian to sin. Sin is forgivable, but not excusable. Such is the seriousness of sin, that as soon as a child of God sins – not when he repents – the Advocate begins to act on his behalf. He is singularly qualified for the task, for He Himself is 'the righteous One' and the propitiation for our sins, vv. 1-2. Fellowship with the Father can be restored, 1. 3; and once more obedience will mark His child. John draws particular attention to one matter that sin would disrupt – obeying the commandment to love his brother, 2. 8-10. Because he abides in the light, he will not stumble his brother: a grave matter against which the Lord Himself had spoken in John's hearing, 'Woe to that man by whom the offence cometh', Matt. 18. 6-10.

John recognizes that not all members of a family have reached the same point of maturity. In the family of God, there are those who are mature enough to be acknowledged as fathers, 1 John 2. 13a, 14a, others less so – the young men, vv. 13b, 14b-17, and the little children, vv. 13c, 18-27. John uses the masculine gender 'fathers' and 'young men', not that spiritual progress is exclusively a male pursuit!

John begins with the fathers because in them we see the progress the Father seeks. They were not necessarily highly gifted, nor of a great age, but they knew Christ in a personal, intimate way. They had learned how valueless everything was compared with Christ. The young men's glory was their strength, Prov. 20. 29, spiritual strength to overcome 'the wicked one' 1 John 2. 14. Their resource was in the abiding word. The little children of this family had come to know the Father. He knew their need and would continue to meet that need.

His Apostles

December 1st   1 John 2. 18-29

Even now there are many antichrists

John outlived the other apostles. Even before his homecall, he was aware of features he recognized as those that will mark the period just prior to the Lord's return to rapture His own to glory. He writes about virulent opposition to Christ, even to denying the very fundamentals of Christianity: that He is the Christ and that He has revealed the Father, vv. 22-23. John names these pedlars of lies as antichrists, and advises the Christians to whom he writes that those who had imbibed their false doctrine were not true Christians – 'they were not of us', v. 19.

Under the guidance of the Holy Spirit, John underscores how God undergirds the faith of His people. Firstly, the saint has apostolic teaching, initially delivered orally; note the verb 'heard', vv. 18, 24. Thereafter, that teaching was committed to writing, now forming the New Testament; note John's thirteen references to his own writing in this epistle. Secondly, the Holy One has sent the Holy Spirit in order to 'guide [the saint] into all truth', John 16. 13. John assures His readers that the 'unction' (anointing), 1 John 2. 20, teaches the truth every Christian needs to hear, truth that will enhance his appreciation of Christ, and form in him features of Christ. When Paul wrote of the anointing, he wrote that God has anointed every child of God with the Holy Spirit, 2 Cor. 1. 21. John now adds that the anointing abides with us, 1 John 2. 27. Christians need not to ask to be anointed by the Holy Spirit, nor to fear the anointing being taken from them, Rom. 8. 9.

John would have us recognize the denial of Christ 'as not merely erroneous teaching but as diabolically inspired' (D. E. HIEBERT). Such false doctrine cannot produce in a life the righteous character of Christ that only those born of God exhibit, 1 John 2. 29. Ultimately, the work of those many antichrists already at work in John's day will culminate in the revelation of the 'wicked one' with 'all deceivableness of unrighteousness', whom the Lord shall destroy with the brightness of His coming, 2 Thess. 2. 8-9. But those born of God have confidence that they will not be ashamed, when at His coming they give account before the One the many antichrists have denied, 1 John 2. 28.

Christ and

1 John 3 — December 2nd

Three times in this chapter, John refers to 'the children of God' (KJV reads, 'sons of God') in a way that would be unrecognizable to Old Testament prophets. They would have been able to recall, 'Ye are the children of the Lord your God', Deut. 14. 1, but were more comfortable being called the children of Israel, for they had not the Spirit of adoption in their hearts, enabling them to cry, 'Abba, Father', Rom. 8. 15. Three different verbs are associated with this term: 'to call', v. 1; 'to be', v. 2, and 'to be manifested', v. 10. John contrasts (1) the child of God's knowledge with that of the world, v. 1; (2) what we are now with what we shall be, v. 2; (3) the children of God with the children of the devil, v. 10.

What a name to have called upon us! No earth-born love could have conceived of, nor could any earthly power have conferred such privilege, v. 1; John 1. 12, 13. The verb 'to call' is a reminder of the Father's gracious initiative, 1 John 3. 1. The world that did not recognize the Lord Jesus as the One sent by the Father, does not understand the relationship into which God's call has brought His children, v. 1.

The phrase 'now are' declares unambiguously that the place in God's family is not a distant goal but a present enjoyment, v. 2. The slave that God had reached and saved still toiled in the same fields, but his destiny was now different. He could not fully explain the difference between his lot as a slave and what he will be 'when he (Christ) shall appear', but he did know that when he would see Christ, he would be like Him. This is the Father's will for His child, v. 2.

Two family traits evident in the children of God are that they do what is righteous and they love others in God's family, v. 10. These are the two features that make manifest that they are not the children of the devil. The devil 'was a murderer from the beginning' and 'a liar', John 8. 44, so his children might hate the children of God and their righteous manner of life, 1 John 3. 12-15. If he is to be true to his calling, the child of God should love like his Father and, like his Lord, be willing to sacrifice everything for his brother, vv. 16-17.

Now are we the sons of God

His Apostles

December 3rd   1 John 4

Not until he had spoken of the Father's love, does John use the word 'beloved', 3. 1, but thereafter he addresses Christians as 'beloved' eight times (ten times in the RV) in his three brief epistles, three times in this chapter, vv. 1, 7, 11. Therefore, before John was to write this epistle, he had been taught of God to love his brethren in the Lord, 1 Thess. 4. 9.

The second occurrence of 'beloved' begins the second section of today's chapter, vv. 7-10, in which are found two unparalleled examples of God's love to us: 'God sent his only begotten Son into the world, that we might live through him' v. 9; when we did not love Him, 'God . . . loved us, and sent his Son to be the propitiation for our sins' v. 10. When we 'were dead in trespasses and sins', Eph. 2. 1, God intervened that we might live through Christ, 1 John 4. 9. When our sins and iniquities separated between us and God, and our sins had hid His face from us, Isa. 59. 2, the loving God intervened at great cost, not sparing His own Son, but delivering Him up, Rom. 8. 32, to be the propitiation for our sins. In order to bring us to Himself, it was essential that Christ should die for our sins, 1 Cor. 15. 3.

John reveals that the loving God seeks a recompense: firstly, in our loving one another, 1 John 3. 11, 23; 4. 7, 11, 12; secondly, in His love being 'perfected in us', v. 12. John shows that God seeks more than mere words, so we should keep His word, 2. 5. Furthermore, He desires that we approach His presence boldly now and in the day of judgement without fear diminishing the enjoyment of our portion in Christ, 4. 17-18. He has placed an obligation upon us: 'we ought also to love one another', v. 11, and seeks our acceptance of that obligation, an acceptance John places in a wonderful setting. John reminds us that no man has seen God at any time, v. 12. But, if we love one another, it will become evident to all men that 'God dwelleth in us'. In his Gospel, we learn that while no man has seen God at any time; the only begotten Son 'declared him', John 1. 18, and men noted that God was with Him. God began this great work in us, for He first loved us, 1 John 4. 19. He will continue to work until the day of account, not just of our work, but of our love.

If God so loved us, we ought also to love

Christ and

1 John 5

December 4th

Sometimes, when health breaks down, or when serious family problems or unemployment overtakes us, doubts begin to arise in the mind. Under the Spirit's guidance John has written that our faith should not be shaken, that we might know that we have eternal life, v. 13. He wrote his Gospel that we might 'believe . . . and . . . have life through his name', John 20. 31. This epistle is written to saints, who in the first century may have been facing persecution fierce enough for questions to arise in the mind. John is reminding them of what they know.

John reminds his readers that the great fundamentals of the faith will support them; they knew the Lord Jesus came into the world 'by water and blood', 1 John 5. 6. Among the pressures then troubling Christians were attacks on the Person of Christ, denying both His incarnation and His vicarious death. What a change faith in Christ had made to those to whom John wrote! John also draws attention to the witness of the Holy Spirit to these great facts, v. 6. When beset with problems, let us remember in particular that God, who so loved the world, has given us this record concerning His Son, John 3. 16; 1 John 5. 10.

Secondly, evidence in a life proves the reality of the new birth: a Christian loves other Christians, those who have also been born of God, v. 1; a Christian keeps God's commandments, vv. 2-3; and Christians don't habitually sin, v. 18. If these traits are evident in his life, a Christian should not have doubts, says John; he has eternal life.

John points again to evidence that they already knew, or should have known. The Christian's prayer-life should be reassuring. He knows that God hears him when he prays. He knows that his God is not an impersonal influence but a real Person with a will, within which the Christian must live. He also knows that God answers prayer and will have experience of the joy of answered prayer, vv. 14-15.

John would approve of RICHARD KEEN's words about victorious Christian faith under pressure:

> 'That soul though all hell should endeavour to shake,
> I'll never – no, never – no, never forsake!'

Know that ye have eternal life

His Apostles

December 5th

2 John

Walking in truth

2 John and 3 John are the shortest letters in the New Testament; but they are more than brief letters. They are admired as beautiful examples of the letter form used in the Graeco-Roman world. This one is also an outstanding example of how an older male Christian would write to a middle-aged, probably a widowed lady with continuing family responsibilities.

John had learned of the spiritual dangers the woman was facing as itinerant preachers arrived at her door, who did not teach what the apostles taught. Those men denied the Christ whom John and his fellow apostles presented. They did not confess that the eternal Son of God took a real body at His incarnation, and will come again in that same body, v. 7. Their intent was to undermine the fundamental doctrine of the New Testament, v. 9. Those false teachers were seeking to draw away disciples after them. Those who followed them would lose the joy of their salvation and blight their fruitfulness in Christ, for those false teachers were not walking in truth.

John had probably come to know about the woman's dilemma through her children, v. 4. From their reports, he may have learned of her reluctance to refuse entry to those who claimed to serve her Lord. At the very time she was troubled by those who did not walk in truth, John was delighting in her children, as was the Father, whose commandment they were obeying. Living their lives, shaped and guided by truth, mattered to John and the Father.

Five times in the first four verses of this brief letter, John uses the noun 'truth'. He also uses it twenty-five times in his Gospel, nine times in his First Epistle and six in the Third. Truth, as taught by Christ and His apostles, offers **clarity of Christian motive** – 'love in the truth', v. 1; forms **a circle of Christian friends** – 'all that have known the truth', v. 1; is **the cause of Christian actions** – what is done 'for the truth's sake', v. 2; lies at **the core of Christian revelation** – 'Grace . . . in truth and love', v. 3. It also determines **the conduct of Christian walk.** What good news for a caring mother to receive; what joy for the Lord's servant to give; what reward ahead for those children!

Christ and

3 John

December 6th

Follow not that which is evil

John's exhortation to follow good and not evil is echoed in both Testaments. Among his fellow apostles, both Peter and Paul commend the same path, cp. 1 Thess. 5. 15; 1 Tim. 5. 10; 1 Pet. 3. 13. These experienced men knew that, from the Garden of Eden onwards, the choice between good and evil has always confronted men and women. But the Old Testament writers made the same forceful appeals. At the end of his last address to his nation, Moses set before them 'life and good, and death and evil', urging them to choose life (and so good), Deut. 30. 15, 19. His successor used not dissimilar language in his appeal, 'Choose you this day', Josh. 24. 15.

Probably, the tone of Solomon's constant appeals across the pages of Proverbs is nearest to the apostle John's. Solomon urged his son to realize that 'a wise son maketh a glad father: but a foolish son is the heaviness of his mother', Prov. 10. 1. Following good was wise; consenting to evil was foolish. Several times in the book he indicates that the kind of company a young man keeps is the determining factor in his choice.

Gaius, the recipient of John's letter was a good man, as brethren had testified to John, v. 3. Clearly, he had made wise choices, as had Demetrius, another good man to whom John refers, as all those associated with John at that time had concluded, v. 12. Sadly, in the circles in which both good men moved, there was a man of a different character – 'Diotrephes, who loveth to have the preeminence', v. 9. So different was Diotrephes from John, Gaius, and Demetrius, that to company with him was 'to follow . . . that which is evil'. Diotrephes refused to allow an apostolic letter to be read to the assembly in an attempt to overthrow apostolic authority, v. 9. He was also given to maligning the apostle and belittling his doctrine, v. 10. We recall that to lie to an apostle was to sin against the Holy Spirit, Acts 5. 3, 4. How much more serious to speak against their teaching!

To follow that which is good does not carry that kind of health warning. We note that there is the guarantee of spiritual health and access to the truth the apostles taught, 3 John 2, 7-9.

His Apostles

December 7th — Jude

Although his is among the briefest letters in the New Testament, Jude is the only writer to mention Michael as the archangel and Korah. But he is not alone in denouncing 'libertines and apostates', as their 'lasciviousness and denying' our only Master and Lord Jesus Christ proved conclusively they were, vv. 4, 16, 18. Peter, John, and Paul also condemn the activities of those holding such dangerous and divisive doctrines. Jude does not name these individuals, but leaves his readers in no doubt that these false prophets brought doctrines that were as cancerous as the 'profane and vain babblings' Hymenaeus and Philetus peddled, 2 Tim. 2. 16-17.

Although Jude does not name them, he does describe their cleverly-disguised entrance; the verb translated 'crept in unawares' literally means that these 'men came in by the side'. They 'crept in' without being detected as false prophets, at some point when watchfulness was less than adequate. The subtlety, stealth, and insidious tactics employed may have deceived the elders in various assemblies. Certainly, Jude does not apportion blame, as he seeks to address the problems those men had caused. However, he does expect the saints to 'earnestly contend' for the faith that has come under attack, v. 3.

Under attack were fundamental matters including 'the common salvation' enjoyed by every believer, v. 3. The teaching they had received in the past would have equipped them to face up to the undermining of their faith. Jude asks them to *remember*, vv. 5, 17. They had learned from the Old Testament that even where there is genuine faith, unbelief can arise, examples of which were seen in the wilderness journey from Egypt to Canaan, in the angels now reserved in chains, and in Sodom and Gomorrha. They were also to remember the doctrine that the apostles taught, and their warnings against ungodly, unsaved men – who were not indwelt by the Spirit – purporting to have new light to offer, vv. 17-19.

In a conflict situation, there are always resources the Christian can use: praying in the Holy Spirit, the love of God, and looking for the Lord's coming, vv. 21-22. These build up faith.

Introduction to Revelation

Unlike his Gospel and his Epistles, John's name is associated with this remarkable book. He is John, but he is not the author, he is the amanuensis of this book, The Revelation of Jesus Christ. The testimony that John records is also 'of Jesus Christ', vv. 1, 2: Christ is the Revelation and the Revealer, not John. When the command is 'Write', John will write, 1. 11 *et al.*; when it is 'Write them not', his pen will not record what he saw or heard, 10. 4. The Revelation is the only New Testament book written by express command of the Lord. Its purpose is to reveal Christ in relation to the present and the future. The unveiling begins with a vision of Christ that John received.

In the book the number seven is important, occurring fifty-four times. We read of seven churches, seals, trumpets, bowls, and last things. The reader also encounters seven revelations of Christ to seven New Testament assemblies. Later, seven remarkable personages are before John's eye: a woman clothed with the sun, a great red dragon, a Man Child, Michael, two beasts, one from the sea and one from the land, and the Lamb Himself, 12. 1-7; 13. 1-18; 14. 1.

One other interesting feature of The Revelation is the involvement of John himself in the scenes traced, sometimes to turn to view something, sometimes to weep or to measure, or to eat a little book. In such scenes, John's role is like that of an Old Testament prophet like Ahijah the Shilonite, or Isaiah, or Ezekiel, 1 Kgs. 11; Isa. 20; Ezek. 4.

Like many books, The Revelation has a title page to tell the reader about the book, 1. 1-3; and a more developed preface, vv. 4-18, followed by an index, which identifies the three sections into which the book is divided. These sections are: 'the things which [John has] seen', ch. 1; 'the things which are' – the seven churches in Asia to which the Lord dictates letters for John to send, chs. 2, 3; and 'the things which shall be hereafter', chs. 4-22.

The major part of the book deals with events that take place after the rapture of the church. It is a prophecy, 1. 3, one that has a special blessing for the public reader and his listeners. The message it conveys in signs, and with the involvement of angels, is of Christ triumphant in earth and heaven.

His Apostles

December 8th — Revelation 1

Alpha and Omega

Four times in Revelation, the first and last letters of the Greek alphabet provide the title 'Alpha and Omega', vv. 8, 11; 21. 6; 22. 13. In each case, the title is used of the Speaker about Himself. In each case, the Speaker uses a parallel expression to reinforce the meaning, 'the beginning and the ending', 1. 8; 21. 6; 'the first and the last', 1. 11. Both phrases are added, 22. 13. Verse 8 also includes a further unfolding of the eternity of the Speaker, 'which is, and which was, and which is to come, the Almighty'. These explanatory expressions are added to enhance their understanding of the divine glory that is His by right.

It is noteworthy that these glories are unfolded by self-revelation. Our English word 'alphabet' combines the first two letters of the Greek alphabet, but the first and last letters form the title 'Alpha and Omega'. All that a learned Greek could reveal on any subject would use the letters including and between alpha and omega. In His self-revelation, the Lord Jesus reveals an all-important truth all must grasp, that no mere man could reveal the wonder of His Person and work. Not surprisingly, in the Revelation of Jesus Christ, He is the Revealer *and* the Revelation.

When the Lord announced, 'Before Abraham was, I am', John 8. 58, the Pharisees would have stoned Him for claiming to be eternal. This title and its accompanying statements restate that claim even more emphatically. Having Abraham for their father was the great boast of His adversaries, but Abraham was not the beginning. The great un-begun Beginning, the original Cause, was Christ; and He is the great End in whom all the counsels of God will be realized. In the Revelation, the Alpha and Omega, who is, and was and is to come, is challenged as to His right to bring the divine counsel to its fulfilment, but as the Almighty, He will subdue all enmity. Men like Abraham, Isaac, and Jacob will be part of the coming scenes, Matt. 8. 11, but the Alpha and Omega will be acknowledged by them and all the blessed of His Father, 25. 34. We will also be with Him eternally, ever learning the wonder of His Person and ever responsive to give Him the glory that is His right.

Christ and

Revelation 2. 1-17 — December 9th

How remarkable that One before whose feet John fell as dead, should choose to speak to a church that had known better days, 1. 17; 2. 5! This One has rights over those He holds responsible – the seven stars, 1. 20; 2. 1. He also moves among the seven lampstands – the seven churches He now addresses, v. 1, so His awesome authority is unchallengeable and His assessment of their state unerring, but, as they are to hear, not coldly critical of their shortcomings.

The Lord of the churches knew that they had experienced the two sides of active service – they had endured wearying toil and exercised the patient endurance that must accompany it, v. 2. He also knew that they had to face up to evil men and false apostles, v. 2. They had great respect for Christ's name in all they did. So much pressure was upon them, yet they did not fail, v. 3, except in one crucial respect: they left their first love, v. 4.

How telling the words the Ephesian Christians now hear! 'I have against thee, that thou hast left thy first love', v. 4 JND. To their credit, they had this, 'Thou hatest the deeds of the Nicolaitans', v. 6. Weighed in the divine balance, their hating evil did not compensate for their deserting their first love. Their abandoning of their first love was decisive and so critical in their relationship with Christ. They were unfaithful to Christ, their first love, their best and peerless love. Surely there would be some response to these things He said.

Will He abandon them? We hear His appeal to them, as if it were to us, *'Remember. Repent. Reinstate the first works'*, v. 5. When Paul had written to them, there had been twenty references to love, none of which reproached them. How far they had fallen from that lofty position! How needful their repentance if they were to continue to be owned by Him, v. 5! He that was speaking desired their first works to be reinstated. He was looking for 'the kindness of [their] youth, the love of [their] espousals', Jer. 2. 2. Without the re-kindling of that love once of prime importance to them, the Speaker, who had loved them (and us) unto death, would sadly have to repeat, 'I have against thee'.

His Apostles

December 10th — Revelation 2. 18 – 3. 6

He that overcometh

In His letter to Thyatira, the Lord Jesus addresses the whole assembly, vv. 18-23; then 'the rest', those who abstained from sins the wicked Jezebel encouraged, vv. 24-25; and finally, the overcomer, vv. 26-28. Clearly, the numbers in each category being addressed would be reducing each time. The Lord's desire was that all would hear the Spirit's appeal to all, in order that in all the churches there might be many overcomers, whom He would generously reward.

The overcomers would be marked by faith in Christ and *faithfulness* to Christ, 1 John 5. 4-5. The Lord promises to be no man's debtor: He will reward the overcomer. Interestingly, the rewards to the overcomers follow a historical pathway from Eden, Rev. 2. 7. The letters to Thyatira and Sardis take us to Jehu who sought to exterminate Jezebel and her seed, 2 Kgs. 9. 1 – 10. 32; and to Judah's return from captivity in Babylon, where they awaited a priest to verify who should be added to the few names whose right to a priest's portion could be substantiated, Ezra 2. 63; Neh. 7. 65.

The promise to the Thyatiran overcomer draws from the imagery of Balaam's prophecy of a star and a sceptre, Num. 24. 17. The Lord speaks of rule over the nations and of the morning star, unfading and glorious. He will fulfil that promise when we reign with Christ, 1 Cor. 6. 2, 3; 2 Tim. 2. 12. His own parable spoke of some reigning over many cities, Luke 19. 17. *Rule* and *radiance* lie ahead for every overcomer.

The difficulties faced in Sardis were no easier to deal with than those elsewhere – lifelessness was its characterizing feature. Like Ephesus, they were to remember better days, 3. 3. For the overcomer, the rewards described were no less encouraging. They are assured of being arrayed in white raiment, of their registration in the book of life, and of their being owned before the Father of our Lord Jesus and His holy angels. *Raiment, registration* and *recognition* in the very court of heaven are more than we could ever have desired. In the minds of believers, there is the realization of how much the Lord has done for them. Yet He speaks of rewarding us for the little we do for Him.

Christ and

Revelation 3. 7-22 — December 11th

He that hath an ear, let him hear

When Moses appealed to his nation, he cried, 'Hear, O Israel', Deut. 5. 1; 6. 3, 4; 9. 1; 20. 3. The nation as a whole was to mark the importance attached to his words, and to respond accordingly. When the Lord Jesus spoke, He often appealed to individuals, saying, 'He that hath ears to hear, let him hear'. He used those inviting words, when He acknowledged the greatness of the then-imprisoned John, Matt. 11. 15; when He outlined the kingdom parables, 13. 9, 43; when He warned the people about the hypocritical Pharisees and scribes, Mark 7. 16, and those who were considering following Him, Luke 14. 35. Now we hear the same appeal to the first hearers of these seven church letters. Three times He makes this appeal to the individuals *before* addressing overcomers, but in the last four letters the appeal is *after* His message to the overcomers.

The Lord's appeal reminds us that the Creator planned for man to hear. In Eden, before Adam's fall, he communed with his God. After he sinned, Adam and Eve 'heard the voice of the Lord God walking in the garden in the cool of the day', Gen. 3. 8. Man still has the ability to hear, but, because of sin, not always is there an inclination to hear what God is saying. Stephen pointed out to his accusers that they were 'uncircumcised in heart and ears'; their own actions in stopping their ears confirmed the validity of his charge, Acts 7. 51, 57. Even Christians may be reluctant to hear 'what the Spirit saith unto the churches', Rev. 3. 13, 22, for which cause the Lord Himself appeals tenderly, 'Let him hear'.

Through the word of God, the Spirit still speaks to the churches. His voice through His servants is as pertinent today as it was in the first century. He may use verbs like 'repent', 'remember', 'rebuke', and 'chasten'. He may comfort, reminding us that He knows, vv. 8-9. He may speak of keeping us, v. 10, or of the Lord's love, v. 19. He may require us to buy gold tried in fire, or prescribe anointing for our eyes, v. 18. His is a varied ministry as these letters show. He has a ministry to meet every need. Where an assembly is not hearing, He may for a time stand knocking and saying, 'Let him hear'.

His Apostles

December 12th

Revelation 4

A throne was set in heaven

Invited by a voice from inside the door that had been opened, John found before him a throne. The voice he had heard was authoritative like the trumpet call that delivered orders during military manoeuvres. Facing him now was the throne from which those orders would have emanated. This is the eternal throne, occupied by the eternal God.

Around that throne were twenty-four other thrones; they also were occupied; twenty-four elders occupied those thrones, v. 4, each of whom was crowned. Daniel had once seen thrones being set, but we read of only one throne being occupied; the Throne-sitter he recognized as the Ancient of days, Dan. 7. 9. Much is said of Solomon's ivory throne, 1 Kgs. 10. 18-20, but little of this throne. Its appearance links it with jasper and sardius stones, materials linked with worlds that once were – Eden and the Levitical world, Ezek. 28. 13; Exod. 28. 17-20. The Throne-sitter is about to bring to light another world whose glory will eclipse all other past glories.

Encircling that throne, John saw a spectacular rainbow, reminding him of the faithfulness of the eternal God, Rev. 4. 3, for He is faithful that promised, Heb. 10. 23. Out from that throne proceeded lightnings and voices and thunderings, Rev. 4. 5, recalling for John Jehovah's descent upon Mount Sinai, Exod. 19. 16, with the unavoidable evidence that God is able to uphold His own standards, no matter what challenge adversaries might make. John was to find that the throne of God would bring to a glorious conclusion a strange work of judgement, Isa. 28. 21, but not at the expense of His promises.

In the Revelation of Jesus Christ, John sees Christ revealed in connection with Israel, the church, and the nations in their apostasy; but also in relation to the throne. Forty-six times the noun 'throne' occurs in this book, but there is never any doubt who will act on behalf of the eternal throne, 5. 6. At the end of the book, that same glorious Person will sit on the throne then called 'the throne of God and the Lamb', 22. 1, 3. As the great Executor of the throne, 'blessing, and honour, and glory, and power' will be ascribed to God and to the Lamb, 5. 13.

Christ and

Revelation 5

December 13th

Some thirty times in Revelation, the exclamatory word translated as 'behold' or 'lo' is used to underscore matters that should be of intense interest to the reader. The two occurrences in this chapter both relate to Christ, 'Behold, the Lion . . . lo . . . a Lamb', vv. 5, 6. No matters of greater interest are to be found in this or any other book.

In the chapter, the same verb is used in respect of things that were of great interest to John; twice the verb is translated 'saw', and twice 'beheld'. He *saw* 'a strong angel' and he *saw* 'many angels', vv. 2, 11. Angels play a larger part here than in any other book in the Bible; their involvement would interest John. He *saw* a book in the right hand of the Throne-sitter, v. 1. The description of that book with its seals allows us to recognize it as a legal document like a will, but in this case the title-deeds of the universe. Jeremiah chapter 32 details what was involved in registering a title to property of any kind. John's eye might have remained riveted on that important book, but, in the midst of the throne and its surrounding throng, he *saw* a Lamb. Well might John's record contain the two interjections, 'Behold! . . . lo!'.

John in the spirit was allowed to witness that climactic moment when the universe which men and demons have treated as their possession is to be returned to its rightful Owner. Men might throw the Son out of the vineyard, but the Owner still had the title deeds and dispossessed the trespassers in AD 70, just as the Lord foretold, Matt. 21. 33-44. The fulfilment of that parable was a foreshadowing of the greater exercise John saw begin in Revelation chapter 5.

The Lion that filled the patriarch's vision, Gen. 49. 8-12, is David's Lord, Ps. 110. 1; Matt. 22. 43-44, the Root from which David sprang, and the sacrificial Lamb who paid the redemption price. None can withstand the Lion's awesome power, or fathom the wonder of His Person, or prove worthy of the adoration that the redeemed universe will give Him. The Lion who has prevailed, whose is the victory, is the Lamb that was slain, Rev. 5. 5, 6, 9, 12. The first 'beheld' stemmed John's tears; the second unleashed wave after wave of praise nothing could stem!

His Apostles

The Lion of the tribe of Judah

December 14th　　　　　　　　　　Revelation 6. 1-17

The great day of his wrath is come

Judgement is God's 'strange work', Isa. 28. 21. He really delights to bless His creatures, but, because He is holy, He must judge impenitent sinners who reject His longsuffering grace in the gospel. Therefore, in this chapter John sees Christ reclaiming the earth for God by opening the seven seals of the scroll containing its title deeds. Each opened seal releases a catastrophic judgement on mankind, to encourage their repentance. The first six seal judgements parallel the disasters predicted in Matthew chapter 24 verses 4 to 14, there called 'the beginning of sorrows', the first half of the seven-year tribulation, which is the prophesied 'day of vengeance of our God', following the present long 'acceptable year of the Lord'. The church is absent from these scenes of judgement, having been raptured to heaven before they begin when Christ returns as our Deliverer from the coming wrath, 1 Thess. 1. 10. But only believers have this hope.

When the first four seals are opened, John sees four war-horses with riders. The first horse is white and its rider a crowned conqueror. This is not Christ, but His counterfeit, Antichrist, the first beast of chapter 13. He will gain world power by indirect diplomatic means and at first appear to solve mankind's problems. But the second, red, horse indicates that soon widespread war will break out with consequent bloodshed. The third, black, horse signifies resultant famine and food-rationing. Then the fourth, pale, horse will spell death and Hades for a full quarter of the world's population by various horrible means.

But the opening of the fifth seal reveals the souls of many martyred believers under the altar calling upon God to avenge their deaths. There will be bitter persecution of all who believe the future gospel of the kingdom during both halves of the tribulation. Faithfulness to God is very costly in every age!

The sixth seal judgement climaxes the series with a great earthquake and cosmic disturbances which will strike terror into the hearts of all unbelievers, great and small, but fail to bring them to repentance. They will ask, 'Who shall be able to stand?' before the wrath of the Lamb who died to redeem them, and try to hide from Him. Tomorrow's reading answers this question.

Christ and

Revelation 7. 1-17 — December 15th

This chapter is a parenthesis in the overall chronological sequence of the book revealing more about those who are saved during the tribulation. They comprise two distinct groups.

Firstly, in verses 1-8, John sees 144,000 Israelites, 12,000 from each tribe, sealed for their protection from persecution and God's judgements by an angel. According to Matthew chapter 24 verse 14, they will preach the gospel of the coming kingdom of Christ throughout the world, a message based on Calvary's sacrifice, but with a different emphasis from the present gospel of grace. This group of God's servants appears elsewhere in scripture as the faithful remnant of Israel, from whom God will remove the partial blindness to the truth about Christ soon after the rapture of the church to heaven, Rom. 11. 25. Literature left behind by church saints and the preaching of God's two special witnesses of chapter 11 may also lead to their conversion. It is unclear why the tribe of Dan is omitted from the list here, and why Ephraim is represented only by his father Joseph. Their idolatry may partly explain this fact.

Secondly, in verses 9-17, John sees a countless multitude of believers from all nations standing before the throne of God and the Lamb, dressed in white robes of purity and carrying festal palms of victory and joy. One of the twenty-four elders, who represent the glorified church in heaven, explains to John that these believers are coming out of the Great Tribulation, having survived its horrors and persecutions, to enter the earthly kingdom of Christ in their mortal bodies. They are probably not martyrs, since nothing is said concerning their deaths and resurrection. Since this vision comes immediately after the vision of the 144,000 Israelite witnesses, this multitude are probably their converts. There will be much gospel testimony during the Tribulation, and many will trust Christ as the coming King. They are seen here worshipping God before His throne on earth.

Then Christ, the Lamb in the midst of the throne, will comfort those who have trusted Him after all their sufferings, refresh them with living water as their Shepherd, and wipe away all their tears. During all the judgements God is still a Saviour!

His Apostles

December 16th   Revelation 8. 1-13

Seven trumpets

The chronological sequence of the tribulation judgements is now resumed. But, first, there is an ominous silence in heaven for half an hour, the time usually spent in silent worship in the Jewish temple during the burning of the incense. The incense here is handled by an angel with a golden censer at the golden altar before God's throne in heaven. It signifies the prayers of believers of all ages for vengeance on their enemies and for the establishment of God's kingdom on earth, as it is in heaven. The opening of the seventh seal by Christ, the Lamb, introduces seven judgements upon earth, more severe than the previous six. Administered by angels, they are called 'seven trumpets', because in them God is declaring His continuing war against rebellious mankind to secure their repentance or submission.

The trumpet judgements, like the seal judgements, are divided into four and three. The first four affect man's natural environment, the earth, sea, rivers, and sun, while the last three are different, and worse. Their distinctive feature is the emphasis on 'the third part', rather than the whole, indicating that judgement is being tempered with mercy in the hope that men will repent. While the language here is partly symbolical, since this is apocalyptic literature, the judgements should be interpreted as literally as possible, as all other scripture usually is.

The first trumpet sends a terrible storm to destroy a third of all trees and green grass. When the second trumpet sounds, a great burning mountain, or meteorite, crashes into the sea, destroying a third of all ships and marine life, and turning the sea into blood. The third trumpet sends a large comet, called 'Wormwood', on to the earth, polluting all watercourses, so that many men die of poison. The fourth trumpet causes further disturbances in the heavenly bodies, reducing their light by a third.

In verse 13, an eagle (RV) flying in mid-heaven announces the three final trumpet judgements as 'Woes', because of their greater severity. In Old Testament prophecy this signifies coming judgement by invasion; for now demonic forces are allowed by God to physically attack all unbelievers. May we learn how futile it is to fight against God, and trust and obey Him instead!

Christ and

Revelation 9. 1-21 December 17th

The fifth and sixth trumpet judgements, described here in vivid symbolical language, will probably occur after the mid-point of the tribulation, when Satan is cast down from heaven and confined to the earth, Rev. 12. 7-9. Then his malevolent wrath against mankind will become fully apparent. But God will overrule his wrath to punish all unbelievers by releasing demonic forces against them. Satan cannot go beyond the will of God, who is always in absolutely sovereign control of His world.

Verses 1 to 12 describe the first woe, the fifth trumpet judgement. Satan must be the star fallen from heaven to whom is given the key of the bottomless pit, the prison-house of evil spirits. From it, amid noxious clouds of smoke, will march out vast hordes of locust-like creatures who have authority to sting men like scorpions, and to torment them thus for five months, but not to kill them. John's description of them is highly symbolical, but literally true, not fictitious. Their king will be Apollyon, the evil destroying angel of the abyss. But they cannot harm believers, who have the protecting seal of God in their foreheads. Even then God will 'remember His own'!

Verses 13 to 21 describe the second woe, the sixth trumpet judgement. Another angel of God gives permission to release four evil angels held captive at the River Euphrates ready for this very time and purpose. Then a huge army of 200 million horsemen emerges to kill a third of earth's remaining population. Unless Christ returns to stop this tribulation holocaust, no one would be left alive on earth. By its end probably over three quarters of the world's population will have died. The obviously figurative description of these bizarre horses suggests that this is another supernatural demonic army, not an ordinary human one, from Asia. Some commentators link this invasion with the one in chapter 16. But that seems different, since it concerns the later final bowl judgements, not the trumpet judgements here.

Sadly, the surviving unbelievers will still refuse to repent. Demon worship, idolatry, violence, sorcery, immorality, and robbery will flourish. What terrible days lie ahead for unbelievers especially! But how hard are their hearts set against God!

His Apostles

December 18th   Revelation 10. 1-11

A little book open

Chapter 10 to chapter 11 verse 13 forms a second parenthesis in the sequence of judgements. Chapter 10 concerns God's purpose in creation. John sees 'another (Greek *allos*) mighty angel', similar to the holy angels in the previous chapters, coming down from heaven with a little scroll open in his hand. Although he is probably not Christ Himself, as many commentators have held, by his remarkable description he clearly has divine authority delegated to him to reclaim both land and sea for his God by means of judgements executed because of the indictments recorded in the scroll. The ensuing seven thunders give warning of the coming cataclysm, but God in His mercy prevents John, by a voice from heaven, from recording it.

This angel now swears by the Eternal Creator, probably indicating that he is a creature, not Christ, that there 'shall be delay (RV margin for KJV 'time') no longer' in executing all God's purposes. The 'mystery of God' referred to, v. 7, is His long silence despite the growing wickedness and rebellion of mankind. This silence has been intended to give unbelievers ample time to repent and believe the gospel preached by God's servants the prophets. But with the imminent sounding of the seventh trumpet His longsuffering will be exhausted, and the judgements which the same prophets also predicted will be consummated. Then all the anguish caused by God's mysterious silence will be ended and explained, as His righteousness is at last asserted during Christ's millennial kingdom. No longer will truth be 'on the scaffold', while wrong is 'on the throne'! J. R. LOWELL.

The voice from heaven then instructed John to take the scroll and eat it, saying that it would be bitter to his stomach, but sweet to his mouth. Although a believer always finds God's word sweet, he finds its message of judgement for his fellow men very bitter. Finally, John was told to continue to prophesy 'concerning' (RV margin) many different peoples and all ranks of society. Thus he was commissioned to complete his warnings of coming world judgement. But are we warning unsaved people around us of the fate awaiting them if they continue to reject God's longsuffering mercy in the present gospel of His grace?

Christ and

Revelation 11. 1-19 — December 19th

My two witnesses

Verses 1 to 13 complete the second parenthesis; then the sequence of judgements continues with the sounding of the seventh trumpet, which is the third woe. First, the mighty angel of chapter 10 gave John a measuring reed to lay claim to the inner sanctuary of the temple, which will be rebuilt in Jerusalem before the mid-point of the tribulation, cp. Matt. 24. 15-18, 2 Thess. 2. 3-4. God will still have a faithful remnant of believers there even then. But the outer temple court was not measured, because it will be dominated by the Gentiles for a further 42 months, the second half of the tribulation.

Then we are told of God's two special witnesses whom He will empower to prophesy for Him in Jerusalem for 1260 days, probably during the first half of the tribulation rather than the second half, although commentators differ here. They will minister in the spirit and power of Moses and Elijah, performing great miracles against their enemies. However, their precise identity is unclear. They are the future fulfilment of the two olive trees and lampstands of Zechariah chapter 4 verse 11, the channels through whom God will sustain the spiritual life and witness of His people Israel, as Zerubbabel and Joshua did at the return from the Babylonian Exile. When their witness is completed, and not before, the Beast of chapter 13 will be allowed to kill them. The whole world will rejoice over their unburied bodies, something quite possible today technologically. But after three and a half days God will resurrect and rapture them to heaven with a shout of triumph. Then the world's rejoicing will turn to terror as a great earthquake kills 7000 people in Jerusalem. Its survivors will give glory to God.

In verse 15 heavenly voices announce that 'the kingdom of the world is become the kingdom of our Lord, and of his Christ' (RV). God is intervening to reassert His rule despite the angry rebellion of men. This will be a day of wrath for unbelievers, but of rewards for all faithful believers. Finally, the temple sanctuary in heaven is opened to reveal the reassuring sight of the ark of God's eternal covenant there. Fellow-believer, final victory is assured in spite of present appearances!

His Apostles

December 20th

Revelation 12. 1-17

A great wonder in heaven

Chapters 12 to 14 form a third parenthesis describing people who will be prominent during the tribulation. Chapter 12 introduces us to two great wonders, or significant people, and to Christ as the Man-child destined to rule the world. The first sign, a woman clothed with the sun, with the moon beneath her feet, and a crown of twelve stars, clearly portrays God's people, Israel. She is in labour, about to be delivered of Christ, her Man-child. The second sign, the great red dragon, who tries to destroy the Man-child at birth, represents Satan, who used Herod to try to kill Christ, Matt. 2. 16. But Christ was caught up to God's throne, thus escaping Satan's clutches. The vision omits reference to the cross, resurrection, and the entire church age, and concentrates our attention on Israel during the second half of the tribulation. Having failed to destroy Christ Himself, Satan will persecute the faithful Jewish remnant, but God will supernaturally protect them in the wilderness, cp. Isa. 26. 20.

Verses 7-12 explain why conditions on earth will become even worse at the mid-point of the tribulation. God's angels under Michael will decisively drive out Satan and his hosts from heaven onto the earth. No longer will Satan be able to accuse believers there. They will overcome him by trusting in Christ the Lamb's shed blood and their bold testimony in the face of martyrdom, which is the secret of victory in every age. Frustrated again, and knowing that his end is near, the devil will vent his wrath on all earth's inhabitants, saved and unsaved alike. He loves no one. All in heaven, however, will rejoice.

Satan will especially target the faithful remnant of Israel. But they will be divinely enabled to find a safe refuge in the wilderness, possibly in the region of Edom, Moab, and Ammon, Isa. 16. 3-4; Dan. 11. 41. God will protect them there from all Satan's malicious attacks, until Christ delivers them at His second coming. So Satan will again be frustrated in his evil designs. This chapter tells us that he is a defeated foe, although still very powerful and fearsome to us as believers. But what assurance and courage this vision of John's should give us in our own testimony to Christ today also!

Christ and

Revelation 13. 1-18 — December 21st

The patience and the faith of the saints

Chapter 13 reveals to us the trinity of evil persons who will persecute true believers during the second half of the tribulation. Verses 1-10 concern a first beast, an evil man who behaves like a wild animal. John sees him arising from the sea of nations with seven heads and ten crowned horns bearing blasphemous names against God. He and his lieutenant, the second beast, or False Prophet, of verses 11 to 18, are Satan's henchmen, and demand that the whole world worship the first beast and the dragon as God. This is the deification of a man in place of the true God, Satan's ultimate objective. His nationality is unclear, but may prove to be half-Jewish, half-Gentile, to gain acceptance by all unbelievers. He bears the features of Daniel's world rulers and derives his authority from Satan. He is elsewhere called the Antichrist, the Man of sin, the little horn, the coming prince, and the wilful king. He will win the world's allegiance as a result of a violent death and a resurrection experience which counterfeits that of Christ. After this he will be indwelt by Satan and claim worship as God. For 42 months he will be allowed to persecute believers, and many will be martyred. This is their great tribulation, for which they will need patient endurance and faith in Christ.

John sees the second beast arise from the land of Israel. He will probably be an apostate Jew. He will support the first beast by performing counterfeit miracles to convince men of the latter's deity. He will set up an image of the first beast in the rebuilt temple sanctuary, and enable it to speak and kill all who refuse to worship it. This is elsewhere called 'the abomination of desolation'. He will also compel all men to receive a mark in their right hand or forehead which enables them to buy and sell. Life will be very difficult for all who refuse to accept it. The mark will be the number 666, the number of a man who falls short of perfection. But the duration of this satanic reign of terror will be strictly limited by God. Satan's men will not succeed in usurping God's place on earth, because God will intervene to save 'His own' at Christ's second coming in glory. This will give believers courage to endure their suffering. Hallelujah!

His Apostles

December 22nd
Revelation 14. 1-20

John now sees seven visions of events during the great tribulation, cameos of salvation and judgement designed to encourage believers to trust and obey God in days of persecution and martyrdom. They predict a final victorious outcome to our conflict with evil. All Christ's followers will be vindicated, but all Satan's followers will be judged eternally. How real and vital, therefore, are the issues whenever the gospel is preached!

In verses 1 to 5 John sees the 144,000 Jewish witnesses of chapter 7 standing victoriously on Mount Zion in Jerusalem with Christ, the Lamb, entirely unharmed by the judgements and persecutions of the day. As they prepare to enter the millennial kingdom with God's name written in their foreheads, they join with the inhabitants of heaven to sing a new song of redemption. They are virgins, untainted by the surrounding defilement, and the first instalment of many other believers. In verses 6 and 7 another angel flying in the mid-heaven proclaims the everlasting gospel in a last attempt to persuade men to repent before the judgements are consummated. A second angel then announces the fall of Babylon, both the literal city and the religious system, in two stages; see chapters 17 and 18. In verses 9 to 11 of chapter 14 a third angel proclaims the judgement of all who worship the Beast and receive his mark. Their fate is sealed: eternal punishment. Reader, on whose side will you be found?

In verses 12 and 13 the Lord comforts all tribulation saints who will suffer martyrdom. He calls them to patient endurance, since they die 'in the Lord', acknowledging His absolute Lordship. They are blessed, and join the martyrs of the fifth seal judgement to await final vindication. The parenthesis then concludes with two complementary visions of Christ's judgement of unbelievers just prior to His second coming. The first likens the judgement to a grain harvest, which Christ reaps with a sharp sickle. It may refer to the bowl judgements of chapter 16. The grain is overripe, rotten with corruption. The second vision is of a grape harvest, also overripe, with rebellion against God. This anticipates the horrific carnage of Armageddon, when Christ will intervene to subdue His foes. Reader, be warned!

They that keep the commandments of God

Christ and

Revelation 15. 1-8 — December 23rd

Seven last plagues

Chapter 15 resumes the chronological sequence of the book with John's vision of the tense interlude in heaven's inner temple sanctuary before God pours out His vial, or bowl, judgements in chapter 16. These seven last plagues, administered by seven angels, are God's direct punishment of unrepentant sinners, and bring the great tribulation to a climactic end.

In verse 2 John sees a sea of glass mingled with fire, representing God's holiness. Beside it stood a great company of saints martyred by the Beast, because they refused to worship his image. They are described, however, as victors over him in their deaths. Do we today think of martyrdom for Christ's sake as a victory? They sing two songs of redemption: Moses' song at the Red Sea, and the song of the Lamb, celebrating His greatness. They praise God's works and ways as the 'King of the nations' (RV margin), and anticipate the day when all nations will fear and worship the Lord. They sing, not of their own experiences or victories in martyrdom, but of God's power and the person of their Redeemer – an example to us today! These martyrs seen in heaven should be distinguished from the 144,000 Jewish witnesses seen on earthly Mount Zion in chapter 14, who will survive the whole tribulation holocaust unharmed.

In verse 5 John sees the inner sanctuary of the heavenly tabernacle of witness opened, so that the seven angels with the seven plagues of God's wrath could come out to administer them upon the earth. Their pure linen clothing speaks of God's righteousness, and their golden sashes speak of priestly service, not now in blessing, but in judgement. Then one of the four living creatures who surround God's throne gave the angels seven golden bowls full of God's wrath. These bowls, like shallow saucers, will be emptied quickly of their contents over a very brief time at the end of the tribulation. Finally, the heavenly sanctuary becomes filled with the smoke of God's glory and power, preventing anyone from entering there to intercede on behalf of earth's unrepentant inhabitants. Their fate is sealed. Unsaved reader, be warned! Repent and believe the gospel before your fate, too, is sealed, and you suffer final judgement!

His Apostles

December 24th — Revelation 16. 1-21

Go your ways, and pour out the vials

The seven vial (bowl) judgements predicted here are the consummation of God's wrath inflicted on unrepentant mankind. Like the trumpet judgements, they are divided into four which affect the earth, sea, rivers, and sun, followed by three different ones, but end with a third great earthquake. God is a God of order, even in judgement. The first angel, then, poured out his bowl on the earth; it became a grievous, possibly cancerous, sore on all who worshipped the beast and bore his mark. When the second angel poured out his bowl on the sea, it became blood. These and others of the plagues are similar to those with which God through Moses afflicted the Egyptians at the Exodus. The third plague turned all the watercourses to blood. This is said, even by the altar, to be a just retribution for all the innocent blood of saints and prophets which men will have shed. The fourth bowl was poured on the sun, so that it became hotter and scorched men to death. The Old Testament predicts this judgement, Isa. 24. 6; Mal. 4. 1. But even this will not result in mankind's repentance, only further defiance and blasphemy.

From the fifth bowl the focus of the judgements is mainly on the kingdom of the Beast, which by this will be plunged into darkness. The sixth angel poured out his bowl on the river Euphrates, and dried it up to allow the kings of the east to invade across it. Then three demonic spirits issuing from the trinity of evil will by counterfeit miracles lure the kings of the whole world to engage in the campaign of Armageddon, unknown to them, by God's own sovereign will. The seventh bowl will result in the greatest earthquake of all time, devastating all the cities of the nations, causing all islands and mountains to disappear, splitting 'the great city', that is, Jerusalem, 11. 8, into three parts, and destroying Babylon the great, as recorded also in chapter 18. How foolish we would be to lay up our treasure on earth, rather than in heaven! An accompanying terrible hailstorm will again fail to produce man's repentance. How incorrigible and ungrateful our natural hearts are! If God's grace in the gospel does not melt them now, even the severest judgements will not do so then. Reader, what is your response?

Christ and

Revelation 17. 1-18 — December 25th

Mystery, Babylon the great

The final parenthesis concerns Babylon the great, man and Satan's city, contrasting with God's city, Jerusalem. It is spoken of in two ways. In chapter 17 it is a prostitute in a wilderness, contrasting with the true bride of Christ, the church. In chapter 18 it is a commercial and political centre. The prostitute is sitting on the Beast, controlling him and persecuting believers. This is called a mystery, which an angel explains to John as a believer. 'Mystery Babylon' appears to be a worldwide religious system which will develop out of apostate Christendom after the rapture of the church. The Beast will allow this evil system to govern his policies during the first half of the tribulation, when, according to verse 18, his capital may be the Rome of John's day, which had accepted the mystery religion of ancient Babylon. The fifth seal judgement in chapter 6 has already mentioned the martyrs of this period awaiting justice.

But at the mid-point of the tribulation, the Beast with his confederate ten kings will, at God's instigation, unknown to themselves, turn against the prostitute, destroy her, and set himself up as the object of universal worship. This will occur after his pseudo-death-and-resurrection experience, when he comes up out of the abyss indwelt by Satan, and is therefore worse than before. His seven heads, or mountains, represent seven kings, probably the world empires which have opposed God's people through history, namely, Egypt, Assyria, Babylon, Medo-Persia, Greece, Rome, and the Beast, who becomes the eighth during the terrible second half of the tribulation. The ten kings are those of Daniel chapters 2 and 7, who will briefly receive power and authority from the Beast as part of his empire. They will make war with Christ, the Lamb, at His second coming, but will be defeated at Armageddon, because He is Lord of lords and King of kings, infinitely superior to His foes. The church saints will return from heaven with Christ to share His victory. By sovereign grace we are described as 'called, and chosen, and faithful'. So we see again in this prophecy of future events that, despite all appearances to the contrary, 'God is still on the throne, and He will remember His own'! Hallelujah!

His Apostles

December 26th

Revelation 18. 1-24

Babylon the great is fallen, is fallen

The repetition of 'is fallen' in verse 2, and the phrase 'after these things' concerning 'Mystery Babylon' of chapter 17, indicate that the fall of commercial and political Babylon predicted here will occur later in the tribulation than that of religious Babylon, which will perish at its mid-point at the Beast's hands. Chapter 16 verse 19 states that the city will be destroyed by God in the seventh bowl judgement, the final earthquake of the tribulation. This chapter confirms that it will be destroyed in a literal hour. Zechariah chapter 5 predicts that the centre of commercial wickedness will return to 'the land of Shinar', Babylon. Therefore, while religious Babylon will be a worldwide system based in Rome, commercial Babylon will probably be centred in a rebuilt city of Babylon in Mesopotamia.

Babylon's sin is spiritual fornication, the misuse of divine truth for selfish ends. In verse 4, a voice from heaven calls all God's people to separate from her, lest they share her judgement. We, too, should separate from all moral and spiritual evil. By the end of the tribulation Babylon's sins will demand summary punishment, for which she is quite unprepared. All the kings of the earth, the merchants, and sailors will stand aghast at her sudden calamity, and helplessly lament the loss of their livelihoods. Their lost merchandise will include many luxury products, and, sadly in last place, the bodies and souls of men. Yes, slavery will be rife, and life cheap, during the tribulation.

By contrast, the inhabitants of heaven will rejoice that God has at last punished Babylon for ill-treating so many of God's servants. In fulfilment of Jeremiah chapter 51 verses 60 to 64, a mighty angel will cast Babylon like a millstone into the sea, so that all normal life in her will forever cease. The Old Testament fall of Babylon in 539 BC did not fulfil these verses. Thus the Lord will prepare the way for the introduction of His true bride, the Lamb's wife, the church of Christ, from heaven. But what great judgements will be necessary before we are united with our Saviour in glory! How serious this world's sins are! Reader, be warned; leave the world's side at once, and trust in Christ, who is our Deliverer from the coming wrath!

Christ and

Revelation 19. 1-10 — December 27th

These final verses of the parenthesis record events in heaven at the end of the tribulation. John hears many people there rejoicing, first, over the just judgement of the false bride, Babylon, then over the marriage of Christ, the Lamb, to His true bride, the church. They sing a fourfold 'Hallelujah Chorus' to God for His salvation, glory, honour, and power, and for His coming omnipotent reign. A voice from heaven exhorted all God's servants to praise Him. Let us today join the twenty-four elders and the four living creatures as they fall in worship before His throne! This is the last reference to the twenty-four elders in the book. From now on they appear to be replaced by the Lamb's wife, who is clearly the church. This probably confirms their identity as the church in heaven during the tribulation.

Verses 6 to 10 anticipate our marriage to Christ in heaven. Verse 8 interprets the fine linen of our bridal attire as our 'righteous acts' (RV) performed during our lives now. Therefore, we need to seriously consider how well we are preparing for our future union with Christ. Certainly, He will have reviewed our lives of service at His judgement seat soon after our rapture to heaven. Verses 9-10 refer to the marriage supper of the Lamb, and the blessedness of its invited guests, who will include both the Old Testament and the tribulation saints. It is possible that this may take place, not in heaven at the marriage of the Lamb, but on earth during the millennial kingdom, since other scriptures seem to portray an earthly, not a heavenly, scene; see Isa. 25. 6; Matt. 8. 11-12; 22. 1-14; Luke 13. 28-30. Consider, however, with what joy Christ will in that day of union view the results of 'the travail of his soul' on the cross of Calvary as all His redeemed surround Him! And what will be our joy, too, when we enter fully into our eternal reward, and, free from sin, enjoy an eternal relationship with Him whom our soul loves!

Following these overwhelming revelations, John was rebuked by the angel for attempting to worship him. He then said that only God should be worshipped; all prophecy is intended to witness to Jesus alone. Christ is the key to its meaning, and His glory its objective. Surely, we say, 'Amen' to that!

Praise our God, all ye his servants

His Apostles

December 28th — Revelation 19. 11 – 20. 6

King of kings, and Lord of lords

The events predicted in today's reading cover one thousand years. John's repeated phrase, 'And I saw', carries us forward in time throughout it. A literal understanding of this passage, which accepts it at face value, allowing for some figurative description, is the one most consistent with simple faith. Non-literal views of it are fatally flawed. John is seeing the second coming of Christ to the earth through an opened heaven to defeat all His foes at Armageddon and establish His millennial kingdom with His saints resurrected at the first resurrection.

John's vision of Christ is awe-inspiring. He comes as the divine Warrior-King on a white war-horse and bears four significant names. He was Faithful and True in His earthly life to God His Father. His secret name may relate to His deity. As the Word of God He reveals God to man perfectly. As King of kings and Lord of lords He alone has the right to rule the world for God. His many diadems signify His sovereignty. The sharp sword in His mouth is His breath, which is sufficient to destroy all his foes. The armies of heaven, the angels and glorified church saints, will follow Him, as He treads the winepress of God's wrath and rules the nations with a rod of iron. Verses 17 to 21 describe the ensuing carnage. With the greatest of ease the ringleaders of man's rebellion, the Beast and the False Prophet, will be seized and despatched to the Lake of Fire. Although God could have crushed our rebellion against Him long ago, He will delay final judgement until all hope of repentance is gone. What grace! But God will ultimately intervene. Be warned!

Chapter 20 predicts the aftermath of Armageddon. Verses 1 to 6 refer to a future literal thousand-year kingdom of Christ on earth, not to the present age. Then, not now, Satan will be bound and imprisoned in the abyss. Then, not now, the resurrected tribulation martyrs and the Old Testament saints will reign with Christ and the church saints, Dan. 12. 2. Non-literal interpretations of these verses confuse our understanding of scripture. Christ 'must reign', 1 Cor. 15. 25! We rejoice that the Lamb rejected and crucified by those whose sins He bore will be vindicated and rule His own creation, acknowledged by all!

Christ and

Revelation 20. 7 – 21. 8 — December 29th

Here we move from the sad end of the present creation into eternity and the glories of the new creation. The final rebellion of mankind after the millennial kingdom of Christ, with its Edenic conditions and universal knowledge of the Lord, will prove that unregenerate men are incurably sinful. They will always be deceived by Satan's temptations, whenever he is permitted, as here, to become active again. So the final dispensation, perfect government, like all the others, will end in failure and cause God swiftly to destroy this present world and set up the solemn great white throne judgement of the unbelieving dead. There the same Christ who died to redeem repentant sinners and put their names in His book of life will judge all who remain impenitent according to their works and consign them to varying degrees of eternal punishment, according to their responsibility, in the Lake of Fire. There will be no escape from attending this assize: all will be resurrected to stand before God and suffer the second death. Reader, will you be in the first resurrection of life, or the later resurrection of judgement? Repentance and faith in Christ makes all the difference.

In chapter 21 we move into the joyful scene of the new heaven and new earth, with which God will replace the corrupted old creation. All will be totally new in character and physical laws; for there will be no more sea. The present life-sustaining water cycle will be unnecessary. John saw the New Jerusalem, the home of God's redeemed people of all ages, descend from God to earth looking like a bride on her wedding day. Glorious sight! At last God will be able to dwell with men and be their God without a rival. All the sorrows of this present life will be banished forever. Finally, Christ from His throne puts the issues of eternity to the reader. All who are spiritually thirsty for the water of life which He offers will be fully satisfied, if they come to trust Him. Believers will inherit all this wonderful new creation. But all unrepentant sinners who refuse to trust Him will suffer the torments of the second death. Reader, the eternal Christ, the Alpha and Omega of all things, is offering you life today. Which will you choose: life or death?

Behold, the tabernacle of God is with men

His Apostles

December 30th — Revelation 21. 9 – 22. 5

No night there

A holy angel now gives John a breathtaking view from a great, high mountain of the eternal city, New Jerusalem, described as the bride, the Lamb's wife, for which all the patriarchs looked in faith, Heb. 11. 8-16. It is free from all sin and darkness, not lit by any created lights, but radiant with the Shekinah glory of the Lord God Almighty and the Lamb. They are its only temple sanctuary, since all is now in accord with God's holiness. It will be a very busy and joyful place, where we as God's servants will serve Him and see His lovely face 'without a cloud between', as we reign with our beloved Lord over the new creation. The redeemed of all Gentile nations will live in its light, and their kings will bring the wealth of the new earth into it. Because our glorified bodies will need no rest, there will be no night there, 'in the land of fadeless day'. Because there is no evil, the city gates will remain permanently open for access.

But what will our eternal home be like? John is describing a literal city using some symbolical language, because we cannot comprehend all its new physical laws. It will contrast utterly with man's city, Babylon the great, and be quite different from millennial Jerusalem. John saw it descending to the new earth, radiant with the shimmering light of many different precious stones, and completely translucent. There is nothing there to hide. The number twelve, denoting perfect divine administration, is stamped on all its features. It is a vast cube of some 1400 miles, like the holy of holies in the temple. Probably both redeemed Israel and the church will occupy it, while redeemed Gentiles will have ready access to it. A pure river of living water will flow from the throne of God and the Lamb to refresh it, and the tree of life on its banks will continually provide all its citizens with healthy food. Its beauty will surpass Eden's; the curse will be forever gone. But its chief glory, joy, and blessing will be its uniting centre, the Lord God Almighty and the Lamb. His very Name will forever remind us of the only basis of our entrance there, the precious shed blood of His sacrifice on Calvary. God will be known in His fullness and worshipped by all the redeemed. Wonderful hope! But, reader, will you be there?

Christ and

Revelation 22. 6-21 — December 31st

Surely I come quickly

The epilogue to Revelation, and to scripture as a whole, is a thrilling, thrice-repeated, and urgent message from the risen Lord Jesus to all believers in local churches. He is coming back to take us home to be with Himself very quickly, as He promised His own disciples and the church at Thessalonica, John 14. 1-3, 1 Thess. 4. 13-18. No other prophecy must be fulfilled before this event, which is therefore always imminent. For the fact that local churches have not been mentioned since chapter 3 further indicates that we shall not be on earth during the tribulation, but raptured to heaven before it begins, cp. Rev. 4. 1. Whilst the Lord promised that He would come to save Israel out of 'the time of Jacob's trouble' as 'the Sun of righteousness', Jer. 30. 7; Mal. 4. 2, Christ here promises to come for His Bride, the church, as the bright Morning Star, which appears before the sun rises. So, as we today see the tribulation storm-clouds gathering apace in the world around us ready to burst in horrific judgements, we can anticipate the blessed hope of the rapture before it starts, and therefore very soon indeed. What an encouragement for suffering and sorrowing saints! Maranatha!

The Lord's message includes both serious warnings for unbelievers and encouraging promises for believers. Unbelievers are warned that their fate will soon be sealed, unless they respond to the gracious invitation of the Spirit and the bride in the gospel to receive Christ's gift of living water: eternal life in Him. Also, no one is to add to, or take away from, this prophecy of future events on pain of eternal judgement. Believers are reassured that their Lord wants us, as His friends and obedient servants, to know 'the things which must shortly come to pass', v. 6 RV. The angel told John not to seal up this prophecy. It is meant to be an open book, understood and acted upon, because the time of its fulfilment is near. The Lord Jesus promises that, when He comes, He will bring with Him rewards for faithful service. While Malachi ended with a curse, Mal. 4. 6, Revelation ends with a blessing of grace from our soon-coming Lord to 'all the saints', v. 21 RV margin. Surely, John's prayerful response is ours also, 'Amen. Even so, come, Lord Jesus'!

His Apostles